i

# Words to the Weary

iv

# WORDS TO THE WEARY
## A Daily Devotional

BY MICHELLE GUNNIN

Scripture quotations are the ESV translation from The Holy Bible, English
Standard Version ®, copyright © 2001 by Crossway Bibles, a publishing
ministry of Good News Publishers. Used by permission.

ISBN-13: 9798572414967


Cover photo by: Mike Hunter
Library of Congress Control Number: 2018675309
Printed in the United States of America

MG PUBLICATIONS

*To the weary and heavy-laden. May God bring rest to your souls through these pages.*

*"Come to me, all who labor and are heavy laden, and I will give you rest. Take my yoke upon you, and learn from me, for I am gentle and lowly in heart, and you will find rest for your souls. For my yoke is easy, and my burden is light."*

*~Matthew 11:28-30*

x

# Preface

Daily devotional books have been a part of my faith journey since I was a child. Even before I accepted the free gift of grace, my mom used to read me and my siblings out of a children's devotional book each morning before school. As I grew in my own relationship with God, daily devotionals were a staple of my development. The authors of these books felt like mentors to me, walking along side me and sharing their wisdom. We were fellow travelers headed in the same direction keeping one another company; each entry was like a stepping stone on my journey. There was always a scripture to get me digging as well as a short explanation to make me think. Each day was like a conversation about God, happening between friends. Written from the perspective of the seeker, these daily moments grew into a routine which has guided my life and created an ongoing pursuit of God.

When I wrote *Words to the Weary*, I decided to depart from the traditional point of view of a fellow traveler and instead, write from God's perspective, using His voice. I did this for a few reasons.

One was because of my audience. I wrote this book specifically for those who have walked extended roads of pain for various reasons. When longsuffering is your path, many well-meaning people offer unsolicited advice. Their guidance is helpful sometimes and other times it is not. I didn't want to add one more advisor voice to the ones already speaking.

The second reason is similar. In a traditional daily devotional, the author's point of view increases the questions in the mind of the reader. Encouraging people to dig deeper in their walk with God is an intentional and powerful objective of this type of book. Yet, when readers are living in an exhausted and heavy place, they need something that speaks not as much to their minds, but more directly to their hearts. They need a word from God. They need encouragement and to be reminded of His love for them. My goal is for the words on these pages to hit the mark and bury themselves deep into the spirit of the reader where they can take root.

Another reason for my departure from a traditional point of view, is that this is how God speaks to me in my own times of hardship. I have had many dark nights of the soul in my life, times where I felt abandoned and all alone. Times where it was difficult just to get out of bed each day. God used terms of endearment to draw me to Himself; His names for me are endless, Beloved, Dear One, My Child…readers will see what I mean. In hard times, I have found God's voice is clearer when He speaks directly to me with tenderness, instead of through the words of others. He knows just what I need to hear and when I need to hear it, so I thought if I wrote from His point of view, others might be able to feel His presence in the midst of their difficulties, too.

You will notice in this book, themes repeat themselves. This is because, during trials and hardships I tend to forget what I know. In my life, God is faithful to remind me of His precious truths and His thoughts towards me. He wants me to know these things every day, so He repeats them often, each time with a little different twist. He is multi-faceted and there are many layers to His truths which He happily shares with me and now I share with you, the reader.

It is my prayer that this work becomes a staple for you during the seasons of long-suffering that you endure. That God would speak deeply into your pain and that His words would bring healing to your heart. That you would be uplifted and encouraged. That you would come to know Him better...really know Him, not just about Him. That in your weariness He would lead you to a quiet place, in Him, where you can find rest for your soul.  Blessings to you, Weary One, as you soak in His words to you each day.

# Introduction

*Words to the Weary* is written for those of you who are exhausted from life. Many people have circumstances which are hard **all the time,** and don't seem to ever go away, but sit heavily on your shoulders. I am speaking of any number of circumstances which leave you physically, emotionally, and spiritually tired, such as: a chronic illness, being a caregiver, parenting a wayward, difficult or disabled child, caring for a parent whose health is failing, navigating relationships which have failed or are strained, or enduring the loss of someone dear. When I started writing this book, I had you in mind because I am one of you. I needed encouragement in my soul. I regularly use words to bless others; why not write to encourage myself, too?

Then the whole world went crazy. A pandemic caused fear and health concerns to be up front for everyone. Financial ruin came upon so many so quickly it took my breath away. Then racism reared its ugly head again; there were riots and people dying. A war of words and division flooded the airwaves like I have never seen before.

Suddenly, everyone was weary. Weary of being shut in. Weary of the hate. Weary of life. Weary of oppression. I was only a few months away from finishing this book when it took on a completely new meaning. Yet, I still was writing it in the same way. Getting up in the morning. Sitting with God. Spilling out my heart and listening to His reply. Writing down His words to me.

This book is my devotional journal for a year. It is the way God and I communicate and converse. It is not a theological work, but a personal one, written from the hard places in which I live. My hope is it that will speak to those in similar places and bring some lift to your life.

# January 1

*Come to me, all who labor and are heavy laden, and I will give you rest. Take My yoke upon you, and learn from me, for I am gentle and lowly in heart, and you will find rest for your souls. For My yoke is easy, and My burden is light. ~Matthew 11:28-30*

Weary One, feel My strength today. Go forward in boldness. Rise up and look up. It is a new day. You have new vision. Things may not be much different in your life, but there is hope because of the fresh beginning set before you. Endings and beginnings are part of the cycle of seasons. Hope comes in and with it there are possibilities of refreshing. Allow me to refresh you and renew your heart.

I long to hold you close. Climb into My lap and sit with me. Let me surround you with My presence. You will feel the strength I offer. It will surge into you and your outlook will lift. Your heaviness will melt away. Going deeper with me is always a boost to your heart. Let me lift the burden from your shoulders. You were not designed to carry it alone. Be My companion this year. Let's walk side by side. Let's share with one another.

If you can let me infuse you with renewed energy, you will find more pep in your step. You will not be buried under emotional weight. You will be lifted up to a higher place, where the day-to-day circumstances are not choking you. You will be able to walk through the days, weeks, and months with a peace that passes understanding. Others will see it and be in awe of how you do what you do. They will see My strength coursing through you and they will wonder how to get it. They will not know all that you have endured to embrace My strength in your weak moments. They will not fully understand how you and I are so close. No matter, it will speak to them anyway. Your revived spirit will flow with joy and peace. You will find your rest in me.

# January 2

*Uphold me according to your promise, that I may live, and let me not be put to shame in my hope! ~Psalms 119:116*

I have the power to sustain you. I can pour it into you and you can walk tall. You do not have to be a slave to shame any longer. Shame is toxic to your spirit. You must learn to recognize its tentacles. It wraps itself around your thoughts and infiltrates how you see yourself. You feel weak when shame rears its ugly head. Shame is why you isolate yourself from those who can encourage you. You pull back when you fail at one thing or another. Setting new goals is good, but what is your plan if you do not meet them? Shame knows. Shame will stand and whisper in your ear that you failed again.

To sustain yourself, you have to lean on me. I am the steadfast one. You can find the strength to meet your goals in me. But, Dear One, go into performance mode and striving. It is not My heart for you to work yourself to death and then to feel defeated if things don't go as you want them to. Instead, be diligent to meet with me. Sit and let me give you your steps. My ways are not always the same as yours.

There is a mindset that is part of a vicious cycle. It manifests this time of year, because after the overindulgence of the holidays it seems natural to want to cut everything out. But shame wants you to set unrealistic goals, to overshoot what is possible. That way you fail more quickly and GIVE UP anything you have promised yourself to move into a better place. I, on the other hand, want you to make your changes with grace as the fuel. Grace for yourself. Grace for the journey...whatever your journey is. Fear and shame should have no place. They drive you into a frenzy that says if you cannot sustain your changes you are of no worth. Those are lies. My grace sustains you. You have to trust in it, not in yourself. I am the sustainer.

# January 3

*Truly, I say to you, whoever says to this mountain, "Be taken up and thrown into the sea," and does not doubt in his heart, but believes that what he says will come to pass, it will be done for him. Therefore, I tell you, whatever you ask in prayer, believe that you have received it, and it will be yours. ~ Mark 11:23-24*

Embrace all that I have for you. It may feel hard to do sometimes, but you already know how to do it. You may not know embracing everything is part of the healing process. It is surrendering. It is acceptance. When you walk in hard places often, embracing them is one of the hardest but most significant things you can do. Let me show you what I mean, Weary One.

You have learned that planning for the future is good, but not always possible, so you embrace uncertainty. You have learned every day has some bright spots, so you embrace hope. You have learned things do not always go the way you had imagined them, so you embrace creativity. You have learned there are immovable obstacles in your path, so you embrace flexibility. Did you know you were doing all of these things? On a journey like yours, these things creep up and you adapt to them. You don't know you are doing it, but I do.

Each and every step you take, there is an opportunity to embrace. Running from or running towards. It may not feel like much, but if every one of My children learned to embrace what life offers, the world would be a more peaceful place. When your heart stops wrestling with all the whys, and the what-fors, it settles down. It makes its own path, directed by My hand. The embracing begins to come naturally, to the point you are unaware you are being shaped and molded for a bigger purpose. If you do not learn to embrace, you will remain stuck. To move forward, embrace what I give you. You will see.

# January 4

*How lovely is your dwelling place, O Lord of hosts! My soul longs, yes, faints for the courts of the Lord; my heart and flesh sing for joy to the living God. ~Psalms 84:1-2*

I want to be your dwelling place, Weary One. I want you to be able to sit with me and know you are safe. I want you to be able to rest. When you come home at the end of a long day, kick off your shoes and relax. I want you to dwell with me.

It can be hard, when you feel there is no safe place. You are in your own world and it is overwhelming. No one else seems to understand what you are going through. I promise you, I understand. A dwelling is a specific place. Your relationship with me can be a dwelling. I am a roof over your head to protect you from the elements that want to rain down on you. I am a door for you to close out things that try to intrude or to let in things that heal. I am windows so you can look around you to see the beauty I place in your life. I am walls that help divide your life into manageable pieces. I am the hearth where you warm yourself on cold days. I am the kitchen when you need nourishment. I am the library when you are looking for words that lift up. I am everything you need.

And, Beloved, do you know what? You are MY dwelling place. Does it surprise you that I picked you? I chose your heart to be the place I reside. It is the roof, the door, the windows, the walls, the hearth, the kitchen, and the library to me. I find what I need in dwelling with you. You open your door for me to walk in. You are my windows to see what beauty is in your life. You allow me into all the different rooms, so I can rest there. You warm my heart on days when the world wants to shut me out. You nourish me with your worship. You lift me up with your praise. You are everything I need.

It is common for people to believe that I don't need anything. Yet, I created man and woman for My own pleasure. I desired a relationship so I would not be alone. That desire has always been within me. It is why I created you with a heart that desires communion. You are a spiritual being, like I am. When I dwell in you and you in me, we connect on a deep level. We have an ongoing conversation, not just one time a day, but throughout the day. Everywhere we go, we go together.

# January 5

*But He said to me, "My grace is sufficient for you, for My power is made perfect in weakness." Therefore, I will boast all the more gladly of my weaknesses, so that the power of Christ may rest upon me. For the sake of Christ, then, I am content with weaknesses, insults, hardships, persecutions, and calamities. For when I am weak, then I am strong.*
*~2 Corinthians 12:9-10*

Beloved, there are so many things you have because of the hard road you have walked. You may not know it or recognize how the journey you are on has shaped you, but it is true. I am using the circumstances to form you more into My image. You are who you are because of all you have been through. Do not discount it or wish it away. Hardship hurts, but it also softens. It forms and transforms. It creates something so beautiful it will take your breath away.

So, when you are crying out for relief, remember you are who you are because of what you have been through. You are compassionate towards others who are walking the same road. You are sensitive to those who are in pain, and those who don't know they are. You are a companion who walks with others and loves them well. You know your frailty and you are not afraid of it. You know your strength and you are not afraid of it either. You have humility that rests on you and makes you approachable. You have scars that point the way to healing. You are faithful, even when you doubt. You have questions and are not afraid to ask them. You wrestle with the darkness. You wrestle with me. You are honest in your wrestling. Your transparency is hard won. Your vulnerability is refreshing to those who live with facades. You are unique in your trials and that makes you special.

I know you long for the burden to lift. It is not wrong to want that Dear One, but I want you to know the burden is transforming you. I want you to look at it from a different perspective on the hard days. It is a tool, not a death sentence. It creates a more beautiful you. Praying for relief is not wrong, and there are times I will grant that request, but always remember My grace is sufficient for what you are up against. Remind yourself of the good in your life and the transforming power of the grace I pour out on you daily.

# January 6

*Finally, all of you, have unity of mind, sympathy, brotherly love, a tender heart, and a humble mind.* ~1 Peter 3:8

Dear One, you may have noticed your suffering makes others uncomfortable. When there are hard things, people search for explanations. Why would something like this happen? Divorce, wayward children, sickness, loss, ongoing trauma, addiction, abuse and other things that are unexplainable all cause wrestling with faith, not just for you, but for those around you.

Unfortunately, if there is not a "reason" readily available, judgement can come towards you. You must have done something that created the trouble you have. My children are the worst at pointing fingers, or whispering behind backs. It is a real problem, but I want to tell you they do not express My heart in their judgements.

Beloved, seek me. Do not allow others to determine how strong or weak your faith is. Do not allow their words to pierce your heart. Tune your ear to MY voice. Walk your path knowing I am with you. My word says that longsuffering is a fruit of the spirit. It is not judgement from me if you have suffering in your life. It is evidence that I am with you and working in your circumstances. The fact that you have walked this hard road for long periods of time is how the fruit of longsuffering is matured.

Those who judge have not walked a path like yours. However, when life hands them some pain, they will understand. They will come to you, because they see this fruit in your life. They will know then that the suffering you have endured has given you a soft heart. They will come and rest in your compassion. They will rethink their ideas about longsuffering, and you will be gracious and extend grace in ways you never received it. That is when you will see your transformation to be like My Son. You will not realize it has happened, but you will see your tenderness is directly related to your forbearance in difficult circumstances. Take heart, not judgement. Know that I am working in you, always.

# January 7

*Therefore, I tell you, do not be anxious about your life, what you will eat or what you will drink, nor about your body, what you will put on. Is not life more than food, and the body more than clothing? Look at the birds of the air: they neither sow nor reap nor gather into barns, and yet your heavenly Father feeds them. Are you not of more value than they? And which of you by being anxious can add a single hour to his span of life? And why are you anxious about clothing? Consider the lilies of the field, how they grow: they neither toil nor spin, yet I tell you, even Solomon in all his glory was not arrayed like one of these. But if God so clothes the grass of the field, which today is alive and tomorrow is thrown into the oven, will He not much more clothe you, O you of little faith? Therefore, do not be anxious, saying, 'What shall we eat?' or 'What shall we drink?' or 'What shall we wear?' For the Gentiles seek after all these things, and your Heavenly Father knows that you need them all. But seek first the kingdom of God and His righteousness, and all these things will be added to you. Therefore, do not be anxious about tomorrow, for tomorrow will be anxious for itself. Sufficient for the day is its own trouble. ~Matthew 6:25-34*

It is easy to get discouraged when the future is unknown. How do you prepare if you don't know how long your challenges will last? The focus is the key. It is like a salmon swimming upstream to live day-to-day, because the world tells you to plan in advance for everything, so much so, that daily living is secondary. Yet, I say don't worry about tomorrow. It has enough worries of its own.

Dear One, plans are not bad. They can be useful, but in your journey, plans cannot be your focus. You do not know what tomorrow holds. The circumstances do not allow for you to have details required to have every moment of your future planned out. Certainly, you can have a loose guide of what you might like to have happen, but make sure that doesn't become your expectation. Letting go of expectations is one of the hardest things about this journey. Learning to trust me in every detail is critical to your survival.

Remember I provided manna in the desert. Not ahead of time, but the day it was needed. I send My provision when you need it. A hug from a friend. A song on the radio. A check in the mail. A kind word. My provision is there to encourage you. You can depend on it. The future is unclear, always. Even if there are plans, they may or may not come to fruition. Worry only sucks the life from you. Trust me with the unknown. It is only unknown to you. I already see what is ahead because I am already there, waiting for you with all the provision you need.

# January 8

*He who has an ear, let him hear what the Spirit says to the churches. To the one who conquers, I will give some of the hidden manna, and I will give him a white stone, with a new name written on the stone that no one knows except the one who receives it. ~Revelation 2:17*

I call you by many names. They are My terms of endearment for you. Just as you are one person with many names, so I am. My facets are endless. If you take the time with me you will see them. Some are listed in My word, but there are many which are not. It is because I want you to seek them out.

As you get to know people more intimately your names for them change. You start with the official Miss, Mrs. or Mr. You move to a given first name. Then a nickname. Then even more specific endearments. The closer you get, the less the terms are shared out. Notice that? A married couple might never share the names they have for one another in public. They are private, intimate, privileged terms. They are not open for everyone to know.

The specific ones are almost secrets, just between you and one other. Those are the names I have for you. They are only between us. You can have names for me that are like that as well. The relationship I desire with you can be seen in some human relationships. They are mirrors of a deeper truth. When relationships on Earth are strained, it confuses the way you see things. My relationship with you is not of this world. I have written your name on the palms of My hands. It is so individual no one else will know it. Ask me for your names. I will share them with you. I love to show you how I see you. It changes the way you see yourself.

# January 9

*But He said to me, "My grace is sufficient for you, for my power is made perfect in weakness." Therefore, I will boast all the more gladly of my weaknesses, so that the power of Christ may rest upon me. ~2 Corinthians 12:9*

My grace is sufficient, Weary One. There are moments where it doesn't feel true, but it is. People confuse My mercy and My grace. Mercy is something I give just because I love you. It is forgiveness when you don't deserve it. It is My choice to love you anyway. My Son made My mercy possible, and I freely give it as an act of My will.

Grace, on the other hand, is the fuel which gives you strength. It inspires you to seek me and to move in what I have purposed for you. It gives you the ability to endure in your hardship and to resist temptation. It flows through you, because I freely give it as well. It is me, in you. It allows you to forgive and show mercy to those who have harmed you. It allows you to grow, even in difficult places. It helps you in your work, in your relationships, and in your day-to-day life. It has been called amazing because it is hard to comprehend.

Mercy and grace are companions. They operate together. They are new each day. Think of them taking your hands and pulling you up. One on one side and one on the other. They walk with you throughout the day. Mercy shows you compassion and kindness. Grace gives you the ability to function in a fallen world, with inspiration. It allows you to persevere.

Beloved, on days when you do not feel My presence, when things are harder than you feel you can handle, you have to lean on My grace. You have to remember it is there for you in the littlest ways. Breathing is My grace. The sunrise is My grace. A song at the right time is My grace. A dog's kiss. A child's laugh. Even in the midst of hard things there are hundreds of little graces. They are put there intentionally, by me, to fuel you to keep going.

# January 10

*But whoever drinks of the water that I will give him will never be thirsty again.
The water that I will give him will become in him a spring of water welling up to
eternal life. ~John 4:14*

What is in your cup? Weary One, if you want more of me in your life you have to
take stock of what is in your cup. You are a vessel. Things can be poured into you and
things can be poured out of you. Your life is so full that when you want to add
something, there is no room. Take stock. There are some things in your cup that can be
removed completely and some that must be rearranged.

Distractions are so common in the culture in which you live, that many cups are
filled with devices. Each device ties you to it in numerous ways and it fills your mind
and heart with distraction. Multitasking becomes a god. Not every device you use is
necessary. Not every task you are assigning time to is needed. Figure out what can be
cut, then ask for the courage to cut it.

The day-to-day of your life is full of things that must be done. Families must be
cared for. You have to go to work. Pay bills. Do laundry. Cook food. Go to the store. All
of these are things that cannot be removed from your cup. Especially if you are a
caregiver, however, they are things that can be organized. They do not have to take all
of your time. When the distractions are cut out, it makes time for essential tasks to
flow in a more efficient, less chaotic, way.

When My Weary Ones ask for more of me, they are often too full for me to fit any
more of Myself into their cups. Then burn out follows. Pouring out some of what is in
the cup is critical. But here is the secret, if you make room for me, what I pour into
your cup will be what sustains you, then you will pour it out to others. My love will
pour in, so you can pour it out. My hope will pour in so you can pour it out. Aren't
these better things to pour out than frustration, burn out, resentment, anger,
bitterness? What is in your cup?

# January 11

*Rejoice always, pray without ceasing, giving thanks in all circumstances. ~1 Thessalonians 5:16-17*

When you talk to me, it is prayer. No need for flowery words, or fancy statements. You do not have to impress me. Your tears are prayers, as are the deep places where there are no words, Weary One. On a hard journey, many times, in the midst of a steep place, or a dark place, breathing is the only prayer you can utter. This communion between us happens when you turn your face towards me. In your grief, you cry out to me. In your depression, when words escape you, you might only be able to think of me. Those thoughts are prayers. Focus on each breath, in and out, in and out...each one is a prayer. Beloved, when you are in a dark night of the soul, you are crying out to me even when you do not know it. Be released from the performance type prayers of old. There is no reason to fill your mouth or My ears with words you do not feel. Rest in me and let your heart do the talking.

When you are not in the deep place of sorrow, I love to hear your thoughts. I love it when you talk to me and pour out your heart. I also like to share My heart with you, so make sure you put in some time to listen to me as well. I speak through My word, and through My servants, and through songs, and the sky, and art, and movement, and so many other ways. I drop thoughts and ideas into your brain. I reside in your smile, which pops up out of nowhere. It is a two-way communication. We are constantly connected.

Do not let fear rule your communication with me. Speak to the fears and release them. You might have to do this daily. When you release fear, it makes room for faith. Speak My word back to me. Pray for others. Pray for yourself. Pray for My purposes. Read the words on My pages. I wrote them for you. Put your name in the blanks and be encouraged. There are all kinds of prayer Dear One. Let me teach you. It is not what you think. There is more. It is a life line and it will rescue you.

# January 12

*For everything created by God is good, and nothing is to be rejected if it is received with thanksgiving. ~1 Timothy 4:4*

Become yourself. I know it sounds silly. Of course, you are yourself. But your true self is who I created. In life, somehow you forget to be you. There are so many voices in the world telling you to be something other than yourself. They are getting louder and louder. They yell into your ears from the television and the internet. They even yell at you from the pulpit. They surround you at work and on the job. Every one of them is telling you what you should and shouldn't be. So much so, that you become a shape-shifter, by trying to fit the mold they want to put you in.

If you look at your life you can see what voices you listen to the most. What are your actions, but more importantly what are the motives behind them. Who are you trying to please? You know you cannot please everyone. If your desire is to please others, you will frantically spin your wheels in many directions. The rub of life is how to do your work and stay true to who I made you to be. But to do that, you first have to know who I made you to be. You have to turn to me and ask, "Who do you say that I am?"

It is a journey to find out. You are already on it. You simply need to pay attention. Who do I say you are? I say you are a strong person. The difficulties you live with make you that way. I say you know how to persevere, because you have had to. My Child, look around you, this hard life you have is a study on who I say you are. Your identity is carved out in the hard places.

People want the characteristics of My Son. They desire His kindness and His love. They want His compassion. No one asks for His tears. No one desires His suffering. Yet to be transformed into His image...to have your identity in Him...those things are a part. You, Beloved, are being formed into His strength. You don't need to look to others to become yourself. You only need to look to who I have created you to be. You are becoming. It is part of your journey.

# January 13

*Put on the whole armor of God, that you may be able to stand against the schemes of the devil. For we do not wrestle against flesh and blood, but against the rulers, against the authorities, against the cosmic powers over this present darkness, against the spiritual forces of evil in the heavenly places. Therefore, take up the whole armor of God, that you may be able to withstand in the evil day, and having done all, to stand firm. Stand therefore, having fastened on the belt of truth, and having put on the breastplate of righteousness, and, as shoes for your feet, having put on the readiness given by the gospel of peace. In all circumstances take up the shield of faith, with which you can extinguish all the flaming darts of the evil one; and take the helmet of salvation, and the sword of the Spirit, which is the word of God, praying at all times in the Spirit, with all prayer and supplication. To that end, keep alert with all perseverance, making supplication for all the saints. ~Ephesians 6:11-18*

Keep fighting, Weary One. I know you are tired. You feel as if you will break. You want to give up and lie down. It seems like it would be easier to quit, but it won't. You must push through. The weary days when all seems lost, those are the ones where it is imperative that you keep moving. Step. Step. Step. One foot in front of the other. Hold onto My hand. Let me guide you and lead you.

Beloved, there are days where surrendering and opening your hand are the appropriate measures to take. There are days when sitting still before me and resting are the most needed things. But there are also days when you need to take up your sword and fight. The enemy wants you to lie down. He longs for you to quit and make his job so much easier. Those are the days you get out of bed and stand. You take more ground. You use My word and you proclaim it loudly. Shout it out. All the truth I speak about you, and about me, and about who you are. Speak it. Do not let the enemy silence you.

Put on your whole armor. The belt of truth. The shield of faith. The breastplate of righteousness. The shoes of peace. The helmet of salvation. The sword of the spirit. Take them all up and use them to protect yourself. They are My gift to you, so you are clad in me. Only I can give you those things. You are a warrior. The circumstances tell you otherwise, but they lie. You are strong and you carry My grace every day.

Days of surrender are when you are holding onto things that are not healthy for you. Those days are the days you are striving and working so very hard. They are the days you exhaust yourself.

Days of battle are days when the enemy wants to eat your lunch. Days when you need to hold fast to the words I have spoken. Days when you need to stand up and speak with your big voice. Do not confuse the two kinds of days, Beloved. There are both kinds, and today is a day of fighting. Swing your sword and fight.

# January 14

*Then He said to me, "Son of man, these bones are the whole house of Israel. Behold, they say, 'Our bones are dried up, and our hope is lost; we are indeed cut off.' Therefore prophesy, and say to them, "Thus says the Lord God: Behold, I will open your graves and raise you from your graves, O My people. And I will bring you into the land of Israel. And you shall know that I am the Lord, when I open your graves, and raise you from your graves, O My people." ~Ezekiel 37:11-13*

Can your bones live, Weary One? They are dry with no life in them. Do you feel brittle? As if you will break at any moment? Do you feel tired and weary, like you are finished? Yes? Then My question to you is this, can you live? Can you rise up?

The answer is yes. You can when I speak. Listen. I speak to your bones and I say, 'Live!' I tell them to come together and they obey My command. They rattle and they join each other to stand. Beloved, you no longer need to lie in the valley of dry bones. I have spoken to your bones.

Now, I speak to your breath. I say, 'Come breath, from the four winds...come and blow into My Weary One. Breath, blow renewal and refreshment into My child.' The breath obeys My command. It does not hesitate. It indwells your lungs, but it also fills your spirit. Hope comes with My breath. Belief comes with My breath. Faith comes with My breath. Consider it My mouth to mouth resuscitation. My breath will save your life. No need to lie there anymore. No need to wonder if you will be dry bones forever. The wind of My breath is here. It is flowing even now. Can you feel it, Beloved? Do not forsake My breath. Do not turn away from it. It will mean peril for you. I want you to live!

Breathe, My Love. Breathe and rise up as a mighty warrior. Breathe. Come to life. Stand up on your feet. Arise. You are resurrected. You are full of My breath and My life. No more valley for you, today you stand up with My breath in you. Today you rise from the bones and you walk.

# January 15

*Neither is new wine put into old wineskins. If it is, the skins burst and the wine is spilled and the skins are destroyed. But new wine is put into fresh wineskins, and so both are preserved. ~Matthew 9:17*

When there is new wine coming you need a new wineskin. Dear One, you have done things the same way for a long time. Your path requires it of you. Routine and structure are not bad, they are necessary. However, there are times when I want to do something new and the old structures won't work any longer.

Most of the time, this isn't regarding what time of day you wake up, or how much time you spend doing things. It is more of old mindsets. Is there someone you resent? That is an old wineskin. Is there some bitterness you are holding onto? Old wineskin. What about self-pity? Or depression? Or outright anger? All old wineskins.

Beloved, I want to give you new wine, but these old structures will not work. My new wine is renewal and revival of your battered and weary spirit. It is the uplifting of your heart. But if My Spirit is poured in, and you are still spewing old hurts and wounds it will be contaminated. The work of encouragement will be short-lived and the old structures will choke it out. Hope will fail to take root.

Do you see how hard things can beat you down? You can feel it, I know. That burned out feeling which tries to steal your joy. Look at your wineskin. Is it holding up or is it old and brittle? Does it leak? Seek me in this. I will show you and help you dispose of it. I will give you a wineskin that is made up of forgiveness and healing. I will give you hope and a future. Then, when My words pour out over you, you can catch them. You can hold them to encourage you on the hard days. Change is hard, but it is necessary so let me work in you.

# January 16

*He said, "Do not be afraid, for those who are with us are more than those who are with them." Then Elisha prayed and said, "O Lord, please open his eyes that he may see." So, the Lord opened the eyes of the young man, and he saw, and behold, the mountain was full of horses and chariots of fire all around Elisha. ~2 Kings 6:16-17*

It seems you are overpowered by circumstances, which never seem to change. They are continually reminding you of this fact. Each day has enough problems to defeat you and leave you broken. You are tired. You are weary and wondering, when will it end? When will there be a breakthrough?

You feel the enemy is more powerful than I am, Weary One. You may not be aware that is what you are thinking, but underneath the layers of woundedness, you can see nothing other than his hand in your life. When you look around you it appears to you as if he is controlling every moment. But you are wrong.

There are more with you than with him. I have surrounded you with My angels. I have lifted you up with My own hand. What you see is not all there is. Look with My eyes, Beloved. See what I see. All around you are warriors of mine. They are your protectors. They fight for you. They cover you. You are defended by My armies.

Do not dismay. Do not allow what you see, or think you see, to determine your worth. Do not shrink back. Be confident that I am with you. Know that I have given you all the help you need. You will not be swallowed up by your circumstances. Your grief will not take over your life. The things you worry about will not fill your mind.

When you see what I see, you will rise up to believe what I say. You will be amazed and your view will change. You will see your value. You will know that I have you in the palm of My hand and that NOTHING can separate you from me.

# January 17

*Whom have I in heaven but you? And there is nothing on earth that I desire besides you. ~Psalms 73:25*

You belong, Weary One. It is every human's deepest desire to belong, because I built a "longing to be" into the DNA. I want every one of My children to understand this. With me, you belong. Automatically. Without trying. You fit. I long to be with you, and hopefully, you long to be with me. It is a relationship which goes in both directions.

So many of the ills of the world boil down to this one thing. So many people are just looking to belong, somewhere, anywhere. Looking in the wrong places. Trying to find a tribe or a group to fit into. You are social creatures who operate best when you are interdependent on one another. Independent is too alone. Dependent is too together. Interdependent is where you lean on one another. It is where the weaknesses and strengths balance each other out. Being with other people is important. Essential even.

However, with me, belonging is a deep place of contentment. It is far from worrying or thinking of others and how they perceive you. It is where you know you are loved because I created you, just the way you are. I accept you, just the way you are. I designed it so you would come to me with your "longing to be." The design is to point people to me. I am the place where you can find your belonging. Show them, Dear One. Show them with your confidence and your contentment. Bring them to the place to have their longings filled in me.

# January 18

*Where shall I go from your Spirit? Or where shall I flee from your presence? If I ascend to heaven, you are there! If I make my bed in Sheol, you are there! If I take the wings of the morning and dwell in the uttermost parts of the sea, even there your hand shall lead me, and your right hand shall hold me. If I say, "Surely the darkness shall cover me, and the light about me be night," even the darkness is not dark to you; the night is bright as the day, for darkness is as light with you. ~Psalms 139:7-12*

You are known, Precious One. Not on a surface level, but a deep one. I know your thoughts, every one of them. I know the number of hairs on your head. I know you because I created you. Being known is another deep desire I built into humans. To be known is to be accepted. To be known is to be cared for.

The problem is you have to be vulnerable to be known, and My children are not always accepting of each other. It is a scary thing to open yourself up. Once you have been mocked or made fun of, vows are made to never open up again. You close yourself off, while inside you are still longing to be known. It is a dilemma to be sure.

May I make a suggestion, Dear One? Open your heart to me. I am safe. I am invested. I will love you, unconditionally. You can trust me. Not to mention I already know you. Before you speak it, I know. Therefore, when you speak whatever is on your mind, I am not surprised or taken aback. I do not snap to judgement. I accept you. I embrace you. I hold you close to My heart.

Knowing you deeply is important to me. You are important to me. In the midst of your life, I know you. My desire is for you to know me in the same way. For you to open your heart and allow me into your world. To see your deepest feelings, so you can feel known. You see, it doesn't matter that I know them already if you don't realize it.

If you think you are hiding from me, you are mistaken. You cannot hide. I am everywhere you are. This is a good thing, My Love. It means you can come to me without words. I understand your hardship. I understand your difficulty. I am a part of you. Turn your face towards me and open your heart. You will feel it. You will be able to rest in being known and loved no matter what. It is My desire for you to KNOW that.

# January 19

*The Lord is your keeper; the Lord is your shade on your right hand. The sun shall not strike you by day, nor the moon by night. The Lord will keep you from all evil; He will keep your life. The Lord will keep your going out and your coming in from this time forth and forevermore. ~Psalms 121:5-8*

Not only are you known, you are seen. The day in and day out life you live does not go unnoticed by me. You care for others and I know your every sacrifice. It is hard to continually be the one pouring out and not always receiving back. Whether you are caring for elderly parents, small children, or those who are homeless or lost, I see. I can see when your heart is breaking. I can see when you are overjoyed. I can see when you are up in the night, feeling alone and invisible.

You are not invisible, Weary One. You are noticed. Your every breath and action are seen by me. Your laundry pile is seen by me. Your nightly actions up and down are seen by me. Your work hours are seen by me. Your home work is seen by me. Your load and all the plates you spin are seen by me. You are never invisible to me. Never.

In the secret places of your life, where you feel alone, you are not. In the heavy thoughts and regrets, do not be dismayed. In the exhausting moments, you are not alone. In the piles upon piles of work you do, to care for all those in your life, every small thing is seen by me. If no one else notices, I do. I am with you at every turn. I am with you in the night season, and in the daily work. I am caring for you, as you care for others. Hold onto My hand and we will do it together.

# January 20

*Therefore, do not be ashamed of the testimony about our Lord, nor of me His prisoner, but share in suffering for the gospel by the power of God who saved us and called us to a holy calling, not because of our works but because of His own purpose and grace, which He gave us in Christ Jesus before the ages began. ~2 Timothy 1:8-9*

Celebrate grace, Dear One. Compounded grace. Grace resting upon grace. Layering one grace-act upon the other until there is a foundation of solid rock. It is beyond feelings. Beyond belief. It is there whether you believe it or not. This grace counters the grief upon grief of the traumas and difficulties of life.

In the darkness, grace is light. In overwhelmed places, grace is peace. When you are surrounded by grief, grace sits with you to hold your hand. When you cannot see in front of you, grace leads the way. This grace isn't warm and fuzzy. It gets down in the mess and mud.

It does not abandon you when you cannot find it. When you cannot feel it, grace is an invisible cloak that covers your lack. Your tears are caught in the hands of grace in the dark night of the soul. It is deep and wide. Unfathomable. When you do not know grace, it knows you. When you avoid it, it chases you. Grace runs to the prodigal, of which you are one. It rescues you from yourself. These everyday rescues compound into evidence of the amazing grace you sing about.

All these little graces add up. They build a fortress for your heart. A solid protected space for you to be. No doing involved. It's all done for you. When you are present to it, grace fills you up. When you are not, it covers you. In the darkest night or the brightest day, grace abides with you. When you have come to the end of yourself, it continues the journey. Grace is a gift like no other. If you sit with it long enough, it empowers you. Grace is the fuel of life.

All is grace. Grace is a person. I am. Grace.

# January 21

*He will wipe away every tear from their eyes, and death shall be no more, neither shall there be mourning, nor crying, nor pain anymore, for the former things have passed away. ~Revelation 21:4*

Wipe your tears, Weary One. I know they are falling like rain. I see them. I catch them and keep them in a bowl beside My throne. I value your tears. They are liquid prayers which fall when there are no words. I am not blind to them. Not one falls without My notice. They are a release of burdens which try to weigh you down. They allow emotions to escape without words. They are a gift.

But there are times, tears hinder you, My Child. There are times you must cry, and then wipe them away so you can move forward. Did you think all tears were the same? Not so. There are multiple kinds of tears. They are tools to help you process life. But some tears are born from self pity. Those are the ones you must not spend too much time with. They remind you of every way you have given without something in return. They remind you that things are not what you wanted them to be. They remind you that life is hard and you are not. They want to weigh you down. Freeze you in your tracks.

Certainly, you need to acknowledge the feelings behind them, but wipe the tears away. You are not pitiful. You are not forgotten. You are not the only one who has it hard. You are stronger than you think. You are more powerful than you know. You are My Beloved and I will not let you sit in a heap while these self-pity tears take over your life. Stand up, My Love. Give these tears to me, and walk on. It is not for you to ruminate. Replaying all that has happened will not help you unless you give it to me. Look to the future. It starts today. Right now. Today is a new day. This is the day I have made and you can rejoice in it. Wipe the tears. Stand up. Rise up. Move forward. Walk on.

# January 22

*We are afflicted in every way, but not crushed; perplexed, but not driven to despair; persecuted, but not forsaken; struck down, but not destroyed; always carrying in the body the death of Jesus, so that the life of Jesus may also be manifested in our bodies. ~2 Corinthians 4:8-10*

Crushing is an essential part of life. Yes, it hurts. Yes, it is difficult. But, it takes breaking the skins of the grape to make new wine. It takes crushing the wheat to make flour for bread. A seed, buried in the ground, breaks open so it can grow and reproduce. Dirt is broken into fine dust to make clay from which vessels are made. Beloved, can you see?

There are people who have been crushed by life. You are one of those. Your circumstances break you over and over again. This is not a bad thing, hard, but not bad. It is one of the ways you have grown. Do not let the breaking harden you, Weary One. That is the choice you have...break you or make you. You can become bitter and resentful of your lot in life, or you can allow me to use it. It can soften you and shape you. It can make you more like My Son.

You can be new wine, or bread, or a seed, or a vessel. I will put you in places where I need those things. You will grow in your hard places, and others, who are also in hard places, will see the way you avoid bitterness. They will watch you be crushed and see how beautiful the process makes you.

It is like incense to me. It rises to My nostrils as an offering. You offer me your tears and your heartache. I accept them with gentleness, because I know they come from places of crushing. I do not take them lightly. I honor your choice to let the circumstances transform you. It is My honor to drink your new wine and to eat your bread. It bonds us together to have shared this communion of suffering. You are a vessel for a purpose that only I know. I am forming and shaping you even now, in the crushing.

# January 23

*For I was hungry and you gave me food, I was thirsty and you gave me drink, I was a stranger and you welcomed me, I was naked and you clothed me, I was sick and you visited me, I was in prison and you came to me.' Then the righteous will answer him, saying, 'Lord, when did we see you hungry and feed you, or thirsty and give you drink? And when did we see you a stranger and welcome you, or naked and clothe you? And when did we see you sick or in prison and visit you?' And the King will answer them, 'Truly, I say to you, as you did it to one of the least of these My brothers, you did it to me.' ~Mathew 25:35-40*

Do you think you have to go around the world to feed the hungry? What about clothing the naked? Are they only far away? No, Dear One. They are in your midst. Those little ones around your table each day, they are hungry. The babies, they are naked. Those who are sick, the elderly, the disabled, they are with you. You do not have to go far.

There is a misconception that missionaries are somehow more spiritual than everyone else, because they go to hard places and do difficult things. Beloved, each one gets the grace they need to do what I have for them. Missionaries have the grace to go. Others have the grace to stay. You have a hard path that might not allow you to go and do. There might be illness, or those depending on you, or grief that presses down. There are any number of things that can keep you from going. But do not believe because of your circumstances that I don't have something for you.

You are a missionary, no matter where you are. You are a missionary in your home as you care for your family. You are a missionary at work as you do your job. You are a missionary at the doctor's office when you are there for treatment. Every place you are, I am there with you.

You can feed the hungry around your table, in your neighborhood or across the world. You can give living water to those you tuck into bed at night. You can show hospitality by inviting people in... not always into your home, into your heart. You can dress the elderly and look after them. You can go to a prison to visit or you can visit with someone who is bound in bitterness. Shackled in selfishness.

Dear One, you do not have to go to fulfill My purpose in your life. You simply have to wake up to it. I can pour Myself out through you wherever you are, if you are aware. Do not be discouraged that you have nothing to offer other than a mundane life in which you feel stuck. Not true! You are not stuck, you are planted in a place where I need beauty to grow. You are My hands and feet right where you are. I might take you on a journey around the world someday, but right now, I have you just where you are needed to feed, clothe, and heal.

# January 24

*Call to me and I will answer you, and will tell you great and hidden things that you have not known. ~Jeremiah 33:3*

Feeling misunderstood can hurt. When others don't see all the details that you deal with, they are likely to jump to conclusions or judgements. They misunderstand your motives. They misunderstand your actions. They misunderstand your need to pull back and they take it as rejection. They misunderstand your need to be with a group, or to be alone. The thoughts run rampant, but My Child, you have no control over their thoughts. Do not take them to heart.

If you are walking with me, I will guide you. You will know when to pull back, and when to push forward. You will know who is for you and who is against. If you internalize their misunderstanding, you will begin to see rejection everywhere you look. You must look to me for your acceptance. I understand you. I cannot miss understanding.

I have a word of caution for you. Do not hold it against them, Dear One. They know not what they do. They are caught up in their own insecurities and it is easier for them to judge and misunderstand others than to look at themselves.

I sometimes give you the opportunity to share your hurt. To explain the misunderstanding to those who don't realize how their comments or attitudes wound. Be open to me in this. I might open the door for you to share, but only do so if I guide you. Otherwise, look to me. I can defend you. I will defend you. You may not always see what I am doing, but know that I am always working on your behalf. You need only to wait on me.

I am not a stranger to being misunderstood. For centuries people have blamed me for every disaster and wrong in their lives. Few take the time to look deeper and to seek me out. My motives are questioned. My actions picked apart. Yet, one day they will all know My love. They will see it. My Son tried to show them, but they treated Him the same as they do me. Mocked. Questioned. Ridiculed.

When others misunderstand you, remember me. Remember they do not know what your life is like or how I have worked in you. They know very little of your inner life. That is between you and me. Do not let them take that from you. There may come a time where they ask you about it. They might need to know someday. Hold to me and I will lead you, because I understand.

# January 25

*For the Lord your God is He who goes with you to fight for you against your enemies, to give you the victory. ~Deuteronomy 20:4*

I never stop fighting for you, Weary One. You may not see it, but that doesn't mean it isn't happening. You cannot know the layers of My plan because it is comprehensive. I work on whole worlds at one time. I am that big. Yet, I care deeply and intimately for each individual. That means you. In your life, even the smallest detail is important to me. I see them all. I see each tear. I see the joys. I know the monumental events and the miniscule ones. I fight for them all.

I also fight for the ones you love. Your prodigals. Your disabled ones. Your mentally ill ones. I fight for your sick ones. Your angry ones. Your lost ones. So many of your prayers are for those. Does it seem to you that I am deaf to your cries? I am not. I weep with you. But I do not weep from hopelessness, I weep at the pain of this life. I weep at how the enemy is wreaking havoc on My children. I weep at how far away from my plan the world has walked. But I am far from hopeless. You see, Dear One, I know the ending. I know how it all turns out.

I know the lengths I will go to for the one. Each and every one. You can know it too, if you read My words at all. I sent My Son to talk to a Samaritan woman. The prodigal father ran to his son. The demoniac was freed from his demons by the shortest mission trip in history. I left the 99 to go after the one. Almost every story has a one in it, and it isn't just in history where I chase after the ones. I still do it today.

I am doing it even now. I am after the one you are praying for. I am fighting for them. I am arranging opportunities for reconciliation. I am planting seeds. I am watering them and nourishing them. I am waiting for the perfect timing. You cannot see all of this, but I promise I am doing it. Beloved, you keep praying and believing. No matter what you see. If you only knew how many praying mothers and grandmothers, parents and friends have impacted eternity. Your prayers make connections for My plan in the spirit. Keep believing and I will keep fighting.

# January 26

*Thus, says the Lord: Do justice and righteousness, and deliver from the hand of the oppressor him who has been robbed. And do no wrong or violence to the resident alien, the fatherless, and the widow, nor shed innocent blood in this place. ~Jeremiah 22:3*

Weary One, I know you are tired. Your exhaustion comes from a life lived under pressure. Sometimes it is from circumstances, other times it comes from oppression. The world you live in is not fair. The enemy does his best to subject as many as possible to his oppression...pressing down. He uses every means possible, skin color, gender, poverty, race, religion, disability, and difference at all is his playground. He is ruthless in his pressing down, and humans join him in his bully games.

Do not despair, Beloved. Injustice will not stand forever. I will see to that. Since the garden, there has been oppression, brought on by sin. Cain and Able are the first examples of injustice and what it leads to. Cain was thinking Able was gaining more of My favor and therefore, murder followed. It was Able's blood crying out from the ground that alerted me to the nature of the crime. It was Cain's attitude of the heart that caused it to be committed. The enemy is still roaming the earth seeking to kill and destroy and still using oppression to do it.

Injustice means not right. There are so many injustices in your world that it is heartbreaking. Beloved, there is no justice without My intervention. I am the deliverer. I am the God of justice. The shedding of innocent blood breaks My heart. The pummeling of precious spirits angers me. I am not a God who turns His head away. My Son's blood covered every person. Every single one. Because I love every single one.

Do not let oppression steal your joy. In the midst of crying out for justice, do not forget me. Do not let the enemy make you think you are not meant for My freedom. Open your arms to me. Open your spirit up and find mine, who draws you to My love. I am the one who will set things right. Stay close to me and despair will not overtake you. Stay close to me and your exhaustion will lift off your shoulders. Stay close to me.

# January 27

*A man without self-control is like a city broken into and left without walls.*
*~Proverbs 25:28*

I am clear, Dear One, I do not desire conflict. I am a God of peace. However, I do expose darkness. I shine a light on the ravages of sin. The cause of power struggles is pride. The cause of oppression is control. The cause of grief is betrayal. I don't need to go on, you get the picture.

The sorrow of this life is the deep pain of sin. That is why I hate it so. It destroys My people. It breaks them. It shackles their hands and feet. What chains you, Weary One? What places in your life do you feel trapped? Can I give you some advice? Take a look at the tender spots. Anywhere you feel a rise in blood pressure, take a look. Is there anger? Look underneath it. Is there sorrow? Look for the cause. Is there frustration? Look at the layers.

I gave you feelings for a reason. They are tools, not tormentors. Every emotion you have is pointing to something. Looking beneath them you will find the sore spots. Unforgiveness lives under anger. Betrayal is deep in the heart as a twisted root of bitterness. Beloved, I can pull these roots out, if you know they are there. If you don't, I will show them to you, but you have to be open to see. Clear your head and look at your heart. Self-reflection with me by your side is a healing place. Don't you want to be healed? Don't you want to be free of the negative emotions so you can have more room for the positive ones?

Come sit with me. Pour out your feelings, then let me show you their cause. Let me into the layers of your heart so we can remove the things that tire you out. Life is never all easy, but it can be easier than it is right now. Will you let me show you?

# January 28

*But thanks be to God, who gives us the victory through our Lord Jesus Christ. I*
*~Corinthians 15:57*

Victories can be big, but they can also be small. The big ones, the grandiose ones, are the ones everyone wants. But do not discount the small ones, Dear One. Each small one is worth celebrating.

Think of the small victories as stepping out towards the bigger ones. Victory. Victory. Victory. VICTORY. It is like muscle memory. The repetition gets ingrained and before long it is automatic. The same is true in your spirit. When you see each small victory for what it is, before long it is automatic to expect the bigger victories.

In your world, a small every day victory might be getting everyone to school on time. Or getting your body to work well enough to get out of the bed. Or turning the other cheek in a hostile situation. Or coming to me first before your grief overtakes you. Sometimes, Beloved, the small victories like these are actually the big ones! The effort it takes to complete them requires all your heart, mind, and soul.

Other times you might pull off a major victory to be celebrated. A whole week of making it to work on time is a major victory for those with autoimmune diseases. An outing with a friend is a major victory for those who are depressed and isolated. Caregivers experience a big victory when they get a break and feel renewed. When you break the gender or color barrier at work, there is since of accomplishment of a job well done. To others these things might seem small, but to me, they are major steps. Do not discount them or minimize their importance. Look for small ones each day, but also find the big ones.

I am with you in these moments. I long for you to be victorious. You are already an overcomer. Do you not see it that way, Beloved? You are. You live in a state of strength-ness- strength through weakness. It is the fabric of victory. The material of which it is made. You have the ingredients you need to be victorious every day. Make today one of the days where you practice victory.

# January 29

*He said to them, "Because of your little faith. For truly, I say to you, if you have faith like a grain of mustard seed, you will say to this mountain, 'Move from here to there,' and it will move, and nothing will be impossible for you." ~Matthew 17:20*

There are mountains all around you. Weary One, you look and as far as you can see, there are tall obstacles in your path. It is enough to make you want to quit moving. It is overwhelming, and here in the valley, the height appears insurmountable. So why try?

I am here today to tell you why. The hike is good for you. It opens your lungs and increases your circulation. It may be a long walk, but it is not without its own reward. There are steps which look impossible, but you will find that you have the strength to do it. One step at a time. I give you enough for one step at a time.

Before you know it, you are standing on the mountain top. You are looking out at the view which takes your breath away. You can look back at the trail and be amazed that you made it. The climb seemed so hard when you were in the valley, but up on top, it seems worth every step. It is exhilarating.

Life is full of mountains. They are not all physical. Some stretch you to your limit emotionally. Others are mental barriers. Mountains stretch your spiritual muscles. They challenge the voices in your head that say you cannot, or that you are less than. Not so. Mountains prove it.

You never have to climb a mountain fast, Beloved. Just keep moving forward. Those big things in your life are there to show you the strength you have. They build endurance. When you get to the top you will see. You will feel the relief of sticking with it and finishing it.

Your mountain will be thrown into the sea...by the small mustard-seed-faith of taking steps. You only need a tiny bit of faith to take the first step. Each next step is another tiny act of faith that has a cumulative effect of removing the mountain before you. Instead of sitting at the bottom and commanding it to move, use your mustard seed to get up and start climbing. It isn't the mountain that is moving, it is your perception of it. Your mustard seed moves you and the mountains are no longer obstacles.

# January 30

*I lift up my eyes to the hills. From where does my help come? My help comes from the Lord, who made heaven and earth. ~Psalms 121:1-2*

And what of the valleys, Beloved? Do you fear them? As you surmount the mountains in your life, do you worry about the trip down again? Life is a series of ups and downs. There is no way to scale the heights without going down into the depths. If there were not differences in elevation, the landscape would be flat with very little variance.

No, My Love, I desire you to see the views. It is not only you who goes up and down, up and down. It is the nature of life. The trick is to keep moving. Do not stay stuck in a valley beyond your appointed time there. Enjoy the strengthening climb out. Soak in the view, and go back towards the valley with renewed vision. Know you are stronger having been at the mountain top.

The valley can be equally beautiful. No, you cannot see far away into the future. In the valley, the vision is up close. It is in the details. There are streams in the valley where you can be refreshed. There is a coolness and a place of rest. All forms of life thrive in the valley, including you. Once you start to see the life flow you can join it instead of fighting against it.

Notice things. Pay attention. In the low places of life, there are details which get missed in the larger picture. In the valley, you can see the trees instead of the forest. The individual places in your life which might need attention show up in the valley. The places of pruning and weeding are clear in the valley. On the mountain, those things are too small to notice.

The valley is a place of growth, Dear One. Do not despise it. It gets you ready for the plan I have for you. Without it, you would not ever progress to your purpose. Each valley gets you ready for the next mountain, and each mountain gets you ready for the next valley. It is a cycle. Learn to appreciate both. Do not stay too long in either place because as long as you keep moving there will be life. You will not stagnate.

I am with you along the path through and over. I show you the beauty all along the way, in the details and in the distances. You are My child and I love sharing it with you.

# January 31

*But they who wait for the Lord shall renew their strength; they shall mount up with wings like eagles; they shall run and not be weary; they shall walk and not faint.*
*~Isaiah 40:31*

Renewal. To become new again. Weary One, you need renewal. A new beginning. A fresh start. It does not have to mean big change. It can be a turning of your heart, from discouragement to encouragement. From fear to faith. From your circumstances to My face.

If you put your hope in me, renewal will come. It will rise like the morning sun at dawn. When you look to another source for your hope, it will not end well. You might determine hope does you no good, because when it is deferred it makes your heart sick. So why hope? Why seek renewal? Because, Dear One, it is on hope you soar. It is hope that renews your heart and breathes life back into you. I am your hope. All other sources will fail you. Hope in your job. Hope in your friends or family. Hope in your abilities. Hope in your talents. Hope in anything outside of me is futile. Do not fall for the lie that hope from other places can save you.

My hope brings the renewal you seek. It is new every morning. You can seek me with all your heart, even your heart with broken pieces. When you seek me you will find me, and when you find me, renewal will be yours. Hope will flow. Your circumstances might not change, but your outlook will. Your heart will beat again.

# February 1

*Now faith is the assurance of things hoped for, the conviction of things not seen.*
~Hebrews 11:1

What is it about the unknown that scares you, Weary One? Is it the lack of control you have? Is it that you are fearful of the outcome? When the future is uncertain, it forces you to trust me. You have to believe I am for you, that I will not abandon you. When you cannot see what is coming it is a hard to trust. A blind trust.

If you do not have a long history of trusting me you will be uncomfortable. Even those who have trusted me for decades sometimes struggle with this kind of deep trust. It is a hard lesson to learn, and harder still to retain. Yet, when you have seen me come through in uncertain times before, you are more likely to turn to me first when they arrive at your doorstep again.

No one knows the future, Beloved. No one. It may appear that all things are moving smoothly in your life, when all of a sudden the rug gets pulled out from under you. Illness comes calling. Financial ruin knocks on your door. Loss breaks into your space. Grief spills out of the windows. No one knows when these things will happen, only that they will. Every life has some of these kinds of challenges. Yours is no exception.

The trick is to remember when I held you up before. It is the word of your testimony which defeats the enemy, the place in your life where blind trust was all you had, and I came through. My faithfulness shows you how much I love you. You are My child and I will never abandon you, even in the unknown-to-you-moments. Remember that the unknown-to-you is the always-known-to-me. When you remember that, you will know I am always trustworthy and true. I have it all in My hand, and none of it is a surprise to me. Blind trust is not misplaced, if I am the one you are trusting.

# February 2

*For whoever has despised the day of small things shall rejoice, and shall see the plumb line in the hand of Zerubbabel. These seven are the eyes of the Lord, which range through the whole earth. ~Zachariah 4:10*

Go back, just for a moment, and remember. There have been days when you thought you would not survive. You wondered if you could continue on. Some days you felt as if you failed. Your dreams shattered. Your future unsure, you wondered why go on? Do you remember those dark nights, Beloved?

Look at you now. You did not give up. You did not give in. You moved forward by inches at a time. Now, you are standing once again. You may not be where you thought you would be before life knocked you down, but you are moving. I know there are days where it is slow going. Days you feel as if life is a waste of your time. But you have made it through all of those days, have you not?

I can look back and I can see your dark nights of the soul. I know the desperate places in which you have been. I heard, every time you cried out. I was there, in the midst, with you. Don't forget that. You have every reason to celebrate your past difficulties because you made it through. Make a memorial in your heart of what I have done. Share the rescue with your children. Tell the story to your friends.

It is the stories which testify. Your testimony is powerful. It lifts others up. To tell the story, you must be able to look back and see My hand at work. Even in the hard things. Even in the dark places. Do not despise your road. It is where all the growth happens. Like a seed in the ground appears to die before it is broken open to sprout new life, you have gone to the place of death and lived. You have been covered in the dark, but you have germinated there. Your shell has been broken into pieces which have nourished your spirit. Now you are sprouting new life, and reaching towards the light.

# February 3

*Deep calls to deep at the roar of your waterfalls; all your breakers and your waves have gone over me. By day the Lord commands his steadfast love, and at night His song is with me, a prayer to the God of my life. ~Psalms 42:7-8*

Persist in My presence. It is easy to skip it. It is easy to rush it. I am not asking for you to check the quiet-time box. It is deeper than that, but it requires less. Sitting in My presence is something to be done intentionally. There are times to converse as you go through your day. That is not what I am talking about here.

You might call it soaking. As if you were in a pool of water, just soak, float, and lie back to rest. You might put on worship music, or you might prefer silence. You might kneel or prostrate yourself on the floor. You might sit and lean your head back like a child does in her/his father's lap. It is a place worth waiting for. In fact, Weary One, waiting is required to get there.

You long to hear me. So, seek My voice. Come day after day. Persist in your efforts to be with me. In me. We are united in spirit, you and I. You may not realize it, but we are. The thoughts that pop in your head are directly related to your time with me. Hearing My heart, seeking My face. When someone you know comes to mind and you feel the need to pray or call. It is My prompting. When you find a scripture rolling through your head at just the right moment. It is My provision. When you hear the wind in the trees whisper, I love you. It is My voice.

Persist. It requires nothing of you other than to turn your face towards me. Tune your ear to My voice. Sit. Wait. Rest. Find me. Climb in My lap. Soak here in My love. Let it flow through every pore. Breathe it in. You will find victory. Hope. Encouragement. Strength. My presence is all those things. It is there for you to partake of. It will nourish you. Partake of My presence. It will bring you new ways and new thoughts. The world cannot touch you here. Here is my secret place with you and me alone. It is your shield, from all of life and its darts.

Once you have found me, you will never let me go. You will come over and over again. I will always be there for you. Soak and let me soften your heart. Let me wash over you.

# February 4

*And we also thank God constantly for this, that when you received the word of God, which you heard from us, you accepted it not as the word of men but as what it really is, the word of God, which is at work in you believers. ~1 Thessalonians 2:13*

I speak to your heart. Can you hear? Weary One, hold on. Do not fret. Do not worry. I am as close as your breath. A whisper away. Sometimes I speak in the noise around you. Your children speak unexpected wisdom. A crowd cheers or sings. A storm blows. There is power in My voice.

But sometimes, I speak in silence. A leaf falling. Your children sleeping. The wind. These are My whispers to you. They tell of My love for you. They tell you that you are not forgotten. In the loudness and busyness of life, My whispers say, "Don't forget to listen."

My words come to you in the noise and in the silence. I can speak in multiple ways. Just as you speak to your children in different ways at different times based on what they need, I do the same for you. It is the tuning into My voice that will draw you to me in those moments.

Dear One, life is not always kind. You know this more than most. It is not fair. It is not easy. Sometimes it beats you up, but in your heart, you know My voice. You know you are not alone, even when it feels I am miles away. You need only to silence yourself for a moment to hear. To know My very breath is in you. It is what holds you together. It is what centers you. It is what will move you forward.

You are not stuck even though it feels so. Do not live by your feelings. They are not always accurate. They can be glorious and they can be brutal, but your feelings are not the final word. I am. I am the one who tells your heart to hold on. Hold on to me and believe me as I speak.

# February 5

*Then you will call upon me and come and pray to me, and I will hear you. You will seek me and find me, when you seek me with all your heart. ~Jeremiah 29:12-13*

Hearts wander from me. Your heart wanders, My Love. It isn't intentional. You do not wake up in the morning and think, I will walk away from God today. No, but it happens. It is a gradual drifting. Circumstances pull you away from me. The busyness of life drags your heart with it. You say you will not leave me and yet, you do. You forget.

I do not say this with a harsh tone, but with tenderness. It breaks My heart, yes. But more importantly it breaks yours. Do you not know it? Some of the brokenness you live with is because you have wandered. There are a multitude of reasons for wandering, but there are even more for returning your heart to me.

Do not let it slip away unnoticed. Think back to your first encounter with me. And then how I wooed you. One question, one thought at a time. It was a dance. You stepped towards me, and I towards you. I moved away and you followed. You looked for me because you felt My presence. You asked me all your questions and I answered. Back and forth we went, until you realized you could trust me with your heart. It was a beautiful thing, Dear One.

You can get back to that place of wonder. The awe and newness of the relationship. It doesn't have to dry up. I am the same God now as I was then. Still waiting and playing hide and seek with you. Only you rarely have time to find me anymore. I sit in different places, waiting to surprise you, but you never come looking. Your heart wants to, but your daily living has prevented it. Can you change that? Can you seek after me?

# February 6

*But we impart a secret and hidden wisdom of God, which God decreed before the ages for our glory.* ~1 Corinthians 2:7

I am mysterious and it is intentional on My part. A mystery is something that is difficult or impossible to explain. So much of who I am is a mystery to you. The human mind is not able to comprehend all of me, but that is the beauty of it. When I am sitting with you, there are parts of me you know, but oh so many you do not. I enjoy introducing you to new facets of My character. There are clues in the scriptures. There is evidence in nature, or people can reveal My character to you. I use so many ways to uncover them for you to see.

Beloved, it is just like when you are getting to know someone, the more time you are with them the more you see what makes them tick. There are friendships where, even years into them, new things pop up that you didn't know about one another. All relationships are this way. So imagine, how much there is that you don't know about me. Every facet is unique to me and I am happy to share them with you.

The issue is that many people focus only on the parts of me they know. They grab a hold of one facet and build an entire theology around it. Yet, there are so many other parts of me that remain unseen. It is why I love being mysterious. The curious seek me out, Dear One. They do not hold onto one or two parts of My character, but continually seek out the others. They are the ones who dig deep. They are the ones who are convinced they know me, but then find there is even more to learn. The curious are not ashamed to say they don't know all there is to know. To them, it is a chase, a challenge to seek me out.

I must say, I do love a good challenge. I leave clues around for them to find. And the curious ones are always aware and looking for who I am. They are never satisfied, until I show them a new part of myself. Then we spend some time together studying My character and how the new fits into the other perceptions. I expand in their eyes. It builds their faith. The mysterious and the curious...we do well together. Are you curious?

# February 7

*You keep him in perfect peace whose mind is stayed on You, because he trusts in You. ~Isaiah 26:3*

Meditate on me. It simply means to think deeply and focus your mind for a period of time on me. Think deeply. Focus on My word. Breathe me in. Rest in me. When you meditate on me, you will find peace. You will hear My words to your spirit.

A parable takes on new meaning. Matthew 13: 45-46 says, "Again, the kingdom of heaven is like a merchant seeking beautiful pearls, who, when he had found one pearl of great price, went and sold all that he had and bought it."

I am the merchant. I seek a pearl. It is you. You are My pearl of great price, Beloved. You are the one I found who is worthy of My all. I have given everything I have for you. I sacrificed it all to purchase your freedom. This is the Kingdom of Heaven. Freedom for captives. Beauty for ashes. Redemption for My high value pearls. I am always seeking them out. I am bringing them into My kingdom.

When you meditate on my word, the merchant becomes more than a merchant. The pearl becomes more than a pearl. The lesson becomes personal. It is clear. Your eyes are open to My meaning. Do not discount meditating on me, Weary One. I can lift your burden and give you insight into how to walk your path. It is critical to meditate on me.

# February 8

*Thus, says the Lord, "Who makes a way in the sea, a path in the mighty waters, who brings forth chariot and horse, army and warrior; they lie down, they cannot rise, they are extinguished, quenched like a wick. Remember not the former things nor consider the things of old." ~Isaiah 43:16-18*

I am a way maker. I create a way when there seems to be no way. Do not doubt My ability to clear a path for you, Weary One. In all the days that go endlessly on, I am working. I can still split the sea. I am a rescuer of My children. And once you have been rescued, you become a rescuer, too.

It is true. I have created you to be a rescuer. Only those who have walked a hard road are qualified to walk beside others along their own difficult paths. To have you, one who has been there, is invaluable. You sit and hold hands. You hold space for others who need it. You do not have flowery words, but words of true comfort, or no words at all. You know the wrong things to say because they have all been said to you. You know how not to be flippant or judgmental to those experiencing difficulty.

You assist me with the rescue. You help me make a way for others. Does this surprise you? Think about it. When you are at your end, and cannot move forward, what lifts you up? Who was there for you? There are quiet steady people who show up because they understand heartbreak. They come and sit with you in the midst of it. They did not run from it. They came and made a way for your feelings to escape. They made a way for you to take a break. They made a way for you to do what you needed to do, no matter what that was. You thought there was no way to enter that room, to file that paper, to hear that report, whatever it was, you didn't see the way. But I sent someone to the rescue, before you even knew you needed it.

I am a way maker, Beloved. But so are you. Sometimes I make a way by splitting the sea, but other times I do it by sending you.

# February 9

*The Lord is my shepherd; I shall not want. He makes me lie down in green pastures. He leads me beside still waters. He restores my soul. He leads me in paths of righteousness for His name's sake. ~Psalm 23:1-3*

I am a shepherd. Shepherding isn't something that is understood in these modern days in which you live. Shepherds take care of their sheep. It is their only job. They protect them. They make sure they have good grazing areas and a water supply. They carry a rod to fend off predators and to move brush out of the way. They herd them along pathways to avoid cliffs and rocky ground. They gather them around at night to keep them within sight.

It is a solitary job. There are other shepherds nearby, but mostly they work alone. They talk to their sheep. The sheep know the shepherd's voice. They know he will be there for them. The shepherd will go after one sheep if it gets lost. But what does he do with the 99? Have you ever thought of that, Beloved?

Sometimes you are the one I go after, and sometimes you are one of the 99. You feel trapped, like you are stuck in a thicket and you are waiting for rescue...but that isn't always true. You cannot always believe your feelings. Sometimes you feel as if you are tangled up, but in reality, you are safe. You are nourished by My words. You drink living water. You are sheltered in My love. You are one of the 99.

Other times you might be drowning in a river which is carrying you away. Or you might be stuck in a thorn bush which causes so much pain you cannot free yourself. At those times, you are the one I go after. Shepherds know the difference between the one and the 99. I do as well. Trust me when I say I lead you in green pastures, still waters, and the valley of the shadow. All of those places are familiar to me. I know the way through. I know the paths to take. Follow My voice.

# February 10

*Listen to advice and accept instruction, that you may gain wisdom in the future.*
*~Proverbs 19:20*

Beloved, do you ever have dreary days? Are there days that seem to go on beyond the 24 hours allotted to them? Those days are the ones that feel as if you are stuck in quicksand and you are being sucked under, like you are trying to breathe through a straw. Those are the days in which you cry out. To me, yes, but Dear One, sometimes you need to cry out to others around you. It is not weak to ask for help.

Asking for help takes bravery. It requires all your courage to seek out one who can guide you. Someone who will pray, yes, but also someone who will listen. Even if all you have to offer is silence or tears. There are those who are listeners. Some are friends. Some are family. Some are professionals. Then there is always me. Do not be afraid to speak.

The fear of exposure is real, but it is also what binds you. You fear that if someone knew of your burden you would be perceived as weak, or unstable. So, you keep it to yourself. You suffer needlessly. The lack of oxygen makes it feel as if you are suffocating. So open your mouth, release your story, whatever it is. It is not too hard, or too shocking. When you share it, you will be able to breathe again. You were never meant to carry it alone.

You have to be the one to ask. I cannot force you to seek help. No one can. You can talk to me, because I already know all about the details. But sometimes, you need to find a person. I have so many possibilities for you. Look around you. Don't hesitate. Do not drag your feet. Find healing. Do not hold yourself back from something I desire for you. Cry out.

# February 11

*Even though I walk through the valley of the shadow of death, I will fear no evil, for you are with me; your rod and your staff, they comfort me. You prepare a table before me in the presence of my enemies; you anoint my head with oil; my cup overflows. ~Psalms 23:4-5*

Are you tired, Beloved? Do you wonder how much pressure you can take before you crumble? The world seems against you. No matter how you try, you cannot seem to catch a break. It is the valley of the shadow. It comes from all sides. You are so familiar with this valley that you have given up ever leaving. Though I am with you, you feel alone. Though I have My rod and staff to fend off your enemies, you have forgotten. The weariness seeps into you like a flood.

It is okay to allow the tears to flow. It does not mean you have a lack of faith. It is honest and authentic for you to let the truth of your feelings out. It is your reality. My staff offers comfort. It leads My sheep to places of safety, even with enemies all around barking and nipping at your heels. Notice it is the shepherd who carries the staff. It doesn't operate on its own.

I give you good things even in the valley of the shadow. You feast at a table when most would be running away. You are anointed for this task. You are designed for this very place. I have poured the oil of My Spirit over you, to empower you in the valley. Let it flow. Eat the feast. Sit at the table. Do not let the pressure of the valley of the shadow overcome you. Instead look to me to give you gifts that run over into your life so that it is obvious you are walking with the shepherd.

# February 12

*But we have renounced disgraceful, underhanded ways. We refuse to practice cunning or to tamper with God's word, but by the open statement of the truth we would commend ourselves to everyone's conscience in the sight of God. 2 ~Corinthians 4:2*

When do you get to take off your mask, Weary One? You know the one. It says everything is fine when it is not. It says you are put together when, in reality you are falling apart. The mask is a facade for those around you. It prevents anyone from getting too close.

It started out as self-protection. Hurt and pain taught you early that it is easier to pretend than to be vulnerable. Vulnerable is dangerous. A mask solves that problem, until it becomes a bigger one. Until hiding behind a mask locks you in a prison.

Beloved, holding all the pain inside, never exposing it to the light, is a trap. Do not fall for it. You think you are safe from judgements and prying eyes when you put the mask on, but it isn't true. The only one you are hiding from is yourself.

My light shatters the darkness. When your pain comes into contact with My light, the heaviness flees. The relief you seek is found. There are ways to take off the mask you wear. With a trusted friend. With a counselor. With a pastor. With your spouse. You know who the safe people are in your life. I know them too, because I put them there for you. Taking off masks requires courage and bravery. I have given you both. You have what you need. You just need to take the step to do it. It is up to you. Freedom will come. Trust me enough to lower the mask.

# February 13

*You know that the testing of your faith produces steadfastness. And let steadfastness have its full effect, that you may be perfect and complete, lacking in nothing. If any of you lacks wisdom, let him ask God, who gives generously to all without reproach, and it will be given him. ~James 1:3-5*

The pressure is building. It is layers upon layers of heartache. It is years and years of grief. With each new layer, comes more weight, until you feel you can no longer bear it. It is tough. It is hard. But stop for a moment and realize that over time, pressure creates beauty.

Diamonds are an example of time turned to beauty. They start as coal, black and dark. It is hidden in the earth. Deep. Under many layers. The pressure is immense. But under it all, a transformation is happening. The dark clears and the light begins to bounce around. The coal becomes the hardest rock. It is dense, but it is clear. When cut, light is trapped inside it and fire swirls around. That sparkle has made diamonds a valued gemstone for centuries.

The truth is not in the stone itself, but in the process. There is a spiritual principle here. In all of nature, really. Pressure creates beauty. The same is true in you, Beloved. The pressure you live under is what creates the fire and light that lives within you. There is nothing else that can transform like this crucible you are in. It is uncomfortable. It is oh so difficult, but it is creating beauty.

It is not outside beauty, but a place inside for My light to dwell and to shine out. The pressure makes it brilliant. The cuts, the polishing, and the light all work together to bring life to the stone. It shines and it says, "You belong with me." It is no wonder diamonds are held in high esteem and symbolize love. They are stunning, just as you are stunning. Even before the transformation of the pressure is complete, you are brilliant. Do not despise the process. Embrace it.

# February 14

*Love is patient and kind; love does not envy or boast; it is not arrogant or rude. It does not insist on its own way; it is not irritable or resentful; it does not rejoice at wrongdoing, but rejoices with the truth. Love bears all things, believes all things, hopes all things, endures all things. ~1 Corinthians 13:4-7*

Do you know My love, really know it? It is different from human love. You might not understand how deep My love for you goes. It trumps any other. It is powerful and empowering once you believe it. Can you believe it, Dear One? Will you choose to believe that the creator of the universe feels this way about you? If you choose me, none of the insecurities of human love can touch you. Don't get me wrong, human love is a beautiful thing, but it pales in comparison to the way I love you. If you are secure in My love all the other is in addition to, not instead of.

Weary One, I am patient. I am kind. I do not envy or boast. I am not proud. I do not dishonor others. I do not seek Myself. I am not easily angered. I keep no record of wrongs. I do not delight in evil, but I rejoice in the truth. I always protect, always trust, always hope and always persevere. I never fail. Prophecies will stop. Tongues will be stilled. Knowledge will pass away. You know in part, Beloved, but when I come you will know the whole. You will no longer behave as a child, but put those childish things behind you. Now, you only see My reflection in your mirror, but one day we will be face to face. You will be fully known. Faith, hope and love...the greatest is My love for you.

Do not shrink back from My attentiveness to you. Do not avoid My eyes as they see deep into your heart. Let me love you, even in your brokenness. My love heals those places. It knits your heart back together. It creates a healing balm which restores health to your wounds. On this day of love, choose the most powerful love there is...My love.

# February 15

*"Put your finger here, and see My hands; and put out your hand, and place it in My side. Do not disbelieve, but believe." ~John 20:27*

I dare you to believe. Weary One, the courage to believe me is more than just saying you believe it. You can believe I love you, but knowing it deep down takes practice. I have given so many promises to you, yet you question if they will ever happen. You wonder if I have forgotten you. You don't believe what you say nor what you tell others. Your faith is empty words.

Hardship can do that to you, Beloved. It steals your belief. You may not even realize it is gone, until something happens that requires you to believe and you find yourself empty. Without hope. Without courage. Without belief. It is often a startling revelation. In fact, rather than face the truth of it, you cover it with religious words that are so convincing you think you believe them yourself.

You say, "God has a plan." Or, "He will get me through." But deep inside you do not believe it is true, at least not for you. Maybe everyone else gets to be loved by me, but you are the one who doesn't meet up to My standard. But, shhhh. Don't tell anyone. Have "faith." Grit your teeth. Smile. Act as if you are My child on the outside, while the inside is crying. Or angry. Faith doesn't work. Not like you expected it to. Not like they told you it would.

Hard things happen. Over and over again. Grief rips you up and spits you out. Love never shows up. The other shoe drops so often you expect it to every single time. You can never relax. You are always on edge waiting for the next hard thing.

I dare you to stop doing that. I dare you to look at the truth and to speak it. I dare you to say, "I don't really believe any of this." And then, I dare you to believe. Not in a religious fake way that is without teeth. No, I want you to step out of your self-imposed clichés, and your comfortableness with discomfort. I issue you a challenge which requires you to be out of your comfort zone. Belief, true belief, requires a step into the fearful unknown. It is where you hash out what you actually believe vs. what you say you believe. Dear One, hardship is such a place. Once you get past the self-pity, you will see your true heart. Your lack of faith. Your doubt. Your false expectations. All of it. Then, the humility of brokenness, will cause you to rethink everything.

In this space, I dare you to believe, I love you. Even the dark places. I dare you to believe I am for you, not against you. I dare you to believe I have more for you than what you are currently experiencing. I dare you.

# February 16

*Now the Lord is the Spirit, and where the Spirit of the Lord is, there is freedom. ~2 Corinthians 3:17*

My Love, you are free. I made you so. Free from fear. Free from sorrow. Free from regret. Free from broken expectations. Free from it all. I know you do not feel it. You continue to walk in bondage. Shackles in your mind hold you captive to your thoughts. The ones that say things will always be this way. You do not look for anything else. You hang on to what you experience by your fingernails. The bigger picture, MY bigger picture, is far from your mind, Weary One.

Beloved, I have unlocked the shackles and the prison door. I have opened the way up before you, yet you sit as if you are still bound. Look around you. If you feel trapped you are missing something. There is an option or a path you have not found, because you are not trapped. You are free.

To find My freedom you merely have to look for it. It is all around you, even in the midst of your circumstances. There is no reason to think you will have it "someday" when this or that is different. You have it now, but you must take hold of it. You have to remove the chains, and walk out of the prison. I hold the keys. I used them to unlock you. Stand up. Walk out your path.

My Holy Spirit is your guide. You will hear, if you listen. Go this way. Make this move. Then the enemy of your freedom will say, "You can't do that. How will you ever…" He will whisper the fears into your ears. You must learn to discern the difference between My voice and his. You must know My voice always brings life and freedom. His brings death and discouragement. Stop. Push those thoughts away. Ask for My help. Listen to what I say. You are already free. You. Are. Already. Free. It is the truth.

# February 17

*We love because He first loved us. ~1 John 4:19*

Nothing separates us, Beloved. There was once a veil between us. Like a bridal veil, it prevented us from seeing each other face to face. It obscured you from me, and it concealed My heart from you. It stood in the way of our intimacy. I couldn't let it continue to be an obstacle in our relationship. So, I sent My Son.

His entire mission was to tear the veil. To remove the separation. It was My heart's desire for you to see me as I am, not as men had made me out to be. The human perception of me will never match with who I truly am. The enormousness of My presence is too great for anyone to understand. I reached down. I initiated contact. There is a reason the veil in the temple was torn from top to bottom and not the other way around.

You see, Dear One, I loved you first. From the very first time I thought of you, I loved you. Before you ever heard of me, I loved you. You have been in My heart from before the foundations of the earth. Yes, that long. I have known of you and longed for the day when you would hear of me. I imagined it. When you turned your face towards me, my heart leapt. It was the moment I had waited for. When you agreed to be my bride, to commit to me forever, I was overjoyed. There was a celebration unlike any other.

Your heart is my home. I seek you, and you find me. It is my way, unlike any other god before me or any who come after me. They are stone, or flesh. They do not reach out to you. I do. I am. The veil is torn. We are face to face.

# February 18

*For I, the Lord your God, hold your right hand; it is I who say to you, "Fear not, I am the one who helps you." ~Isaiah 41:13*

Take heart, Weary One. When trouble comes in like a flood, take heart. When everything seems to remain the same, take heart. When you are tired and cannot take another step, take heart.

How do you take heart? What does that even mean? It means to regain your courage. Not find it the first time, but RE-gain it. Gain it again. It means, Dear One, that you have had courage before. You know courage. You simply need to find it again.

Go back to other times you have had courage. Remember those times. Remember how everything felt hopeless and then you found the ability to rise up. To face the storm. You can do that again. Picture floating down a raging river. You are trying to keep your head above the water. That is your only focus. Keeping your head up. While it is out of the water, you are scanning looking for anything to hold onto to help you keep your head up. A rock. A tree branch. Anything.

You see a branch hanging low across the water and you take heart. You regain your courage and you grab onto it. Barely hanging on, the water continues to rush around you, but you have the branch. Suddenly, you take heart that it is not all over. Still in survival mode, you are able to rest momentarily and regroup. You can wait here for rescue. You wedge yourself into the branches and you wait.

Taking heart looks like this, Dear One. It is finding your courage again in hard situations. It is waiting on rescue. It is knowing you are not done yet. You have more life to live and more relationships to build. You are stronger than you think. Take heart.

# February 19

*Peace I leave with you; My peace I give to you. Not as the world gives do I give to you. Let not your hearts be troubled, neither let them be afraid. ~John 14:27*

What is the worst that can happen? Think on that for a minute. In your current situation, what are you most afraid of? I ask you to consider it because sometimes your fear gets so big it paralyzes you. So, if you take a minute to think about your biggest concerns, it can put them in perspective and take their power away.

Now, think about what you can do to change the circumstances you are afraid of. Is there anything? If not, it is time to let go. In letting go, you are entrusting me with your fear. You are giving it over to me and saying, "I cannot do this on my own. I have no power in this situation. I give it to God who has all power and will always finish what He starts." A weight will lift off of your shoulders when you hand things to me. Your prodigal children. Your difficult relationship. Your diagnosis. Let go of what you cannot change.

What about the things you can change? Wait on me to show you how, but then move forward with the steps I show you. The result of inaction in an area of your life is sometimes worse than the fear. Let's say, you need to make a job change because of a toxic workplace, but you are afraid to lose your security, so you stay put. The result of your inaction is far worse than the loss of security. Your health will suffer. Your family will suffer. Your mind will suffer. All in the name of "security." That doesn't sound so secure to me.

If you trust me, and wait, I will lead you past the fear and into the faith. Faith that when you make changes, I will direct you. I will catch you. I will not forsake you and leave you hanging. It is My character to help My children find their way. Trust in My character as a good father, Dear One. This is not all on you. I know it feels like you are in this alone, but it is simply not true. I am with you, always.

The worst that can happen is you will never make a change. You will never grow. You will stay miserable forever. You will not find your purpose. You will never be happy. Those are some pretty bad outcomes, all because you are afraid to move. So, listen to My voice. Follow My direction. You will find courage to keep going and to look past your fear.

# February 20

*We who have fled for refuge might have strong encouragement to hold fast to the hope set before us. We have this as a sure and steadfast anchor of the soul, a hope that enters into the inner place behind the curtain. ~Hebrews 6:18-19*

I am your anchor. When storms come, tether yourself to me. Anchors are heavy. They are solid. They dig in and hold fast. They are not taken lightly, because they keep the entire boat from drifting away. The anchor is the most important piece of equipment on a ship, because it is what keeps it in place.

When you hold fast to me, Beloved, you will not drift. You will not sink. You are bound to me and I hold. Storms can come. Waves can batter. Wind can blow. Yet, you will not be moved.

The secret, is that you don't know how important the anchor is until you are in a storm. Before that, you might think it unnecessary. It sits on deck, or hangs from the side of the ship. Heavy and bulky. The chain that holds it takes up space and is wound around and around in circles. But when the storm comes, or when the ship needs to be secure in an insecure place, the anchor drops. It sinks to the bottom of the sea, and it rests there. The weight, size, and shape, make it strong enough to hold an entire ship in place.

I am an anchor for your soul. When the night is dark and your soul cannot find rest, I am your anchor. Tie yourself to me. Throw me overboard, into the waves of doubt. Let me sink to the depths of the dark night of the soul. When the circumstances of your life seem to overtake you, it is then you realize your anchor is critical to your survival.

The importance of maintaining the anchor before the storm cannot be overstated. If it is rusty, or the chain tangled, when you throw it overboard you will find yourself tossed on the sea. Your spirit is lost and seeking, in the middle of the storm where you cannot tell which way to go. In that situation, insecurity causes doubt to rise up. Hope is blown away by the wind. When you lose hope, all is lost.

If you hope in me, and you know I am your anchor, you will stay the course. You will not be blown away. You will hold firm and wait out the storm. When it clears, you will hoist the anchor and continue on your voyage, knowing that if another storm blows up, you are tied to me.

# February 21

*And he said to them, "Come away by yourselves to a quiet place and rest a while." For many were coming and going and they had no leisure even to eat. ~Mark 6:31*

Weary One, take a breath. Another one. Another one. Breathe in My calm. Breathe out your worry. Let the tears flow. Let them roll. I am not afraid of your tears or your emotion. They are an outlet for the feelings which are building inside of you.

I created you to experience life in full. Without these emotions, your life would be flat. Robotic. You are designed to be immersed in the sights, sounds, and smells around you. These experiences paint a vivid picture. They saturate you and yes, sometimes overwhelm you.

It is okay to be overwhelmed. Do not fault yourself when you cannot take in one more stimulus. It is My design that your tears flow when you are most tired. It is an indicator that you need rest. Like a check engine light for your soul. Stop. Take a moment. Sit with me. Assess the situation. Give it some attention. Is your tank empty? Are you overheated? Is your fluid level low? Do a check of your gauges. What are they telling you?

Beloved, there are so many times you just push right through difficult circumstances in your life. You feel that everyone is depending on you, so you cannot stop and take stock of your condition, but I tell you, the world will not fall apart if you take a moment to rest. Gathering yourself is not a weakness. Finding a time and a place to rest will actually strengthen you to carry your load.

Just like if you ignore the check engine light in your vehicle it will break down, it is the same with your physical being. I have given you warning signals. Do not ignore them, or you will find yourself in need of extended service. Those tears that rise up to the surface and overflow are signals. That physical feeling of being drained and unable to function is a signal. You are running on fumes. You are in danger of a breakdown.

I long for you to rest. To sit with me and let me minister to your soul. To sleep. To pull back as much as you can. To unburden your heart to me and to take My breath within you. I hear all your excuses of why you cannot take the time. Those excuses will not serve you well, My Love. They will prolong the pain and increase the intensity of your breakdown. Melt downs are part of the warning system that is built into you to prevent a total breakdown. Take a moment. Do not delay. Stop what you are doing. It is an emergency. Check your gauges. Rest. Refill your tank. Breathe. Sit with me.

# February 22

*I know how to be brought low, and I know how to abound. In any and very circumstance, I have learned the secret of facing plenty and hunger, abundance and need. ~ Philippians 4: 12-13*

Dear One, flexibility is defined as the ability to flex. Simple enough. It seems as though that such a simple definition would be easy to carry out. Not so. There are days when life doesn't go as planned. Interruptions happen. It is important to be pliable. I am not merely talking about circumstances. Flexibility applies to spiritual matters as well as interruptions in a daily schedule or a delayed appointment.

Digging your heels in and not being able to be malleable in your spiritual life does nothing to help you grow. In some ways, flexibility gets a bad rap because it seems to some people to be associated with compromise. But, Dear One, when I am working it requires a supple heart not a hard one. It requires an open spirit to move with My spirit.

A rigid tree breaks off in the wind, but one that bends with the wind does not break, it flows. It joins the movement of the breeze. I need you to be flexible like the trees in the wind. Swaying with changes in direction. Flowing with the pivots which are required in day to day life. Staying open to My words to you. Taking steps when I show you situations where you need to forgive. Listening to me when I point out an error or a thought pattern that is contrary to My heart.

This is not compromise, it is transformation. This is not concession, it is grace. This is not giving in, it is humility. Learning to be flexible is a sign of growth and maturity. Relinquishing control of the way you see things and bending to My instruction and My vision is the ability to flex at its best. Stretching yourself is healthy. Flow, Beloved. Do not be scared of My movement. Trust My words. Trust My heart is for you. Flex with me and you will see.

# February 23

*Every valley shall be lifted up, and every mountain and hill be made low; the uneven ground shall become level, and the rough places a plain. ~Isaiah 40:4*

I am your rescuer. I have said it before. I will say it again. In impossible situations, I am working. Behind the scenes. When you can't even see it, I am making a way. You feel all alone, but nothing could be further from the truth. I go before you and I sit with you. I have your back at all times.

How could I not, Weary One? You are My treasure. I value you more than you can possibly understand. You are My prized possession. I have not abandoned you. I will care for you, always. So, do not despair in the midst of suffering. Do not give up or fall apart. Your meltdown will not change things. Be at peace. I am working all things for your good. You might not believe me, but do not discount me. You cannot always see My hand in action. One day you will look back and see clearly, but for now, just believe me. Take me at My word.

When you least expect it, I will rescue you. When you cannot fathom how your circumstances will work out, I will work them out. I am the calm in the midst of the churning sea. Worry will only cause you to sink. Lift your eyes, Weary One. Look for me in unexpected places. I am moving mountains for you. You do not see it now but one day you will.

# February 24

*Before they call I will answer; while they are yet speaking I will hear.* ~Isaiah 65:24

This too shall pass. Whatever Big Thing you think you cannot overcome will not remain big in your life. It may or may not be removed, but it will not continue to block your view. When obstacles come into your life, they loom. Especially ones that knock the breath from you. The phone call. The court papers. The accident. The diagnosis. Those BIG ones will take a huge chunk from you. The wound will be great; the pain earth shattering. The healing slow. Resurrection of the heart takes time, Beloved.

You must give yourself grace. I do. There are seasons for grief. Seasons of pain. If you cannot just get up and move on, it is not time yet. Allow yourself the time you need. It feels as if your world is collapsing, but it is not. It is changing. Acceptance of change, especially the hard changes and losses you don't choose, is the most difficult thing about life. Changes make you weary. Giving yourself grace to feel the deep pain, to allow it to do its work in you, is important, Dear One. You must allow yourself some space.

But there will come a day, where you will wake up and the wide-open wound will be a scar. The scar tissue will form around it and it will no longer rule your days. Your first thoughts of the day will not drift to the Big Thing anymore. It will "pass" and you will begin a new day. The scar will remain as a reminder. Grief never fully goes away. It is the consequence of loving deeply. But, Beloved, grief will not always be the Big Thing in your vision. It will take an appropriate place. You will look back on your dark days with heartfelt emotion. You will walk forward with the shadow of those days behind you as you face the sun.

# February 25

*Where shall I go from your Spirit? Or where shall I flee from your presence? If I ascend to heaven, you are there! If I make my bed in Sheol, you are there! ~Psalms 139:7-8*

I will run after you. There is no place you can go, Dear One, where I will not follow you. It is the opposite of what you might think. Most people think they have to run after me, but they do not realize I am already chasing them. I long to have their whole heart. Every part. Every room within it. If you try to hide, I will find you. If you run away, I will chase you. You are worth every step I take. I choose you. I will always choose you.

Some people think they can walk away from me, but I never walk away from them. I follow. So, if you have gone your own way and you are far from me, you are not far at all. I'm as close as your breath. Merely acknowledge me. I am right beside you. I am holding your space for you until you return to me. Does your heart pound harder when you hear this? You are never out of My sight, nor My heart. I love you with an everlasting love which cannot be quenched or forgotten. Ever.

If you are with me, but feel as though you are failing at following me "correctly," stop. Stop putting more weight on your shoulders. Stop performing. You don't have to jump through hoops for me. You do not have to run after me...I live inside you, Beloved. My grace is sufficient for you.

Don't get me wrong, I love to be pursued. I love it when you want to talk to me about what is going on in your life. I love to tell you what is on My heart. This conversation between our hearts is refreshing to me. But pursuing is different than performing. Pursuing is turning your heart towards me. Allowing yourself to be caught. Pressing into My advances and letting me take you deeper in me. I will run at full speed towards you if you are far. I will race to you if you are close by. I will follow you anywhere and everywhere. Always.

# February 26

*For you did not receive the spirit of slavery to fall back into fear, but you have received the spirit of adoption as sons, by whom we cry, "Abba! Father!" ~Romans 8:15*

You are not an orphan. You are a son or a daughter. Dear One, do you not understand what that means? You don't have to earn My approval. You already have it. You don't have to fight for a place with me. You already are established in My family. I created you. I give you breath. I nurture you. I grow you. Because you are My child. I am a good father.

An orphan spirit will tell you that I do not love you. It will tell you that I love everyone else differently than you, that you are somehow an imposter. That because you go through hard things it is what you deserve. The enemy loves to trick you into believing you are illegitimate. The spirit of rejection chimes in to say you will never fit in. You will never be a part or belong. Shame joins the chorus by making you feel less than. You are embarrassed by yourself. You hide your true self behind a mask so that no one else will see you. This triad of the enemy is his most effective tool. It is at the base of so many lies. If he can get you to believe it, it is the foundation of all the other mess he makes.

I am here to knock down what the evil one has built and clean up his mess. I am here to tell you that you are not any of the things he says you are. You need a new foundation. You need renewed thoughts.

So, let me breathe some life into you. You are mine. You are loved, just as you are. Yes, really. You are My treasure. You make me proud. You are not a failure. You do not embarrass me. You are not being punished by me. The things you go through have nothing to do with your position as My child. I do not rank My children. Do you rank yours? Each one is individually unique. Each one has a special relationship. Each one is a delight. Do you want your children to all act the same? I don't either. I want mine to be themselves. To learn and grow into the beautiful creation I have made.

You are not an orphan. You are legitimate. You are intentional. You are not an accident or a mistake. Find your identity in me. Believe what I say and it will break the power of the tirade of the enemy who is trying to destroy you from the inside out. Listen to My voice. My Child, you are not nor will you ever be, an orphan.

# February 27

*Commit your work to the Lord, and your plans will be established. ~Proverbs 16:3*

Do you look for divine encounters? I have set them up for you. They will happen in unexpected places. At the store. In the break room. Around the table. In the laundry room. Be aware. Look for them. They are appointments, appointed times of interaction.

What is a divine appointment? It is a connection which I have pre-ordained for you. An intersection between heaven and earth. My Spirit that lives inside of you, reaches out and touches the heart of another. Or you, weary and beat down by life, suddenly find yourself face to face with hope in the shape of another person. Both parties in such an interaction benefit.

I arrange these times to build you up and encourage those involved in them. It can be total strangers, or close friends who know just when to obey My prompt to call you. The man in the grocery store bagging your groceries can make one statement that hits your heart. Or you can give a smile and a kind word to your server at a restaurant. These appointments are small nods that I am with you and that I use you, or someone else, to bring about My hope.

There are other divine appointments. A song can come on the radio at just the right moment. A scripture can jump off the page. A phrase uttered in a movie can hit your heart in such a way you know it was a message from me. These kinds of encounters are proof that I am near. They are sweet nods from me to you. My way of showing you that before you even knew where you would be, I had a plan to meet you there.

# February 28

*Rejoice not over me, O my enemy; when I fall, I shall rise; when I sit in darkness, the Lord will be a light to me. Do not gloat over me, my enemy! ~Micah 7:8*

I am one who wars. That might not sit right with you, since warfare means killing and death. It is a hard thing to reconcile My love and My wrath. They seem so opposed to each other, do they not? It might even make you uncomfortable, to think of me as both a loving father and a ruthless warrior. Yet, you can see in My word that I am.

Would it help to think of yourself as both a loving parent and a mama or papa bear? What makes you come out swinging regarding your children? Do you protect them? My guess is you would fight to the death for their lives. That is a warrior spirit. You want evil far, far from them. Remember that I fight on a spiritual level, not a natural one. In fact, fighting in the natural is not as effective as ripping out the root of the problem.

Today, much of what fighting for your children looks like has gone awry. Instead of paying attention to the spiritual fight, parents have opted to fight the people who are around their children. The boxing match that has followed is one where nobody wins. Hateful words are spoken by protective parents at ballgames, in classrooms, and at conferences. All in the name of being a warrior for their children.

Beloved, being a warrior has nothing to do with accusing others. It has everything to do with knowing your enemy. He will kill, steal, and destroy and sometimes he does so by destroying relationships with others, so in accusing them, you are playing right into his hands.

I war for you, My Child. I fight for your freedom. I fight for your wholeness. I do not let the enemy destroy you. He comes and accuses you day and night but I do not listen. You are mine, and I refuse to let him taint My love for you with his words.

A warrior spirit is not about death, or killing. No, it is about standing up when everything around you wants to knock you down. It is about continuing on even when the enemy is roaring around you. It is about not giving up or giving in to his taunts. My warrior Spirit rises up in you when the enemy tells you that you cannot continue on.

When he says you are down for the count, it is the thing inside you that crawls to your knees, pulls your bloody and battered self to stand up and plant yourself in front of him. He pounds you, and you refuse to let him take you out. Over and over again, you stand before him, with your gloves up...ready to go...ready to knock him out. Your willingness and determination are My warrior Spirit rising up inside of you, because I am a warrior and I fight for you.

# March 1

*Whoever goes about slandering reveals secrets, but he who is trustworthy in spirit keeps a thing covered. ~Proverbs 11:13*

I am your confidant. One who keeps your secrets. Does this surprise you, Beloved? I do not desire to expose you. It is not My mission to drag you into the streets and accuse you before a crowd. No, I am gentle in My rebuke. I am restorative in My correction. I do not throw stones, I keep secrets. A secret is something that is kept or meant to be unknown and unseen by others. It is something I do to protect you.

My heart is to commune with you. To have such a close relationship that you will tell me your secrets and I can tell you mine. Your biggest fears do not scare me. Your heartache doesn't make me want to run away from you. Even your sin and its consequences do not push me away. I am always ready for your secrets, whatever they are.

A confidant is one you trust with your secrets. One who you can confide in. You can trust me with your private thoughts. Just as you know your best friend will not gossip about you, you have the same assurance with me. Even more so. I am able to keep your deepest thoughts between the two of us. We are companions, who understand one another.

If you can keep a secret, I will share mine with you. Yes, Weary One, I have secrets, too. I have feelings like yours, you are made in My image after all. I have deep heart desires, and I have places where I have been wounded by My children. I tell you this so you will know, you are not alone. Confidants know this. They hold nothing back from one another. A good confidant brings health to your bones. It makes relationships a safe place. It requires trust, vulnerability, and stepping out in belief. I am all those things. I am a safe place for you. I am a secret keeper.

# March 2

*Therefore, my beloved brothers, be steadfast, immovable, always abounding in the work of the Lord, knowing that in the Lord your labor is not in vain. ~1 Corinthians 15:58*

What does it mean to be steadfast? Is it possible in the difficult places of life? To be unwavering, when you feel nothing but instability? To be loyal when you feel like quitting? To stand firm, when the ground under your feet seems to be quaking?

I tell you, Weary One, it is possible. It is actually who you are. The hardships of life require steadfastness in order to get through them. Putting one foot in front of the other is part of the journey. It is an especially important part. Step. Step. Step. Even when it seems impossible to move your feet, you step.

How do you learn to be steadfast? You watch me. I never give up on you or your circumstances. I never back away. I never leave you or forsake you. So then, you must never leave or forsake yourself. Follow My model. Stay. Stand firm. My promises are a solid foundation to stand on. Hold tight to them.

Being steadfast means you are immovable on the course I have set for you. Hard days, difficult circumstances, and seemingly impossible trials require you to be immovable. On days when it feels as if the wind could blow you over, stand strong. Find a friend to hold you up if you have to. Call out to me. I am with you, there in the midst holding you up.

Never have I said to do this on your own. Never have I said you must have it all together, or that you should not wrestle. In fact, you are better equipped when you are together with others who support your path. They help you to be steadfast. They remind you of who you are. They hold you to it. Being steadfast is not a once and done situation. It is an ongoing choice to be firm in your convictions. It is doing what you know I have planned for you. It is holding onto the rock of your faith, because it is the only immovable thing in your life. When you plant your feet on what I have shown you, you will become an immovable force.

# March 3

*Therefore, if anyone is in Christ, he is a new creation. The old has passed away; behold, the new has come. ~2 Corinthians 5:17*

Do not be called away. Do not go back to the things that move you to unhealthy places. Any area of life can pull you; mentally, emotionally, spiritually, or physically. You are an overcomer. I have placed the ability within you to overcome hard things. To walk away without the smell of smoke upon you, because I am with you in the fire. You do not walk alone. When things heat up in your life, stay the course. Hold onto what I have promised you. Do not allow the enemy to get into your head.

You are My Beloved. You are valuable. You are worthy of My love. I have covered you. When you are tempted to fall back into old patterns, remember they will not cover you. They expose you. They pull you away from the path I have made for you. It is not hard to see this fact, but it is hard not to follow them.

Patterns come from past hurts. They engrain themselves deep. Usually they are related to self-protection or numbing some wound from the past. You live in a sin-filled world. It is full of pain. Every one of My creations has felt the pain of life. No one is immune. How you handle the pain is what creates the patterns of behavior. Unhealthy patterns cause more pain, not less. They are originally designed to protect your heart or mind, but they eventually become a prison from which you cannot escape.

When you see the path I have for you, hope rises up. You begin to believe there is a way out of the dark places. It requires vulnerability, transparency, and trust, which you usually give up when you go into self-protect mode. To move forward, you have to develop those skills. Practicing transparency isn't easy. It requires you to face your fears. Trusting me in the midst of the changes you make is the only way to avoid falling back into old patterns.

I will walk with you when you let go of past hurts. I will give you the power to forgive painful memories. You will walk out of those places empowered to move in a new direction that is healthy. Let me guide you, Weary One. Let me help you stand strong in your new patterns.

# March 4

*For the Lord of hosts has purposed, and who will annul it? His hand is stretched out, and who will turn it back? ~Isaiah 14:27*

I am sovereign. I possess ultimate power, which means nothing happens without My knowledge. Nothing. There are no surprises for me. Each event is part of the overall picture. Sometimes it looks as if everything is lost, only to have things change into something entirely different.

Beloved, I do not cause terrible things to happen. Many of the bad things are brought in by a sin-filled world and a free will population. Others are the enemy trying to do his business of killing, stealing, and destroying. Life is hard.

I have the capability to interrupt the laws I created. I could stop gravity the moment a plane is about to crash. I could remove disease from a body designed to heal itself. I could do a lot of things. On occasion I do. You can read about these times in My word, but I do not do these things often.

What you need to know is that even if I do not interrupt the laws I created, it doesn't mean I am not unaware. I allow nature to take its course for bigger reasons than you can see. The depth of the world's pain is the only thing that causes people to look up to me. If all was smooth and easy, there would be no need for me to be around. In your children, do you smooth the way for them? Or do you separate them from their choices? Sitting down and looking at issues which bring pain is one of the main goals of parenting. Making sense of hard things.

I do the same with My children. I sit down with them. I listen to their heartache. I try to give them words of encouragement. I do not cause harm to My children any more than you do. I do not rejoice when bad things happen to them. I grieve. I wait for them to come to me for comfort. I love too much to wish harm on My kids.

Do not let anyone tell you that My sovereignty means I bring all the bad things on people. That is not what sovereignty is. Sovereignty is ruling over all, not causing all. Just as a king rules his subjects, but does not control them, so I am sovereign over your heart. I rule it, if you allow me to. I do not force Myself on you. I do not control your behavior you are the one to do that.

# March 5

*I believe that I shall look upon the goodness of the Lord in the land of the living! Wait for the Lord; be strong, and let your heart take courage; wait for the Lord!*
*~Psalms 27:13-14*

What have you given up, Weary One? What has your life forced from your grasp? Your dreams? Your hopes? Your future? Hard places force you to let some things go. Holding onto everything only causes heartache, so you open your hand. It is not willfully, it is under duress. Examine what you have given up. Examine how you feel about it.

Resentment is poison. Self-pity is toxic. When you are forced to give up things important to you, there is a plan in place to bring you down to the dark places. When you mull over and over in your mind all that you have lost, you absorb the toxins. Once in your system, it is a slow and gradual death of your dreams. Anger follows. Deep hurts cause hot anger to rise up. Giving up on important things sends you on a spiral of downward thoughts. You find yourself miserable, and you may not even connect the feelings with the losses.

I am here to tell you, letting things go is not always bad. Sometimes it takes letting them go in order to recognize the deep desire that resides within you. Sometimes abandoning your plans, your ideas, your way, makes room for mine. Beloved, if you have fire in you to do a certain thing, it is likely that I am the one who put it there. When you let that thing go, be it a dream or a plan, you make room for me to work it out for you. It will look differently than you had imagined it. But I have not given up on it, and neither should you.

Allow dreams to be dormant for a season. To put down roots in the dark places. Let me nurture it imperceptibly. Then one day, when you are content with your life as it is now, not how you thought it should be, I will resurrect the dream. It will come full circle and all that you abandoned in your moment of trial will come back to you. It is actually surrender. You give it up to me. Then I give it back to you. All the promises I made will be fulfilled. You will see.

# March 6

*For this reason, the Father loves me, because I lay down my life that I may take it up again. ~John 10:17*

Giving up, but not forever, just for a season. Laying down something willingly in order to draw closer to me is common this time of year. Many will put something away in order to have it resurrected later on. This giving up is different than the kind where you had no choice. This giving up is a decision. It is a desire to deny yourself in order to grow closer spiritually to me. Some have given up sugar, others meat, still others technology. Each decides for him/herself what they want to remove from their lives.

Willingly sacrificing areas of your life which are important in order to spend more time with me is a beautiful practice, but not everyone replaces their sacrifice with me. Beloved, anything can become a habit and not a heart commitment. However, when you abandon some comfort or another for a season, I will show up. I will honor your sacrifice by being present in your day-to-day. But truth be told, I am there in your day-to-day already. It's just that when you give up something important to you, you become more aware of My presence.

Giving up requires you to lean on me. That leaning into the discomfort you willingly chose, will connect you to me in a new way. Your eyes will open to new and different priorities. I will show you Myself, and because you have laid down your comfort, you will see me in places you were blind to before. Giving up things is fasting, and fasting is a practice which enhances spiritual growth. Allow yourself to abandon and lay things down that prevent you from seeing me clearly. It is a spiritual discipline which is neglected in modern times, but it is more needed than ever before. Give up. Surrender. Fast. Deny yourself. A season of sacrifice can change your life.

# March 7

*He gives them security, and they are supported, and His eyes are upon their ways.*
*~Job 24:3*

I see you washing your tears down the drain in the shower. I see the puddles on your pillow. I see you swallow hard and smile when someone asks you again about your situation, whatever it is. I see you hold your chin firm when they whisper behind your back, thinking you cannot hear them. I see you on the mornings you struggle to get out of bed because the pain of the body or emotions is too great. I see you squeezing pennies together to try to make it. I see you caring for those in your life beyond your strength to do so. I see every grimace, tear, and every time you grit your teeth.

I see YOU. Not the circumstance in which you are living. I see YOU. Not the reputation. Not the details of your loss. Not the ongoing saga. YOU are My beloved. YOU are My precious child.

I SEE you. My eyes are open to your heart. I SEE you. The internal struggle with which you wrestle daily. I SEE you. The ongoing sadness. The hardship of living in pain. I SEE the parts of you, you think no one knows about. You are not alone. You are never alone.

You are so strong, yet you feel weak. You don't know how much longer you can go on, but you do. Every day. You continue forward. You do what has to be done. You put one foot in front of the other. I see you. Today I simply want you to know, you are seen. Not forgotten or forsaken. Seen.

# March 8

*For though we walk in the flesh, we are not waging war according to the flesh. For the weapons of our warfare are not of the flesh but have divine power to destroy strongholds. We destroy arguments and every lofty opinion raised against the knowledge of God, and take every thought captive to obey Christ. ~2 Corinthians 10:3-5*

Whose voice are you listening to? In other words, what are your thoughts telling you? Do you wake up in the morning dreading the day because you think you know what lies ahead? Do you assume things will be the same today as they were yesterday? Those thoughts, the ones that are on automatic pilot are setting the tone of your life. That is a pretty important thing to pay attention to.

The feeling of being "less than" originates with a thought. If you feel you will never get better, check your thoughts. If the drudgery you walk under doesn't lift, it probably began with a thought. The resentment you carry set up shop in your thoughts. Are you getting the idea, Weary One? Your thoughts are vital to how you see your circumstances. And who controls your thoughts? Why, you do, of course.

A thought can be planted in several ways, but you are the gatekeeper to let it continue or to shut it down. The enemy whispers in your ear, "You are not enough, you are never going to make it, you will always be less than." Do you let those thoughts take root? Worse yet, do you repeat them to yourself?

The voices of the world say you are not pretty enough, rich enough, or successful enough. If you chase them down, even to prove them wrong, you are giving your thoughts over. They will direct the course of your life.

I tell you, you are valuable, you are worthy, you are loved, you are cared for, you are beautiful, and you are special. Do you listen to My words like you listen to the others? Do you let these thoughts take root and grow to direct your steps? For some reason, My words are harder for you to hear than the others. Why is that, Dear One? You banish the thoughts I plant in your mind. You think they are untrue or not for you. It is killing you to push My words away.

There are some ways to check thoughts which are dominating your mind. Ask some questions. Is this thought true of what God says about me? Can I find it in the word of God? Does this thought bring me life? Does it lift me up?

Beloved, if your thoughts are something other than what I say about you, it is not the truth. Banish it. Put it down. Do not allow it in. Be the gatekeeper of your mind. Close the gate on thoughts which are contrary to what I say. You will find your life, attitude, actions, and behaviors will shift. You will begin to believe the truth about yourself and that will change everything.

# March 9

*For by grace you have been saved through faith. And this is not your own doing; it is the gift of God, not a result of works, so that no one may boast. ~Ephesians 2:8-9*

What is life supposed to look like, Dear One? Differently than it does? There are things you expected which never happened. There are things that happened which you never expected. The expectations are the problem. A strong belief that something will be a certain way in the future, and holding onto that belief above all, causes so much grief in life.

In our society, it is hard not try to meet expectations. When you don't live up to them, it causes comparisons, not only from others but in your own mind. You feel somehow left behind when everyone else is "ahead" of the life timeline. School, job, marriage, kids, house, on and on it goes. But how many people actually follow the timeline? Not as many as you think.

It might appear to you that everyone else has it all, but it is simply not the truth. Some who "have it all" are miserable. Most didn't go in order, or do things the "right" way. But who determines what is right? When you hold to what your life is supposed to look like in your eyes, but then it doesn't, it is a recipe for depression and resentment.

When you heap expectations on others such as your spouse or your children, the relationships suffer. Unmet expectations are a big source of breakdowns in relationships. If he would just... If she could ever... These thoughts create an invisible standard which leads to accusation and communicating becomes next to impossible.

Beloved, let go of your expectations. On yourself. On others. Everyone is different and has a different path. Everyone will go their own way and it will not look like the world says it should.

Even your relationship with me is held to high expectations that you will perform a certain way. That you will do certain things and not do others. That perfectionistic way is impossible to meet. I don't expect you to do it. My Son gave His blood so you don't have to be perfect. There is grace enough for you to be yourself. I give you grace. Give some to yourself and those around you. Drop the expectations and embrace the freedom I give you.

# March 10

*Behold, I have engraved you on the palms of My hands; your walls are continually before me. ~Isaiah 49:16*

I don't give up on you. Weary One, there is not a time in your life I have ever given up, and I will not ever. Somehow you feel as though I am there for everyone else and that I am not there for you, but you are wrong. There is nothing you can do to make me give up on you. When you have a bad day I am in the midst of it cheering you on. Even when you are making bad choices for your life, I am praying for you to turn things around. I am offering other choices to help, always.

There may be people in your life who have let you down and thrown in the towel. You might have pushed them out. You may have let yourself down. Don't punish yourself. Don't think you can never make it out of whatever bad place you find yourself. The God of the universe is in your corner. I do not ever give up.

Even if you are in circumstances beyond your control, I never give up and neither should you. If you have a physical ailment or an emotional one. If you are grieving or depressed. If you are confused or spinning your wheels. Even if you are spiritually distant from me or have walked away all together. I will never give up on you.

Humans somehow think My actions depend on theirs. It is not true. My ability to stay with you, to fight for you, to live among you, to care for you, even to love you, isn't dependent on you at all. It is dependent on me. My character is one of tenacity. I don't give up. Not on you. Not on the people I created. Not on the world.

Remember, I am the one who designed all of it. There is a plan. It includes you. I never leave you out of My plan. You cannot make me forget you. You are carved on My heart. You are written on My hands. I will never give up.

# March 11

*Humble yourselves before the Lord, and He will exalt you. ~James 4:10*

Can you give up the need to be right, Dear One? There are times in your life you can look back and see you believed something that wasn't true. But at the time you were dead set it was true. You would have fought for it because you believed it so deeply. Yet, now you look back and laugh, it could be as simple as when you were a kid and you believed in the Tooth Fairy or Santa Claus. At some point, reality was showing you the truth, but you refused to believe it because you wanted the lie to be true so badly.

"Yes," you say, "but those around me reinforced the lie. They actually participated in it." Do you think it is any different now, My Love? I am talking about what people believe about others. Or what people believe about you. Or what they believe about me. There are lies all around you. When you choose to believe them instead of My word, and then you stake your life on them being right you are setting yourself up for heartbreak.

In the divided culture in which you live, everyone believes in one side or another. You are willing to forfeit relationships to stand on your sandy ground. You think you are standing on the rock, but just as the Tooth Fairy flew away and was replaced with reality, so too will the false beliefs you are holding onto. The reality will come and so will the understanding that the disagreements are distractions and not worth the time wasted.

Give up your need to be right, Weary One. Consider that you might not be. In any given situation, you might be the one who is not seeing things clearly, but that is okay. It is okay to change your mind and to realign your beliefs. How many relationships in your life could heal if you asked forgiveness, or you forgave? How much stress could you reduce if you didn't dig your heels in so deeply? Beloved, it is worth laying down your pride and reconsidering your need to be right all the time. It is worth changing your mind.

Even if you still believe your perspective is the right one, consider the perspectives of others who have their own backgrounds and life experiences. Diversity is My creation! I don't want everyone to be the same or to think the same way. What if you are wrong? Better yet, what if it doesn't matter? What if all the time you spend researching or rehashing your beliefs about a topic or a person could be spent loving people? What if you are falling for the lies of those around you instead of getting on with the truth? Life is too short to declare yourself right all the time. Come to me. Trust me to show you. Humble yourself.

# March 12

*For God gave us a spirit, not of fear, but of power and love and self-control. ~2 Timothy 1:7*

Fear is a liar, Weary One. When you are ruled by fear, anxiety is your companion. Wild thoughts fly through your mind. The more frenzied your fear becomes, the harder it is to control those thoughts and before you know it the fear has complete control of you. You might even know it is irrational, but you cannot seem to stop it from taking over your life. If someone tells you to stop being afraid, it is futile. You know it is not healthy. You know it is causing a huge obstacle in your life, but you cannot stop it.

Beloved, I say perfect love casts out fear, but you have to believe it. I say do not be afraid a million times, and you can acknowledge My words, but not feel them. The enemy uses fear as his main weapon. He knows he can immobilize you. He can stop you in your tracks. That is his entire goal. To stop you from moving into My plan for your life.

I know there are scary things in your life. The diagnosis. The loss. The phone call. The divorce. The spiral of depression. The trap of addiction. The oppression. The disappointment of life. The news of the day. There are literally hundreds of things that cause panic every single day. The enemy works so hard to make sure you come into contact with fear as often as possible. He does this until you are so saturated in it that you are paralyzed.

Saturate yourself in something other than fear. Something that will speak truth to you. My word can reset your mind to things above. Prayer is not just for some "quiet time" checklist. When you talk to me I can reassure you of My love for you.

Trusted friends or counselors can help you to see the enemy's web and how to cut your way out of it. The main thing is to know fear will take over if you let it. You have to choose not to let it. It is a hard battle, but it is one I have already won. It is a victory I want you to walk in, Weary One. It will decrease the weariness of your soul. Let me show you the truth. Keep watch over the gate of your mind. Shut the door on alarming sources and come to me. I will walk with you.

# March 13

Beloved, disappointment is a hard pill to swallow. When something is appointed, it is as if you have an appointment, it is crushing to be dis-appointed. It is like a wish unfulfilled. It crushes you. All the time and effort you put in vanishes when cancellations happen.

Disappointment is different than expectations, though the two are closely related. Expectations are usually unspoken; more like thoughts about how things will go. Sometimes you are not even aware you have expectations until they don't happen. Disappointment on the other hand, is when something falls through. Something tangible. Expectations need to be let go. Disappointments need to be grieved.

Dear One, it is okay to grieve when you are disappointed. In fact, if you don't grieve the loss, you can get stuck in it. Whatever it is that you worked so hard to accomplish. A new job you trained for and didn't get. A relationship you worked on that fell apart anyway. New treatment options that failed. Life's disappointments can weigh you down if you don't process the grief of them, Weary One. They rise up like a mountain in front of you that seems impossible to climb.

Yet, I can take those mountains and use them to build strength and resilience into you. You can bounce back, once you have properly acknowledged the pain that disappointments cause. They are the building blocks of a strong foundation. Yes, pain is part of the process, but it strengthens the base so that your life doesn't crumble with the next disappointment that comes at you. They become a tool in My hand to shape you and make you into a strong person, who learns to face disappointments with grace. To process them with honesty. To go beyond them with new determination.

Disappointments...the changing of what is appointed...is a life skill. It is never easy, but it is necessary to adapt and learn healthy ways to process. I am with you in the process. Cry out to me and I will be near. I will walk with you and bring you to the appointed times of life.

# March 14

*In peace I will both lie down and sleep; for you alone, O Lord, make me dwell in safety. ~Psalms 4:8*

What is stealing your peace today, My Love? I see your furrowed brow. I hear your heart beating faster. I know there are tears just behind your eyes waiting for the moment to overtake you. You are trembling. The enemy has your mind and he is stealing the truth from you.

There is nothing I do not control. There is no famine or sword that has escaped My notice. There is no illness or injury I have not seen. There is no loss I have not known was coming. You are held in the palm of My hand. Even when you don't feel it. Even when it seems the world has gone crazy around you. Even when everything is upside down.

There is no need to panic. There is no need for frenzy. There is no need to speak. Sit in silence with me. Let me speak to the storm and to your heart. "Peace be still." I say it over you. "Peace be still." I say it over the waves in your life. "Peace be still." I say it over your life. "Peace be still."

My peace is a blanket which comforts you. It covers and warms you in the midst of a storm. It bores down into your soul and takes up residence there. If I am with you, and in you and surrounding you...so is My peace. If you do not know it, stop, take a moment and breathe. Breathe in My peace. Breathe out your worry. Breathe in My peace. Breathe out your anxiety. Breathe in My peace. Breathe out your fear.

I have it. I have it all. In. The. Palm. Of. My. Hand. Trust me. Breathe.

# March 15

*Then I turned my face to the Lord God, seeking Him by prayer and pleas for mercy with fasting and sackcloth and ashes. ~Daniel 9:3*

You will rise from these ashes, My Child. I am always working, even in the fire, because I am the fire. There is always hope. The fire burns, but out of the ashes I bring new opportunities. You are right to grieve the loss, but do not get stuck there. Open your eyes. Let My creativity flow through you. You will begin to see new life rising up. You will see possibilities you would have missed before.

When you walk through fire, it is hard. You are blinded by the smoke. You cannot see the other side. When the fire is extinguished, you see the devastation. You see the ruins of what was. You mourn with your face to the ground. But, after a time, you begin to see the freedom from the old for what it is, a chance of the new.

It is similar to a blank canvas. You can pick any color. There are new materials. You can try new textures. You can experiment and grow. You are free to create a fresh look that ties all the experiences you have into a new form. Things may not work as they did before. You may have to rethink your process. Rework your patterns. Adaptation is part of it all. Going forward means creating a new path, not rehashing an old one.

The good news is that I am with you on your journey through the ashes. I can point out the places you need to stop and sit in a sackcloth for a bit. I can get you past those places in healthy ways. I can give you pause as to how the hard things have made way for the gifts I have developed in you.

Empathy you use in your daily life to encourage others came from these ashes. Perseverance to put one foot in front of the other, when others would simply give up, came from these ashes. The ability to love others well, despite their imperfections, came from these ashes. Do not despise your ashes, Beloved. They have made you who you are.

Now is the time to rise up into who I created in the process. Find your footing. Walk out of the ashes, not with tears, even though there have been many, walk with your head held high. With the eyes of your heart opened to the future. With your sensitive spirit awakened to needs around you. Be My hands and feet in the midst of the storms of life. Rise from your ashes to new life.

# March 16

*When the Spirit of truth comes, He will guide you into all the truth, for He will not speak on His own authority, but whatever He hears He will speak, and He will declare to you the things that are to come. ~John 16:13*

Do not be afraid of the unknown, My Love, for it is only unknown to you, not to me. I live in the unknown places of your life. There is not a shadow for me. I see clearly, always. Where you see foggy misty landscapes, I see crisp and clear pathways. I lead you in those paths, through the valley of the shadow. Take My hand. Let me guide you.

It is difficult to walk your own way when you cannot see in front of you, is it not? Especially when things are not ideal, and you don't know what is happening around you. There are seasons of turmoil and trouble. You cannot see My plan in these seasons. You only see and feel the pain of them, Weary One. That is why you need to hold My hand. Trust that I have it, even when you are blind. No need to grope around when I can lead you.

Your confidence must be in me, Dear One, not the circumstances around you. Have I ever let you down? You have experience with me. We are in a relationship and I have your back. I will take care of you, no matter what is happening in the world. It is the shadowy places, where things are unclear, that you need to fall back to what you know to be true.

I love you. I will not leave or forsake you. I am your guide, through this present trial, just as I have been through the past ones. I do not abandon My children. You are My child. I provide. I am always working. There is always hope.

You know these things, you simply have to remember them. Sometime in the future, you will look back and see that once again, I was working. You will see how My hand guided and protected you. You will be amazed at how all of the current unknown territory has become familiar, and how it became a part of the story of your life that I am writing.

# March 17

*You are the light of the world. A city set on a hill cannot be hidden. Nor do people light a lamp and put it under a basket, but on a stand, and it gives light to all in the house. In the same way, let your light shine before others, so that they may see your good works and give glory to your Father who is in heaven. ~Matthew 5:14-16*

Let your light shine, Weary One. I know you are tired. I know hard things suck the life from you, but do not let the enemy steal your light. You may think the things you have been through disqualify you from serving me, but I tell you the opposite is true. They absolutely qualify you. Your pain, your grief, your loss, your bad choices, your hardships, all of these are redeemed by My Son's blood. They are your scars, which means you have lived a little. You have seen life from the side of suffering.

Look around you at the world. What do you see? Suffering, yes? When the whole world is spinning out of control, you know the anchor of My presence will hold because you have lived it. You know My heart is for you. You know that in hard times I am with you. You know I will lead you. You have learned these things for such a time as this.

Those who are unfamiliar with My ways do not know how to handle hardship. They are ruled by their fear. They run to and fro as they try to figure out what to do. You are My light in the darkness of the unknown. You have the experience they need of holding My hand, of trusting My path through the rough places, of learning I am for you. Do not hide your scars. Do not hide the skills you have learned in the hardness of life. Shine, Beloved, shine.

Take My light, with you wherever you go. Give it to those around you. My servants have always done so. Whether it be to another nation, as St. Patrick did, or in their own backyard, they have taken the light and shared it. Do not hide it, but put it out there for all to see.

# March 18

*Fear not, for I am with you; be not dismayed, for I am your God; I will strengthen you, I will help you, I will uphold you with My righteous right hand. ~Isaiah 41:10*

I take care of you in a crisis, Dear One. There is never a time in history where I didn't care for My people. Passover is but one example. The death angel literally passed over them because of the blood of the lamb. Now, the blood of My lamb covers you. You are safe underneath His sacrifice. Whatever comes, you will be spared.

That doesn't mean there won't be pain or suffering. That doesn't mean it won't be difficult. My people fled Egypt in just a few hours. Everything they had known changed in an instant. Their enemies chased until they were backed into a corner. I opened the way before them, and they watched their enemies thrown into the sea. Their freedom was assured, but it was 40 years in the desert before they claimed it. Hardship was involved every step of the way, but I delivered My people.

Do not fret. Things around you may be upside down, but I am not. Things in your household may be crazy and unclear, but I am not. Your health may be in question, but I am not. Your emotions may be shaky and unstable, but I am not. You might be in a crisis situation, but I am not.

I do not change. I was with My people in Egypt. I was with them in the desert. I was with them in the Promised Land. I am always with My children. That includes you. That includes today. That includes whatever is coming. I am with you.

# March 19

*I have said these things to you, that in me you may have peace. In the world you will have tribulation. But take heart; I have overcome the world. ~John 16:33*

Do not fear the unknown, Weary One. You cannot know all. No one can. There is just too much to know for a human brain to comprehend. When things are uncertain, and you do not know what is happening, fear takes a foothold. Anxiety surfaces, keeping you awake at night. It is a kind of limbo land and it is stressful. Uncertainty freezes you in your tracks. You don't know which way to step, what path to follow, or what will happen to you. You are like a trapped animal, unsure, and afraid, so rather than move you freeze to assess the situation. You stand like a stone, too afraid to move forward.

Or when a big event happens out of the blue and many people are facing the unknown, panic can set in, causing a frenzy. Fighting over silly things ensues. Instead of being frozen, groups of people look to each other to see how to react. One follows the other and soon nothing makes sense, but people keep on going, like sheep without a shepherd. They would go right over a cliff if the first one in line did so.

Freeze or Frenzy? Beloved, neither of these responses to the unknown is healthy. In both of them fear is the foundation. To avoid feeling like a trapped animal, you have to breathe a minute. Calm your body. Breathe in. Breathe out. Seems simple, but in fearful times it is hard to remember to breathe.

Calm your mind. You cannot know the future, so quit inventing one in your mind. Stop thinking of all the possible things that could go wrong. Quit imagining all the worst-case scenarios. Clear your head of all thoughts. Fill it back up with My word. You believe in a God who doesn't cower in the face of the unknown. That is because it isn't unknown to me. You can trust in your own knowledge, or you can trust in mine. You can trust in your fearful thoughts, or you can trust in me. Faith, not fear, will win the day.

I am not saying you will suddenly know what you cannot currently see. I am saying it won't matter that you don't know. Fear will not rule you if you heed My words. Peace will come, despite the fact you are facing the unknown. You can look the unknown in the eye and stare it down. You can trust that I am working always, and wait for me to show you the way out of limbo land.

In the meantime, you can sit with me. Listen to My voice. Trust My word. Breathe in. Breathe out. Think. Rest. Be at peace. I have overcome the world. Fear and frenzy are included in the things I have overcome. Nothing is unknown to me. Put your trust in that fact.

# March 20

*Hear my cry, O God, listen to my prayer; from the end of the earth I call to you when my heart is faint. Lead me to the rock that is higher than I, for you have been my refuge, a strong tower against the enemy. ~Psalms 61:1-3*

I am a strong tower. I am your refuge. I am a fortress. Weary One, when you are tired and exhausted from life, I am your safe place. I will protect you. It is a mandate I put upon Myself. I am always aware of what you need and I provide it for you. You need only turn to me and run to My strong tower.

A tower is high, above the fray. Towers of old were built for their strategic advantage, so the king could see the enemy approach. The kingdom could prepare for battle by sizing up the foe on the ground below. I do that for you, I allow you to see into the battle before it comes. When you sit with me, inside My tower of protection, I will share with you the battle plans. How you will win against your enemy. Even when you feel weak, Beloved, I will strengthen you.

Being in a fortress offers security like no other place. The walls are stone. The doors are thick. A fortress is perched on the side of a high place. It is not easily accessed. The enemy cannot come unannounced. Those inside have time to prepare for what is coming. My love is a fortress. You can hide within it. It surrounds you like the high tall walls of a castle. My heart is multidimensional just as a fortress has intricate pathways and levels of protections. It is deep. It is wide. It is all inclusive.

In all of this, I am a refuge. A safe place you can go. When everything is topsy-turvy, when life is uncertain, when difficult times come...I am your refuge. I may not give you every answer, but I am the solution. I may not show you the whole path, but I am the way. You can trust me to be your refuge. I am your shelter, if you run to me. I offer you a place of being safe from pursuit. The enemy cannot touch you here with me. Stay with me.

# March 21

*For you shall go out in joy and be led forth in peace; the mountains and the hills before you shall break forth into singing, and all the trees of the field shall clap their hands. ~Isaiah 55:12*

Dear One, be brave. There are things beyond your control. Scary things. Bravery will be required to face them. Being brave doesn't mean you don't have any fear. It means you move despite your fear. You find your resolve and determination to move even when you are scared to do so.

When you acknowledge your fear to me, I carry it. Sharing your heart with me sets you free. It doesn't mean the scary things go away, but you are empowered to meet them face to face. You won't back down, because I don't back down. When facing the unknown, admit how uncomfortable it makes you. It will make you feel better just to speak it. It turns on the light and the shadows flee.

As long as you hold it inside, it will manifest in anxiety, or depression. It will wreak havoc in your mind. Worry will overtake you. But, Beloved, your worry changes nothing. The circumstance you are in stays the same, no matter how much you fret. So, lay that fear down at My feet. You might have to do it daily for a particularly rough season. It is hard to walk when fear freezes you in your tracks, so bring it to me. Over and over if you have to.

Replace worry and anxiety with My truth. Perfect love casts out fear. Be not afraid, I am with you. There are so many thoughts you can plant into your own mind, Weary One. Do not let your ongoing troubles steal My peace from you. Do not let fear rule your mind. Retrain your thoughts. Do not listen to those around you who are fearful. Guard your heart...and your ears. I am with you. I surround you and give you peace.

# March 22

*Let me dwell in your tent forever! Let me take refuge under the shelter of your wings! ~Psalms 61:4*

Birds find their shelter in trees. They build their nests in the crook of the branches to provide support and protection. The foliage keeps them hidden from danger. Other animals find holes in the ground or caves to shelter themselves and their offspring. Shelter is required for them to live and keep physically safe.

You require shelter, too, Dear One. A roof over your head and a place to get out of the storms. It doesn't have to be a fancy shelter. Its purpose is protection. Safety. Some live in mud huts, or cardboard shacks. Others live in mansions or high-rises. Each chooses their own place, but it comes down to the basic need of survival. A good shelter ensures you will go on, a poor one isn't as accommodating. Security and peace of mind come from knowing your shelter will hold up to whatever comes.

I am a shelter for your soul. You can run to me in times of trouble when you are downcast and burdened by life. Shelter comes from the word shield; I provide a shield for you. A place you can take a deep breath. A place you can hide to wait out the storm. You can hold me up in the battle and the enemy's blows will be turned back. You can cover yourself with me and I will blanket you with peace. My shelter is for the deep places inside of you. The places you think no one sees or knows about. They are safe with me.

The term shelter-in-place is a new one, brought about by a crisis. It means to stay in your shelter, wherever it is, until the danger has passed. It is designed not only to protect you, but also those around you. If everyone shelters in place, the disease will pass by. Actually, sheltering in place is what I had My children do in Egypt when the angel of death passed over them. They took refuge under the blood of the lamb. They survived because of it.

The blood of My Son still offers shelter today. It is not new. It is your shield. It supports and secures you. It repels the enemy's blows. It is a covering provided for you by me. When you run to it, I hide you in the palm of My hand.

# March 23

*Blessed be the Lord, my rock, who trains my hands for war, and my fingers for battle; He is my steadfast love and my fortress, my stronghold and my deliverer, my shield and He in whom I take refuge, who subdues peoples under me. ~Psalms 144:1-2*

You are a fighter. Do you know how I know that, Beloved? Because you get up every time life knocks you down. The barrage of losses and disappointments keeps coming and you keep rising up. There are times you want to stay down for the count. There are times you have had to lie on the mat a bit longer than others, but you have never given up.

It takes guts. It takes courage and determination. It takes strength. It takes an indomitable spirit to keep going in such times. Like an elite athlete trains and pushes through the pain in their body, so you push through the pain in your soul. Not by ignoring it, but by recognizing its power to shape you for the better.

You fight. For yourself. For your family. For those who cannot fight for themselves. It is a calling. You probably don't see it that way. You would rather not be the one taking the punches over and over again. Yet, having so many come your way, has made you strong. The fight has given you the strength to overcome hardship. It has given you practice and experience to dodge the blows and when to throw one.

I see the toll it takes on your heart. I know the hardships beat you down. I am aware of your pain. I understand when you don't want to take one more step or one more punch. Let me bind your wounds, Weary One. Let me wrap your heart with bandages while it heals. Just because you are a fighter, doesn't mean you don't take time to heal. Let me train your hands for battle. Let me hold you up when you feel you cannot stand.

Being a fighter gives you the ability to see others in pain. You can see when the knockout is coming. You can see them go down and you know what to do. You know when to get the smelling salts and infuse them with courage. You know when to throw in the towel to fight another day. You understand how to pull back and nurse your wounds and then get back out there for the next round. You have expertise, from all your years of fighting.

You know how to get up. You know how to rise up. You know how to stand up. I know how to hold you up. I know how to back you up. Together we win the fight, every time.

# March 24

*Arise, shine, for your light has come, and the glory of the Lord has risen upon you. For behold, darkness shall cover the earth, and thick darkness the peoples; but the Lord will arise upon you, and His glory will be seen upon you. And nations shall come to your light, and kings to the brightness of your rising. ~Isaiah 60:1-3*

I speak to your spirit, Weary One. I say you are not too tired. I say you are not too weak. I say you are not lazy. You are strong. You carry strength with you, wherever you go. There is something inside of you that you are not even aware of. It rises. It grows. It breathes. It urges you on. It shouts from the inside, "You can do this!" It calls to you, "You are a warrior!" It is your spirit man.

Do not let your physical body hold you back. It will tell you, "I am too tired." It will tell you, "It is too hard." Do not listen, Dear One. Your spirit knows when it needs to push through and when to rest. Your spirit knows My voice. Your spirit is wise, because I am wise. Your spirit is strong, because I am strong. When you are joined with me, I am in you. I abide in you and you abide in me.

The enemy wants you to quit. He wants you to think you are weak and worthless. He wants you to look at your circumstances and be overwhelmed. I say, "No!" We are strong when we work together. We are capable of big things. I in you and you in me.

Your spirit knows the truth of who I say you are. It might have been buried under a mountain of hardship, but it has not been forgotten. Take a moment to remember. You are My child. You are compassionate. You are brave. You are worthy. You are beautiful. You are the apple of My eye. You have stolen My heart. You are My warrior. You are bold. You are strong. You are powerful. You are resilient. You are tough. Rise up, Beloved. Rise up to be who you are. Let My Spirit speak to yours. You can do whatever I put in front of you. You can make this journey you are on. You will do it. You will see.

# March 25

*When you pass through the waters, I will be with you; and through the rivers, they shall not overwhelm you; when you walk through fire you shall not be burned, and the flame shall not consume you. ~Isaiah 43:2*

There are clouds on the horizon. They bring shadow. They bring a flood. But before that, I bring hope. I bring light. The sun rises. The day is born. What will you do with it? It is a gift to you. Do not despise My gift. Use it to create. Use it to connect, with others, with yourself, with me. Use it to construct the life you want instead of the life you have. Use it to craft something new.

You have been given the gift of more time. It is what you have always wanted, isn't it? You have said, "If I just had more hours in the day." You do, so now what? A new day. A new dawn. All yours. Inspire. Design. Invent. Plan. Prepare.

Every storm has a calm. Every hurricane has an eye. Sometimes I hold back the storm, but others I do not. Sometimes the storm is needed to clear the air. In those moments, Dear One, I hold you. I embrace you and let the storm rage around you. In these times I am closer than your breath. When you do not know the outcome, I am with you in the midst.

You have had many storms in your life, Weary One. They have raged and you feel windblown and battered. Yet, you see I have been with you. The bigger the storm the more you hold on to me; you know what is required to survive.

Now I ask you to share your knowledge. Help those who do not yet know how to sink into me while their own storm is raging. Help them find peace that passes understanding. Help them to find the eye. Give them some of your strength. Then they will pass along their knowledge.

# March 26

*Let me remember my song in the night; let me meditate in my heart. Then my Spirit made a diligent search. ~Psalms 77:6*

When you are tired or burned out, Dear One, listen to the rhythm of your own heart. I put desires and dreams deep inside of you. They course through your veins until life shatters them or disappointment pushes them down. You forget. It is unintentional most of the time. Your circumstances overwhelm you and somewhere along the way you lose yourself. You are swallowed up.

I didn't give you desires and dreams to have them buried. I gave them to you to find your passion. Dreams cannot be stolen from you. You make a choice: push them away, or give up on them altogether because they feel impossible. I assure you they are not. They may take a different form than what you expected. Those expectations always get in the way. You might not have a white picket fence life, but the heartbeat I put within you is still there.

Listen to it. Bapum. Bapum. Bapum. Just listen for a moment...

What is your heart telling you? What does it desire from you? Where are the lost parts of you? How do you get them back?

Let me show you, Weary One. Let me pick you up and put you on your feet again. Let me breathe life back into you. Did you put down your art or your music? Did you give up on your career? Did you put your self-expression aside? I am the one who gave you a unique way to express yourself. I am the one who made you to be just who you are. I want ALL of you. Even the part you have hidden away. Even the part you think is lost forever. Find that part. Write that part down. Talk to me about that part.

Find your courage to pick up the palate again. Be brave and write your songs. Sit with me and I will show you how. I will encourage you to move in those things you have given up. It can be done, even in your busy complicated life. Small steps to regain the rhythm of your heart. You will know it when you find it. It is when you feel most alive. Search me with all of your heart and you will find me...then you will also find yourself.

# March 27

*Thus, says God, the Lord, who created the heavens and stretched them out, who spread out the earth and what comes from it who gives breath to the people on it and Spirit to those who walk in it. ~Isaiah 42:5*

Who is it that gives you breath, Beloved? It is I. When you were born I blew the breath of life into you. It was not an accident, nor a mistake. It was My wish for you to live. I put My breath inside of you to make it happen. I am not one to take back My gifts. Your breath, every one of them you take, is a gift. Do not let the enemy tell you otherwise.

You are My representation on the earth. You are made in My image. But, Dear One, bones and muscles do not make life. It is the breath that makes you who you are. Without it you are declared dead, with it you are alive. I put that within you.

Your respiratory system is a miracle that I created. It filters the air. It defends you. It takes oxygen everywhere you need it to go. It takes in what you need and it pushes out what you don't.

Spiritually, it is the same. Your spirit filters what comes into your heart. It protects you. It feeds and nurtures you. It shapes your thoughts. It knows what to take in and what to push out. That is by design. My design.

When I breathed into you, I did so into your physical body, but also your spirit. You need both to function properly. I did not do this by accident. You are on purpose. You have purpose. It is why you are breathing still. Breathe in life. Breathe out toxicity. Breathe in purpose. Breathe out negativity. When you focus on the gift of breath, you will see My hand. You will hear My voice. Just breathe.

# March 28

*He who dwells in the shelter of the Most High will abide in the shadow of the Almighty. ~Psalms 91:1*

Don't forget the secret place, My Love. You can always get back there during hardship, and even when things are uncertain, especially then. Brokenness draws me to you. Doesn't it draw you to your children? I come to you to soothe you, to comfort you, when you are hurting.

In the secret place with me you will find out what you believe and what you do not. There is grappling and sometimes shouting, along with lots of tears. Fear seems to be a pre-requisite on the hidden path to this place. Honesty is another. Exposing your fearful heart is not a choice during these times, it is impossible to keep it hidden. It bleeds all over the place, and you can do nothing to stop it.

The secret place isn't neat and words are not carefully chosen. In fact, there usually are not many words at all. It is messy when you are working through suffering. Your mind is unable to wrap around My thoughts. Your heart explodes with uncertainty.

It is here...in this messy place...where I meet you. I come, without your call. It is here where I become your shelter. It is here, once your tantrum is over and your feelings are played out, that you find me ready to hold you and say to you, "Shhh...It's going to be okay. I've got you."

Beloved, you will recognize this place. What once was uncomfortable for you because of the intensity, has become a shelter. You have learned and are learning to run to it when times are tough. You can soak in My presence because all other options are futile. It is the only place you can find me. It is where the false beliefs fall away and you find the truth.

I am trustworthy. I am the provider. I am the healer. I am the lover of your soul. I am your dwelling place. You live in the shadow of My wings and the hollow of My hands. It is the secret place...and you are safe here.

# March 29

*Thus, the Lord used to speak to Moses face to face, as a man speaks to his friend.*
*~Exodus 33:11*

One of the beautiful things you might not know about the secret place is that I tell you My secrets there. The name makes you think it is the place that is secret, but it is also a place to tell secrets. I like the play on words. When you come to the secret place, you can tell me yours. You are safe. My ears are open for your cries, your tears, your shouts. You can tell me how you really feel and what you really think. Anything that you are holding onto, or holding back is welcome in this place.

I listen. I hear. I wait for you to do the same. I share My love, but also My wisdom. I make corrections when needed. I hold hurt hearts as well. I point out sin. I welcome repentance. I forgive freely as I set you free. The secret place is a beautiful place of healing, hope, and honesty. It is a place you are free to be yourself, the way I made you.

It is also a place for me to tell you My secrets. Did you know I have some too? I know the end from the beginning. I see the state of hearts. I have feelings. You are created in My image, correct? If you have feelings, I do as well. We are more alike than you know.

In the secret place, once you have wrestled and found peace, I will share the things which are on My heart with you. I will show you the pain I carry, and the love I share. I will tell you things which I hold dear and I will show you things that make me angry. I do this not to burden you, but to have someone to share with.

It is My way of communing with you. Letting you get to know me more intimately. The more you learn of My heart, the less likely you will be drawn away from me by untruths. The enemy wants you to believe so many lies about me, and I combat those by sharing who I am with you. Once you know me, no one will be able to convince you I am against you or anyone else. You will know My secrets.

# March 30

*As a deer pants for flowing streams, so pants my soul for you, O God. My soul thirsts for God, for the living God. When shall I come and appear before God? ~Psalms 42:1-2*

Precious One, does your soul long for me? Are your difficulties weighing you down and keeping your soul bound up? I can tell you that I long for you. I long to sit with you, to be in your presence. Does that surprise you, Weary One? It feels backwards doesn't it, for the God of the universe to say He longs to be with you? But it shouldn't.

From the very beginning I created you to be with me. I put a place in your heart that cries out for communion with me. You can fill your heart up with so many things, but it is not satisfied with just anything. It is only filled by me.

Your hardships try to fill that place. They clamor for your attention. They leave very little time for anything else. I know what it is like for you to be in survival mode, Dear One. Everything seems urgent and so very important. The details of the current issue are on the forefront of your mind. But, Beloved, it is battering your soul, leaving you tired and overwhelmed.

Your soul is weary and there is no longing there. It is dry and cannot find its way. You are dehydrated spiritually. So much so, that you don't even recognize the signs. Dehydration makes you weak. It clouds your mind. It causes your body to begin to shut down. The same is true for your spirit. Without living water and being in My presence you will dry up. You will be weak and unclear as to what path you are on. You will shut down.

I cannot tell you how much this breaks My heart. I so long to be with you, to fill you up. To saturate you with My presence, but Beloved you have to long for it too. Come to me. Sit with me. Put me on the keys to survival list. I will be here waiting for you.

# March 31

*He was despised and rejected by men, a man of sorrows and acquainted with grief; and as one from whom men hide their faces He was despised, and we esteemed Him not. ~Isaiah 53:3*

I know suffering, My Child. Do not believe you are the only one who suffers. Your pain is not lost on me. I feel every heartache. I see every tear. There is no time where I am closer to you than in your suffering. I draw near to you in the hard times. I am acquainted with grief. The heavy places in life are where you will find me closer than your breath.

When tragedy and crisis happen, I am there in the midst. I can calm you in the times you are most fearful. I can bring you peace like a river. Your soul can know My heart, because I have known pain. I know it, still.

Dear One, there is so much suffering in the world. I bear it all. Every one of those who cry out in their hardship, their voices reach My ears. It is overwhelming to hear so many having such difficulty. I don't like it when My children are in pain any more than you like it when yours are.

My Son bore the weight of it all. He knows every sorrow. He feels every pain. In that, you know that you are not alone. The rejection, He felt it. The hurt, He had that too. The sorrow of the world was on His shoulders. But, more importantly than how He carried it all, is why He did it.

He did it for you. His love for you was so great He chose to experience what you do, so He could connect to you. So, WE could connect to you. He poured out His blood, and conquered death so you could be with us.

The trying times you live in, the daily battles you face, are temporary. They will pass. Remember that. No suffering lasts forever. Even the sorrow that you bear in your heart at loss will lessen over time. Pain leaves scars, but it also builds relationship between us. We bond over shared pain.

Brokenness is the thing that humbles you, and healing makes it beautiful. Makes you beautiful. Your sorrows are your clothing. Your garments are created by your tears. You are covered. I cover you as you weep. I weep with you. I surround you when you are struggling. My presence is always there, because I don't want you to be alone in your grief. Cry out to me and you will find I understand you more than you know.

# April 1

*Can you find out the deep things of God? Can you find out the limit of the Almighty? ~Job 11:7*

I live outside of boxes. Beloved, what box have you put me in? Am I in the God-only-heals-other-people box? Or maybe the God-loves-me-when-I-am-good box? What about the boxes you put yourself in? The I-will-never-be-good-enough box? Or the God-has-abandoned-me box?

Weary One, it is time to do away with the boxes. I understand you want to make sense of things. I know that putting things in boxes somehow orders them in your mind. But when your boxes become hindrances to freedom, it is time to throw them away.

I must tell you, one of my favorite things to do is to crumble boxes. I do new things just so you can see me in a new way. The old ways were good in their day. They brought life but when they become immovable traditions I am put into a box. People build an altar and worship the tradition rather than me.

Part of the beauty of being in a relationship with me is that it is alive. It breathes and moves with us. Do you and your other friends always do things the same way? Do you think it is wrong to change the way you relate to one another? No. You pick different meeting places. You have serious times together and fun times together. You pray together and you play together. Yes, you have traditions which are meaningful to you, but that is not all you have.

It is the same way with me. I long to be outside the boxes. I love to keep the mystery of our relationship going. You never know what I will do or how I will do it. It makes you seek after me, to figure me out. The same for you, Dear One. You put yourself in boxes of what you can and cannot do. You believe there is only one you and you will never change or be different. But you are not stagnant. You are always moving and growing. You are learning. You are capable of much more than you believe.

You are not separated or abandoned by me. We are together. Let's get out of our boxes. Let's look for new ways to connect to one another. Art. Music. Research. Prayer. Find me in new places. See yourself in a new way.

# April 2

*The point is this: whoever sows sparingly will also reap sparingly, and whoever sows bountifully will also reap bountifully. ~2 Corinthians 9:6*

Weary One, you need to cultivate your heart. The word cultivate means to prepare and use the land for planting. Of course, it is a gardening term but I am a master gardener. To prepare the soil for seed takes time. It requires removing debris. Rocks, trash, sticks...all sorts of junk that prevents the soil from being a healthy place for seeds to grow. It is time consuming. It takes work.

After the soil is cleared, it has to be tilled. The chunks are broken into smaller pieces. The weeds and roots that are underground are turned up into the sun where they dry out and die away. Fertilizer is added and mixed in. The soil is raked and shoveled and made from a rough place into a smooth one. It is more work. More time.

Then the plow makes rows where the seeds will be planted. It breaks the dirt into an organized pattern for growth. Rows upon rows of freshly plowed soil make the planting an easier task. The sower goes down each row with a seed and plants it into the healthy soil, which has been so carefully prepared.

The seeds get water from the rain. The sun urges them to rise up. The food in the soil feeds them. In a miraculous event, they grow. They put down roots, they send up sprouts. They get bigger and soon they are bearing fruit. The fruit of each plant provides food.

Your heart is the same, Dear One. It takes removing blockages. It takes tilling and breaking up the hard places of your heart to make good soil. It takes plowing the rows so I can plant the seeds. The seeds of hope, faithfulness, righteousness, love, compassion, gentleness...all the fruits of My spirit. Those seeds will take root in the soil once I have prepared it. They will be watered by My spirit, and fed by My fertilizer. My Son will cause them to rise up. And oh the fruit they will bear. It will bring you life. It will feed your soul and the souls of others. You will see, when you allow me to cultivate your heart. There will be a great harvest.

# April 3

*Every branch in me that does not bear fruit He takes away, and every branch that does bear fruit He prunes, that it may bear more fruit. ~John 15:2*

You know I am a gardener, which means I know when to plant and I know when to prune. Planting is all about preparing the soil. It is knowing the times and seasons. It is fertilizing and watering, and nurturing the seed. It is staking and protecting the new plants. It is about watching them grow.

However, Dear One, it is also about shaping them and helping them to provide the best fruit. Pruning is an artform. Knowing when and where to cut. Knowing how much and at what angle. All of it is very specific. I do not just lop off at random. It could kill a plant to do that. It is all very controlled and believe it or not, it is what is best for the plant. It produces more growth and a healthier harvest.

When I prune hearts, it is not to break them. It is to grow them. When I cut back dead weight, oftentimes you don't even realize it is there, until I cut it. You cannot feel the weight of overgrowth until it is removed.

Other times you can barely move because of the weight. Heaviness is a companion you have grown accustomed to. Circumstances make it feel as though you are walking through quicksand. I don't always prune the situation, sometimes I prune the heart in the midst of it. The times when nothing has changed on the outside but everything has changed on the inside, are times of pruning.

This time of year, it is common to lay things down. In an act of temporary self-pruning, you put away temptations and shackles that bind you. In this season, freedom can be the result if you will let me make it permanent. Why pick something back up that you are dependent on in unhealthy ways?

I do not desire for you to make temporary changes in your heart. I desire transformation. I desire new growth. I desire healthy fruit. I see the baggage that needs to be dumped. I see the open wounds that need to be healed. I see the burdened life you live. Allow me to prune you, Dear One. Though some of the dead stuff I cut off might sting for a bit, it will set you free in the long run. I know the correct time. I know the correct way. Trust me in this.

# April 4

*For we are His workmanship, created in Christ Jesus for good works, which God prepared beforehand, that we should walk in them. ~Ephesians 2:10*

I am a gardener, but I am also an artist. I not only cultivate, I also curate. How could I not be, after creating so many masterpieces? My creativity has no limits. Just look at the natural world to see it. Waterfalls, rivers, trees, sunsets, sunrises, the night sky, all the animals...so many animals...the sea, the wind, the waves, the desert. All of it has to be curated. I select each piece. I put it on display. I organize the collection. I care for each creation.

Now, Beloved, look in the mirror. You are a masterpiece. You were selected for such a time as this. I knew you were needed at this time. I created you just the way you are, because you fit in the collection. The whole piece would be less without you. It would be incomplete. Do you find that hard to believe? Do you think I am overstating your importance? I am not. Your place here is essential to the completeness of the piece.

Not only that, but individually you are a work of art. I know you complain each time you see yourself in the mirror. That hurts My heart. When I created you I picked specific colors, textures, and features. I love diversity and you are unique. There is none like you. I did that on purpose, Dear One. Please do not despise My work. Celebrate it. You need no 'fixing' to be beautiful. You already are. I should know, I am a master artist and craftsman.

A curator selects pieces of art which compliment each other. They are a cohesive whole. It is part of the job to make sure of it. A curator also knows how to arrange things and how to care for them. You will not find a museum with fine works of art that are in disrepair. It is because the curator is so gentle with them. Keeping the temperature just right, wrapping them when moving, shining the light on them at just the right angle to highlight their best features; all of it is to care for the artwork. To keep it in good condition so it can be admired and appreciated.

You are such a piece. I want you to be admired and appreciated just the way I created you. No need to add or take away anything from My work. I will put you on display so that you will be stunning. No need to worry. A painting doesn't have to work at hanging on a wall. It just stays where it is put. It just is.

You may feel overlooked. You might not see yourself as a masterpiece, but you are not the artist, and you are not the curator. I am both. I am the expert on fine art. I assure you that you are fine art. Worth a high price. I willingly paid it to have you in My collection forever.

# April 5

*Why do you spend your money for that which is not bread, and your labor for that which does not satisfy? Listen diligently to me, and eat what is good, and delight yourselves in rich food. ~Isaiah 55:2*

What is your daily bread, Beloved? What I mean by that is, what nurtures your spirit? Is it a constant stream of bad news? Do you fret over circumstances and gorge yourself with worry? Do you eat the bread of idleness? There are so many things to feed upon. Things that will stuff you to overflowing, until you are sick. Things that will taste terrible and cause you harm.

Weary One, it is up to you what you take in. You can choose to take in unhealthy nourishment or you can choose good food. The good food is uplifting for your spirit. It is a joyful outlook. It is a positive attitude. My word provides peace and wisdom. My presence provides peace. There is life when you choose the daily bread I provide.

Put away the junk food the world offers. It has fillers and preservatives and other things that clog your spirit. Over time, a diet of junk food will bring depression, anxiety, sorrow, and a hard heart. Tenderness, compassion, and empathy will be lost. Self-pity and self-centeredness will prevail. As you add baggage to your life, it is a gradual weight gain, until you can hardly move forward in your heart. Lethargy and apathy set in.

Precious One, that is not what I have for you. It is not My best for you. I offer bread that brings you life. Whole spiritual food that builds you up and sets you free. It is worth the search. It is worth putting away the convenient but poisonous food of the world. What I give is substantive. It is filling and does not add to your already heavy plate. It frees space for your heart and gives life to your spirit.

You can feel the difference. You know which kind of food is which. In your spirit you can feel it when something you are taking in is not healthy. You simply have to pay attention. What do you listen to? What do you watch? What do you physically eat or drink? What do you set your hands to? Where do your feet take you? They are all your choices. I empower you to make the best ones for yourself. I trust you to find what works for you. I will provide you with your daily bread. Will you eat it?

# April 6

*If you then, who are evil, know how to give good gifts to your children, how much more will your Father who is in heaven give good things to those who ask Him!*
*~Matthew 7:11*

Do you have some hard questions for me, Weary One? The whys? The where-are-yous? The are-you-cruel? The did-you-do-this? The can-you-stop-this? The answers to those questions have been difficult from the very beginning. They roll around every time suffering occurs.

I can tell you, I am always with you. Always. I never leave or forsake you. I can tell you I am not cruel. I give good and perfect gifts to My children. I do not cause suffering, I use it. The world is tainted by sin. The enemy prowls around seeking to devour. Hard things happen. Suffering and painful events take place. Some on an individual level and some in large groups, in nations, or globally.

These circumstances are not comfortable, but I care more about your character than your comfort. Hard places form your character. Resilience is born in such places. Strength is birthed in hardship. I am a parent who sits with My children to dry their tears. I comfort. I hold. I explain. I lift your head. I pat your back and send you back out into the world again.

Why bad things happen isn't the right question. The better question is what? What do I do now? What does this mean for me? How do I respond? Beloved, you are My light. You are My hands and feet. You respond as I do. With compassion. With love. With care. For others. For yourself. For your family. For your friends.

Mental gymnastics over who is to blame, or why a thing has happened do not help. They prevent you from coming and sitting with me sooner. The sooner you stop worrying about the why, the sooner you will be at peace. You have to trust me, despite what you see and feel. You have to know me well enough to know I am for you. How do you learn that truth? You walk through enough tough stuff to see a pattern of My behavior. You sit with me so many times you know what I will do and say. You learn My ways. You learn My heart for you through hardship.

# April 7

*Now the serpent was more crafty than any other beast of the field that the Lord God had made. He said to the woman, "Did God actually say, 'You shall not eat of any tree in the garden'?" ~Genesis 3:1*

In times of trouble go back to what you know about me. The first thing the enemy does in hard times is get you to question My character. Look back to the very beginning. He asked, "Did God really say…?" He wants you to think I am holding out on you; that somehow, I am punishing you; that I am not loving; that I don't care. So many lies he spreads. He knows that if he can get you to doubt me, he has won. He has gotten your focus off of me and onto yourself and what you are or are not getting.

To combat his age-old, but very effective strategy, you have to look back. You have to see My hand in your life over and over. You have to recognize the pattern of My character. You have to see the lies he has spoken in the past are just that…lies. When My hand is on your life, you can look back and see it might not have been obvious, but that I have been protecting you all along. There has never been a time where I have forgotten you or abandoned you.

Go back, Dear One, to what you know. I love you with an everlasting love. I have hope for you, and a future. You are the apple of My eye. I adore you. You are paid for with My Son's blood. I love you that much. There is never a time I am not working things for your good. Remember these things.

If your memory fails you, go to My word and read what I say about you. Sing songs that lift your spirit and speak truth to your soul. Meet with friends who will remind you who I am and who you are. Make a memorial when there are breakthroughs. Do not forget. There are so many ways to go back and remember.

Go back to what you know to be true about me. Study My character. Notice that it never changes. Pick one trait, faithfulness, and study it. Then pick another, compassion, and study it too. The more you learn about My character, the less the enemy will have to hold against you.

You will see the patterns of My work in your life. You will know those things that seemed random were anything but. They were orchestrated by me. Don't let the enemy twist things and bring up questions for which he has already planted the seeds of doubt. He is the one who brings suffering, either blatantly or he convinces you to make choices which bring it.

I am the one who constantly is using the efforts of the enemy to sway you; to make something beautiful. I work all things for your good. I pick up the pieces of his work and create a masterpiece out of them. It is who I am. So, Beloved, go back to what you know. Go back and remember.

# April 8

*Death has been swallowed up in victory. Where, O death, is your victory? Where, O death, is your sting? ~1 Corinthians 15:54*

It's a season of contemplation. A time to consider the Holy things. A time to give up things and to seek My face. Beloved, this practice has been around a long time. So long, it has become commonplace to many. The reflection, the seeking, the longing which started as a spiritual act, has given way to ritual. Tradition is not bad, but when it makes heart issues into routine behaviors you need to take a look.

Fasting is the practice of denying yourself so you can draw closer to me. I love for you to be more aware of My presence in your life. I love for you to spend more time with me, sharing your heart and listening to mine. I long for it actually. But if you give something up, and never draw closer, never seek me out, what is the point? What did you give up?

This is the season to celebrate the gift I gave you. Life instead of death. The stone rolled away. Love winning. My Son sacrificed. He fasted being divine for a season. He drew closer to me, dependent on me for His every move. He sought me. He listened to me. He pulled away to hear. He became human so death could die and you could live. It was His choice to do so.

Take some time to contemplate. Take some time to reflect. Then, celebrate! It is a wonderful season of life. A season of waiting, turned celebratory; a season of fear, turned bold; a season of confusion, turned clear. My heart was made clear during this season. A heart dying to love you.

# April 9

*Continue steadfastly in prayer, being watchful in it with thanksgiving. ~Colossians 4:2*

Watch and pray. Dear One, be sensitive to My spirit. You will know the time and the hour to pray. Keep your eyes open and your heart tuned to me. There are some seasons which are more intense. Seasons of suffering. Seasons of loss. Seasons of grief. Seasons to fight. Seasons of wrestling. Seasons of confusion. Seasons of heartache.

When you find yourself in one of these severe seasons, Weary One, watch and pray. Talking to me in the midst of one of these times is critical to survival. Not only that, but it bonds us. It is these times you will one day look back on to remember My faithfulness. You will build a foundation of relationship you can count on in times of trouble.

Watch for clues. I leave them for you all the time. There are hints of My presence in the sunrise. You notice your heart quicken when you hear the laughter of a child. Your gut tells you when something is off and you need to be wary. I give you love as well as discernment. I show My delight in you, as well as My hopes for your future. It is a grand treasure hunt to watch for me in all seasons, Beloved.

Do not forsake watching and praying. They are two of the ways I communicate with you. When you have a deep friendship with someone you know when they are happy, but you are also aware when they are upset or going through heartache. They don't always have to tell you, because you can see it. You know them so well that you recognize when something is bothering them. You watch them. You communicate with them. Talk to them and have a conversation. You can do all of this with me, Dear One. Watch and Pray.

# April 10

*Now on the first day of the week Mary Magdalene came to the tomb early, while it was still dark...and saw that the stone had been taken away from the tomb. ~John 20:1*

The darkest of days are also the hardest. They are the ones when you question me. Beloved, I don't mind. When things are beyond your sight, I love it when you ask me for sight. When things don't make sense, I love it when you ask for wisdom. When it seems, the whole world has gone crazy, I love it when you ask for My intervention. I am here for you, Weary One. When you need My ear, you have it. When you need My shoulder, you have it. When you need My heart, you have it. You have always had it.

Dark nights of the soul shake your foundation. They are heavy and scary. You wonder if I exist or if you have been wrong about me all along. It doesn't anger me for you to feel this way. I don't feel offended at the lack of faith...because I don't see it that way. I see it as real faith that you would talk to me in such times. Even if you are shouting at me, it shows you believe. If you question me, it shows you believe.

I know what a dark night feels like. I know grief. I know pain. I know heartache. I know what it feels like to wait for the Son to come up. Even I, know.

But in the darkest night, the light still exists. Just because you can't see it doesn't mean it isn't there. The Earth still turns. The stars still hang in the sky. Even while you are wondering and crying out, I am still on the throne. Even when you are not sure I am alive, I am there, in the dark night with you.

# April 11

*Trust in the Lord with all your heart, and do not lean on your own understanding. In all your ways acknowledge Him, and He will make straight your path. ~Proverbs 3:5-6*

There is a mess in the middle. After diagnosis, but before healing. After grief, but before joy. After job loss, but before new provision. After divorce, but before new life. After disability, but before adaptation. Do you see what I mean by the middle? It is all so very messy, Dear One. Hard.

It's where the wrestling happens. Trust is born in the middle. Hope is found. Desire to seek me is fueled. In the unknown places, control is replaced with surrender. In the in-between, hard hearts are tenderized. Humility finds its way into the cracks. Lamenting births repentance. Repentance brings forgiveness. Waiting becomes an opportunity.

After death, before resurrection. Is hell. I know this from experience. But it is also where the battle is won. It is where death is defeated. It is where freedom begins. So, do not despise the messy middle, Beloved. Much is to be gained here. More than you can comprehend. Believe me when I say it. The middle is where I do My best work...in you, as well as on your behalf.

Wait for me here. Let me into the messy places. Trust me. Rest in the wrestling. It is a place marker. You will look back to this place and see My hand. You will testify of all I did in you. It will change your life. It is the trial of transformation.

# April 12

*The steadfast love of the Lord never ceases; His mercies never come to an end; they are new every morning; great is your faithfulness. ~Lamentations 3:22-23*

A new day is here. Difficulty always leads to new places, Beloved. The hardship is a temporary step along the journey. It requires reassessment of priorities. It requires taking stock. It requires humility. Suffering peels off layers of old thought patterns. It upends the mundane life. It exposes the lies you believe; about me; about you; about life. And right when you think everything is lost, the new day arrives. Winter always leads to spring.

The old wineskins would burst if I tried to fill them with the new wine I have for you. There is freedom in the new. Hope. Grace. In places of beginning, the burden you carry is lifted. The tomb is empty. Light and life rush to meet you. Groping in the dark is no longer needed, because in My light you can see again.

You can see the results of the pain. You can see the ways your heart has changed. You can feel your spirit rising up. The exhausted and weary soul which has carried you is infused with hope. The stirring is real. It is the wind of My Spirit blowing on the ashes. It is the coals that have been buried sparking to life again. A small flame increases to a roaring blaze. The heart is alive and beating again. The blood coursing through your veins. You see My provision for you. You see My design. You feel My love.

Dear One, you will not go back into the old. You cannot because once you have been raised from the dead, you are infused with My life. It lives inside you. Even on bad days, My breath keeps you going. Even in hardship, My grace is in your heart. The way you look at things will be different. The way you respond will change. Your spirit will lead because My Spirit lives within you.

Before, this would not have been possible. After, all things are possible. Before, you would have been suffocating. After, you can breathe freely. Before, you could not push your way out of the dark places. After, you walk unhindered. It is a new day! It is a fresh wind! It is freedom!

# April 13

*At that time His voice shook the earth, but now He has promised, "Yet once more I will shake not only the earth but also the heavens." This phrase, "Yet once more," indicates the removal of things that are shaken—that is, things that have been made—in order that the things that cannot be shaken may remain. Therefore, let us be grateful for receiving a kingdom that cannot be shaken, and thus let us offer to God acceptable worship, with reverence and awe, for our God is a consuming fire.*
*~Hebrews 12:26-29*

When things are shaking, Beloved, what do you do? How do you handle your life when everything is falling away? When all that you know is in question? Difficult places are made more difficult when outside circumstances press in on you. But just because you don't understand what is happening around you doesn't mean that I don't.

Look to me, Dear One. I know what is happening. I know the bigger picture. Trust me. The key is to be grateful for what you do know. To give thanks for what you have been given. There are so many with so little, yet you have so much. Take heart.

It isn't about materialism. No, I am not talking about your stuff, even though you have an abundance of it. I am referring to all that you have in the spirit. Your relationship with me is rich. You know and hear My voice.

Humble yourself before me in the midst of trials. There are times to rejoice, and there are times to lie low. There are times to dance, and there are times to sit in sackcloth and ashes. In the shaking, the worship becomes repentance. The repentance becomes forgiveness. Because when quakes of life happen, they shake away bitterness. They shake unforgiveness. They shake greed. They shake selfishness. I said I would shake ALL things. The shaking exposes them.

Beloved, you have to see the darker places in your heart before you can deal with them. Shaking is the great leveler. When it happens, it is for everyone to see their flaws and faults. It is for everyone to take stock. Shaking reveals that you are small and I am big.

I am calling you back to your first love. Back home to me. Back to fellowship with me. Back to the secret place. Back to intimacy. All else falls away.

# April 14

*But the fruit of the Spirit is love, joy, peace, patience, kindness, goodness, faithfulness, gentleness, self-control; against such things there is no law. ~Galatians 5:22-23*

I have something for you, Weary One. A promise fulfilled. You cannot see it yet, but I am working. I know it seems I am far away sometimes, and that I am not aware of your circumstances, but that is not true. I am very much aware. You are in a hard place and it seems you are always suffering.

Long suffering is a fruit of My spirit. It is the one no one wants. Yet, I give it freely, just as I give the others. Some call it forbearance, others say patience but no matter what you call it, it is a gift. It is common to want joy, peace, and kindness. Normal even. Goodness, faithfulness and gentleness are much desired. However, when it comes to longsuffering, just the name brings fear. No one likes to suffer, much less for a long time, but oh the fruit. Forbearance means bearing with something for an extended period, and the result is worth it.

The reason forbearance is listed with the fruit of the Spirit is that it requires sacrifice. To handle difficulty requires humility and laying down your own desires to deal with hardship. It puts things on a slower time table. Grief requires patience. Dealing with sickness requires putting your schedule aside to wait on healing. Unforeseen events cause plans to be cancelled and goals to be lost.

Unexpected things are part of life. When you have multiple things all at once that last a long time, it requires you to pace yourself. To give yourself grace. To be kind to yourself. Dear One, longsuffering is part of a long list of My gifts. You cannot have one without the others. They go together. Just as kindness and gentleness go together, so do peace and longsuffering. If you have longsuffering, but lack the other gifts, you have not surrendered yet.

What I am bringing to you requires all the gifts. It is a promise. When My Spirit breathes on you, these gifts follow. That does not mean they are easy. It means you have to be empowered by My Spirit to receive them. Including longsuffering. Maybe even more so with it than the others. Be patient. You will see.

# April 15

*The sacrifices of God are a broken spirit; a broken and contrite heart, O God, you will not despise. ~Psalms 51:17*

There is prayer, and then there is prayer born of desperation. The first kind is often done out of obligation, because you are 'supposed' to pray. The second is a cry from deep pain. You, Weary One, are more familiar with the second type. I love both types. Anytime one of My children turns towards me, I am happy.

However, the desperate cry catches My ear. It is the same when one of your children cries out in the night, and your feet hit the floor before you are even fully awake. You run to them. It is instinct. Protect. Nurture. Soothe. Comfort. Where do you think you get those attributes? You are made in My image, after all.

These kinds of prayers are uttered in the night. They are made in the shower. Someplace where tears can flow unchecked. Somewhere you are alone with your pain. Someplace your heart can bow down.

These prayers are not for others to hear. They are between me and you. Your chin is down, not up. Your face is to the floor. You might be on your knees or lying on the ground. You are spilled out, worn out, and tired out. You lay yourself upon the altar. You sacrifice yourself there and give me your broken heart. You are contrite. Lamenting is your food. Tears are your drink. These prayers are heartfelt.

I draw near to these prayers and those who pray them. They are not intellectual. They are not head prayers, they are firmly in the realm of the heart. These prayers move me with compassion. They stir me to action. In hardship, your prayers bond us together in a way a well-written prayer cannot do. When everything is pulled out from under you, prayer becomes a lifeline. Do not fear prayer, Dear One. Let it overtake you and pour it out. I will never despise a broken heart.

# April 16

*Then my enemies will turn back in the day when I call. This I know, that God is for me. ~Psalms 56:9*

I am for you. No matter what is swirling around you, I am for you. Don't let your mind tell you otherwise. In unknown times, I am for you. In difficult times, I am for you. In hardship, in suffering, in uncertainty, I am for you.

That means I stand in your corner. I have your back. I support you. I defend you. I encourage you. I fight for you. I lift you up. I am always working FOR you. Even when it doesn't feel like it. Even when it feels like I might be against you, I am not.

Beloved, there are so many layers in life. I am working on so many levels at one time, you cannot always see what I am up to. That is why you have to trust me even when you don't know what is happening. It is especially important in the unknown seasons, that you hold this truth close.

I am a good father. I do not abandon My children. You must believe it. It is who I am, a father who stays. In the mess, in the grief, in the frustration...I stay. I am faithful. I am steadfast. Sometimes it requires great faith for you to believe these things about me.

Doubt sneaks in and causes you to question if it is really true. My character is put on trial in hard times. It is somehow assumed My job is to keep things smooth and comfortable. So, when they are not, fingers get pointed to me. "He could stop this. He could fix this. He doesn't love you enough. You are not important to Him." All the lies that run through your head are not from me. Do not listen to them, Weary One.

Instead, speak the truth. I am for you.

# April 17

*Do not be anxious about anything, but in everything by prayer and supplication with thanksgiving let your requests be made known to God. And the peace of God, which surpasses all understanding, will guard your hearts and your minds in Christ Jesus. ~Philippians 4:6-7*

Be anxious for nothing, those are words you have heard often, Beloved. They seem impossible, don't they? How do you stop from worrying? In a life filled with hardship, it seems like a cruel command. Anxiety is replaying possibilities over and over in your head. The problem with worry is that it focuses on things that haven't happened yet, and possibly won't. It is a waste of time.

Surely, it is wise to consider possibilities and be prepared. But there is a difference between preparing and being fixated. There is a difference between making a plan and being in a panic. Wouldn't you feel free if you could stop worrying all the time? My heart is for you to be free.

So, enter into a conversation with me about your worries. As you talk to me, you will see more clearly that worry gets you nowhere. However, focusing on what you have in your life, instead of what you don't, will build thankfulness. It is a matter of renewing your mind and training your eyes to see all that is good, noble, just, true and beautiful.

I am not asking that you blind yourself to the problems of life, but I am asking that you not camp there. I am asking that you take notice of all the good things because they far outnumber the bad. In your mind, thoughts roll around and around unless you stop them. Worry is a pattern of thought. It has to be stopped.

My peace can stop the cycle, but you have to seek it out. When you talk to me, I give you My peace. I help you see all that you have through grateful eyes. I show you more than possibilities of what could happen in the future. I show you the faithfulness of the past. How I have come through repeatedly. When you remember, gratitude refreshes your soul. It reminds you of the truth...which is peace that starts with a prayer.

# April 18

*Be not wise in your own eyes; fear the Lord, and turn away from evil. ~Proverbs 3:7*

What are you taking for granted, Dear One? Assuming something to be true before it happens can be dangerous. Do you assume everything will always be the way it is now? If all was stripped away, would you be able to go on? Am I enough for you, Beloved?

You assume your family will always be there. You assume your friends will stay with you. You assume you will have an income. You assume you will have a place to live and food on the table. Do not take these things for granted. They are gifts for you to appreciate, just as is the breath in your lungs. Each day is a precious gift and there are no guarantees for tomorrow. Set your mind set on gratitude and it will keep you grounded in today.

I want to talk to you about false assumptions, too. You assume your life will always be hard. You think suffering will be your constant companion, because it always has been. Do not assume you know what is coming...good or bad. My Precious Child, your trauma has made it hard for you to expect anything else. You wait for the next crisis like some people await the rain. You watch for the clouds to form and you think you know what is coming.

You assume the storm is coming before it happens. Your thoughts are tainted by your past, and maybe by your present circumstances. Don't do that. As hard as it is, setting your mind on what you believe is coming can drag you down. You have given up on hope. You have accepted the fact that hardship seems to follow you. You have resigned yourself to it. Don't do that.

A poverty mindset says you will never have more. You will never have enough and you don't deserve more. Those are lies. It is a way of thinking, based on your experiences, but it is false. You deserve every good gift I give you. You have many. Don't you see them? They are all around you. Your family. Your friends. Your food and shelter. Your blessings. And me. You have me. I am enough. If you have nothing else but me, it would be enough.

# April 19

*If you abide in My word, you are truly My disciples, and you will know the truth, and the truth will set you free. ~John 8:31-32*

Weary One, I cannot lie. Did you know that? I am the truth teller. This means whatever I say is the truth. What I say about the world is true. It can be redeemed. It is worth dying for. What I say about you is true, too. You are the apple of My eye. You are My beautiful creation.

There is a problem when you do not believe what I say about you. Dear One, when you are down on yourself, when you look at yourself in the mirror and find fault, you are calling me a liar. You are in essence saying I am wrong in the things I say about you. This hurts My heart.

Fault finding means you believe the enemy over me. He is the father of lies, not me. He is the deceiver, not me. His plan is to steal your peace. He uses all manner of lies to do so. When you believe any of his lies you are teaming up with him. If you believe anything he says about your neighbor that is untrue, you are working for him. If you believe anything that I did not say you are deceived.

How do you know if you are working with the accuser of the brethren or not? First you have to know the truth. Do not study the lies, study the truth. What do I say about you? What do I say about your neighbors, or the world? When you know the truth, it will set you free from his lies. Once you know what I say, when you hear something different you will stop and think, 'That does not sound like my father. That is not the truth.' My sheep know My voice.

# April 20

*"I have heard the grumbling of the people of Israel. Say to them, 'At twilight you shall eat meat, and in the morning, you shall be filled with bread. Then you shall know that I am the Lord your God.'" ~Exodus 16:12*

I am your daily bread, Beloved. My words to you are your sustenance. Just as you eat food to keep you alive physically, My word keeps you alive spiritually.

When My children were wandering in the desert, I gave them manna to eat. It was a picture of the truth that you are dependent on me for bread. I have new words for you to pick up each day. They are enough for one day, no more, no less. They nourish your spirit. Without them you would starve spiritually. It is unnecessary for you to go hungry, because I provide fresh manna daily.

Manna doesn't mean bread, it means 'what is it?' My people were amazed to see bread all over the ground in response to their complaints. They wanted to go back into slavery in order to have food, so I sent them manna so they could stay free. It was sweet to eat. It was in the middle of the desert and it was confusing to them. They wondered, 'What is it?'

When you arise in the morning, or sit in the evening with My word, you can ask me, 'What is it?' What is it you have for me today? What is it you want me to know? What is your word for me today? I will show you what you need. It's freedom. It is nourishment. It is My hand providing. Every breath that proceeds out of My mouth is there for you to pick up. You will always have just the amount you need.

Be careful you do not complain about My manna like My children did. They grumbled and I responded, and then they grumbled more. Nothing was good enough for them. The enemy always wants to get your eyes off of what I have done for you. He prefers that you focus on yourself rather than on me. He wants you to get bored with your freedom. He wants you to wish for more because if he can make you discontent he knows you will run for bondage. Don't let him fool you, Beloved.

My manna for you is enough. Just enough. What is it? It is My hand, providing and protecting you. Take it. Eat it.

# April 21

*But be glad and rejoice forever in that which I create; for behold, I create Jerusalem to be a joy, and her people to be a gladness. ~Isaiah 65:18*

Anticipation is closely aligned with hope. Hope is the mother of faith. When you hope for something, you desire it. When you anticipate it, it is the beginning of belief. Anticipation is hope plus longing. It is desiring more than just seeing.

Beloved, when you are in a hard season, anticipation feels like an enemy. It creeps in and fills your mind with possibility. When the possibilities of life become impossibilities, it seems anticipation is a cruel companion. But in those times, the stirring you feel is My way of gently moving you forward. It is My whisper in your ear that life is not over.

Being stuck, in ways that do not go away makes it hard for you to understand that I still have more to give you. Sit with me and wait. You will see what I have for you. Open your hand. Let go of your grief. Receive your gift. It is different for each person, but I promise you it is exactly what you need, when you need it.

Look for life. Anticipate seeing it. When you focus your eyes on me, the Giver of Life, you will find clarity. You will understand what is next. You haven't been abandoned by me. You are being prepared. To walk with me. To stand. To testify. To be a witness.

Do not wait in vain. Do not waste this time with me. One day you will look back and see all that was imparted to you in the time of anticipation. It will make the day of fulfillment of My promise to you a sweet one. You will be overwhelmed by the gift I have for you. Anticipate it.

# April 22

*All the earth worships you and sings praises to you; they sing praises to your name. ~Psalms 66:4*

Go outside. Does that seem like an odd request? Some of My best work is outside. The fresh air will do you good, Weary One. When you get out there, take some deep breaths. Walk around a beautiful place near you, one where you can see My creation.

Notice the trees. They are tall and reach their arms up in praise. Their leaves unfurl and face the sun. They bask in the warmth. Turn your face up. Can you feel me? Does the warm light bathe you in comfort? Follow their example. They will show you what to do.

Notice the grass. It grows like a green carpet under your feet. Sit on it and feel it with your fingers. Does it tickle? Is it cool and soft? It grows quickly when it has water. It reaches up to the sky. It moves with the wind. It hugs the lay of the land. Can you feel me? Do you move with the wind? Hug the ground like the grass. Be humble. It softens you. Be like the grass.

Notice the flowers? They are all around. Wild or cultivated doesn't matter, lean over. Take a whiff. Can you smell me? The flowers open themselves up. They blossom and bloom. They spread fragrance and color. They create beauty. Can you see me? Do you create beauty? Open yourself up. Spread your color and fragrance to the world around you. Learn how from the flowers.

Notice the water? Is there water nearby? A creek perhaps? Maybe a lake? Or possibly the ocean? Something rushing, or still? Water flows. It moves from the mountains to the sea. Always going lower and lower with such delight. Stick your toes or your fingers in. Do you feel the current or see the ripples? Can you feel me? Do you flow and move? Be still like a lake. Rest in My stillness. Or flow like a river. Moving with My rhythm. Watch and learn from the waters.

Beloved, anytime you feel overwhelmed, go outside. Spend some time interacting with me there. It will do your heart good. It will lift your spirit. I will teach you who I am.

# April 23

*Bear one another's burdens, and so fulfill the law of Christ. ~Galatians 6:2*

You love to give. You will lay down your life for others around you, Weary One. I love your generosity. I love how you love others well. I love how you look for ways to help. If someone has lost a loved one, you are there. If someone has welcomed a new baby, you are there. If someone has surgery, lost a job, or broken a leg, you are there. You come alongside and express My heart to them. You demonstrate the gospel message, to love one another as I have loved you. It is a beautiful thing you do.

But Beloved, I have a question for you. Why is it so hard for you to receive? You have such a great understanding of what it means to help, but when you are the one who needs help, you refrain from asking. If anyone asks to help, you shy away from accepting. You don't want to put anyone out. You don't want to be a burden. You don't want to cause any trouble. But that isn't the real reason, Dear One.

The real reason is you don't want to need help. It is humbling to need. It feels weak, like you can't handle things on your own. But the truth is, you can't. You aren't supposed to. I created you to need others, just as they need you. It is interdependence at its best. When you are giving, you say you are doing My work, and it is true. So, when someone gives to you, they are also doing My work.

When you refuse help, you are refusing me. I know that sounds harsh but it is the truth. I put you on someone's heart. They hear My voice and respond by calling to ask if you need anything. You say no, which isn't true. They assume they heard me wrong. They wonder if they have somehow missed me, when in reality, they are My hands and feet in the situation.

I give everyone the opportunity to be a blessing. I answer your prayers for rescue by sending others to help. So, when you refuse it, you are blocking your own prayers. When you try to do everything yourself, you get exhausted and burned out. You wonder why you are so tired. I will tell you how to fix that, ask for help. Humble yourself and reach out to someone. Tell them you cannot do it alone and that you need help. It will change your life.

Your heart will grow. Your pride will go down a notch and you will appreciate people so much more. To graciously receive from others is to receive from My hand. I love you enough to send you the gift of help please learn to receive it.

# April 24

*The Lord is my strength and my song, and He has become my salvation this is my God, and I will praise Him, my father's God, and I will exalt Him. ~Exodus 15:2*

You, Beloved, are beautiful. Even in stressful times I can see the beauty that lies within you. I see it when you don't see it in yourself. I know it is there because I put it there. I am not talking about outward appearance, but inward beauty. You radiate from the inside out. Truly you do.

I want you to see what I see. I want you to see the strength you possess. You must put it on. My joy is your strength, so step into it. Your hope in me is your strength, so cover yourself. I give strength to the weary...which means you qualify! My strength is your rock, your deliverer, your stronghold and your refuge. When you seek My face, you gain My strength.

The power of My strength creates the inward beauty. It creates a resolve to stand even in the midst of a crisis. It causes you to seek healing in the midst of trauma. The places you need strength in your everyday life receive it when you seek me. I am talking about the ability to rise up, to get out of bed on the days you want to hide. I am talking about the desire to keep moving when everything in you wants to quit.

The kind of strength I give is the supernatural ability to persevere. It is beyond what you think you can do. And you are right, you cannot do it on your own. It requires trust and allowing me to use your weak moments to show up. My strength gives you a reason to keep going.

See My strength. It is available to you. Open your eyes and see it. Wake to its ability to move you forward. Wake to its ability to get you through hard days. Wake to its ability to sustain you. Wake to its ability to reside deep within you, even when you feel broken to pieces. Look to me and let me open your eyes, Dear One.

# April 25

*"Be still, and know that I am God. I will be exalted among the nations, I will be exalted in the earth!" ~Psalms 46:10*

Beloved, sometimes you need to just be still. Life goes at such a frantic pace that it is easy to lose sight of what is important. Especially when you are trying to hold it all together. But, Dear One, you cannot hold it all together. It is not possible, so you might as well lay it all down and sit for a bit.

Stillness is simply the absence of movement, and it sounds quite easy, but it isn't. I know that. When you sit, all manner of circumstances call for your attention. Then thoughts begin shouting at you. The laundry lifts its voice. The children begin to argue. The pets demand attention immediately. The phone calls you. It is difficult to just be still in today's world.

However, I promise you it is worth it. Unplug. Refuse the cries of the laundry and the phone. Give the kids a snack. Put the pets in the yard. It is important they all know your time with me is a priority. Your silence is sustenance. Just to listening to your breathing in and out will calm you. To remember My promises to you will infuse you with hope. To share your heart with me will heal you, and to hear My heart for you will empower you. It is a divine exchange of your weakness for My strength.

You will know me better. You will learn My voice. You will not believe the lies but you will know the truth. In unsure times, in hard times, in anxious times, you will know I have your back. You will feel My peace. Stillness is fuel. Refill your tank before you run out of gas.

# April 26

*For freedom Christ has set us free; stand firm therefore, and do not submit again to a yoke of slavery. ~Galatians 5:1*

I break every chain. Every shackle. Everything that tries to hold you captive. I am the one who sets you free. Weary One, your freedom is very important to me. It is why I sacrificed My Son.

The things that bind you are sometimes your choices. In those instances, renewing your mind will begin to loosen your bonds. When you believe lies, or tell yourself lies, you get trapped. The insecurities make you feel as if you deserve imprisonment. For example, you may think you are not worth rescuing, so you settle for less than ideal relationships. But it isn't true. You are worth every drop of My Son's blood. To break these shackles which hold you back, you have to believe what I say about you.

Other times, the things that hold you are circumstances beyond your control. You are a caregiver for a child with special needs, an injured family member, or an elderly parent. You have lost someone close, like a child or spouse. In these instances, the chains are different. You are bound but it is love that binds you. You do not walk away but sometimes the grief of the situation has you locked up. I break every chain.

Beloved, these chains are not relational, they are emotional. The bonds are suffering, sorrow, resentment, anger, disappointment, emotional exhaustion, and they are constant. There are no vacations from your circumstances and that is why they are hard to handle. I do not always take the circumstances away, but I set you free in your spirit in the midst of them. I help you to see beyond the immediate right in front of you and focus on the eternal. You can be free and content while you continue to love. The emotions do not have to "go away" for you to be free of them. I will teach you this and break the hold they have on you.

Sometimes your chains are physical limitations you have. Your body doesn't work properly. Illness of one kind or another holds you back. It is discouraging and frustrating. You see others walking in wholeness and you long for it too. You are bound by your body. Even in this, Weary One, I can set you free. If not with direct healing, then with a freedom of Spirit that transcends physical confines. Every morning when you wake up you can soar with me, even if you are bedridden. Seek me and I will show you. Freedom is My plan for you, in all its forms. Let me break your chains.

# April 27

*Know therefore that the Lord your God is God, the faithful God who keeps covenant and steadfast love with those who love Him and keep His commandments, to a thousand generations. ~Deuteronomy 7:9*

My covenant with you still stands, Weary One. A covenant is a promise. My promise. It is initiated by the stronger party, that would be me. It is accepted by the weaker party, that would be you. The one who stretches out to offer the promises guarantees protection, strength, covering, shelter, and identity. I do that for you.

Long ago, when a covenant was made there was a swapping of robes, so that at a distance anyone could see who was in covenant with whom. To see the color of the robe was to know if they were friend or foe and what strength they had. It was their identity.

In our relationship, I have offered you My robe, My identity. Those who are in a covenant with me are known to be in My household. As you live your life, those around you can see that you are mine. Your identity is wrapped in mine and mine in yours. You are My child. I am your father. We belong together. From a distance My robe of righteousness is visible. Anyone who sees it knows My power is behind it. When they see you coming, they know where you get your help because they know you couldn't do it without me. They see. All of My protection. All of My shelter. All of My covering.

My promises didn't end with the old covenant. They were extended and enlarged. Now, more than just protection, I offer relationship. More than just outer appearance, I offer an inner peace. More than a shelter, I offer a dwelling place. More than law, I offer grace. All that I have is yours. We are in communion together. I vow to care for you always.

Covenant isn't an old-fashioned idea. It is as current as the sun that rises each day. Do not forget My covenant with you. Do not wonder if somehow, I have forgotten it or broken it. I will never break it. You can count on that, always.

# April 28

*And suddenly there came from heaven a sound like a mighty rushing wind, and it filled the entire house where they were sitting. And divided tongues as of fire appeared to them and rested on each one of them. ~Acts 2:2-3*

Have you heard of the fire baptism? My followers were all together when the rushing wind arrived. Tongues of fire rested on each of them. Since that time many believers have prayed for the fire of heaven to fall. They deem it powerful and associate it with boldness, which are both true. However, there is more to the fire than they anticipate.

Fire burns up the dross. It purifies. It is hot. It is uncomfortable. Fire is a tool for refining. You know the fire, Beloved. You have lived in it. You know the heat. You know the pain. You know that fire is more than a catchy cliché. It is serious business to invite My fire.

Soon after the fire fell, My disciples spoke with boldness, but they also experienced persecution like never before. Trouble came upon them. They were chased, imprisoned, and stoned. They were beaten. Yet, they got bolder with each testimony. Each time they were asked to speak, they were empowered by My Spirit.

The fire you walk in is making you bold. You have to hold onto me to survive, on a daily basis. You know what it is to be under pressure. You know what it is to depend on me for each step. You know how it feels to believe you are done for and you cannot go on. But that is part of your testimony. When you bear witness to My work in your life, you have My fire in your eyes. No one can take My love from you. No one can break your belief in me. You have too much experience with My fire for that.

You have been purified. Is it over? Probably not. There will always be more dross to remove, but the beautiful thing about the fire is that it melts down so that the impurities rise to the surface. No digging is required. The dross rises up to be scraped off. Then the shine is so bright I can see My reflection, which is My goal.

There is a reason for the phrase 'baptism by fire.' It means you are thrown into something over your head and you figure it out as you go. No advanced planning really, just thrown in. Weary One, sometimes life just throws you into something when you least expect it. You know this better than most. You adapt and you keep going, but don't forget I am in the fire with you. And when you come out, I will be with you still.

# April 29

*For from His fullness we have all received, grace upon grace. ~John 1:16*

Error on the side of grace, Weary One. Both in the giving and receiving. There is an endless supply. Giving it away is one of the most precious gifts you can give. When someone hurts you, give them grace. If you are offended, extend grace. Do not harbor ill will. Unforgiveness only drags you down into a pit of negativity and bitterness. You do not need that in your life.

Giving someone grace doesn't mean you ignore wrong actions; it means you cover them. By doing so, you are empowering them to be better. To make different choices. You are quite possibly building trust they may have never had before. Of course, this will not be true of every person, but give grace anyway. Your extending it doesn't depend on their response, positive or negative. It depends on your choice to extend it.

There are times giving grace will seem impossible. That's okay. Give it anyway. Think of it as if you are the one in need of it. How would you want others to treat you in the same circumstance? Grace wins every time. Even when you don't feel it. Even when you are offering it and it is rejected. A seed is planted and one day in the future it will bear fruit.

Now, to receive grace is harder still. It requires that you believe it's available for free. It is a hard concept for humans to grasp. It seems everything in the world costs something. So, grace, for free, is countercultural. It seems too good to be true. But, Dear One, it is true and it is free. To receive it from me, you simply ask for it. I give it. That's the whole process. Free gift. From me to you.

When you have some sin or behavior you are ashamed of...ask for grace. Then receive it. To open your hand is humbling. To accept it requires seeing yourself in a new light. Not as a slug or slime, but as a child. Not as a rebel, but as a son or daughter. You are cleansed by grace. You are welcomed by grace. Grace is amazing.

Once you have accepted it from My hand you have to give some to yourself. Instead of replaying old memories in your head, you have to cover them in grace. Forgive yourself for whatever wrong I have already forgiven you for. It is all under My grace. Covered. Ended. Over. Now, once you have sealed it, move on. Walk in grace, both giving it and receiving it.

# April 30

*Keep your heart with all vigilance, for from it flow the springs of life. ~Proverbs 4:23*

Align yourself with me. Go to My word. Read it. Find what I say to you and about you. Align yourself. I know you are stressed. I know you are under pressure. Things do not always go your way. To keep from spiraling, align yourself. When you do, you will remember adversity brings growth. You will remember suffering is temporary. This too will pass. In the midst of it, these things are hard to remember. When you align yourself on a daily basis, it keeps the important things up front in your mind.

Weary One, the main source of weariness is misalignment. When your focus is on your circumstances, you are focusing on the wrong thing. Concentrating on your losses will pull you down. Certainly, you need to process events that have happened, but dwelling on them beyond the healing does not align you with me. Forgive liberally. Extend grace. Establish boundaries.

Do not think of yourself as a victim. I do not think of you that way. I know you can rise above. I know you can fly. My word tells you this. Read it. Post it. Memorize it. Whatever you need to do to align yourself to me. In an uncertain world, My word is certain. I do not change. Everything around you can be in upheaval, but I am solid. Finances can be in question, but I have everything you need. Relationships might be crumbling, but I will never leave you. I am present if your health isn't good. I am with you if you lose one you love. No matter what it is, I am there. My word tells you this.

Align with what I say. Align with who I am. Weariness will fade. Strength will rise. You will see it, when you align.

# May 1

*Are not two sparrows sold for a penny? And not one of them will fall to the ground apart from your Father. But even the hairs of your head are all numbered. Fear not, therefore; you are of more value than many sparrows. ~Matthew 10:29-31*

Weary One, you are worth so much more to me than a sparrow. But even the sparrows catch My attention. They are small, but I know every move they make and every song they sing. Do you think that is possible? For me to know every sparrow? That is how big I am. It is how much I love My creation. All of it. That includes you. A sparrow cannot fall to the ground without My notice.

You may think I do not know you, or care about you. You may think you are insignificant to me you couldn't be more wrong. Do not listen to the lies. I tell you the truth, I know every single hair on your head. I know each moment of your tiring days. I know every one of your heart's desires and I know the details of your biggest fears.

So, there is nothing you can tell me that would be a surprise to me. There is nothing that is too big or too horrible for me to hear. Dear One, that should be a relief to you. Your hardships are not lost on me. I see every single difficulty. I see every tear you hold back. I know every part of your heart that is broken. Do not hold it back from me.

Pour it out. Let it flow from your mouth to My ears. It will be a relief to let it out. I will comfort you, as only I can. I will remind you of who you are to me. My child. My precious one. The one I care about.

When you hear the birds sing, remember I know every note of their song. I know every feather. If I can know that much tiny detail, I can know you...really know you. I am bigger than you can comprehend. I am vast and beyond compare, but even with My all-encompassing knowledge of creation, I am still in the minute details of life. Your life. You do not walk alone. I will not let you fall. Like a father who follows behind a bike without training wheels, or who stands behind the swing, I protect you. I cheer you on even as I watch over you. Even when you don't know I am doing it. I am alert to your needs. I am aware of your surroundings. Always. Rest in that knowledge. Do not be afraid. I will always have your back. I will watch over you.

# May 2

*When I was a child, I spoke like a child, I thought like a child, I reasoned like a child. When I became a man, I gave up childish ways. For now, we see in a mirror dimly, but then face to face. Now I know in part; then I shall know fully, even as I have been fully known. ~1 Corinthians 13:11-12*

What masks do you wear? Some masks are made to protect you from germs. They keep you from breathing in germs which could hurt you. Other masks are created to hide your face. They are to help you to pretend to be someone else. Still others are made to help you celebrate one event or another. Which kind do you wear?

Weary One, your masks will wear you out. I am referring to the ones you put on for others to see. These masks hide the truth. They keep you in shame. How you really feel stays hidden behind these kinds of masks. You don't speak about many things because you fear judgement or condemnation, or you condemn yourself by thinking you should be beyond whatever it is in your life that is holding you back, but you aren't. And you feel bad about that. So, you smile and say things are going well, when nothing could be further from the truth. It is exhausting to mask the truth. It is harmful to you, Beloved.

Masks are objects of self-protection. You think they are necessary, but they shouldn't be. They are objects of deception. They deceive others around you, even those who love you. They make them believe everything is fine, when it most definitely is not. Masks even deceive you. You have worn them so long that you believe they are who you are. You have even deceived yourself.

Take them off. Peel them back. Let me see the real you. There is no need to hide from me. I love you, as you are. Let me show you who that is. You don't even know yourself because you only see your masks in the mirror. You are not the person you believe yourself to be. Let your guard down and let me show you the true you.

# May 3

*And he said, "Go out and stand on the mount before the Lord." And behold, the Lord passed by, and a great and strong wind tore the mountains and broke in pieces the rocks before the Lord, but the Lord was not in the wind. And after the wind an earthquake, but the Lord was not in the earthquake. And after the earthquake a fire, but the Lord was not in the fire. And after the fire the sound of a low whisper. ~1 Kings 19:11-12*

Don't be distracted, Weary One. It is so easy in the world to get your focus off of me and onto all the things around you. It may feel like you don't have a choice, but you do. Take Mary and Martha as an example. My Son spoke to Martha, "You are worried and upset by many things, but only one thing is necessary." She was worried and upset about many things. Mary chose only one thing. Who do you think had more peace?

That verse still holds true even today. You are worried and upset by many things. Our jobs. Our health. Our family. Our world. So many things are crying out to burden you. Feeling this burden and unsettledness is actually one way to tell whose voice you are listening to. If you are worried and upset, you are not hearing My voice. When your gut is churning and frazzled, that is a clue.

Only one thing is necessary at this moment in time...sitting at My feet and listening. To me alone. Personal, deep relationship. Intimacy = into me see. Letting your walls down. Cleaning the inside of your cup instead of the outside. Taking off your masks. Opening up...yourself. Knowing that I am your safe place.

Resist being driven to distraction. Resist the frenzy. Refuse the tsunami of worry. Shut out the noise. Cut off all voices. Stop it all. Just listen. You will hear My love. You will feel My peace. You will breathe more easily. Open your heart to me. Let me heal it. Let My words be your bread. I am the provider of all you need and the remover of distractions.

# May 4

*My people will abide in a peaceful habitation, in secure dwellings, and in quiet resting places. ~Isaiah 32:18*

Come home. Do you know I am your home, Beloved? I am a place as well as a person. I am the place you can go when you are overwhelmed. I am the place you can go when you are sad. When you are depressed, come home. When you are grieving, come home. When you are afraid, come home. When you are struggling, come home.

Home is a place where you feel safe. Do not let past experiences with others mislead you. My people are not always the best representation of My heart. I am working on that. But you need to know deep in your spirit that I am safe. I am accepting and I understand you better than you understand yourself. I do not condemn you. Conviction and condemnation are two different things. My ways are gentle. My goal is always to restore. I want you near me, so I do not push you out or away. One way you can know My voice is if it is gentle and you feel drawn to it.

I want what is best for you. That is what home is supposed to be. A place where you are encouraged and built up. There are times that home requires serious conversations, and there are times that home is full of laughter. But always, always, there is love. Love is the foundation of what home should be. If your home has not always been a safe place, learn anew from me how home should be.

You can relax at home. Drop all the facades you carry out in the world. Drop all the insecurities and just be. You can do that because you are highly valued and accepted at home, as you are. No pretenses. You are worthy of love. I know your strengths and weaknesses. I love everything about you. Areas that need smoothing out are not problems for me. I know how to smooth them. You can breathe easy with me. You can sit in comfortable silence, or you can talk until your tongue is too tired to speak. Either way, I will love you.

Weary One, you are known at home. Every moment. I know you. Who you are. Who you will be. The you that you don't like and the you that you do. I am for you. I am with you. There are times when you are confused about yourself, but I never am. I created you. You are one of My best designs. Believe it. Do not hesitate. Come home. Run to me. You are My child and I will be your home forever.

# May 5

*Draw near to God, and He will draw near to you. Cleanse your hands, you sinners, and purify your hearts, you double-minded. ~James 4:8*

Stay close. When a parent says, "Stay close" to a child, it means danger is near. Whether it is because there is a lot of traffic, or they are walking on a dark path, or there is a large crowd. "Stay close" -words of warning. Do not stray. Keep me in view. It is a parent's nature to draw their children close to them in dangerous places. Once again, you are made in My image, so it is also true for you.

I say the same to you, Weary One. Stay close. When you are tired and life is overwhelming there is a temptation to wander away. Intense circumstances cry out for relief. You just want a moment to yourself to forget. Come to me in those moments, do not go to the usual numbing activities. They simply put off the inevitable. At some point or another, the reality will come to light and it will be hard to find your way back.

When you are bored the same is true. You look for other interesting things to do. You wander away in search of "more" only to find it doesn't exist, not really. More is found inside of you because that is where I am. When you allow me to peel back the layers, the boredom goes away and you see your potential to find adventure in the normal everyday parts of life.

Stay close. Do not stray. Keep me in view. Otherwise, you will look up and have lost your way. You will search but will be unable to find me. It is scary to be on your own in dangerous places. Of course, Beloved, you can always call out to me. I will always run to you. But how much better never to have strayed. How much less pain will there be for you if you are always by My side? Stay close.

# May 6

*The Lord is my strength and my shield; in Him my heart trusts, and I am helped; my heart exults, and with my song I give thanks to Him. ~Psalms 28:7*

A shield is something you hide behind when danger is present. It absorbs the blows that come your way. It is mobile and can be pivoted from side to side or over your head. Wherever the battle is, the shield is there to guard and protect. It covers the essential parts, while still allowing one arm to move freely. It is a defensive part of your armor. Without it you would not be able to stand for long.

The shield of faith works in the same way, Beloved. Faith is your belief. When lies come at you, put up your belief of the truth. When depression tries to overtake you, hold up your shield and renew your mind. When loss is overwhelming, sit behind your shield as you cry. Sometimes the shield is heavy. It is hard to hold onto. You are tired and your arms are weak from the battle. It is tempting to drop the shield. To take your chances without it. It is cumbersome. It is awkward.

If you drop your shield, Weary One, you will regret it. You will be overtaken in a moment. The shield of faith is the most important piece of armor. It is an active piece, though you might not realize it. It moves with you. Whatever position you take, the shield is attached to cover you. Your faith is a covering, like the shield. Dear One, do not put it down. Do not leave it behind. Do not think, "I don't need this today." You need it every day.

There are some who only pick up their shield when the battle is imminent. They set it to the side at other times. But when they do it that way, they are out of practice and not as effective when the battle comes. Some take their shield everywhere, but they don't use it properly. They only hide behind it. Never moving forward, never making changes needed for it to be used successfully. It becomes a rigid piece of metal, hard over their hearts. Never shifting, never agile, they are stiff. Using your shield requires faith that doesn't waver, and knows the truth. It anticipates the enemy's blow and it arrives in the proper place just before the strike.

I will teach you to use it. I will give you the intuitive motion you need by My spirit. In times of trouble, use your shield. Believe when you cannot see. Hope when you cannot feel. Speak words you don't think have power. Trust promises made. Hone the use of your shield so that when the battle is raging around you, there is a way to survive. You are a survivor, because you have a shield. You will survive again, because you have a shield. I am your shield.

# May 7

*Thus, says the Lord to you, "Do not be afraid and do not be dismayed at this great horde, for the battle is not yours but God's." ~2 Chronicles 20:15*

Speaking of armor, let's talk about the helmet. It is the protector of your head. Without a helmet, a warrior would be eliminated immediately. Inside your skull is one of My most advanced creations. It runs everything about you. Without your brain, your body would cease to function. So, in battle it is vital to have your head covered.

In spiritual battle the same holds true. The helmet of salvation protects your thoughts the same way a regular helmet protects your brain. Your thoughts are the controller of your actions. Every single one of them is important to how you move, Dear One. Forward or backward. If you hesitate or take a bold step it begins in your thoughts.

When you are under stress, Weary One, it is hard to remember to put on your helmet. Thoughts come at you like arrows. You hold your shield trying to block them, but some still get through. What you do with them determines the course the battle will take. If you allow them to penetrate, they will take you down. If you focus on your sorrow, you will be depressed. If you focus on your loss, your grief will overstay its welcome. If you focus on your anger, it will bloom into bitterness.

I am not saying just grit your teeth and think happy thoughts. That is too simple an answer to a strategic plan of attack. No, that will not work. The helmet of salvation is more than just thinking about what will save you from the onslaught. It is more than memorizing scripture and quoting it when you are under the barrage, though that is a powerful tool.

I am saying you need to know; I mean really know, the author of your salvation. If you know me deeply, you know My voice and you will hear it in the battle. It will implant My thoughts into you for your strategy. Sometimes it tells you the scriptures you need at just the right time. Other times it may tell you to sit still, or maybe to run ahead. Like a coach, calling the plays needed to beat an opponent, I am a master strategist. I am the voice in your helmet. There are no two battles that are just alike, so your response will be different each time.

Everything depends on your thoughts. Everything depends on who you know and who you listen to. Although your helmet of salvation, will save you, but it's not the helmet itself, it's the thoughts. When you let me direct them, the battle will be won.

# May 8

*God is spirit, and those who worship Him must worship in Spirit and truth. ~John 4:24*

Let's continue with the armor, Beloved. The belt of truth is crucial. Truth is the foundation. It is fitted to you and worn by you. It holds things together. Without a belt, pants are loose, shirts are not tucked, there is no place for the sword to hang. Without truth, everything is based on lies. Nothing fits together.

My truth is what girds you up. It is the core. My Child, if you can't find the truth in your world, it is because you are looking to the world to give it to you. There are times when elements of My truth are there, but the world almost always twists it in some way. If you cling to My words alone, you will be strong.

In the world it has become commonplace to say whatever you want. Media makes up stories based on partial truths. Friends lie and betray confidences. All the systems of government stretch the truth to paint a certain picture. Family members speak their own truth to avoid reality. Sometimes you even lie to yourself, Dear One. It has become normal for truth to be relative to the circumstances.

But that isn't how truth works. Truth is reality without bias. It is factual, without emotion. In a battle, the truth is that there is an enemy who wants you dead. He is well equipped. He is stronger than you. You are an underdog. Saying you are more powerful than him doesn't make it true. Saying you will win hands down doesn't make it true. Neither does saying you have no possible way to win. Neither does saying the world is conspiring against you.

In the heat of battle, it is easy to let emotion overtake the truth, and it seems true at the time. That is why you cannot let feelings cloud your vision. Once you know where you stand, do not deny the truth of your circumstances. You must prepare rather than let your emotions dominate. I am the only one who can win the battle. If you align yourself with me you will be victorious. Any other way is a lie. Fasten the belt of truth around your waist. Let it hold all things together. Let it be the foundational piece of armor.

# May 9

*Put on shoes for your feet, having put on the readiness given by the gospel of peace. ~Ephesians 6:15*

Go, with your feet fitted with the readiness that comes from the gospel of peace. Shoes of peace. Every place you put your feet, every step you take, brings peace, or does it? It is easy, when things are difficult, to let the circumstances steal your peace. When that happens, Beloved, you carry your burdens with you. The heaviness affects the atmosphere around you. If you are weary, you bring weariness. If you are anxious, you bring anxiety. If you are depressed, you bring sadness. Your feet carry what you bring into every environment you enter.

Fit your feet with peace. Be careful where you walk. Be careful what you carry. Be ready in season and out of season. There are times I bring you into places where I need My peace to reign. Walking the path I have planned for you involves being My hands and feet on the earth. You bring the kingdom with you. My kingdom is not like the world. I need My representatives to show others the ways of walking in peace when the world is in chaos. I need My representatives to be alert and ready...to be interruptible in their daily walk, to be easily moved to help others. To pivot when I need them to shift from their daily activities to show compassion.

Dear One, sometimes the cashier at the store needs My peace. Sometimes the lady in the waiting room needs a compassionate word of peace. Sometimes the teenager at the restaurant needs to be seen through eyes of peace. The need is all around you, all the time. Just take your eyes off of your own hardships long enough to look up. You will see what I see. A world that is desperate for something to calm the anxiety and fear.

People need you to show them. They need the steps you take to usher in peacefulness into the situation. They will even ask you how you are so calm. You can tell them, but it all begins with showing them and walking with them. Fit your shoes. Tie them up tight. Hit the road in your shoes of peace.

A warrior needs these shoes even in the battle. Ultimately, they carry a warrior to push through to the peace. Warriors don't fight just to fight...they fight to bring peace to all men. The foundation of their armor is the shoes.

# May 10

*Stand therefore, having fastened on the belt of truth, and having put on the breastplate of righteousness. ~Ephesians 6:14*

Let's talk about the breastplate, Dear One. All armor has a breastplate to protect the vital organs. It covers the heart and lungs. It protects the liver, spleen, and pancreas. Any of the organs that are essential to keep your body running are under the breastplate. That is by design. It is a defensive piece of armor.

In spiritual armor, your righteousness is your breastplate. It is what protects your heart. Righteousness doesn't mean you are always right or always do the correct things. It is a character trait which always looks for the higher ground. In life, it will serve you well to choose to do the right thing in a given situation. It is when your choices are questionable that you get into trouble.

The consequences of making bad choices are that they leave your heart exposed. In times of hardship, it is important to stay aware of your choices. Most of the time, you know the right thing to do. It is the doing it that challenges you. It is hard to choose the right thing when you'd rather do something different.

Doing the right thing can be costly, so sometimes you take the easier way, and your breastplate slips. Exposing yourself to the enemy is not wise. When you are wallowing in self-pity, your breastplate has slipped. When you are gossiping about others, your breastplate has slipped. When you are enraged from impatience, your breastplate has slipped. In these times, it is best to stop and take stock of your actions.

A warrior checks his breastplate BEFORE the battle starts. Think of it as a bulletproof vest. If it doesn't fit properly, or it isn't attached right, all is lost. To have it in place before the battle begins is the only way to survive. If you wait until the arrows have started flying, you are too late. It is a part of the preparation for battle.

When you practice righteousness...doing the right thing...all the time, it is a natural response when things get tough. Like muscle memory. It is automatic. Beloved, after things you have been through, doing the right thing is a relief. It is releasing the burden of self and picking up the lightness of My righteousness.

You can't be righteous on your own. You know this better than anyone. Hardship shows the need for supernatural strength. You understand it in ways others cannot. Choosing to do the right thing is something I put into your spirit. The desire. The motivation. The ability. You do have the strength to choose rightly. I have given it to you already. Reach out and accept the gift and then walk in it.

# May 11

*For the word of God is living and active, sharper than any two-edged sword, piercing to the division of soul and of spirit, of joints and of marrow, and discerning the thoughts and intentions of the heart. ~Hebrews 4:12*

Don't forget the sword, Weary One. It is your only offensive piece of armor. It must be sharp enough to divide soul and spirit, joints and marrow. My words carry power. When you read them, make sure you apply them. It is so easy to use My sword against others, but not use it in your own life. It is not meant only for the enemy. Does that surprise you?

Certainly, My sword helps when the enemy comes. It will be your primary means of survival. When your mind is under attack, My words will pop into your thoughts. When you are in a tough place, speak My words with your voice and you will see their power. The enemy flees at the sound of them. The relief is quick. The blow is fatal. He turns away from tormenting you. He leaves you to me to heal. The battle is real and his weakness is My sword. He hates it when you use it effectively.

However, the sword can also be used in your own life. It helps you determine what is flesh and what is spirit. It is not always the enemy who is trying to take you down. Your flesh is strong and it fights against things of the spirit. Your flesh is all about itself and getting what it wants. When you read My words, they show you if you are aligned with me. They expose the flesh and the desires that are not healthy for your spirit. Sometimes, Beloved, your internal battle is bigger than anything that comes from the outside. Learn to wield the sword in your own life.

Weary One, I give you a word of caution here. Do not use the sword on My people as a weapon. There are more of My children who have been butchered by it than you would believe. It is not to be used in this way on My little ones. Use it as an encouragement, not as judgement. Trust me to do the correcting. Please, do this for me. My word will go much farther in spreading My love if it is used properly.

My sword is an empowering part of your armor. When you use it properly, you become a warrior of strength. You do not back down or turn away. You face the challenges before you, confident in My words. You know them. You use them. You apply them. They bring you life.

# May 12

*The prayer of a righteous person has great power as it is working. ~James 5:16*

When you are on your knees, you will find me. It is so easy to talk about me, but to know me, you have to spend time with me. In a trial, survival mode kicks in. It has to. You are in the immediate situation with immediate needs. At a hospital, or in a courtroom. Working with a counselor, or weeping on your own. Whatever the situation or circumstance, when you are barely able to breathe, moving forward is difficult. You are working on details and trying to keep living in the midst of hardship. Not an easy task.

This is why you have to spend time with me. I am not talking about a rigid schedule to keep. I am talking about time to sit with me and soak. Time to pour out your heart and your words. I am here to listen. It is why being on your knees is such a powerful place. Therefore, you have to do it intentionally.

Humans tend to be strong on their lips, but weak on their knees. It is easier to speak without taking the time to sort things out first. Especially in a crisis. Thoughts swirl around, begging to be spoken. Dear One, speak to me first. I can help you sort what is coming from the circumstances and what is coming from me. I will guide you. That is what prayer is. A conversation. A back and forth. You speak, I listen. I speak, you listen.

Being strong on your knees doesn't mean you are super spiritual; you don't have to be, you only have to be genuine. You only have to be honest with me. Just as you want your child or loved one to be honest with you and share their heart, I want that for you. Just as you would rather your child to consult with you before they run ahead and speak, so I want that for you. I am your biggest fan. I want the best for you. Being strong on your knees means you acknowledge that. Then you can speak on My behalf because you know me. You will make it through your trial because I am with you, holding you up. I am speaking life into you when you are sitting with me. Prayer is your lifeline. Make time for it.

# May 13

*Has the potter no right over the clay, to make out of the same lump one vessel for honorable use and another for dishonorable use? ~Romans 9:21*

Do not be dismayed or discouraged, Dear One. I am in control. You cannot see all that is transpiring. I am moving things around. Adding things, removing others. It feels as if everything is coming apart, but remember demolition comes before rebuilding. Consider it like a renovation of the heart.

I position My children for such a time as this. It is not an accident. I do not randomly throw things together and hope they will work. I am strategic in My ways. Your hardship for the past years has prepared you. It has built strength into you that you are not aware you have, until a crisis comes. Then you will rise up in strength. You have been trained how to do hard things. Not for naught, for now. For today.

In your dark places, on the hard days, you are not alone. I am with you. I am speaking and shaping. I am molding. Clay requires fire to be functional. Metal requires heat to be purified. Everything beautiful goes through the transformation process. Your hardships have refined you and prepared you for now.

Beauty is not the finished product. What is most beautiful is the process itself. In the kneading of the clay, of the sitting on the shelf, in the staining, and in the baking in the kiln. One step is not more important than the other. They all serve the purpose of creating both beauty and strength. This period in time is exactly where you were born to be. You are a vessel to be poured out. You will make a difference no matter what stage of transformation you are in. I use all things for My glory.

It is so with all art, isn't it? Glory in the process. Do not be impatient with your stage. Do not take it as rejection or abandonment. It is part of the process and it is beautiful in and of itself. Even if paint splatters. Even if somehow, it isn't looking like what you planned. Do not despise the work of an artist. Perfection isn't the goal. You will never be perfect, but you will always be beautiful and bring your beauty to the world around you. I am not finished with you yet, but I always finish what I start. I promise.

# May 14

*Awake, awake, put on your strength, O Zion; put on your beautiful garments.*
*~Isaiah 52:1*

Awake, awake, Weary One! Stay awake at all times praying for strength. I am pouring out a deposit. Will you receive it? The strength you need. The eyes to see. The heart of joy. The place of rest. A deposit, to be withdrawn in the days to come. A deposit of compassion. A deposit of hope. A deposit of courage. A deposit of My power.

Awake, O sleeper and arise from the dead, so the light of Christ will shine on you. Anything that is visible is light. I will illuminate the darkness for you to walk through, as if it is day. It will be clear to you, when you awake, your vision will not be hindered by the shadows. I will shine and you will carry My light into the night.

Put on strength, as the arm of the Lord. My arm carries burdens. My arm removes obstacles. My arm lifts up. I will rescue you. The hour is upon you to stand up in My strength.

Put on your beautiful garments. I have prepared them for you. A garment of praise. A garment of joy. A garment of truth. A garment of light and life. They are layered and they flow over you, like My presence. They were made for such a time as this.

Awake! Do not sleep as others do. Do not take your vision lightly. Be alert. Look for me amidst the chaos. Look and you will find me, in the eye of the storm. Peace, peace. I am the peace. Open your eyes to see me.

Awake! Prepare your mind for action. Set your mind fully on the grace of Christ. Guard your mind. Focus on me alone. Protect what goes into your mind. Your thoughts steer your life. Let me guide them. Center them on me.

Wake up, watch and pray so you do not fall. The spirit is willing but the flesh is weak. I speak to your spirit to rise up, and be strong. Clothe yourself in strength. Your adversary the devil prowls around like a roaring lion, seeking someone to devour. Do not let it be you.

All will be well. All will be as it should be. I am the light in the darkness. Awake and walk with me in the garden. I will show you the way to walk with your eyes open.

# May 15

*But in your hearts honor Christ the Lord as holy, always being prepared to make a defense to anyone who asks you for a reason for the hope that is in you; yet do it with gentleness and respect. ~1 Peter 3:15*

Get ready. Dear One, I am preparing something for you. It is especially designed with you in mind. It is geared towards the person I have made you to be, not what you do for everyone else. It is for you alone.

When you walk a difficult road, you know what it means to be alone. Caregiving, physical limitations, broken heart, whatever your lot, you have walked on your own. There are others around you, but they cannot walk your path, just as you cannot walk theirs. Life is a solitary journey. But in that journey, I have built you into who you are. The trials and tribulations you have experienced have shaped you.

Now, I am asking you to get ready. Do not sit and sulk. Do not worry and fret. None of those things help you at all. Self-pity is a life stealer. Resentment is a destroyer of peace. These things are not becoming on you. They do not lift you up. Check your heart. Years of walking hard roads can take a toll on your spirit. They create a hardness of heart that will hold you back from what I have for you.

If you nurture the hard places, and you feed the hurt that lies deep inside you, the tenderness I am pouring out on you will be quenched. You will not see compassion rise up. You will wallow in your troubles. I know it is hard to see past them sometimes, but you must. You must take stock and look at the true state of things. You are more than your circumstances.

When I say to get ready, I mean to examine yourself. Like cleaning your closet, throw out anything that doesn't fit you anymore. Throw out lies. Throw out attitudes that do not serve you anymore. Throw out hurts. Replace these things with truth.

Replace them with healed hearts. Do the work necessary to make the exchanges. It is a deep work to exchange lies for truth. It requires grit to replace negative thought patterns with positive ones. Just to be aware of your self-talk, requires concentration, to change it, requires focus and commitment. When you personally do what is required to clean the inside of your cup, what you pour out will be pure. Your words will not be tainted, nor will your thoughts.

Get ready. I have something for you. Do the work to get ready. I will present you with new places, new opportunities, new ways of being, new areas to explore. You may never leave home, not every opportunity is "out there" somewhere, some of them are "in here." Sit with me and let me show you how to get ready for what I have for you.

# May 16

*Jesus spoke to them, saying, "I am the light of the world. Whoever follows me will not walk in darkness, but will have the light of life." ~John 8:12*

I am the light and just like a flame moves, I move. The core of the flame is steady, so am I. Yet, the flame moves around the core. There is a reason throughout scripture I am described as the light of the World. I illuminate things. I bring life within the flame. Light is warm. It glows.

When the sun rises, life rises up. The natural world opens up. The birds sing. Leaves unfurl. Sunflowers and morning glories turn their faces to me. It is their natural way. It is part of My creation. Physical light is required for nature to thrive.

Spiritual light is the same. It rises in your heart because I live there. I created you as a spiritual being. Yet, all the challenges of your life are physical and emotional. They can get heavy and if you only live in that place, it is all you will feel. However, if you let My light shine, if you take the time to pay attention to your spirit and bathe it in My light, you will find relief. You will find peace. I will show you things you do not know, or that are difficult to remember when you are in your physical day-to-day.

It is My light which clears the darkness away. Do you feel like you live in shadows, Weary One? Like I have forgotten you? It is not the truth. Look to My light. Run to it. It will wipe away the darkness. In the midst of pain, your load is lightened because light has no shadow. The light dispels the shadows.

Just as I always do, what I have, I give to you. I am the light of life and I give it to you. It radiates out of My words to you. It shines on your heart. It shows you the path to travel. It bears witness in your spirit when you feel it. It warms you and lifts you up. That is what light is for-illumination.

Candlelight is used as a representation of me in all kinds of ceremonies. Candles are lit as prayers. They are lit as a unity candle to join a bride and groom together with me. They are lit in remembrance of someone.

Dear One, a single candle can shatter the darkness. You can be that candle in your world. Many can remove shadows all together. Bonded with others, the light becomes a powerful force. I am the light that lives within you. Using a flame to represent me is a picture of the reality of My presence. It moves, but remains in one place. I am always moving. My Spirit spreads life throughout the world, and yet, I am always the same, steadfast and faithful. Follow My light, Beloved. In whatever dark place you are walking, follow My light.

# May 17

*Count it all joy, my brothers, when you meet trials of various kinds, for you know that the testing of your faith produces steadfastness. ~James 1:2-3*

Dear One, I am cultivating you. I know it can be painful to have old roots torn out. It hurts to have the hard ground broken up. Trust me, I wouldn't do it unless it were necessary. But if the new seed is to grow, I must prepare the soil of your heart. I am a farmer after all.

As a farmer, I know it is a waste of time to plant new seed if the ground is not prepared first. If the soil is rocky, I reach down and remove the heart of stone and replace it with a heart of flesh. Hard heartedness is soil that requires intense labor. It is some of the most difficult to tend.

First, I remove any debris by pulling out the hard-stony places. Then I use tools to literally break it apart, which requires precision and strength. I must remember what I am working towards in order to complete the task, otherwise I would give up when it started to hurt you.

Once the clumps are broken up, I pull out any old roots that have been exposed by My tilling. Those roots are from things that were planted long ago. Some of them were planted before you surrendered the ground of your heart to me. They are still dug in deep, even though the plant on top has died. Beloved, these roots are hard to remove, because since the top has been cut away, you can no longer see the plant on the outside. It is deep inside the heart where it appears. Bitterness, resentment, self-pity, all of the underground roots will destroy any new seed I plant, so I rip them out.

I fertilize the ground with My word, and I till it again to make sure the food is spread evenly throughout. The dirt becomes soft and free of obstacles. I allow your heart to rest for a season, so it can heal from the hardness and all the labor. As it sits it soaks up the warmth of the sun and absorbs the water from the rain. Sitting with My Son and the Holy Spirit always heals the heart. They minister to the formerly broken places and bring them back to rich pliable soil.

Now, My seeds will grow unimpeded. The soil is finally ready to receive. Weary One, do not despise the cultivation. It is necessary. Rejoice as the hard places are pulled out and the ground is broken up. It means there is a fruitful season ahead.

# May 18

*Then the kingdom of heaven will be like ten virgins who took their lamps and went to meet the bridegroom. Five of them were foolish, and five were wise. For when the foolish took their lamps, they took no oil with them, but the wise took flasks of oil with their lamps. As the bridegroom was delayed, they all became drowsy and slept. But at midnight there was a cry, "Here is the bridegroom! Come out to meet Him." Then all those virgins rose and trimmed their lamps. And the foolish said to the wise, "Give us some of your oil, for our lamps are going out." But the wise answered, saying, "Since there will not be enough for us and for you, go rather to the dealers and buy for yourselves." And while they were going to buy, the bridegroom came, and those who were ready went in with Him to the marriage feast, and the door was shut. ~Matthew 25:1-10*

Have you read My parable of the ten virgins who go to meet the groom? They all have oil lamps with them which are burning, but only five of them took an extra oil supply. When they fell asleep, someone called to them that the groom was coming, and they woke up to trim their lamps. The five without extra oil found that their lamps were getting low and asked the others to share their oil, but there was not enough for all of them, so they said no.

Weary One, trimming your lamp is important during a hard time. The wick is what carries the oil to the flame. As the flame burns, the used wick gets charred. The burned part must be cut away so the fresh wick will burn brighter. If it is not trimmed, the light gets dull and smoky and you cannot see.

I am the oil, the fuel for your lamp. I flow from within the container, which is you, to the outside world. Then My flame lights the way through the wick of your heart. It transports me as it lights your way.

As you live, Dear One, your wick burns and the hardships of life make your flame dull. Trimming your lamp is when you cut back the used-up places of your heart. The bitterness of life will give you less light, unless you cut it away. The sorrow of suffering will steal your light as well. Holding onto those things will not allow you to clearly see the path in front of you. Like the five foolish virgins, you will not be prepared for what I have for you.

In addition to remembering to trim your lamp, you must also have enough oil. You do not know how long it will be before I arrive, which means if you do not continually fill yourself with me you will dry out. I am working in your life as it goes through seasons of fruitfulness and seasons of dryness. There are seasons of sorrow and seasons of joy. If you do not supply extra oil by abiding in me, when the hard seasons come, you will be unable to see clearly. Your light will be dim, or go out completely. Your heart will wither and you will be useless to yourself and to me.

Beloved, trimming your lamp is not for me to do, it is for you. It is taking care to keep the light burning brightly. It is taking care to be prepared when hard times come. You know all about hard times; you know the need for the light in the darkness. Heed My words to you. Prepare your lamp so you can transport My love, My grace, My hope, My words, My heart to the world.

# May 19

*And David came to Baal-perazim, and David defeated them there. And he said, "The Lord has broken through my enemies before me like a breaking flood." ~2 Samuel 5:20*

I am the God of the breakthrough. Do you not believe me? Or does it seem, Weary One, that the breakthrough you need always goes to others? I know when a sudden, important discovery or development is needed. I know when the pressure of holding yourself together is too much. When you feel alone, like the enemy is going to overcome you, I know just the right time for a breakthrough. You must trust me in this.

To break a line means to make a forward movement through the obstacle of an enemy. As in battle, this requires a fight. Determination to hold the line is one thing, but to break it is when the victory begins. Pushing through the line is forward movement.

Dear One, you have been holding the line for a long time. You have battled and held your ground. You have been solid and steadfast. But it is tiring to constantly hold the line without breaking through it. It can almost seem like defeat when you never move forward. Chronic hardship feels like defeat, but what you don't know is that you have actually been growing stronger. Your constant defense of the line is building a warrior.

In the right time, you will push through the line. Beyond holding the ground, you will begin to take it because I am with you. When this happens, you will see it quickly. The nature of a breakthrough is that the fight is wearing down your enemy. I know you feel worn down, but in reality, you are wearing him down. Then suddenly, there will be a turn of the tide. You will see. The strength you have gained in the battle will rise up. I will use it to turn the tide. Like a flash flood it will come quickly and wipe out everything the enemy has set in its path. It will be a turning point.

You deserve a turning point. Do not let your enemy convince you otherwise. I have not abandoned you on the battlefield. You do not fight alone. In your mind, you are less than only because you don't see the breakthrough. But I am here to tell you, it is time. It is time for you to push through the line. I am the Lord of the breakthrough.

# May 20

*Put on then, as God's chosen ones, holy and beloved, compassionate hearts, kindness, humility, meekness, and patience. ~Colossians 3:12*

Are you interruptible, Beloved? If I put someone in your path who needs encouragement, do you see them or walk right by? Are you so caught up in your own trials that you miss opportunities to be a blessing to others? It is easy to forget why you are here. In the midst of life and its hardships, it seems like everything revolves around taking care of your own life. How in the world could you stop in the middle of a task to speak to a stranger?

But I want you to think for a moment. How many times has someone spoken encouragement just when you needed it most? In the hospital, or at work, or in the retirement community, or the funeral home? I have sent people to you specifically to speak life when you were in a hard place. They were interruptible. They stopped what they were doing and came to visit you, or gave you a call.

My people can be interrupted when they realize their purpose is to bring life to those around them. Until that happens, they will be caught up in their own details. Life will be egocentric and everything will revolve around them. Interruptions cause frustrations or disappointments. A car breaks down and frustration overflows to others. Or a doctor's appointment takes hours and the nurses pay the price of a bad attitude.

What if these types of interruptions are not random? What if they are opportunities to show kindness or to lighten someone's load? What if you smiled at the person who bags your groceries and asked about their day? What if you helped an elderly person with the door? What if you asked nurses how they are doing instead of the other way around?

Weary One, paying attention and being interruptible actually lightens your own load. It seems contrary I know, but instead of making life harder or more hectic, it brings lift to you. Compassion is the best antidepressant. Kindness soothes anxiety. It is one of My greatest secrets. But it's not really a secret. It is just a forgotten truth. Stopping and taking a moment to be kind will do a world of good for you. Try it and see.

# May 21

*See what kind of love the Father has given to us, that we should be called children of God; and so, we are. The reason why the world does not know us is that it did not know Him.  ~1 John 3:1*

I want to talk to you about striving, Weary One. Striving is when you over work yourself trying to make something come to fruition. It can be something you love, but it wears you out. Usually striving is served up with a heap of expectations and comparisons. You look at the lives of everyone else and you feel you don't measure up, so you strive to do better, to be more. You work hard at it, but it feels as if you never arrive at your destination. Frustration arises and you are left with that not-good-enough feeling.

My Child, it doesn't have to be this way. You were not meant to be like anyone else. I designed you to be unique with your own personality, your own strengths, and your own way of being. When you try to be something other than yourself, you end up feeling burnt out and run down. Striving does that. It makes sure you never feel good enough or rested. It is the opposite of My grace.

When My grace covers you, you have the strength you need to do the work in front of you. Whether it is an actual job, or taking care of things at home, you feel My pleasure and favor. It's not that the work is easy, but it just feels lighter than when you are weighed down by striving.

Learn to recognize the differences. Work is work. How you feel about your work is where you get clarity. If you are miserable and you feel like you will never meet the standard set before you, take stock for a moment. First, is the standard set by someone else, or are you the one setting an impossible goal? Next, is the work something you love or something that doesn't use your strengths? Do you feel My favor? Are you able to put aside the things you don't like about it to walk it out anyway, or does it weigh you down? Answering those questions can give you insight into yourself. The answers can show you if you are operating in My grace.

If you find, upon reflection, that you are striving and the strife is causing burn out, you might need a change. If My grace has lifted from your work, the only thing left is to continue to strive. Finding work that allows you to both, work hard and to do so in a spirit of rest and peace is vital. Again, this is not about a job...it is about your life's work.

If you are in a circumstance where you cannot make a change you must learn to rest. Work at your home isn't something you can walk away from. It is your family. It is your health. It is your life. In learning to rest, you will find My grace. Striving to keep all the plates spinning will not bring you peace. Learning what plates to drop, and how to say no goes a long way to finding the grace-flow you need.

Another way to cease striving is to stop chasing an impossible standard you have set for yourself. Quit comparing your life. I didn't create you to live someone else's life. I don't expect you to be perfect, so why should you expect that from yourself? Find who I made you to be. Find your purpose. Align yourself with what I say about you and what you know about me. You are loved, as you are. You are valued. You are worthy of My love. You are a treasure. Stop striving and rest in me.

# May 22

*Be strong and courageous. Do not fear or be in dread of them, for it is the Lord your God who goes with you. He will not leave you or forsake you.*
*~Deuteronomy 31:6*

You can do hard things, Dear One. Your resilience is amazing. Do not be afraid. You are stronger than you know. One of the advantages of having survived trials and suffering is that it shores you up. You learn to hold on, one day at a time. You learn to press into My strength when you are weak. That experience teaches you how to face hard things in the future.

Remember you possess courage to go forward in difficult times. Courage doesn't mean fear is gone. It means you go forward despite it. You have learned what you desire is on the other side of it and you gather yourself to you push through.

Beloved, when you gather yourself, breathe me in. Breathe out the anxiety. Breathe in My strength. Breathe out your fear. Breathe in My courage. It will make movement forward possible. I am with you in the hard things. I am right beside you as you walk into the unknown.

It will be okay...even these hard things will be okay. The beauty of this is that you already know this. Your previous experience with hard things allows you to KNOW this is true. It may take some time. It may not happen immediately, but in some time when you look back you will see that it is okay. You are a survivor. You will survive the new hard thing just like you did the last one. You have survived every hard day in your life thus far, and in every hard season you have walked out changed. Take courage in that. Hold to it. Say to yourself, "I am a survivor and I can do hard things."

# May 23

*So, if the Son sets you free, you will be free indeed. ~John 8:36*

Freedom is a gift. But freedom isn't simply living in a place where you can do as you choose. Just because you are free on the outside, does not mean you are free on the inside, Beloved. Not everyone lives free. Some are bound to their homes by illness. Others are confined in caring for those they love. Still others are tied to sadness and grief from a monumental loss. Some are trapped by addiction or stuck in unhealthy relationships. Some are oppressed and beaten down. There are a multitude of ways not to be free. It has always been this way.

Freedom has always been worth fighting for. There are battles that have been fought in order for people to live free. Soldiers have sacrificed their lives for it. Given up time with family. Given up their last breath for it. Soldiers do it, even though you might never know who they are.

Freedom of heart is the same. I have battled for your heart, Dear One. I have sacrificed time with My Son. I have given Him up to death for your freedom. He laid down His glory and walked among you to bring you freedom. You may or may not know of His sacrifice, but He did it anyway, so you could be free, truly free.

Even when you are not walking in freedom, you have it. You can be in chains and still be free, Weary One. Freedom is possible in your life. When your heart is free, you are free indeed. Clear your mind of captive thinking. Line up your thoughts with My word and you will find freedom for your soul, no matter what your life walk is. It is My gift to you to set your spirit free.

# May 24

*And I tell you, ask, and it will be given to you; seek, and you will find; knock, and it will be opened to you. ~Luke 11:9*

How do you posture yourself, Weary One? What is your particular way of dealing with life? Do you go through with a clenched fist or an open hand? Life hands out some rough situations. It can cause you to harden your heart, creating a prison of bitterness. I long to set you free, but if your hand is closed I cannot do it.

Assume a posture of grace, Beloved. To do so, you have to let go of the things you cling to. Let go of resentment and bitterness. Let go of unforgiveness. Let go of controlling everything around you. Release your grip. Actually, open your hand physically to release negative feelings. Then you have room for the new things I want to give you.

I want you to have new opportunities. Just ask. I want you to have hope and be free from the things which are holding you back. A posture of grace is one which receives from me. It is an open heart. An attitude of waiting for me to move on your behalf. Still yourself. Listen for My voice. Open your heart to it. My grace is sufficient for your needs. It is also what empowers you to move forward.

When you feel stuck, check your posture. When you feel down and defeated, check your posture. When you are grieving to the point you have lost yourself, check your posture. It is important to know how to humble yourself and open your hands before me. Give up and then ask me for what you need. Offer up what you are holding onto as a sacrifice. When you willingly give it, I receive it. Then I pour out grace to carry you. I pour out new gifts into your hands. Receive them with a posture of grace.

# May 25

*The angel of the Lord encamps around those who fear Him, and delivers them.*
*~Psalms 34:7*

You are surrounded. You may feel overwhelmed, like your enemies could take you. Grief, disappointment, unmet expectations, broken dreams, depression, anger, bitterness, resentment...they are all circling around you, Weary One. They are why you feel so weary. They are trying to get a foothold into your thoughts and attitudes. You feel their pressure. You feel them at every turn.

But when I said you are surrounded; I wasn't talking about them. I was talking about me. You are surrounded by My presence and it comes with all of My attributes. Hope, love, faith, strength, courage, freedom, self-control, patience...all the fruits of My Spirit. If that is not enough, I also send warring angels to protect you. They are more numerous than you know. Their purpose is to battle the enemy who is trying to defeat you.

Of course, the war is won already. It is not in question, but there is still a battle for your mind and heart. It is being fought daily, but there is no need to worry about it. There is victory. When you chose me, you chose wisely. I surround you always.

# May 26

*You have turned for me my mourning into dancing; you have loosed my sackcloth and clothed me with gladness, that my glory may sing your praise and not be silent. O Lord my God, I will give thanks to you forever! ~Psalms 30:11-12*

I am a redeemer. I compensate for your faults and weaknesses. When you are with Me, you are whole. I make amends. I pay what is necessary to clear your debt. I regain possession of you; My Son is My form of payment.

Dear One, I redeem all things. Time you think you wasted, I redeem it. A job you did poorly, I redeem it. Relationships you think are beyond repair, I redeem them. Redemption is one of My favorite activities. So much seems impossible in your life. Your circumstances seem beyond help, but I tell you I can redeem them.

Your loss can become your gift of compassion to others. Your broken relationship can become sweet forgiveness. Your physical brokenness can be healed. Your emotional wounds can be sealed up. I can redeem it all.

Take heart, My Love. You are not impossible to redeem. The seeds from your past sometimes bloom into something other than what you planted. They bloom into what I say. Out of your suffering comes strength. Out of your rebellion comes redemption. Out of your mistakes comes My plan. I use all things for your good, and mine. I am the God who can create something out of everything. I can use the worst times of your life for My purposes. You are never too far from redemption.

The question is, will you let me be your redeemer? Will you allow me to do My redemptive work? Or will you sink yourself down into the miry pit? Will you beat yourself up for your past? Will you say there is no possible way for me to redeem your circumstance?

I give you a choice. When you choose to receive what I offer you, there will be redemption in your life. When you walk away from the internal dialogue of defeatism you will find hope in redemption. Open your heart to me. Let me turn your weeping into joy, your ashes into beauty, your mourning into dancing, your death into life.

# May 27

*Death and life are in the power of the tongue, and those who love it will eat its fruits. ~Proverbs 18:21*

Watch your tongue, Weary One. There is power in the words you speak. When you talk about others negatively it brings death. When you hold things against them it binds them. The tongue has more power than you realize, that is why scripture has so much to say about taming the tongue. The words I am referring to are ones that you say with your mouth, but also the ones you type onto a screen. So much of your culture is shaped by the words spoken, and you see the result of not taming the tongue in the daily news reports.

Just as important as watching your words about others, is being careful of the words you speak about yourself. Do you look in the mirror and find fault with My creation? Do you speak about what you deem unacceptable about yourself? Do your words bring life or death?

When you speak negative words over yourself, you are not aligned with me. You are in essence cursing yourself. This is not appropriate for you, My Child. Any child of mine is worthy of My love and grace. To say otherwise is to utter a curse. Why would you do that?

And what about your circumstances? When you complain, you are not remembering that I am using them to transform you. When you believe things will never improve and you speak those words, you are bringing death. I am not saying to act as if everything is wonderful when it is not; I am saying to be careful of the attitude you carry and how it influences your words.

The tongue is a measure of what is in your heart. It is an overflow. Therefore, if your tongue is speaking death over anyone, yourself or your circumstances, it is time for a heart check. Are you saying you believe one thing and then acting as if you believe another? Your words reveal where your heart is. They expose lies you believe. Pay attention and watch your tongue.

# May 28

*Surely there is a future, and your hope will not be cut off. ~Proverbs 23:18*

You've done the best you could, Beloved. Do not beat yourself up. Do not live with regret for how things "should" have been. You cannot change the past, but I can redeem it. When situations don't turn out as you planned, it is not a time to let your mind wander to all the things you could have done differently. You did the best you could with what you had at the time. You would have made different choices if you had been a different person maybe, but you were not. The past is the past.

If your children's lives did not go the way you expected, it isn't up to you to fix it. It is up to me where they end up. I am not finished. I am not giving up. I am still working. Not for your plan, but for mine.

If your marriage isn't what you thought it would be, remember I am not finished yet. It is still a work in progress, no matter how many years it has been broken. I am the healer of broken things.

If your friendships are on shaky ground, stand on the rock. I can redeem the hard places. I can restore or remove. You have walked in both of these places. You have done the best you could. Trust me with the result.

Carrying the situations around with you and always rehashing them is why you are weary. Disappointment is a heavy load. It can steal life from you. Let it go. Remove your expectations as best you can. Lay them at My feet and trust Me to work things out for the good of all involved. There are many layers you cannot see.

I am always working. It is not all up to you. Let that sink in. I ask you to partner with me...with me. So, we are in it together. Meaning, I have it. You may not be able to imagine your future, but I can. Do your best and let that be enough.

# May 29

*Choose this day whom you will serve, whether the gods your fathers served in the region beyond the River, or the gods of the Amorites in whose land you dwell. But as for me and my house, we will serve the Lord. ~Joshua 24:15*

Choose you *this* day whom you will serve. It's not a one-day choice, Dear One. It is an every day one. Each and every day you must choose. Will you seek life or death? Will you put healthy food in your body to bring life, or junk that will move you closer to death? Will you pour into your spirit, or will you take away from it? Will you have compassion on yourself, or will you condemn yourself?

It is always your choice. Life is always available to you, Weary One. Always. Seek it. You will find it. What is holding you back? Is it your circumstances or is it you? Don't let hardship prevent you from finding life. The difficulties are not blocking your path although you may feel like they are. Your journey may have to change direction depending on what is happening in the moment, but if you look for life you will find it.

My word is filled with regular people who had tough circumstances, yet they found me in the midst. The woman caught in adultery found grace. The man possessed found freedom. The Roman Centurion found resurrection. The woman at the well, found truth. Their lives were interrupted by life. All they had to do was choose to believe the words of My Son.

You can choose hope over hopelessness. You can choose love over hate. You can choose compassion over hardheartedness. You can choose forgiveness over bitterness. You can choose consideration over selfishness. You can choose love over fear.

In your thoughts. In your words. Beloved, every moment offers you a choice. Your body might not work the way you want it to, but you can choose to strengthen your mind. Your heart might be broken, but you can choose to serve others while it heals. You might be limited in your ability to go outside of your home, but you can create a safe space within it. No matter your circumstances, look for life. Look for ways to seek it out. I will show you how. Just ask. I will be happy to walk beside you and show you how. Choose you this day whom you will serve.

# May 30

*For He wounds, but He binds up; He shatters, but His hands heal. ~Job 5:18*

I am the friend of the oppressed. I am the God of the marginalized. I walk with those who feel invisible. I do not walk away from you, Weary One. I do not see like others see. I look deep into the well of pain. I see the wound. I call you out of the infectious places which fester in silence. I shine the light on the things hidden.

At first, it is ugly when you see what has been under the cover of darkness. But, Beloved, the light must come to remove the pain. Like a splinter which goes deep and spreads infection, oppression brings contamination, and it increases over time.

My way of healing is to expose the disease to the light. Opening up the wound is the only way to drain it. It is painful to see and to feel, Dear One, it takes courage to allow Me to do the healing. But if you know My work will ease your suffering, won't you let me do My work? Your circumstances have held you back for so long, but even now I have a plan of healing for your heart. Even in the midst of hardship, I can still excise the pain. Do not fear My work. Do not shrink back from the required surgery.

Trust me. Know that I will not leave you unhealed. Open your heart to me. Climb on the operating table and let me expose the broken places. Let me cut out the poison. Let me transform your heart to a healthy one. I am the great Physician. I can be trusted when everything around you is upside down. Seek me. Listen to My voice. Follow only me. I will direct your paths.

# May 31

*Glory in His holy name; let the hearts of those who seek the Lord rejoice! Seek the Lord and His strength; seek His presence continually! ~Psalms 105:3-4*

Do not let anyone hinder you from growth. When I am putting My finger on areas in your heart, pursue me in this process. I am always promoting your forward movement. If you want to go deeper with me, Dear One, it requires an openness to change. An openness to listen to My voice and to follow me into uncomfortable places. Even though these areas are between you and me, there will be those who will try to prevent you from making changes.

Change is hard. It is hard for you. It is hard for others. When one person changes and others are not ready, sometimes it causes conflict. But I am for you. When you are following me, I will not lead you astray. I work on many levels at one time. You are not alone. When you seek My kingdom first, you will face opposition. Keep seeking anyway.

When you see things in a new way, you will be a light to those around you. Testimony is My greatest tool. It is how I spread the good news. It is how I grow My children in wisdom. When you receive new insight into My Spirit, it changes you. When you testify of that insight, it changes others. It can be a messy process, however. Especially if what you are changing challenges old systems.

It is normal to want to stay in one place. People do it all the time. But those who seek My kingdom are never stagnant. They are always searching out My mysteries. I do love it when you do that. I love giving you a clue and watching you seek it out. I love sharing the deep places of My heart with you. You know, Beloved, not everyone will seek me until they find me. Many only seek me when I align with what they believe. Then they stop and plant themselves. No one, not even me, can move them after that.

I am alive. I give you breath in your lungs. I am always moving. Will you follow me? Will you put aside your hardship and suffering long enough to seek me? When you seek me with all of your heart you will find me. Even if others do not agree, you will see more of me and be more like me.

# June 1

*Therefore, since we are surrounded by so great a cloud of witnesses, let us also lay aside every weight, and sin which clings so closely, and let us run with endurance the race that is set before us, looking to Jesus, the founder and perfecter of our faith, who for the joy that was set before Him endured the cross, despising the shame, and is seated at the right hand of the throne of God. ~Hebrews 12:1-2*

Momentum creates a flow. I am the momentum you need, Dear One. I am the wind in your sails and the breath in your lungs. Be assured that I will always keep you moving forward. Even in seasons of waiting, or hardship, when you feel as though you are sitting still, I am moving you forward. It is My momentum, not yours, that will see you through.

Beloved, when you try to stir up your own forward movement, it will fade away. It doesn't last long because it is born out of your own strength. Real momentum rises up from My Spirit living inside of you. It empowers you. The grace you get to live your life flows from me. Therefore, if you want momentum, seek Me. Feed your spirit and you will feel My energy rise up inside of you. There will be a hunger in your heart. You will seek Me, and when you find Me power will be released.

What slows your momentum? Negativity. Fear. Self-contempt. Lack of confidence. Anger. Circumstances? No. Circumstances come and go. If you let them stop you in your tracks, it's difficult to re-gain momentum. When things are uncertain, there is a tendency to stop. To put everything on hold. Survival mode will do that to you. Weary One, you must not let things stop you. I don't mean activity; I mean in your spirit. Focus on that.

When all the world has gone crazy, when your news is bad, when you feel terrible, when you are caught up in the worries of life, do not let it stop the momentum I have created for you. Nurture your identity in me. During hard times you forget who I say you are. Shore yourself up by reminding yourself who I have made you to be. Proclaim My promises to you...out loud. Speak over yourself, your family, and your circumstances. Pour out My words. They never come back empty. I will show you where to find them. They are a tool to increase momentum in your life. Trust me in this.

# June 2

*So also, the tongue is a small member, yet it boasts of great things. How great a forest is set ablaze by such a small fire! And the tongue is a fire, a world of unrighteousness. The tongue is set among our members, staining the whole body, setting on fire the entire course of life, and set on fire by hell. ~James 3:5-6*

If the rudder of the ship is the tongue, where is it you are steering your ship? That rudder is so small, Dear One, but it controls the direction of the entire vessel. Your complete attitude is controlled by your tongue. When you speak negatively, there will be hopelessness. There will be depression, sadness, frustration, anxiety, and fear. All of these emotions are attached to your words.

When you speak harmfully of others, a blanket of filth settles over you. Not them. You. It works its way to your heart, eventually creating a bitterness that will only burrow deeply into your entire belief system. Then out of the heart the mouth will speak more unforgiveness. It is a cycle. The mouth speaks. The heart takes it in. The heart hardens. The mouth speaks. Before you know it, Beloved, you are hopelessly tangled up in your own words. Your attitude plummets. Your mental and emotional health suffer. All because of that little tongue.

Not to mention the strife it causes between people. Name calling and blaming don't serve anyone. Those kinds of words tear people apart. Gossip and lies break hearts. Words of rejection and abandonment are the source of so much pain that anger flares up and ugly sin rears its head in the discourse. It is not becoming in any way. This rudder has steered entire countries to war. It is that powerful.

And when you speak negatively over yourself, it has the same effect. You go to war with yourself. You speak. Your heart hears. Your heart breaks. Your heart believes your words. You sink down, down, down into self-pity, self-hatred, self-loathing. Notice each of these begins with SELF. Lies always lead to self. A tongue in service to the enemy will always destroy.

Instead of speaking negativity, speak My words. Commit to follow them too, because positivity is also a cycle. The mouth speaks. The heart takes it in. The heart is healed. The mouth speaks. See? It works the same way. It is worth learning how to steer your ship in the right direction. Test it, Beloved. Find some words of mine. Speak them. Watch what happens. Hearts, yours and theirs, will be healed. Hope will be born. Trust will rise up. Watch and see.

# June 3

*All things were made through Him, and without Him was not anything made that was made. ~John 1:3*

I use a variety of colors in My creation. It is one of My favorite things, Dear One. It brightens things up and keeps them from being boring. My mind rolls with creative ideas. Just look around you. Look at the intricacy of insects, or the detail of the flowers. I am in the details.

Look at your own body for that matter. How specific. Down to the smallest cell and its function. I long to create things that show My artistic talent. It is why I use the entire palette of color. Even in My creation of humans. You will see all shades of color, all types of personality. No two are the same, because I keep creating and creating. My ideas never end. The combinations cannot be exhausted. The thoughts and ideas of each one mirrors me. You are all created in My image, Dear One. You are My image bearers. When you are looking at another person, you are looking at me.

Even those you consider to be your enemies bear My image. Does that surprise you? They didn't create themselves, Beloved. I created them just as I created you. With hope and a purpose. With potential and all the beauty in My creation. They may not know it yet, but if you look, you can see My signature somewhere. Find that part. Find the part that looks like it might be me. Love that part. Speak to that part. Find me wherever you can.

There is a reason I love diversity of color. There is a reason I don't make everyone the same. There is richness in variety. It brings depth and beauty. Unlike a piece that is monochromatic, multiple colors add depth and interest. All masterpieces have many layers of texture and color. When you see My finished work, you will understand. For now, love one another. Trust My brush. Look for me.

# June 4

*And if one asks him, "What are these wounds on your back?" he will say, "The wounds I received in the house of my friends." ~Zachariah 13:6*

Scars are important, Weary One. You have many of them. Life issues them without preference. There is not one human who will escape without some scars. Do the wounds you carry feel like open sores? Do you feel they will never heal? I assure you they will, but scars will remain. A reminder of victory over pain. A reminder that I am the Great Physician. A reminder of resurrection and renewal. I make all things new.

My Son kept His scars. Have you ever thought about that? He didn't have to. He could have wiped away all evidence of His human journey, but He kept them. He is easily identifiable by those holes in His hands and feet, even now. He wants you to see. He wants you to know that He knows what pain feels like. He can fill in your scars with His glory and make them part of your story.

He identifies with suffering and pain. He knows betrayal. His sorrow is yours and yours is His. Many will identify Him from His miracles, or His works of greatness, but not you. Not those who walk a hard journey of pain. You will know Him by His scars. They will stand out to you because you are full of your own. Scars are not weaknesses as you may suppose. They are marks of death. They are resurrection repurposed. Do not diminish the weakness you feel in your painful circumstances, Precious One. There is not one wound that is invisible to me. Not a circumstance, not a betrayal, not an attack, not a hardship I do not know. I see every one of them. I even see some you do not.

Let My Son's scars speak to yours. Let His understanding and compassion wash over you. He knows. He sees. He feels. Let Him fill in your scars with His glory, making them marks of hope. Then they will be a memorial of survival. They will be a part of your testimony of My healing. Bear your scars well, My Love. They are beauty marks.

# June 5

*And a great windstorm arose, and the waves were breaking into the boat, so that the boat was already filling. But He was in the stern, asleep on the cushion. And they woke Him and said to Him, "Teacher, do you not care that we are perishing?" And He awoke and rebuked the wind and said to the sea, "Peace! Be still!" And the wind ceased, and there was a great calm. He said to them, "Why are you so afraid? Have you still no faith?" And they were filled with great fear and said to one another, "Who then is this, that even the wind and the sea obey Him?" ~Mark 4: 37-41*

Lift your head. I can never say it enough, Dear One. When the world around you has burst into flames, or crashed into the sea, or feels like a whirlwind, don't forget to look up. Somehow when things are not going as expected and things are hard, it is easy to get caught up in the immediate. Sometimes you just have to take a breath and a pause to look up.

When you lift your eyes from the path at your feet, you see My creation around you. It makes the troubles fade. No, they will not disappear, but you will gain some perspective. When you gaze into the ocean, you cannot help but feel small. When you glance up to the mountains, your problems shrink. When you listen to birds' songs, you can get lost in their joyous attitude. The breeze on your face wakes you up to the fact that this too will pass. Whatever is bothering you, it is temporary.

The sun will come up tomorrow. The world is still turning. Most importantly, I have not dropped the ball. I have not abandoned you. Not in any way shape or form. You simply have to look around you to find me. I am standing right next to you. I will always be right next to you. Even when you don't believe it. Even when you haven't asked me to. Even when you are unaware of me, I am aware of you. Every step you take.

You can praise me in the storms of life. Whatever they are. You can look and see me and I will comfort your soul. I say to your heart, peace be still. Peace be still. Breathe in. Breathe out. Peace be still.

156

# June 6

*Then the eyes of both were opened, and they knew that they were naked. And they sewed fig leaves together and made themselves loincloths. And they heard the sound of the Lord God walking in the garden in the cool of the day, and the man and his wife hid themselves from the presence of the Lord God among the trees of the garden. But the Lord God called to the man and said to him, "Where are you?" And he said, "I heard the sound of you in the garden, and I was afraid, because I was naked, and I hid myself." ~Genesis 3:7-10*

The wind and waves know My name. They listen to My voice. I cannot tell you Weary One, how important it is to know My voice. There are so many voices. Too many. If you listen to them you will be pulled from the path I have for you. I speak to you with love. I speak with gentleness. I am not harsh. I speak with peace. I am not violent. You can tell if it is me by learning My ways.

That is not to say I don't correct or point out areas that need attention. One of My goals is heart transformation. You cannot transform your own heart, and it cannot be transformed if you do not examine it beneath the microscope of My words. I will tell you the truth like no one else will. I point out sin that clouds your vision, not to shame you, but to bring you into alignment with My heart.

Shame is different from conviction, Beloved. Shame is harmful. It can be toxic because it keeps thoughts in the dark. It eats at you from the inside. It says you are not good enough and will never be, and that if anyone knew what you had done they would reject you. If they found out who you really were, they would walk away and abandon you. Shame is based in fear. Fear that you are an imposter and you can spend a lifetime trying to keep yourself hidden from others.

Conviction, on the other hand, is firm but gentle. It comes from a broken heart that recognizes a wrong. I do not try to harm you when I correct you. I simply show you the truth about a situation. I let you know how I feel about it, and that I long for better for you. Your heart feels this pain I feel and it moves to change it. It turns towards the truth. The light comes in and heals the wound from the sin. It is a beautiful process.

You must know My voice to discern the differences. If you feel rushed, it is not My voice. If you feel dirty, it is not My voice. If you feel harshness, it is not My voice. My goal is always redemption. Restoration. I long for our relationship to be whole and honest. It is My aim when I am doing My transformational work. Listen to My voice, Dear One. You will hear.

# June 7

*It is the glory of God to conceal things, but the glory of kings is to search things out. As the heavens for height, and the earth for depth, so the heart of kings is unsearchable. ~Proverbs 25:2-3*

I am expansive. The span of My hand is beyond your universe. Look to the heavens and you will see. It is why people are drawn to study the stars. The width and breadth is bigger than the brain can understand, but it wants to. I built the curiosity into it. Those who follow the curiosity learn more and more, but they know there is always more to learn. That's because I never end.

And what of the sea, the depth of it and all that lives there. Millions upon millions of creatures, you will never even know. Those who dive and study can only tell you a portion of the secrets of the sea. Curiosity is built into them. They desire to find out more and I will always provide it.

The core of the Earth. The depth of the center and all the layers to get there. The events which have to take place for mountains to appear and landscapes to change. Curiosity is leading the way. Finding new artifacts, always studying. I am uncovering and providing clues to keep them digging for more.

Beloved, where is your curiosity? What makes you want to find more? I planted it in you. I put the seed there for you to grow into knowledge of an area. I span all disciplines. You might be interested in the human body, or maybe just the brain, or lungs. You might be fascinated with sounds and music, and experiment with new ones. There are so many parts of My expansiveness. I never end.

Do you want to know more about My heart? It is the biggest mystery of all. Are you curious about what makes me tick? I put that desire within you, to wonder about the unseen things. To want to know more about Me and My ways. It is built into you. Just like all the other areas of exploration, I am open to show you more about me.

When you are walking through hardship and suffering, find your curiosity. Don't put it to the side. It reminds you of My expansiveness. It reminds you of My ability to create the smallest, tiniest details in the midst of the enormous world. Curiosity is universal and it is one of the greatest weapons against heartache and weariness. Scientists and artists alike find solace in My expansiveness by using their curiosity.

# June 8

*I will feed them with good pasture, and on the mountain heights of Israel shall be their grazing land. There they shall lie down in good grazing land, and on rich pasture they shall feed on the mountains of Israel. I Myself will be the shepherd of My sheep, and I Myself will make them lie down, declares the Lord God. I will seek the lost, and I will bring back the strayed, and I will bind up the injured, and I will strengthen the weak, and the fat and the strong I will destroy. I will feed them in justice. ~Ezekiel 34:14-16*

There are times, Weary One, when tiredness is overwhelming. Fighting daily battles becomes a hardship which requires more energy than you have. You must not give up on these battles, the physical due to illness or mental with great challenges. Emotional struggles come from every direction. Usually, there are mixtures of all of these facets of life.

You are a human. You have a soul, and when you are tired mentally, physically, and emotionally, you are soul-tired. The crushing weight of all you carry bears down on you. It feels impossible to go forward, to even have the courage to try. When you are operating in your flesh instead of your spirit, difficulties become hindrances. Obstacles feel like mountains. A daily activity feels as if you are pushing a boulder uphill. You understand what I mean.

In these moments, Dear One, you must feed your spirit. Whatever the circumstance is, no matter how long it has lasted or will last, you must feed your spirit. Find me. Look for me. I am there. Read My words. You will feel your spirit start to rise up. Sing/play a song and you will know My strength. Create with colors or words and you will feel your spirit stirring.

Feeding your spirit creates energy to keep you moving. If you are too tired to feed your spirit, find someone who is feeding theirs and ask if you can tag along. Put yourself in a place where others around you are feasting. If you don't know, learn how. I have many who can show you. Talk to them. Watch them. Or talk to me. Watch me.

Building your spirit is like exercising a muscle. If you don't do it, it will not get stronger. In a dire situation, the strength you need will fail. But if you prepare and saturate your spirit, mingling with mine regularly, you will endure the tough times. Even when your soul is tired, you will be able to stand, because your spirit is strong. All the heroes and heroines of the faith knew the secret. Feed the spirit.

# June 9

*That which is born of the flesh is flesh, and that which is born of the Spirit is spirit.*
*~John 3:6*

Do not invite me into your space, Weary One, come into mine. When you are weak you will not find strength anywhere else. It seems contrary to what you would think. Wouldn't you want me to intervene in your world? Couldn't I do that for you? The answer, of course, is yes. I could. But I have found it more effective to open My heart and invite you into it.

When I interrupt consequences and bring My glory, there is great commotion, to be sure. Although healings and miracles gain attention, they do not foster intimacy. The fanfare dies away and things go back to the way they were because this world is sin-tainted and temporary. My realm, on the other hand, is eternal. When you enter into worship, you are entering My realm and intimacy follows.

Sometimes it takes hardship in your world to lead you into mine. Your wounds turn to scars here with me. When that happens, you can speak out of your scars and it is powerful. If you neglect to come to My space, your wounds will stay open and fester. They will bleed and ooze on those around you as the infection spreads. Look at your world, can you see what I am saying? Do you see the spreading of pain?

The humility you gain when sitting with me will be your greatest weapon against the heartache you see around you. You cannot forgive without it. You cannot get past wrongs committed against you, unless you walk in it. This humility is required to enter My presence, not because I command it, but because to find this place you have to lay your pride down.

It is a delight to My heart when you seek me for me. Not for your agenda or for the things you need. Not for your ministry or your authority. You know, Dear One, ministry without intimacy is idolatry. When you come and seek me, you are choosing to lay down your idols and your unguarded strengths which lead only to downfalls.

Be relentless, My Love. Seek me out and do not relent until you have come into My presence. Find My realm and sit with me there. It may not change your world, but it will change you.

# June 10

*O Lord my God, I cried to you for help, and you have healed me. ~Psalms 30:2*

Let it go. There are times in life, Beloved, when you just have to let things go. Sometimes it is a relationship with a person. Often it is a job. There are even times you need to let go of your dreams. You can also release hurt, or grief, or sorrow. You can let go of expectations, or maybe, attitudes. How about bitterness and unforgiveness? There are so many ways to let go and I will guide you into which ones are relevant for your life.

I don't mean you have to let go of memories. If a relationship has shifted or ended all together, be it a death or divorce, you have to release it. Keeping memories alive is not part of that. Letting go doesn't mean you erase that part of your life. It means you carry it forward, rather than sitting with it. There are times to sit and hold space while you grieve, but only for a season. Once that season is over, you no longer need to sit in it. You rise up and you move forward.

The same applies to your dreams. You may miss what comes next if you hold on too long when a dream doesn't pan out. I am the fulfiller of dreams, but My timeline and yours are often miles apart. Let the dream go. Shed the expectations. I might bring it around again later in a different form. You must trust me in this.

Letting go of attitudes, fear, pride, and bitterness is never a bad thing...but it is hard to do. Apply My word to your heart like a healing balm. Rub it in. Let it do the work and these attitudes will not weigh you down. When you open your hand, you allow me the space to remove the splinters that have dug their way down deep. I want to give you so much more life. Freedom. Grace. Abundance. Favor. Health. All good things. But first you have to let go.

# June 11

*And let us not grow weary of doing good, for in due season we will reap, if we do not give up. ~Galatians 6:9*

You are resilient, Weary One. You may not feel like it, but you are. You have the ability to spring back when stressful situations come your way. You bend. You stretch. You are pliable. When you are under pressure, you are not rigid, you are moldable.

Do you know where that ability comes from? All the hardship. All the suffering. All the heartache. Those who fall apart under pressure have not learned that tough times are the birthing places of resilience, where the ability to bounce back is born. You may walk with a limp afterwards, but you walk. Out of the trial. Out of the wrestling. You come out stronger.

In the midst of difficulty, remember that you will grow and get stronger. One day, you will feel the strength, but for now, just remember you are changing. Your circumstances are shaping your future self. I designed it that way. I walk with you in it.

The patina you gain from living your life makes you beautiful. It takes the scars and makes them marks of victory. You think you are weak, but then one day, you find you are stronger than you thought. You can endure more than you knew. This strength is built into you as you go through life. Don't despise the pain that is part of your growth.

There are bumps and bruises along every path, but each time you arrive at your most recent destination you will find it worth the pain. Not that pain is fun, but it does develop fruit if you hand it over to me. I can grow grace from the smallest pain. I can harvest hope. I can develop healing. All of the attributes you seek are found at the end of resilience.

# June 12

*The Lord is a stronghold for the oppressed, a stronghold in times of trouble. And those who know your name put their trust in you, for you, O Lord, have not forsaken those who seek you. ~Psalms 9:9-10*

Sometimes you have to take a stand, Beloved. For others or for yourself. The enemy seeks to oppress. His goal is to keep people in bondage, whatever way he can. He uses deception to do it. If he can keep you blind, he can keep you bound.

When you put yourself down, he has you deceived into believing you are worthless. When you refuse to see the beauty, I have created in you, you are playing into his hands. When you only see the bad in your life circumstances, he has you deceived into believing that is all there is. He weaves a sticky web for your mind.

Also consider how you view other people. When you judge them for their behaviors, it is part of his plan. If you see someone else being put down and you say nothing, he has you right where he wants you. His deception makes you believe there is nothing you can do. He keeps you from seeing the truth so you will believe everything is how it should be.

I tell you, Dear One, oppression is everywhere. Open your eyes to it. I will show you, but once I do, you have to take a stand wherever you see it. Standing up isn't always an easy task, yet freedom for all is My heart. To be free is to allow My love to seep into the wounds of the oppressed.

It may be uncomfortable to take a stand when you see the oppression of others. It might require hard conversations. It might be inconvenient. It will require you to listen. It will require you to open your heart. I will lead you in all these things. You have to trust me.

If the oppressed is you, it will require you to replace your own thoughts about yourself. You will need to listen to what I have to say. You will have to open your eyes to see as I see. That means letting the scales fall off and standing on the truth rather than the lies of the enemy. Can you do that, Weary One? Can you stand up?

# June 13

*He heals the brokenhearted and binds up their wounds. ~Psalms 147:3*

You are tired, Weary One. So very tired. The circumstances of life have pummeled you for years. Every hit wears you down further. Every impact takes away not only your breath, but your hope. It is battle fatigue. It makes you want to quit trying. Quit your life and run far, far away. But you know, Beloved, that is not possible. You teeter on the edge of despair. Your defenses are worn down. Your fight has all but disappeared. It is easier to be a victim and let life happen to you, than to be a warrior and stay in the battle.

At this point, you need a support system around you, Dear One. You cannot go it alone. When life is difficult, knowing who you can call makes all the difference. There is a reason I made you for community. You need each other. I called it a body of believers for a reason. You are but one part. When you are hurting, the whole body is hurting. Let them come around you while you heal. Let them help you learn to rest properly. Let them pour into you when you cannot do it for yourself.

I'm not referring to every person you meet, but the ones you are connected to in heart. You know the ones. The safe ones, the ones who get it. Unfortunately, not all of my children will, but there are a few in your life who do. They will love you unconditionally. They will stand with you. Those are the ones who you reach out to when you are weary. You can be honest with them.

Beloved, if you don't have those people in your life, find some. Seek them out. I will show you who they are. Trust me. You cannot go it alone. It is why you are so tired. Feeling misunderstood is exhausting. Having to explain yourself and your circumstances to people over and over wears you down. When you don't feel like talking and you want to just be silent, you have me. You always have me, of course, but in the weary times I am so close. As close as your breath. I am with you no matter what. You can rest in me. Let me bathe you with My Spirit. Let My healing balm restore your soul.

# June 14

*Or do you not know that your body is a temple of the Holy Spirit within you, whom you have from God? You are not your own, for you were bought with a price. So, glorify God in your body. ~1 Corinthians 6:19-20*

Take care of your body. It is vital to care for your spirit but do not forget the body. When your body is wearing out, you will always struggle spiritually. If you do not sleep, it wears down more quickly. If you do not eat properly, it will affect your mental state. You are a triune being: body, soul, and spirit. Each of these parts is important. Do not neglect any of them.

To fend off weariness, you need to get rest. I designed sleep to be restorative. It heals wounds. It builds immunities. It restores energy. You need it, every single night. When crazy things are happening in the world around you, do not cheat sleep. Your mind will try to steal it, so find a way to still your mind. Set it on Me and My word. Shut off the outside voices. List the things that want to rise up at night, so you can deal with them tomorrow. Exercise your body enough that your physical being will be tired enough and shut down to rest.

To fend off disease, you need to move. Your heart and lungs need to pump. Your muscles need to be strong to keep your body operating properly. You do not have to be a bodybuilder, or a marathon runner, Beloved. You just need to take time for your body. If you don't have time, make some. Get up earlier, or step out for a walk at lunch. After dinner, go for a swim, or a hike. Work it into your schedule. It is important. Really important.

Eat the right food to fend off depression. Food is medicine. It can lift you up or bring you down. Your choice. What you put into your body matters. No need to beat yourself up about what you eat. Just figure out what makes your body work the smoothest and stick to it. I designed your body to be amazing. It is a factory that produces the energy you need to live. It can run efficiently, or it can get bogged down and prevent you from functioning. I have given you the ability to take care of it without guilt.

Your spirit rides around inside your body. Just like a vehicle, your spirit may break down if you don't maintain it. All the prayers for healing will not be able to undo the damage caused by neglecting your body. Let me teach you. Let me direct your physical being, as you let me direct your spirit. It is important, Dear One.

# June 15

*And after six days Jesus took with Him Peter and James, and John his brother, and led them up a high mountain by themselves. And he was transfigured before them, and his face shone like the sun, and his clothes became white as light. ~Matthew 17:1-2*

Did you know sometimes you have to pull things apart to put them back together? It's true. Your thought processes are built upon a foundation. If your foundation isn't solid, you will have to take it apart and rebuild it. Some of your thoughts stem from childhood. From before you were even old enough to know you had thoughts. For some, they are born out of traumatic events. For others, they come from the environment you were brought up in. Some people made their own vows while they were still young. "I will never…." "I won't be like…" These promises to yourself shaped your thoughts. Now they have become patterns and some of them are not healthy.

To take apart your thoughts and analyze them is hard work. You have to sit with your thoughts, some of which you don't know you have. You have to allow me to show you. Then you have to hold them up to My light. Look at them, see if they line up with My words. See if they are a part of your foundation that needs to be removed. If so, you will have to replace them with My thoughts. My ways. My actions.

If you challenge the status quo in your life, it might change your life. If your life changes, there are some who may not like it because it unintentionally shines the light on their own foundations. You must do it anyway. Take a stand. Remove what I show you. You answer only to me. Stay close to My voice and you will see transformation in your heart. You will see growth. Your stagnant ways will fall to the side and you will move forward. All because you pulled yourself apart into pieces and waited on me to show you your heart.

# June 16

*For everyone who asks receives, and the one who seeks finds, and to the one who knocks it will be opened. ~Luke 11:10*

I have spoken to you about identity many times, Beloved. It is a subject near to My heart. I want you to fully understand that your identity is in me alone. It is not in the voices that tell you that you are not enough or are somehow less than. It is not in the person you see in the mirror. It is not your body type or size. It is not your appearance at all. It is not in your ability to charm others. It is not in your personality in any way. It is not in your failures. It is not in your success. It is not in your good works or in your thoughtfulness. It is not in your frustrated days or your depression.

No, Dear One, it is not in any of those things. It is only in me and My righteousness. I come back to this over and over because I want you to get it, because if you get it, you will be free. When you feel as if you have failed or somehow your circumstances are a direct result of My disfavor, you are missing the point. When you respond in one way and then discover your motives were not what you thought, you are not defined by selfishness. I am working in you.

Give yourself grace. If you see your motives were not pure, it is because I wanted you to see, so you can give them to me and be free. You are not always good, but I am. Therefore, you are good even when you are not. When you see some mistake, submit it to me. Lay it at My feet and then pick up My goodness. When you falter, stop and lay it down. Then pick up My righteousness. The secret is humbling yourself when you see you are placing your identity in things other than me.

You have a divine exchange which you did not initiate. I willingly give you My life. It replaces all that is weak about you, but it also replaces your strengths. When you find your identity in things other than me you will eventually find your foundation crumbling around you. Your eyes will be opened to the fact that you do not even know why it is you do the things you do. Your motives are hidden, even from you.

I know your motives, Precious One. I see them and I reveal them to you when you let me. I do not desire you to wallow in self-pity or to stand tall in self-assurance. I long for you to rest in Me and My work. Me and My glory. Set yourself aside and be in me. When you are in me, and I in you, your identity will be wrapped in mine. You will walk as I walk, think as I think. It is a lifelong process. It sets you free from all the other ways you try to be. You are found in me.

# June 17

*For everyone who asks receives, and the one who seeks finds, and to the one who knocks it will be opened. ~Nehemiah 8:10*

Is there joy in your heart, Weary One? Do you know how to find it? Even in the midst of hardship, I give joy. Maybe it's been awhile since you experienced the sensation you get when you feel great pleasure. It is warm. It is a deep place in your heart. There is a sense of well-being when you feel joy. A place of contentment. Do you remember it? Can you tap into it? It is important.

If you have lost your joy, you have lost your strength. When the world around you is in turmoil, you must be able to pull back into your joy. Even when circumstances are not going your way, the joy I give will sustain you. It is easy to look all around you and see the negative, the broken world, the hardship. It is easy to get caught up in it all and forget your joy is not in this world. Heaviness tries to overtake you. It is then that you need to seek joy, not happiness, joy. There is a difference.

Joy rises up when you hear a baby laugh, when you see your kids playing. When you hear a beautiful song. In the morning, when the birds are singing, there is joy. They sing no matter what is happening around them. It is built into them.

Joy is like that. I built it into you, too. You have to turn your intention to it. You have to remember it is there, inside of you. Laughter is only a part of it. There are times you feel it as a sense of well-being. Or as a warmth of heart.

Protect your joy, Dear One. Do not let the world steal it. Find moments of joy in every day, even the little things, especially the little things that bring you a sense of loving life. Do not forget.

# June 18

*My son, be attentive to my words; incline your ear to my sayings. Let them not escape from your sight; keep them within your heart. For they are life to those who find them, and healing to all their flesh. Keep your heart with all vigilance, for from it flow the springs of life. Put away from you crooked speech, and put devious talk far from you. Let your eyes look directly forward, and your gaze be straight before you. Ponder the path of your feet; then all your ways will be sure. Do not swerve to the right or to the left; turn your foot away from evil. ~Proverbs 4: 20-27*

Hold your ground. Do not let anyone tell you that where I have placed you is the wrong place. If you have sought me and heard me, stand strong. There will come questions. There will come accusations. Do not let them sway you from the path I have given you.

When you have doubts, from someone's words, come to me. Seek me. I will lead you in the path of righteousness. Humble yourself to seek My will. Then act on it. Beloved, the enemy is not a person. The enemy is not flesh and blood. When seeking destruction, he prowls around like a lion. Remember it is a spiritual battle when people are coming against you. You fight, not with them, but on your knees in prayer.

You can only control one person's actions, and that is your own. You cannot change another person or how they think. You cannot change the behavior of others. However, you can work on your own heart. You can let me do the deep work inside you, and once you have freedom, hold onto it. Do not let someone else try to pull you backwards.

The enemy would love nothing more than to suck you back into areas from which you have escaped. Stand firm on what you know. Stand firm on who you are. Stand firm on the ground you have taken. Stand firm on your boundary. Like a watchman on the wall, pay attention to the enemy's movement. Recognize it for what it is. Seek me. I will show you the strategy for guarding your heart. For out of the heart there are springs of living water.

# June 19

*There is one body and one Spirit—just as you were called to the one hope that belongs to your call— one Lord, one faith, one baptism, one God and Father of all, who is over all and through all and in all. ~Ephesians 4:4-6*

You are gifted. You are called. Rise up and take your place. Weary One, when life knocks you down, if you push yourself up from the ground, you will see your calling. You may not know exactly where it leads...yet.

I have created in you a person who has a combination of abilities no one else has. It is the way I do things, to create unique beings who fit My plan. No one else is like you. No one else has been through what you have been through. The compassion and empathy your journey have given you could be found no other way.

When you walk through the valley of the shadow of death, you navigate all the things which live in the valley. Depression. Sorrow. Grief. Ache. Conflict. Frustration. Bitterness. Resentment. Anger. Sadness. Suffering. These are your companions in the valley. They walk beside you. You have come to know them well. If you learn about them when you are under pressure, you will find that the fear of them fades away. You begin to recognize these dark companions from the valley and deal with them appropriately. You do not allow them to take you. You rise up and push them away. You walk forward and keep moving...through the valley instead of camping out there.

When you rise out of the canyon, you find you are stronger for it. You are more resilient. You relate to others in new ways that bring grace to them in their own pain. You know the path and you bring hope to those who are behind you on it. Beloved, your journey will take you through the valley often. It will not be all smooth sailing. I am building faith into you. Faith is not some mystical invisible force you gain by study. Faith is practical. It is using your gifts to walk through your life. It is belief made visible.

Take your place. Lead others as you rise up. They need an example. They need a way to use faith as more than a religious exercise. Use your gifts, Dear One. You are called.

# June 20

*Let us then with confidence draw near to the throne of grace, that we may receive mercy and find grace to help in time of need. ~Hebrews 4:16*

Beloved, take care not to put others down. In your world right now, it is popular to speak words which are designed to elevate yourself and discount others. The definition of oppression is the pressing down of "the other." The "other" is anyone who is not like you. Doesn't think like you. Doesn't believe like you. Doesn't look like you. Color, politics, religion...it matters not the way they are different, only that one feels superior to the other. If you feel you know the "right" way, you are in danger, Weary One. Your weariness from life makes you more susceptible to this temptation, so beware.

Only I am the righteous one. Only I am the judge of hearts and intentions. You cannot even determine the motives of your own heart without me. It is best to always remember that how you judge others is how you will be judged. Keep that in your mind at all times, to help you find more grace than criticism. Your agreement with each other is not as important as your agreement with me. My grace covers a multitude of sins, including yours.

Self-righteousness does not become you, Beloved. In fact, even your good works are as filthy rags to me when done to elevate your own agenda. The human way to fight oppression is to rise up. Speaking out for injustice is a righteous cause, one that is dear to My heart. But be careful in your rising that you are not pressing others down in the process. Lifting up is the opposite of oppression. To rid the world of oppression is to give grace to "the other." It is hard, Beloved, but it is My way. Seek My face to learn My ways. Then walk in them.

# June 21

*Let all bitterness and wrath and anger and clamor and slander be put away from you, along with all malice. Be kind to one another, tenderhearted, forgiving one another, as God in Christ forgave you. ~Ephesians 4:31-32*

Beware of resentment, Weary One. It is the child of comparison and the cousin of bitterness. When your eyes are not fixed on me they will wander to others around you. You will wonder why they have what you do not. You will compare your life with theirs. You will resent them. The feelings of displeasure and ill will come from the idea that you have been wronged in some way. They are persistent and never leave your mind for long, and they can blossom into full blown bitterness if you are not standing guard over your thoughts.

I warn you of this, My Child, because negative thoughts and feelings can steal life from you. So constant are the feelings that they become a normal emotional state. They take up room that was reserved for joy. Many times, resentment is pointed towards others, who appear to have it better than you do. Someone with more money or someone who got the promotion. Someone who wronged you in some way. A relationship that failed. A system that is an obstacle in your life. Something you want but do not have, and it appears you cannot get it.

But, Beloved, the deeper issue is when you resent me. Ultimately, you know I could "fix" the problem and give you what you want. When I do not, you consciously or unconsciously hold it against me. A seed of resentment is planted in your heart by the enemy who always says, "Did He really say....?" It is the voice of the serpent, making you question My goodness to you. "If God was really good, would this be happening to you?" "If God really loved you, how could He withhold these things from you?" Am I right, Dear One? Do you recognize these questions?

The opposite of resentment is contentment. When your circumstances are hard and continuous, finding contentment is most difficult. To lay aside your desires. To let go of your hurt. To forgive others for their wrongs and to forgive me for not rushing in to fix it right away, is the key. To do so involves trust.

You have to trust that the battle isn't over, but it is not up to you. Trust that I am aware and working in your circumstance. Remember that the things you want may not make you as content as you think they will. Believe that the circumstances you are in are part of My plan to develop you, and that when the time is right, I will change them.

# June 22

*Be watchful, stand firm in the faith, act like men, be strong. ~1 Corinthians 16:13*

Do not give up, Weary One. It is easy to become discouraged. It is easy to think nothing you are doing matters, when you are in the midst of hardship. When everything around you has let you down you think, 'Why try?' I will tell you why, because when you keep going you will eventually reap a harvest. Even when your circumstances don't seem to ever change much, I am still working.

The one you are caregiving might be more challenging than ever. I am working on relationship. Your sick child might not get healed right away. I am working on stamina. Your grief might not let up. I am working on compassion. Your body might not be functioning properly. I am working on your spirit. The world might seem to be against you. I am working on endurance.

You do not always see what I am doing. That is where trusting me comes in. Discouragement presses down on you. It brings heaviness. It takes your courage. To live the human life takes courage, Beloved. Just to get up in the morning requires bravery and belief that it is worth the effort. When discouragement comes in, it is like a blanket that covers everything.

However, I am removing the blanket. I am pulling back the darkness. I am infusing you with courage today. You have what it takes to thrive this day, because I have given you the courage. Whatever you face, when you feel the courage rise up, it is me. Indwelling you. If I am for you, who can be against you?

# June 23

*Open your mouth for the mute, for the rights of all who are destitute. Open your mouth, judge righteously, defend the rights of the poor and needy. ~Proverbs 31:8-9*

I gave you a voice, Beloved. Use it. You are an advocate. For your loved ones. For those in your community. For yourself. When your children need you to stand up and speak for them, you should. When the elderly parents you care for need you to speak on their behalf, you should. If you are a caregiver in any capacity, you speak for those you care for. The same is true for others around you. When you see someone, who is being mistreated at work or at school, stand up for them.

My Son did. He not only spoke *to*, but He spoke *for*. He stood with the adulterous woman in the midst of a circle of stones. He sat with the woman at the well. He ate with the tax collectors. He spoke up to the authorities. He demanded change, although not in the way people usually viewed change. He didn't fight a revolution, but He quietly led one. He made his opinions known, while still serving others. He spoke truth, some of it hard truth, as He challenged the laws of the heart. His was an inner revolution that led to an outer change. A work of the heart, in the hearts of all He came into contact with.

When hearts change, Weary One, lives change. When you use your voice, eyes can be opened leading to the kind of heart change which transforms the world. It is not a screaming match I am referring to. It is the story you are living. If you share it, there will be an impact on those around you. That is what I hope for. They will listen to you when they will not always listen to me.

Can you speak what I share with you? Can you tell them what I am doing in your heart to soften it, so they will begin to soften theirs? That is what I mean when I say you have a voice. When you stand up, those in your circle of influence listen. You may not always know it, but they do. You are having an impact. Leave the results to me. All I am asking is that you use your voice as I direct you to. Can you do that, Dear One?

# June 24

*Create in me a clean heart, O God, and renew a right spirit within me. Cast me not away from your presence, and take not your Holy Spirit from me. Restore to me the joy of your salvation, and uphold me with a willing spirit. ~Psalms 51:10-12*

Renew your faith, Weary One. Renew your faith in mankind and in yourself, but more importantly renew your faith in me. The world you live in can be a cruel place. It seems the news is bad everywhere. It is disheartening to watch humans destroy humans. It is not the way I designed it and it breaks My heart.

However, Beloved, I created man in My own image. There is the capacity for great love and deep compassion within humans. Sin draws men away from My design. Try to see others through My eyes. Look for the best in people, not the worst. You will find the human spirit is strong because I made the inner man resilient. When it is bonded with My Spirit there is supernatural strength, and it is a beautiful thing.

Renewing faith in yourself is hard when you are down. When things are not going your way, it is easy to assume you are somehow less than. Beloved, I made you, just as you are, so you can never be less than. Believing in yourself as I have made you is not humanism. It is choosing what I say about you over what the enemy says. That is all. Sounds simple, but it requires you to renew your mind. Take your thoughts captive. When you control your thoughts, you also choose to have faith in yourself.

Renewing faith in me is another matter. If your hardships and suffering have turned your faith cold, if you feel I have abandoned you to your plight, if you feel rejected by me, renewing your faith will require you to trust me.

Trust me with all your feelings. Trust me with your circumstances. Trust that I am working and I am with you. Read about me. Read about My faithfulness. I have given you so many stories of those who thought all was lost only to be rescued. I put those stories in My word just for you, today. Go find them. My words will encourage your heart. When you see what I have done for others, even if I haven't done it for you yet, it will help you realize I am bigger than your circumstances.

# June 25

*Many are the plans in the mind of a man, but it is the purpose of the Lord that will stand. ~Proverbs 19:21*

My purposes cannot be thwarted, Weary One. You can make plans. You can even make mistakes, but they are merely stepping stones that lead you to My purposes. There is freedom in the fact that I use every opportunity to move you forward. Even when you feel stuck, I am moving you towards your purpose.

In fact, the purpose of your life isn't an end point. You have purpose every single day. It is not far off in the future somewhere; it lives with you. It is getting up today and going to work. It is taking care of your children. It is sitting with a friend. Purpose is everywhere. It is in the small details of life. Don't give up, My Love. Don't see yourself as a failure when things are not lining up to what you thought you would do.

When you are discouraged, remember there is purpose even in the little things that are part of your everyday life. You can make plans, but even if they don't go as you designed them, even if you fail or fall; My purposes will not. You cannot mess them up. You cannot stop them. They are as sure as the rising sun.

So be free, Dear One. Be free to live your life in the daily moments I provide for you. See your purpose all around you. Walk in it. Quit waiting for someday, move in your purpose today. Now.

There is only one like you. All of your past has made you what you are, you're your successes and mistakes. Today is making what you will be in the future. You are unique. There is no one else who brings what you have to the table. Embrace it. Watch and see what I will do with you.

# June 26

*You have kept count of my tossings; put my tears in your bottle. Are they not in your book? ~Psalms 56:8*

There are times when you have to do hard things, Weary One. Things that will hurt your heart. Decisions which are in your best interest, but will bring great pain in the process. Relationship decisions. Job decisions. Decisions for loved ones. Life decisions. To leave or to stay. To move or not. To leave behind the season you have been in sometimes means leaving things you love and walking into the unknown. Is it any wonder so many never make the hard decisions?

There is a season of preparation that goes before the decision. If you have lived enough of life, you already know this, Dear One. You can feel one season winding down and you know a change is coming. A scary but necessary change. Before it happens, you begin to feel uncomfortable. You feel a shift, or a lifting of responsibility. Or maybe a loss of interest. Your heart is no longer invested as it once was. This is the beginning of change. It is when you know you can no longer remain as you are.

Every decision you make in these kinds of situations will bring some level of pain. But don't forget, at the end of every season there are some sweet times left behind. Memories of what was. Good times, good friends, good partners, good places you have been. Cherish these memories. The fact it hurts to move on from them means you have loved well. You have been in a place where your heart connected. Some people go their whole lives without such memories. Be grateful, Weary One. Know that these times were a gift.

When the next hard time comes, memories will sustain you. They will be your help when you are walking forward in pain. The lonely days before your next season begins. It is okay to grieve season changes, Beloved. In fact, it is healthy to do so. I designed grief to give you a release for pent-up emotions. Tears are a release valve. Sorrow can be cleansing. On your way to the new season, make space for the grief.

You know the decision has to be made. You will make it when you are ready. You will know when the time comes. I will be with you. I will walk beside you and catch every tear.

# June 27

*Either make the tree good and its fruit good, or make the tree bad and its fruit bad, for the tree is known by its fruit. You brood of vipers! How can you speak good, when you are evil? For out of the abundance of the heart the mouth speaks.*
*~Matthew 12: 33-34*

Be careful with your words. I command you to love your enemies. Dear One, this is not an easy task. It is much easier to hate than to love. To love requires putting down your own agendas. It requires putting aside yourself and what you want, or what you think about a situation. It is so difficult to love one another, impossible really, without depending on me. Loving others is important to me because you must lean into me. When you are wronged, to love is the opposite of what you want to do. Yet, it is My wish for you to express My heart.

True kindness isn't practiced often in the world. There are all kinds of pretenses which masquerade as kindness, but they are false. Smiling and saying things you do not feel is not loving. It is not kind. It is a lie, because it is not from the heart. It is not real. In order to make kindness genuine, you have to forgive and allow me to change your heart. It is a deep work and it is not quick. True love is never quick.

How do you know if your loving kindness is authentic or not? One way to figure it out is to pay attention to what your mouth is speaking. Out of it come words of life and love, but also death and criticism. When you think about a topic or a person, what comes bubbling up? Is it love, joy, peace, patience, kindness, goodness, faithfulness, gentleness or self-control? Or is it something else? What is in your heart, Beloved?

Ultimately, you cannot know your motives. Only I can show you. Therefore, to be loving, you have to seek me first. To show kindness you must first have kindness in your heart. The fruit of the Spirit is only obtainable by spending time with My Spirit. It is an overflow of your relationship with Me.

Hate is easy. It requires no real work on your part. Just feel and let it take you. Love is a real challenge. I do not say to love only when you are loved in return. It is not a conditional command. It is a real inner working of transformation that has to happen. You cannot bring it about on your own. It is too hard to do it alone. This is important to me, My Child. Do not ignore My command to love. Seek me out in this. You must have me to help you, to show you, to open your eyes.

# June 28

*For in this hope we were saved. Now hope that is seen is not hope. For who hopes for what he sees? But if we hope for what we do not see, we wait for it with patience.*
*~Romans 8:24-25*

There is always hope, Weary One. Even when it appears the world has gone mad. Even when your own life is in shambles. Even when it seems all is lost. Even when grief seems to overtake you. There is hope.

Hope is what fuels all of life. It is an intangible force which cannot be seen but is felt in the core of your being. To be hopeless, or without hope, is to be cut off from life. It seems when your hope is gone, that nothing is worth doing. Like a shroud, hopelessness covers you in darkness, clouding your vision, making every effort like walking in quicksand. Dear One, when you are hopeless you feel lost, but you are not. I am always with you even when you cannot feel me.

I walk beside you even in the darkness. There is always a spark and when I breathe on it, hope will rise to flame again. Do not give up, Beloved. Wait for me to blow on the spark. While you are waiting for me to do the work, sit with me. Be with me. Tell me your troubles. Share the hardship with me. Let the fearfulness out of your system, by giving it to me. I am with you always so you might as well pour out your concerns. They will not fall on deaf ears. I promise I hear every thought as a prayer. Every sorrow. Every regret. I will not strand you in a hopeless place, but you must trust me with your hopelessness. I can transform it.

Hope will return. It might take some time but it will. Don't let it go. Hold on. Whatever shred of hope you have left, hold on to it. Let me show you how. Let me encompass your thoughts and your heart. I will bring you hope.

# June 29

*Cast your burden on the Lord, and He will sustain you; He will never permit the righteous to be moved. ~Psalms 55:22*

Bring your offering to Me. Lift it up. Place it in My hands and see what I will do with it. You can offer your gifts. You can offer your talents. You can offer your children. You can offer your parents. You can offer your job. You can offer your grief. You can offer your pain. All of it. You can hold it up to me and give it as an offering.

Dear One, giving an offering means letting go and letting me have it. It is a sacrifice. You cannot control everything in your life. You may try to do it, but you will never be able to do it all. When you give me an offering, you are relinquishing control. You are opening your hand and releasing your gift to me. When you offer me something you have held, I consider it an honor and I bless it.

If it is a gift I have given you and you give it back to me, I bless it. If it is pain and sorrow you lift up, I bless it and use it in your life to make you stronger. If it is a person in your life, I bless them. Think about it, Weary One, when you give money to a charity or an organization, they spend it to further their vision. I am the same. When you give something to Me as a sacrifice, I use it to further My kingdom. I use it to further My purposes in your life.

You cannot miss by bringing offerings to Me. The more you realize they are safer in My hands than in yours, you will grow in your trust in letting things go. The more freedom you will have. The more grace you will walk in. It is My way to let things go in order to gain them. My ways are not your ways. Once you learn My ways, you will not go back to yours. You will offer everything up to Me.

# June 30

*Agree with God, and be at peace; thereby good will come to you. ~Job 22:21*

There is a time to fight and there is a time to surrender. When you are weary many times it is due to the fight. The constant battle with pain of all kinds. Holding your own. Holding your space. Standing for your loved one. Sitting in the grief. It is all a fight. Some days it is a battle just to breathe. You know this place. It is a bone-weary place, Beloved. It is a dry place where it is an effort just to take one step.

These battle-weary places lead to places of surrender. Just like in a real battle, when you are worn down fight after fight and your stores are empty, there is little choice. Retreat or surrender. In a retreat, there will be great losses, whereas with surrender you live another day. Dear One, surrender is not weakness as you suppose. It is a necessity.

When you surrender to me, you are safe. Remember that. I am a safe place to go when the weariness is draining your life away. When you surrender you make time to rest. You replenish your stores while in My protection. You lay down all your work, your battle plans, your strategy and just sit. I can tell you it will not be forever. The surrender can hurt. It goes against your will to continue on fighting. It feels like you have lost, but that is not so.

In surrender, you will find freedom. You will cease striving and let go. Letting go is not always a bad thing, Dear One. Let go of bitterness. Resentment. Relationships that are toxic. Let go of weariness. Let go of the last shred of the end of your rope. Fall into My arms. Let me catch you. Let me restore your heart. Let me heal your wounds. I will bind you up with My strength. I will renew your hope. Give me time. Sit with me. You will fight again when I infuse your spirit with My purposes. But for now, rest Beloved. Just surrender. Put your hands up. Wave the white flag. I will come for you. I will protect you while you rest.

# July 1

*For everything there is a season, and a time for every matter under heaven: a time to be born, and a time to die; a time to plant, and a time to pluck up what is planted; a time to kill, and a time to heal; a time to break down, and a time to build up; a time to weep, and a time to laugh; a time to mourn, and a time to dance; a time to cast away stones, and a time to gather stones together; a time to embrace, and a time to refrain from embracing; a time to seek, and a time to lose; a time to keep, and a time to cast away; a time to tear, and a time to sew; a time to keep silence, and a time to speak; a time to love, and a time to hate; a time for war, and a time for peace. ~Ecclesiastes 3:1-8*

There is an ebb and flow to life, Weary One. Like the sea rises and falls, so does the day-to-day of life. Sometimes there are stormy waters, other times they are calm. Constant battering causes doubt to rise. When the calm seems far away, it is like trying to stand in rough surf. Just when you think your feet are under you, another wave comes to knock you down. In that circumstance it is not you but the waves which are causing the trouble. You instinctively know it is not your fault that you can't stand up. You don't sit in the water and blame yourself for the waves. Neither should you in life.

Big waves come. You begin to wonder what you did to deserve the storms, as if they are somehow your fault. I am not talking about the consequences of your actions. That is different. This is when the circumstances are beyond your control. Losses of great magnitude. Or uncertainty and unrest. Doubt looms in these bigger waves, waiting to crash over you. To make you wonder, to make you question, to make you feel as if you are somehow responsible for things that could not possibly be your fault.

Why do you do this to yourself? Do not let the enemy steal from you, Dear One. He would love nothing more than to have you walk in regret for something that has nothing whatsoever to do with you. His ploy is to pull you off track into your own head and get you thinking in circles. No, these waves are not your fault. You will have difficulty trying to balance in them and it is futile to try. If you cannot balance, and you cannot stand, and you don't want to run away, what are you supposed to do? I hear the question ringing in your head.

Swim, Dear One. Swim in My love for you. Float on My grace. Paddle past the breaking point and ride the storm out. No storm lasts forever. The ebb and flow of the waves promise that calm is coming again one day. Until then, swim with me.

# July 2

*Blessed are you when others revile you and persecute you and utter all kinds of evil against you falsely on My account. Rejoice and be glad, for your reward is great in heaven, for so they persecuted the prophets who were before you. ~Matthew 5:11-12*

Weary One, do not become discouraged when others come against you. Check your heart with me. Trust me to show you areas that need correction. Then when you have submitted yourself to me, let the words of others roll off of you.

Remember hurt people, hurt people. When a heart is wounded there is pain. It has deep places which are unresolved and unhealed. When those places are touched the pain spills out. It can come in hurtful words. It can manifest in ugly behaviors. It shows up in disproportionate reactions to events. Relationships are destroyed, not by direct arguments, but by unresolved pain that has been festering for years. There is a reason I say do not let the sun go down on your anger.

Weary One, I know you have walked a long road, but do not let it poison your heart. Do not let it make you a bitter person. Many bitter people do not know how their actions affect those around them. They do not realize how selfish they are acting because they are caught up in their pain. Extend grace. Show understanding. Getting defensive only makes their pain spill out onto you. There is no need for that. You can prevent it by showing compassion.

You cannot change anyone's view or attitude. Only I can do that. But you can pray for them and for you. Pray for healing to wash over hearts. Pray for the balm of My love to seal the wounds. It is the only way forward. It is not up to you to fix the hurt. It is between me and the other person. Do not let their hurtful actions pierce your heart personally. They do not know what they are doing. I have experience with this, trust me. It is not about you. It is about me. They are wrestling with me and you are catching the overflow of that. Pray, Dear One. Pray.

# July 3

*Everyone then who hears these words of mine and does them will be like a wise man who built his house on the rock. And the rain fell, and the floods came, and the winds blew and beat on that house, but it did not fall, because it had been founded on the rock. And everyone who hears these words of mine and does not do them will be like a foolish man who built his house on the sand. And the rain fell, and the floods came, and the winds blew and beat against that house, and it fell, and great was the fall of it. ~Matthew 7:24-27*

You cannot let your feelings lead, Dear One. They will give you a run for your money. They will batter you to and fro like the wind. In the midst of trials, when you are down in the trenches, feelings will not serve you well. Oh, you will feel them all right. They will rage and demand your attention, but they should not influence how you make decisions. They should not be in control of your actions.

When you are in a hard place your emotions are heightened. They are more intense. It is tempting to run with them and let them rule the day. Stress causes this response. Similar to fight or flight, your brain increases emotional responses when hardship comes along. I am not saying to ignore your emotions, they are there so you can express and relieve some of that stress you are carrying. There are healthy ways to process grief.

However, I am saying do not let your emotions rule you. Acknowledge them. Express them, but do not let them lead. If you have decided to quit your job for emotional reasons, you will regret it later on. Keep your head. Think things through. Decide based on your goals. Act on the purposes and plans I have put in your heart.

Emotions want you to quit everything so they can have center stage. Some people call it drama. When you choose to go forward, to put feelings in an appropriate position, even the hard places get smoother. When you look to me as you make your decisions, you will find solid ground. Emotions shift like the sand. Any home built on sand will fall. But if you put me as your foundation, if you choose to move even when you don't feel like it, you will not regret it. You will get to the other side of those feelings more quickly. Build your foundation on me.

# July 4

*The Spirit of the Lord God is upon me, because the Lord has anointed me to bring good news to the poor, He has sent me to bind up the brokenhearted, to proclaim liberty to the captives, and the opening of the prison to those who are bound; to proclaim the year of the Lord's favor, and the day of vengeance of our God; to comfort all who mourn; to grant to those who mourn in Zion—to give them a beautiful headdress instead of ashes, the oil of gladness instead of mourning, the garment of praise instead of a faint spirit; that they may be called oaks of righteousness, the planting of the Lord, that He may be glorified. ~Isaiah 61:1-3*

Freedom is a beautiful thing, Weary One, but you may not have considered its true meaning. It is not doing whatever you want. It is not freedom *to*; it is freedom *from*. From bondage. From oppression. From the sin-tainted world. From darkness. From captivity. From mourning. From despair.

People have it backwards. They run to say what they want. They run to do what they want. When their freedoms are taken away they demand them back. But Dear One, I tell you, people can be or do whatever they want, but still be bound in chains. The physical freedoms are only one kind and when they are elevated over spiritual freedom, they become bondage. Is it strange to you that freedom itself can become bondage?

When freedom is worshiped over me it becomes self-centered. Idolatry. Hearts are not humbled or grateful, but they become entitled and haughty. They demand. They refuse to consider others for fear that their own freedom will be infringed upon. However, you can be in prison and still be free. You can live with hardship and walk out of your chains. You can be financially poor and still be free.

I make it possible to find freedom no matter what country you live in, no matter what your station, no matter what you have done or not done, no matter your status or your level of oppression. When you find me, you find freedom for your soul. You come to see this world is a temporary home, and it is short and momentary. You can walk in freedom from the pull of this world.

So, do not despise where you are. Do not think you cannot be free because you don't have resources. Do not think you cannot be free because you are trapped caring for others. Do not think you cannot be free because grief follows you around or because you are brokenhearted. Freedom is not limited because I am not limited. Seek me and you will find true freedom.

# July 5

*And the Lord answered me: "Write the vision; make it plain on tablets, so he may run who reads it. For still the vision awaits its appointed time; it hastens to the end—it will not lie. If it seems slow, wait for it; it will surely come; it will not delay."*
*~Habakkuk 2:2-3*

When I put an idea on your heart, Beloved, make steps to achieve it. Set it as a goal. Then take one small step at a time. Before you know it, you will have made it to the end. I give big dreams which seem so enormous, many never even step out because they think it will never happen. I tell you, the goals I want you to achieve, the visions I set before you, are achievable when you depend on me. I put together the pieces that seem impossible. I order the steps. I make the connections seemingly out of nowhere. It is one of My favorite things to do.

You look at those who have accomplished so much and wonder how driven they must be. How can one person change the world, and others not hardly move their own feet? Some are driven and they strive their whole lives. Then there are the ones who put their vision in My hands, who know I will do the work if they will simply step out when I lead them to take the first step. They are the ones who know it isn't actually their vision, but mine.

When you have a burning desire to accomplish something, it is likely me putting it in your heart. It is up to you to take the first steps. You may not know what to do after that, but I will show you. I will direct you each step of the way.

You will be awash with joy when the task is complete. You will see what I saw at the beginning. You will endure the hardships to get to the goal. You will learn along the journey to the dream. How to do hard things. How to push through when you don't feel like it. How to keep going and persevere. More importantly, you will be transformed in the process. What starts as a step will lead to bigger things where you will need to have My heart. The journey develops your heart, Dear One. It is not intended to wear you down; it is to prepare you for the future. It is to build you up and help you find contentment in me. When everything feels overwhelming, you learn to sit with me. When the goal seems too far away, you learn to hold it up to me. When you are ready to give up, remember I am in control. Weary One, it is not up to you to create the whole vision. It is only up to you to take the first step.

# July 6

*When Pharaoh drew near, the people of Israel lifted up their eyes, and behold, the Egyptians were marching after them, and they feared greatly. And the people of Israel cried out to the Lord. They said to Moses, "Is it because there are no graves in Egypt that you have taken us away to die in the wilderness? What have you done to us in bringing us out of Egypt? Is not this what we said to you in Egypt: 'Leave us alone that we may serve the Egyptians'? For it would have been better for us to serve the Egyptians than to die in the wilderness." And Moses said to the people, "Fear not, stand firm, and see the salvation of the Lord, which He will work for you today. For the Egyptians whom you see today, you shall never see again. The Lord will fight for you, and you have only to be silent." ~Exodus 14:10-14*

Oh, Weary Soul. Do not be downcast. Lift your eyes to see all that you have been given. Every minute of every day is a gift. Do you not perceive it as such? I am as close as your breath. Breathe in. Breathe out. Can you feel me? You are not alone. You have never been alone. I am right here with you in the midst of your battle. I can carry the heavy weight of it…lift it off your shoulders. You need only to release it to me. Open your hands…even when you feel you cannot. It will be worth the effort, I promise.

You don't see the outcome, but I do. You cannot see the future, but I can. The dark and weary spaces are the hardest ones because you are blind here. It requires trust in me to walk in heavy places on a daily basis. Trust. Not control. There is not one thing you can do to change the circumstances. Striving and grasping to fix it or to go back to the way things were 'before' will do nothing but exhaust you.

So, open your hands. Release it all. Physically lay it down before me. Then breathe in My grace. Breathe out the stress. Breathe in belief. Breathe out hopelessness. Breathe in My truth. Breathe out discouragement. Breathe in faith. Breathe out heaviness. Soak in My love. Allow My joy to be your strength. Let a smile brighten your face today. Let My light in. Make space for it to grow. In the stillness. In the quiet. My light will make a way in the darkness.

Weary One, I will not strand you in the wilderness. I will not allow the enemy to swallow you up. I did not lead you here to watch you die in the desert. I brought you here to show you My power, in all things. In hard things. In impossible things. In things no one can see but you. Wait for me here. Do not despair. Wait and see what I will do.

# July 7

*And your ears shall hear a word behind you, saying, "This is the way, walk in it,"*
*when you turn to the right or when you turn to the left. ~Isaiah 30:21*

Beloved, all around you are voices. Even today, you will have the opportunity to listen to a multitude of them. Every moment, there is a choice you must make. What voice to listen to. The doctor? Social media? The news? Your friends? Your enemies? Your children? Your teachers? Your pastor? Your counselor? Your internal voice? The taunting voices? My voice? Do you know My voice, Beloved? Or has it been drowned out by all the others?

Listen to what I say. You are loved. You are a complex and beautiful creation. You are unique, one of a kind. You are the apple of My eye. You are not forsaken. You are not abandoned. You carry My authority. You are inspiring. You have gifts. You are not invisible. You are cherished. Can you feel these things stirring in you? Do these words bring tears to your eyes? You are parched for words of life. You are thirsty, My Love. Drink deeply from the well of My words to you.

The heaviness of life tries to steal the truth. It weighs you down. It begs you to compare yourself to others. It pleads with you to give up. It tells you the pain will never end. It silences the voice of hope. It covers you like a wet blanket. The voices of the world swirl around in your head and increase your distress. Do not listen to them. They are not for you, but I AM.

To which voices should you listen? If the voices do not echo what I say about you, push them aside. Plug your ears. The ones that uplift and encourage are from me. They call you to be more fully who I created you to be. They stir your belief in me, in the future, and in yourself. They increase your desire to persevere. They infuse you with determination to keep going. Beloved, choose wisely.

# July 8

*You know when I sit down and when I rise up; you discern my thoughts from afar. You search out my path and my lying down and are acquainted with all my ways. Even before a word is on my tongue, behold, O Lord, you know it altogether. You hem me in, behind and before, and lay Your hand upon me. ~Psalms 139:2-5*

You are not the only one, My Child. Many people feel overwhelmed, overworked, and alone. Their walk-through life is like struggling through waist-deep water that seems to zap the strength out of them. Every step of every day requires tremendous effort.

In the battles of life, you feel as if you are losing. Barely able to raise the sword of the spirit, much less to wield it. Your armor is barely on and so every day is heavy with effort and every night filled with sleeplessness. You wonder if anyone sees you...really sees. Not the smile and "I'm fine," that you use to cover the pain, but the hollow exhaustion in your eyes. The overwhelming disappointment with how life turned out and the blows that life has dealt you.

The walk you walk, putting one foot in front of the other is the only way to move forward. You cling to hope and faith by a thread. You wonder if anything would even change if that thread broke.

You think you cannot do another day when you are constantly tending to another, or when all hell breaks loose. I am with you. You are not alone. Ever. I see. I know. I feel. The pain and sorrow of your life can be unbearable. Do not carry it all on your own, My Child. Let me walk with you, let me lighten your load.

Come to me all who are weary and heavy-laden. Rest. Still your heart, when you can, and know this. I know when you sit, sleep and rise. I know when you pace and worry. I know your thoughts and how alone you feel. You have not even spoken it, yet I know the thoughts. I understand abandonment. I know betrayal. I have carried grief. Disappointment has been My bread. Yet, I am still here. With you. My hand is on you. I blanket you with My presence. I go before and behind. I walk beside. There is nowhere you can go, where I am not there already. Hold tight to that truth, Weary One. Look for me in all the hard places. In the night. In the grief. In the loss. In the hardship. In the pain. I am with you.

# July 9

*God is our refuge and strength, a very present help in trouble. Therefore, we will not fear though the earth gives way, though the mountains be moved into the heart of the sea, though its waters roar and foam, though the mountains tremble at its swelling.  ~Psalms 46:1-3*

Hello Valley Dweller. I know from the valley you long for the mountain top where the view is far and wide. From the top of the mountain the way is clear. The view allows for a 360-degree perspective where you can see what lies behind and what lies ahead. From above, you can make out the trail and how it weaves around, but also where it leads. Yes, the mountain top is a spectacular place to be because everything is beautiful. Once you arrive at the summit, the work it took to climb is over...forgotten with the panoramic, stunning, view of the scenery below. Ah yes, the mountain top is a wonderful place, but it is not the only place.

Those who dwell in the valley look up in longing. They wonder what it would be like to live above, where everything is in clear view. They wish they could have a chance to find out. It must be better than living in the valley where you cannot see very far.

In the valley, it may seem claustrophobic, with trees and undergrowth all around. It is shady and there are shadows that change and move with the wind. It feels shifty and unstable. When the rains come, the valley fills up. The ground under your feet erodes as the water rises. It seems as if the wind and rain have conspired against you, and though the top of the mountain is hidden in the fog, it stands steadfast in the midst of your flailing. Climbing the mountain is a worthy goal for you, Valley Dweller. It is something to aim for. But...

But, what if there is more life in the valley than you have seen? What if living in the valley doesn't hinder you as you suppose, but it brings you growth? Sure, life in the valley is different from the mountain top, but it has its own beauty.

You can see it if you look. The rains, which are frequent as storms roll through, bring rushing rivers which nourish the foliage. When there is a break, the leaves reach to the sun and unfurl in worship. The lush and fertile dirt provides nutrients to all who live in the valley. Plants mature and animals thrive here. The shadows which seemed so ominous, offer cool shade under which to rest.

Valley Dweller, do not be dismayed. The valley is a place of life and growth. Do not believe otherwise. Although it is a place of hardship, it is also a place where I meet you on a daily basis. I draw you to put your roots deep, so the storms cannot move you. I teach you to find rest while you are in the midst of difficulty. I provide for you in ways you would not recognize if you were on the mountain top. I cover you with My presence. I hold you, so you can feel My presence rather than see it. I guide you to know the truth...I am with you in the valley.

# July 10

*Bless the Lord, O my soul, and all that is within me, bless His holy name! ~Psalms 103:1*

Rest can be elusive when you carry the world on your shoulders, but rest does not always mean what you think, Beloved. It is not napping or sitting still, though those are both good things. Rest is not defined merely as a lack of activity. When you enter into My rest, it is possible to be at peace even with a whirlwind swirling around you. It is possible to be full of activity and still have calm pervade your days.

When you take care of everyone else before yourself, it drains you. When you carry grief or loss, you can be overwhelmed in an instant. When you are in pain, the days feel years long. One more item on your to do list threatens to steal your mental health. These places in which you find yourself are soul-crushing. They pull at your whole being, until you are done. Over it. Just trying to breathe and sometimes wondering why you try so hard. To rest, you need so much more than sleep, My love. You need your soul to be healed.

It is a dilemma when you cannot just turn your life off for a bit. You may not be able to quit, but you can practice soul awareness. Learn to recognize before you get to the last straw. Seek me, not in a checklist of dos and don'ts, but in the deep places of your heart. The places you don't allow anyone into.

Are you surprised I know about those Weary One? Ah…don't be. Everyone has closed off places with walls to shut out pain and self-protect. But in protecting yourself I am relegated to the sidelines or the quiet time. I am so much bigger than just the quiet time.

I long to pour healing into you. To whisper that everything is going to be okay. To hold you close and let you cry. To give you time to let down your guard. I can do that if you want me to. If you will let me. It doesn't have to be a set time of day. It can be anytime the stress is threatening to spill over.

Turn your spirit towards me. It is an intentional turning, and it can happen in the carpool line, or driving to the doctor, or sitting with a therapist, or while cooking dinner. There is no "right" place or "correct" way to pour out your heart to me. Once you have opened the door to the protected places, listen to My voice. I spoke and the universe was created. Do you think it will be any different when I speak rest to your soul?

# July 11

*For God alone, O my soul, wait in silence, for my hope is from Him. He only is my rock and my salvation, my fortress; I shall not be shaken. ~Psalms 62:5-6*

Dear One, I invite you to intimacy (into-me-see). It is a place you can drop your goals, your facades, your visions for the future, the person you try to be, and simply be who you are. You can be transparent with Me. I have opened My heart to you to show you that it is safe for you to open yours to me. You can put off the false and open your soul to me. Here is where I expose the dross and remove it with My love. It is the place where you find who you truly are despite all that you walk with and through. It is the place you come into agreement with me, about you and about me. The truth lives here.

Here, in the into-me-see, I open Myself to you. I invite you into My heart. It is a sacred space, a place that is tender. Do not take it lightly, and do not be flippant with this gift of intimacy. I trust you with it. I allow you to feel some of My pain at your circumstance as well as My overwhelming love. Beauty resides here. Do not get so busy with your work, your burden, your load, that you walk right past this place. It is where healing begins.

Your eyes cannot see it. You do not allow yourself any time to spend in this place. I want to sit with you and pour out My heart's cry. Did you know I have pain in My heart too, Dear One? It seems opposite from what you are used to...you pouring out your heart to me, wanting me to do something. Instead, in the quiet place I want to show you My secrets, the pain of a jilted lover, the agony of a rejected father, the hope of redemption, the faith I have in My plan, and the overwhelming love for you that cannot be quenched. It is all too much for you to comprehend, but I want to share it anyway. It is a privilege for you to be in this place with me.

I am the only one who can rescue you. Only I can carry you. Only I can set you free from your weary world. Only I can pour into your soul to revive it. Only I can create beauty in you so that it shines forth, even in the dark places. Only I can expose your heartache, remove it, and be your lover at the same time. Only I can open your eyes. Only I can reveal the secrets of My whispers to you. Only I can bring you to a place of compassion. Only I can humble you. Only I can wipe your tears. Only I can cover you with a blanket of comfort. Only I can raise you up.

Will you sit with me? Will you be in this space with me and let me be with you? In this place you will be transformed. You will hear My heartbeat and it will be life to your soul. You will see My pain, and I will see yours. You will be undone by My compassion. It will shape you. My acceptance will purify you. You will find your place. It is here that you belong...here you long to be.

Refreshing begins in My heart. Thank you Dear One for sitting with me and being with me. Thank you for hearing me and looking into me to see. Intimacy is where we commune together and where your soul finds peace.

# July 12

*Blessed are the poor in spirit, for theirs is the kingdom of heaven. Blessed are those who mourn, for they shall be comforted. ~Matthew 5:3-4*

You are neither hopeless nor helpless. You are not weak. You only feel so. My strength lives in you, otherwise you would not have survived thus far. I hold up the Valley Dwellers. It is one thing to visit the valley from time to time. It is quite another to live here. The day-to-day looks different than life on the mountain top. Do not compare the two; it will only lead to discouragement. The life of a Valley Dweller cannot be compared to others. Hardship takes many forms in the valley; chronic illness, a grieving heart, caregiving for another, loss of one kind or another, a disability, generational poverty, addiction, oppression, and the list goes on and on. The Valley Dwellers are many. That fact alone can be a comfort. You are not isolated. There is a multitude.

While adversity and suffering are common in the valley, they are not the only things which grow here. The tears that water the soil make it fertile. It is rich in compassion. It overflows with empathy. Gratefulness sprouts in the valley like a weed. Grace blossoms and faith in the unseen flourishes. The joy that matures here is unlike any other. It finds even the smallest place to put down roots and hold the ground.

Contentment is another fruit of the valley. Those who have lived here a long time have cultivated it and learned how to harvest it well. Valley Dwellers live in the present, because they have no other choice. Each day is new, with new challenges. Looking back and wishing to change things, or looking forward to what may not ever be, doesn't benefit those who live here. Today has enough worries of its own. Seeds of trust are fostered here. They take some time to develop, but their roots intertwine with every other plant to infuse strength to them. It is a delicate biome, this valley, but it is rich in fruit.

Valley Dwellers help one another. The strong today help those struggling to find their strength. They know tomorrow it may be their turn to need help. There is no apology for needing help in the valley. All the residents know it is the only way to survive here. The interdependence here is one of the things that makes it so beautiful.

I say, those who hunger for and depend on me are fortunate. For your life is a place where My fruit grows. I say, those who walk with daily grief are blessed. For you will be covered and held up by me.

# July 13

*This is the day that the Lord has made; let us rejoice and be glad in it. ~Psalms 118:24*

Today is the day I have made. Rejoice, O Weary One, and be glad in it. Walk with an awareness of me by your side. I am always there. I will give you My eyes to see what I see. Ears to hear what I hear. I will give you a voice to speak My words and discernment as to what to put your hand to today, and what to leave undone. I will arrange your steps and order your day.

My wind blows outside your window and in your heart. Can you feel it fanning the flame I have put there? Blowing on the spark of hope I planted and growing it into something bigger; a place of hope, which lives inside of you. Anywhere I am, hope resides, and I am in you. Can you see me working in you? Orchestrating your steps?

Prepare your heart, Beloved. I have put hope in you because you need it. All that seems so important, is not as you think. All you see is not as it appears. Cultivate hope. Darkness comes to try to steal My light, but I am planting it inside of you where it can grow, even in darkness. Fan the flame. Build a community of hope where you are. Do not isolate yourself. Do not be overcome with fear. Do not cower. Do not be discouraged. Be wise in your movements. Be shrewd in your steps. Watch and pray.

Build up other Valley Dwellers and Weary Ones. Support one another. Link yourselves together. Arm in arm, but more importantly, heart to heart. It is the communion of shared pain. Connection happens here. You will feel what I feel. And love what I love. Life for you, not death. Hope, not depression. Grasping for something...or someone, called hope. It is me. In your connection with one another, I will be seen. Love and care in a world where love and care have taken flight. Be My hands and feet to one another, but more so, be My heart.

# July 14

*Seek the Lord and His strength; seek His presence continually! ~1 Chronicles 16:11*

Clothe yourself, My Love, in what I provide for you. Humility, purity, holiness, righteousness. These are the garments you wear under your armor. You cannot provide them for yourself, rather you must receive them from me alone. Otherwise they are self-righteousness, which is filth to me. I offer these garments in My way and in My time. Kneel to receive them from me. They are chainmail under your armor, yet they are intimate garments. Do you not think that could be true? You are a warrior bride, are you not?

My Love, you must ready yourself. To do so you do not need to visit the armory. You need to come into My chambers. You need intimacy with Me. My ways are not your ways. To disrobe and remove the layers with me, behind closed doors, is the only way to find what you need. It is not out there somewhere. It is in surrendering yourself to me that you will find it.

Then, when you are in unity with me, I will clothe you with the garments you need to go out. I will clothe you with humility that is found in intimacy without even looking. I will drape you with purity of heart, which can only be found in intimate innocence. Holiness will rub off of me and onto you and My righteousness will become yours. Only then can you take up your armor to do daily battle. Any other way and the order is all wrong. The gown of a bride is not meant for battle; it comes after the battle is won.

Beloved, clothe yourself. Come to me. Lay all your troubles at the door to My chambers and leave them there. Come to me and let me see you. All of you. Do not hide in shyness, or embarrassment. Do not let your weariness keep you from me. Do not walk away from me. I already know. You are known by me. Will you let me show you Myself? Will you allow yourself to see My heart for you? In this place, the garments you seek are found. Seek me alone.

# July 15

*And He said, "My presence will go with you, and I will give you rest." ~Exodus 33:14*

Dear One, I don't think you know your own strength. The daily burden takes up so much of your life you cannot look up long enough to recognize the power you have. Your feet trudge along, step by step. If you look up you will see the wide-open sky over you. The clouds have no hindrances. They float and move seemingly at will. Sometimes it appears they are dancing. Others they hang lazily barely moving at all. It looks like they are moving on their own, but the reality is they are subject to the wind. The wind carries them. Just as I carry you. Can you feel me lifting you up? Or do you feel your weakness so heavily that My wind rushes past?

I have a secret to tell you. Your weakness is your strength. I know it is counterintuitive, but it is the truth. You see, My Child, your time enduring hardship has stripped you of bravado. It has taken pride from you and replaced it with humility. The days you can barely lift your head are the days I have carried you. In your inability, My ability rises. In your heartache, My joy slips through the cracks into your broken heart. Do not fret. Do not fall prey to the hopelessness. Look up.

You walk in My power alone. My presence goes with you. I hover over the face of the deep places in your heart. I infuse you with hope. I fill you with compassion. Wipe your tears, Beloved. You are courageous. Each day requires you to be brave. You are a powerful warrior. A secret weapon of mine. Do not worry that you do not have a place on a stage. Do not think that your life has made you invisible. You are not invisible to me. I SEE you. I KNOW you. There may not be a platform for you now, but there is a place for you. A place where your sweetness overflows to others. A place where you dwell in wisdom. A place where you sit and hold space for those, who like you, feel discarded.

Here is another secret...you are My invisible army. Invisible in the natural, but giants in the spirit. You are seen and feared. There is no hiding your strength in the realm of the unseen. Do not allow this world to worry you. The spiritual realm is more real than anything on this earth ever will be. One day you will know this to be true. For now, trust me when I say you are a force to be reckoned with. What you perceive as weakness is the very thing which makes you dangerous to the enemy. He wants you to feel stuck, when in reality, the depth of your burden puts you in the most dangerous place to him...at My feet.

# July 16

*The crucible is for silver, and the furnace is for gold, and the Lord tests hearts.*
*~Proverbs 17:3*

You may have taken hit after hit in life, but that doesn't mean you are somehow cursed. I am more powerful than any curse! I took every curse upon Myself. The price has already been paid. Do not let a performance mentality steal from you. There is nothing you can do to make me love you more or less. That is the truth. Even My disciples had a hard time grasping this truth. Remember the blind man? Born blind?

"Rabbi, who sinned, this man or his parents, that he was born blind?" Jesus answered, "Neither this man nor his parents sinned, but this happened so that the works of God would be displayed in him." Yet everyone is asking why this happened to him. Who sinned? Who's to blame? Weary One, placing blame on others, on yourself, or on a curse isn't the point.

Things happen to you so I can be acknowledged to the people around you. Sometimes that means supernatural breakthrough. Physical healing. Emotional peace. Other times it means walking through the hard stuff in such a way that others are amazed at how My light shines in the darkness around you. Sometimes it means your maturity and understanding of your identity speak volumes, because you really KNOW it is not about what you have or have not done. You walk each step in humility and grace.

Wave after wave crashes over you and you are disoriented from the never-ending pummeling, remember it is life. It is hard. Arrange your thoughts in an attitude of grace. Grace for yourself. Grace for your circumstances. Grace for others. The sooner you learn a grace-filled attitude, the better even the difficult times will be. I leave the choice of attitude in your hands.

When the next wave comes, and the one after that, do not ask why this happened to you. Instead ask, "What do I do now? How can this help others?" Ask me for strength to endure. It isn't always about finding relief or jumping out of the fire. It is about allowing the impurities to burn off and leave you as gold. You live in the furnace of the world. My Spirit lives inside of you, so you are made of incorruptible material. The fire does not kill you, though at times you think it might. It only burns out the parts of you that are not like me. The impatience. The hurt. The selfishness. The resentment and bitterness. Eventually, these hinderances will soften and be scraped away, leaving compassion, hope, contentment, and love behind. Watch for them to surface while you are in the fire.

# July 17

*Behold, I have engraved you on the palms of My hands; your walls are continually before me. ~Isaiah 49:16*

How could I ever forget you? Could I erase your face from My mind? Could I blot out your spirit from My own, where they are intertwined? I tell you it is not possible for me. My love for you is too great for me to ignore it. Even when you walk far from me, I will never leave or forsake you. Your mind cannot comprehend the kind of love I have for you. It is never about what you do or do not do. It never has been. That is the way others want you to perceive My love, but I assure you it is much bigger than that.

I will never forget you. I have engraved you on the palms of My hands. I have scars which bear your name. They go deep, beyond My skin and into My Spirit. They are permanent reminders of the kind of love of which I am capable. Sacrificial love. The consequences of this love were nailed to a tree. My scars prove the truth of love. It is a free gift. I said, free. Without penalty. Without condition. Love without consequence.

So, on this day, remember My engravings. Remember the name I carved into My scars. It is your name. Beloved. Child of God. Compassionate one. Faithful one. These are the names I call you. These are the things I see in you. If I can see them, shouldn't you too? Shouldn't you believe My scars?

# July 18

*Yet you do not know what tomorrow will bring. What is your life? For you are a mist that appears for a little time and then vanishes. ~James 4:14*

When you dwell in the valley, you are familiar with hardship. Every way out is up. A climb to get above the valley floor uses energy you do not have. But if you are familiar with the valley, you also know there is a lushness there. It can be a beautiful place. Even the fog, which rests in the low places, can have its own sort of misty beauty. It is all in how you look at it.

Foggy places can be frustrating because you cannot see what is in front of you. The mist is so thick you wonder what is just ahead. It could be dangerous and you would be caught off guard, unsure of what to do. But it also could be something unexpectedly lovely, like a rainbow in the droplets.

In life, there are foggy seasons, where you don't know what is around you. They are disorienting and keep you on guard. These are the times you must remember I am with you. You are not alone in the fog. Instead of focusing on what you cannot see, focus on what you can feel around you. You can hear My voice. You can feel My presence. You can sense the path. Fog causes you to slow down. It forces you to be alert and intentional.

Dear One, taking small steps and sometimes even waiting to step until things clear a bit is part of living in the valley. It is training you for later on. It is causing you to be dependent on me. Your fog might be a decision you need to make. It might be the day-to-day living without knowing what is coming next. It might be a new season where you are unsure of where you stand. It might be suffering you have endured for years with no end in sight.

The good news is I am with you. Your steps are ordered, even on this day, there is a plan for you. Do not be discouraged in the fog of life. Change your perspective and see the beauty in the mist.

# July 19

*All that the Father gives me will come to me, and whoever comes to me I will never cast out. ~John 6:37*

There is a spirit of rejection which tries to follow you around, Beloved. It says you are not accepted by your peers. It says your family merely puts up with you but doesn't truly want you around. It tells you that people at work don't approve of you or think you are inadequate for the job. This spirit creeps into your thoughts and soon every action you observe around you verifies what you think you know, which is rejection.

Do not believe it for one minute. When you think these thoughts regularly you must combat them with My words to you. In fact, feeling rejection is a signal to pay attention to your thoughts. Taking them captive is the only way to defeat this foe.

You are not rejected. My Son made sure of it. His suffering was to assure you a place at My table. You belong with me, in high places. You are received by me as you are. When you humble yourself and present your heart to me, I will not deny it. I will embrace you always, no matter how far away you find yourself. Do not let the enemy tell you that you are too far for me to care. It is simply not true. I will go to the ends of the earth to make sure you know you are accepted. You are known. Every thought and action is known by Me, and yet I do not run from you, but towards you. I catch you in My embrace and I draw you to My heart.

You are My heartbeat. You are My love. You are My creation. Perfectly made and perfectly accepted.

# July 20

*He has delivered us from the domain of darkness and transferred us to the kingdom of His beloved Son, in whom we have redemption, the forgiveness of sins. ~Colossians 1:13-14*

Do not let your mistakes define you. Every human I have ever created has made mistakes. It is a part of the fallen world in which you live. It is not uncommon, nor it is surprising to me. Perfectionism is a trap. Striving to be perfect, or expecting yourself to be, is an impossible task. When your shortcomings replay themselves over and over in your head, stop the train. Stop the thoughts which beat you up. I am a forgiving God. My Son is the only perfect one, and he made a way for you to walk free from perfectionism. You do not have to be a superhero with the weight of the world on your shoulders.

You say, "But God, you don't know how big my mistakes are! What I have done is unforgivable! I have hurt people. I have hurt myself. I am slime on the belly of a snake. What I have done cannot be undone, and it is beyond fixing. It is beyond my ability to control. I have destroyed my life."

Oh, really? I cannot know how bad it is? I promise you I do know. I know every detail, even beyond the behavior...to the heart. I also know these mistakes enslave you. You punish yourself every single day. It is time to stop, My Child. Do you not think My forgiveness is real? Is the grace My Son offers not enough to cover you? Do you mock His sacrifice by holding onto the mistakes he has forgiven? The guilt you carry is false. Once you have left the mistake at the foot of the cross, it is gone. Guilt does you no good. It is actually a form of pride, Dear One. Guilt says you are so important that your mistakes cannot be forgiven. The antidote for this life-crippling guilt is humility. It is reaching out to receive your free gift of forgiveness. It is believing that My Son washed away your mistakes.

I assure you His blood was real. It was our plan all along to rescue you from yourself. From your mistakes. From your failures. We wanted to erase them, from the beginning. It has always been our plan to carry them away from you. We know the power they can have in hindering you from the life you were born to live. It is important for you to know that your mistakes are erasable. It is also important that you know apologies are not the same as flogging yourself. A humble heart admits the errors. It makes restitution for pain it caused, but that is different than annihilating yourself. If you have hurt others, make it right with them. You can only do that if you have received the forgiveness I have for you. Otherwise, it will ring false in the ears of those you hurt.

Believe me when I say, you will continue to make mistakes. But knowing My heart on the matter will help you to run to me quickly. Allow me to wipe them away, then stand and walk forward. Do not rehash the past. It is past, let me leave it there, where it belongs.

# July 21

*A voice cries in the wilderness, "Prepare the way of the Lord; make straight in the desert a highway for our God." ~Isaiah 40:3*

The desert is different from the hardship-laden but fertile valley. This wasteland is a desolate place, where nothing seems to grow. The heat is suffocating. Everything is dry and shriveled up, including your heart. Desert Dweller, you are parched. The thirst for the water of life is nearly unbearable. You seek it at every turn, only to find sand which slips through your fingers. You know without water; death will come to your soul. You see others who appear to have found the springs in the desert. They are moving slowly, but still moving, while you are barely alive in the wilderness. You have no energy to move. Sweat rolls down your face, until there is no more in you. You cry out for water only to be met with silence. Does no one hear you? Is it your fate to end up dry bones in this place of heat?

It is here I met my foe, Beloved. I have been here, where you are trying to stand. It is a place of hot silence. It drains you. It pulls you low and makes you willing to do most anything to survive. Your parched lips crack and peel with the need for fluid. The words you speak must come from the deep well inside of you. The place where you stored them in better times. You think they are not there, but you are mistaken.

My words are never void. Speak them, Desert Dweller. Speak them out to the dry and barren place in which you find yourself. Speak them loudly. Each one of them is a drop of water that will turn to a torrent, if only you can speak them out. This place is where the dry bones come to life. This place is where all else but my words fall away.

My words are the water of life you seek. Do not let the weakness of this place stop you from speaking them. They may not even make sense to you in the moment, but speak them anyway. You may not remember I am with you always, but speak them anyway. Keep speaking them. I am using them to breathe life into you, just as with the dry bones in the desert I will breathe My life into you. I will open your grave and bring you out of it. My Spirit will be in you and live through you. My words of life are breathed by My Spirit who lives and moves and has His being within your heart. Do not let the desert steal this truth from you.

Behold, I am doing a new thing; now it springs forth, do you not perceive it? I will make a way in the wilderness and rivers in the desert for you, My Beloved. Have you seen the desert after the rain? It is a place of life and great beauty. Flowers where there was only sand. Animals who had remained hidden, dance in the rain. There is no starker contrast than the desert before and after the rain. I have not left you here to die. This wilderness will not kill you. It will strengthen you. It will bring out the beauty I have planted within you. Hold tight to My hand, Desert Dweller. Do not let me go and you will find your breath.

# July 22

*He heals the brokenhearted and binds up their wounds. ~Psalms 147:3*

You are not the only one with a broken heart. I know it hurts and sometimes it seems as if the brokenness of your life will never end. You feel in a desperate place and you just want the pain to stop. But I can tell you, you are not the only one. My heart is broken too. Does this surprise you, My Love?

My children are stabbing each other with words. They kill one another with guns and bombs as well. They do not recognize me in each other. They cannot see. Being blind makes My desire to show them Myself even greater, but they choose not to see. Instead they run for their lives. Into hard places and away from everything they have ever known. They flee the enemy who wants to snuff them out.

Children are going hungry. All over the world, they are doing without and starvation is rampant. Where are My people? Bickering over nothing. Considering themselves more important than the little ones who are dying daily. My heart cannot contain the pain. It spills out onto those who turn their faces to me and incline their ears to My voice.

The poor...are everywhere. Poor in material goods, poor in spirit...just poor. These have My heart. They go forward each day, with so very little. They are more content than those with much. The beggars. The widows. The orphans. The oppressed. They are desperate, too. Their hearts are broken, as they cry themselves to sleep at night. They are not so very different from you in their longing for love.

Prostitutes sell themselves to feed their children. Other slaves, without freedom, work to live. Do they wonder why? Do they question the point of slavery, or do they just do what they must to survive? The desire for life overrides their yearning for freedom. It is easier not to think of it because the pain is too great.

If you want to feel less pain from your circumstance, or your sick body, or your loss, or your addiction, or your grief, find the poor, the weary, or the refugees. They will share your load. They will show you the way to put one foot in front of the other. Truly, they will show you My broken heart. No, you are not alone. We are all with you.

# July 23

*For no good tree bears bad fruit, nor again does a bad tree bear good fruit, for each tree is known by its own fruit. For figs are not gathered from thorn bushes, nor are grapes picked from a bramble bush. The good person out of the good treasure of his heart produces good, and the evil person out of his evil treasure produces evil, for out of the abundance of the heart his mouth speaks. ~Luke 6:43-45*

Pruning is a part of the growth process, Beloved. It is painful, but necessary. I am a gardener. There is a reason My relationship with man began in a garden. There are so many parallels between the soil and the heart. The planting and the fruit. My ways are not quick, and patience is required to see growth. I want good fruit for you, Dear One. I do not want rotten fruit, so I prune. I cut back what is not needed.

I know it seems as if I am cutting back good things at times. A plant which appears to be flourishing is not always as it appears. Sometimes to continue to grow, the nutrients have to be redistributed. When the branches are cut back, it gives the nutrients new places to be absorbed. They bring what is needed to produce good fruit.

It may seem to you to be a death of sorts. It may even look like one, but I assure you there is health on the other side of pruning. Do not despair when I have to cut back in your life. It hurts, I know, but I wouldn't do it for no reason. I do it for your benefit.

Let it go. Whatever it is, I am cutting away. Trust me. I know what I am doing. I am a master gardener. I will not cut away anything that is needed to bear fruit.

# July 24

*I am the vine; you are the branches. Whoever abides in Me and I in him, he it is that bears much fruit, for apart from me you can do nothing. ~John 15:5*

Rest, O Frenzied One. I see you rushing here and there. I see your constant movement and your inability to stop the whirlwind that is your life. If you do not rest, burnout will be upon you before you know it. You are aware that rest doesn't mean standing still, right? It is not a lack of activity. No, My Child, rest is when you learn to abide in me despite all that swirls around you.

When you feel out of control of your schedule, take note. When you feel panicked and frantic, take note. The turmoil inside of you is an indicator of your need to rest. Consider it a signal that you have stepped away from me as your source. You have turned outward to look like everyone around you, in a race to nowhere.

Stop. Breathe. Take a minute or 60 and ponder. What is all your activity leading to? Is it joy? Peace perhaps? Is it a feeling of being in the center of where I want you to be? Or is it a chore, to hang on by the skin of your teeth? Learn to discern. Your life can be full and fruitful, or it can be frenzied and futile. Which one do you choose?

When you are in the center of what I have for you, there is grace for the tasks. You can be busy from sun-up to sundown and not feel overwhelmed. You can walk in each activity and know you are in the right place doing the right things. My grace hovers over you and enables you to put your hand to what I have given you to do. Even hard things seem somehow easier in this space of grace.

When you have stepped outside of what I have for you, life becomes harder. You are exhausted with each step. Even the smallest daily tasks seem heavy and you feel loaded down. Life becomes a burden. Even the good things seem to suck you dry. When this happens, it is time for a realignment. A time to sit with me and reprioritize. What is so important that you are willing to sacrifice your health and well-being? It isn't something I have chosen for you; I can tell you that. I do not create chaos. I do not give you things which run you into the ground or confuse you. I am not the author of those hardships. Did you hear me, Beloved? I am NOT the author of those events. Learn to discern.

I can help you with your plate. I can fill it. I can empty it. I can show you what to remove, if you ask me. I can put things on it that are good for you, if you let me. However, I will not help you spin it. Nor will I give you multiple plates to spin, because spinning plates only ends in broken pieces lying at your feet. My desire is *for* you, not *against* you. Slow down a minute, Frenzied One, and listen to me. Align yourself in me. Rest in me. Abide in me.

# July 25

*Have I not commanded you? Be strong and courageous. Do not be frightened, and do not be dismayed, for the Lord your God is with you wherever you go." ~Joshua 1:9*

Do you feel forsaken by me? Rejected perhaps? Is it like I have left you on your own? I promise you what you feel is not the truth, My Child. I could never leave or forsake you. It is not possible for me to deny the love I have for you in My heart. My scars prove this to be true. I could have walked away, but instead I stood firm. I took the lashes, the nails and the crown, so you would know how much I love you.

Do not be afraid of those things which seek to destroy you. I know it feels as if they have the upper hand, but that is a lie. I have already defeated them. You merely have to walk it out with me. Although it may not be easy, you know that I will not leave you and you can count on me. If you are confident that I cannot forsake you, the courage you need to face your hardships will be there. I will infuse you with it. You will walk with your head held high, as one who knows the truth. Bravery will be your clothing and it will cover you because I have wrapped you in it.

There will be tears, but they are liquid prayers. I will answer them with My own tears. When you hurt, Beloved, I hurt. When you are shaking in fear, I quiver for you. I want you to understand I am in it with you...always. Whatever the dark place, the hard place, the dry place, the fiery place...I am with you.

The terror which grasps at your throat is but a wisp of smoke and mirrors when I am with you. The giant, like Goliath, who towers over you, has nothing a few of my stones cannot take care of. The Pharaoh, who is chasing you, has no power because you have My staff of deliverance. As the one who holds your life in My hands, I cannot snuff you out, because I have already been laid upon a tree in your place. You are enveloped in courage and walk with confidence. You are My Warrior. Stand firm and KNOW that I am right beside you, in the fight, in the trenches, in the moment you most need me, I am with you.

# July 26

*For He is our God, and we are the people of His pasture, and the sheep of His hand. Today, if you hear His voice. ~Psalms 95:7*

Today is the day I have made. For you. It holds nothing you cannot handle with My grace. Nothing. There are no surprises here. Maybe for you, but not for me. Your every breath is recorded. Every hair is known. You are surrounded by My presence on this day and every day. Take a minute and feel it. Breathe it in. I am as close as your breath.

Do you trust me? Do you trust that I am in this day, no matter what it holds? Because I am. Whether it is a good day or a bad day`, I am here. The bad days try to steal your hope. They conspire against faith. They make you feel that I am not trustworthy, and plant seeds of doubt. On bad days, disastrous days, you discover what you truly believe, not just what you say you believe. Bad days are where the hashing out of your faith begins. Not a service or a ritual, but the REAL beliefs that rise to the top when things are not going your way.

Your job is to sort the truth of what I say from the lies you believe. On bad days, the lies bubble up to the surface, and My character is questioned. Did God really say__? Why didn't He stop___? Is He really for you? And this is how He shows it? What kind of God allows this? He is an abusive Father. He does not care. He is harming you. He has left you alone. This day is one He has no control over…or does He? He could make this easier for you, but He didn't. He could prevent the pain, but He won't.

Do you recognize these lies, My Child? Now listen to what I say. You are the apple of My eye. I will never leave or forsake you. My love is an everlasting love. Nothing happens without My knowledge and nothing can destroy you. I have made you and you are My beloved. I am with you, always. Even on bad days. Do not let your foe tell you differently. Do not allow him to manipulate your feelings. Feelings are fickle. They ebb and flow based on circumstances. While they are sometimes glorious and euphoric, they are not always reliable because of the way they change constantly.

I do not change. I am faithful. I am steadfast. I am love. I am compassion. I am holy. I am trustworthy. I AM. I am in you, am I not?  Therefore, you ARE. You are all the things I am. We are united, even on the bad days. When we are together in spirit, bad days become good ones. Maybe not in the emotions, but in the REAL beliefs…the honest heart to heart where you cry out to me…that is a good day. A very good day indeed.

# July 27

*Cast all your anxieties on Him, because He cares for you. ~1 Peter 5:7*

Worry does not become you, My Love. I know it is easy to do, without even thinking about it. However, to allow your mind to give way to unease, to dwell on the negative, to rehearse calamity in your thoughts will not assist you in your life. Trust me on that. The cares of this world will weigh you down and cause you to feel defeated. Is it any wonder? There are so many cares! But if you cast your cares on me you will find peace for your soul. It sounds simple, doesn't it? So why then, do so many of My children find it so difficult? Do you not know what worry does to you?

Worrying is one of the most toxic activities in which you can participate. It steals your health, as most diseases are rooted in the soil of anxiety. They fester there until the sprout begins to grow and the roots begin to spread to all of the bodily systems. That is not how I designed it. And mentally, when your mind replays scenes from the past or imagines them in the future, the repetition crowds out the good thoughts and encouragement. It is like an old road with ruts in it; the deeper they go, the harder it is to get out of them.

So how do you get unstuck from worry? Change your thought patterns. To do that you must learn My thoughts and My ways. I clothe the lilies of the field. I feed every sparrow. I put the stars in the sky. There is not one aspect of creation that I am not aware of, to the smallest detail. Do you think I do not know your problems? Of course, I know them...but I also know you. You are known in the deep places and loved immeasurably more than you realize. Every thought you think is of utmost importance to me, because you are valuable. My desire is for you to know how much care I take with you. The mindset of a victim is not how I want you to feel, like being in a loop of anxiety. It leads nowhere.

Trust Me with your thoughts. Get help if you need to retrain them. Read My words to you over and over again, until you begin to think like me. I talk about worry and anxiety more than any other topic because it is an obstacle for My children more than any other thing. All the stuff stuck in your head is holding you back. It is not as important as it feels. Take a risk. Step out and believe what I say. It will be transformative.

# July 28

*You gave them bread from heaven for their hunger and brought water for them out of the rock for their thirst, and you told them to go in to possess the land that you had sworn to give them. ~Nehemiah 9:15*

You are a warrior. I know sometimes it doesn't feel like it. Your picture of a warrior is one of bravery, strength, and running into the battle with sword drawn. Sometimes that image is a true one, but not all warriors run into the fray. Some sit back and plan. Some supply those who are in the battle. Some think of strategy. There are many kinds of warriors, and not all of them look like what is depicted in the movies. The courage and bravado don't always overflow with a battle cry.

Often courage is in the day-to-day continuation of breathing in and out, or walking step by step. Sometimes bravery is looking at the fear in front of you and moving towards it instead of away. There are days when loss hangs over you like a shroud, and you choose to get out of bed anyway. That is when you are a warrior.

A warrior is one who engages in conflict between two opposing sides. One side wants what is best for you: health, joy, fulfillment, and purpose. The other side wants you to be miserable, angry, sad, and ultimately to see you destroyed. You are on the side that fights for your survival. I am on that side too. Anything you do to keep moving forward is an act of war. Some days it might be getting out of bed. Others it might be putting on your armor and facing the enemy with a fire in your eyes. There are many ways to do battle, My Love. Not all of them are forceful. Some are holding the ground.

I know you feel weak. I know you feel you are not cut out for battle. I know you watch champions of the faith and feel less than qualified to stand with them. However, in My realm things are upside down. The weak are the strong. The quiet are powerful. The warriors are on their knees. Do not let this backwards view confuse you. Are you moving? You are a warrior. Are you showing up every day? You are a warrior. Anything you do that fights against your destruction is a battle in the war for your soul.

Anything you do that encourages another to continue fighting is a strategic move. Your feet move in the rhythm of My grace, stepping one in front of another. Your hands reach out in mercy, wiping tears and holding hands. Your eyes express compassion when they see pain. Your mouth speaks hope into hopelessness. Your ears hear My voice and the whispered hurts of others. Your heart is heavy, but not too heavy to feel My love and to share it.

Each day is another chance to be My agent of healing and grace. Each day you receive from me enough strength for the day ahead of you. No more, no less. It is like the manna of old. Gather what you need for today. Share it freely because you know there will be plenty again tomorrow. If you don't know that, you will find out as you give yours away. It will multiply. You, My Warrior, will not stand alone. You will be a part of an army of those who fight to survive against an enemy of destruction. Do not join him in his quest; instead, keep breathing, keep stepping, keep falling to your knees, My Powerful One. You will find me there and your weakness will become strength.

# July 29

*Finally, brothers, whatever is true, whatever is honorable, whatever is just, whatever is pure, whatever is lovely, whatever is commendable, if there is any excellence, if there is anything worthy of praise, think about these things.*
*~Philippians 4:8*

Does confusion rule your days? Or maybe you don't have any idea the way forward in your life. I am not the author of confusion. No, the enemy is the one who throws all the mixed-up thoughts at you. He tries to shroud your mind with opposing ideas until you are in a whirlwind of frustration and you cannot see your way forward. His goal is to paralyze you. He wants you stuck, so you cannot move. If you do not move, he doesn't have to worry about your life's work being completed.

I have gifted you and called you for such a time as this. You are uniquely made by me, for this time. You have something the world needs. It is powerful. It can be small, such as being kind to others. Or it can be big, like inventing the cure for cancer. In fact, I would say that the small things are the big things. Big things are made up of a line of small ones. If you are confused, start small.

Can you do something kind for someone today? Try it. You will begin to see more clearly. What are the things you love? Working with your hands? Snuggling with a baby? Creating beautiful music? Cooking for a crowd? I have given you these passions. Begin to use them, and the way will make itself clear.

Of course, daily obligations will still require your attention. You have to pay the bills. And that means you have to have a job, or source of income. You live in Caesar's world and it is one of commerce. However, even in that world, there is room for your gifts. Especially in that world.

You bring a smile. You shine My light. You make a difference, not by what you do, but by who you are. So, who are you? The lift in someone's day? The reminder of hope? The encourager? These are the small things that are really the big things. They are the things that begin to get the wheels turning. They are the oil in stuck gears. Look around you. Where can you add light to your current place? Add it. Look for those who have no one, and be the light. Share your lunch. Give a kind word. Before you know it, you will feel better. Then life will not seem so dark and confusing. Remember who I have created you to be. The more in tune you become with what I say about you and the ways I have gifted you, the more you will walk out of the confusion.

My love gives you a sound mind, but only if you recognize it and seek it out. What are you putting in your head? What thoughts do you feed? The world wants you to feed fear, anxiety, anger, discouragement, and negativity, so the clouds of confusion swirl in your mind. It is the opposite of what you need to dwell on.

# July 30

*For you formed my inward parts; you knitted me together in my mother's womb. I praise you, for I am fearfully and wonderfully made. Wonderful are your works; my soul knows it very well. My frame was not hidden from you, when I was being made in secret, intricately woven in the depths of the earth. Your eyes saw my unformed substance; in your book were written, every one of them, the days that were formed for me, when as yet there was none of them. How precious to me are your thoughts, O God! How vast is the sum of them! ~Psalms 139:13-17*

I am a star-breathing God. When I speak, whole worlds are created. When I said, "Let there be light," there was, and the Universe is still expanding because I never said stop. The heavens, the Earth, the animals, the birds...all of it, came about upon My word. So, My Love, if I spoke you into existence in the secret place of your mother's womb, how can you doubt your worth? If I deemed you worthy of life, why do you sometimes show disdain for yourself? You revile your body. You complain about your hair. You despise your lack of certain abilities, but do not give yourself credit for your gifts.

Your complaints are disheartening to me. By My hand and by My word you were created, you are as valued as any mountain, star, or sea. You are as unique as every bird, raindrop, or snowflake. The combination of and complexity of you is a work of art. Every single thing about you is individual. You are made in My image, so every complaint, every criticism, every murmur against yourself is an accusation of me. Did you know that? By having a low opinion of yourself, you are questioning My choice to create you.

The pain in My heart when you do not see your worth cannot be measured. My Son died to show you your value, and yet you persist in trying to convince me and others that you are somehow flawed. It is simply not true, but the more you speak negativity over yourself, the more you believe it. The more you believe it, the less you believe me. It is a slippery slope. Before long, you dread looking in the mirror. You want to avoid seeing your image...which is My image. You avoid having your picture taken. You hide yourself whenever possible. You wonder what it would be like to be more beautiful or handsome. You long to be noticed and sought after, and somehow that is tied to your appearance.

Beloved, I seek after you. I long to be with you, as you are. In all your glory. Make no mistake, you glow with glory. How could you not? You are a masterpiece I have created. There is NONE like you. Why would you desire to be someone else, when there is NONE like you? If you could change yourself into someone else, you would be less than you are right now. Because, as you are now, you are a priceless treasure.

You are rare because you are one of a kind. Imagine discovering an excellently crafted piece of furniture, or an exquisite piece of art that is the only one of its kind and its value is enormous...because there is only one. You are the only one like you. That means you are of utmost value. See yourself through My eyes. Look deep into the mirror and into your own eyes and see me there. I am in you, and if you look, you will see me. Read My words and see them through My eyes.

# July 31

*Humble yourselves, therefore, under the mighty hand of God so that at the proper time He may exalt you, casting all your anxieties on Him, because He cares for you. Be sober-minded; be watchful. Your adversary the devil prowls around like a roaring lion, seeking someone to devour. Resist him, stand firm in your faith. ~1 Peter 5:6-9*

What are you carrying today? The cares of the world? Is your burden heavy? Do you wonder and worry? About your job, your children, your parents, your friends, your bills, your future, your mistakes... How long will you live in anxiety? Do you feel as if you are drowning? Head under, breathing through a straw?

Allow me to throw you a rope. Seek me and you will find me, and when you find me you will know that I care for you. Every hair on your head is numbered. Every breath is tallied. Every thought counted for. If I know you this intimately, don't you think I know all these details of your life?

I know how you worry, but so does the enemy. He knows he can plant thoughts which will keep you up at night. He is lazy. He'd rather not have to harass you constantly, so he sows seeds which he knows will grow in your mind. Then he can sit back and let your thoughts do the work of devouring you. It is a brilliant strategy on his part, to let his enemies destroy themselves. My Love, don't let him do that to you. Resist those thoughts. Replace them with My thoughts towards you.

I know sometimes life is overwhelming. So much so, that you cannot even bring yourself to think past the rolling turmoil in your head. In those moments, be assured I am not silent. I am calling to you. I am reminding you of your secure place where all things work for your good. Reminding you that I have walked where you walk, before you. My Son carried the burden of anxiety...to the cross. He could go to that place because He knew on the other side of the tomb, I could bring you life. Freedom from all that threatens you. It was worth it to set you free. It was our plan all along for you to be free from the taunting of the enemy. He has merely started the thoughts churning, and I can stop them...if you will let me. Look to me and know that I will lift your head. I will raise your eyes off of your worries and set them on hard-bought freedom. Do not deny me that free gift to you, Beloved. Relinquish your bothersome thoughts and receive My peace of mind.

# August 1

*He answered and said, "But I see four men unbound, walking in the midst of the fire, and they are not hurt; and the appearance of the fourth is like a Son of the gods." Then Nebuchadnezzar came near to the door of the burning fiery furnace; he declared, "Shadrach, Meshach, and Abednego, servants of the Most High God, come out and come here! Then Shadrach, Meshach, and Abednego came out from the fire. And the satraps, the prefects, the governors, and the king's counselors gathered together and saw that the fire had not had any power over the bodies of those men. The hair of their heads was not singed, their cloaks were not harmed, and no smell of fire had come upon them. ~Daniel 3:25-27*

Sometimes life is a furnace. The flames lick your feet and you think you will die if it gets any hotter. When another stressor is added to an already flaming fire, it seems like I have abandoned you. You look everywhere for relief. You long for a rescue, and you beg for it. It's not that I don't hear you, Beloved. I do, because I am standing with you in the fire. All the stuff that rises to the surface when you are in the fire is the stuff I am scraping off. The dross, they call it.

In metals, there are impurities which decrease the value. They are embedded within the solid lump. When heat is added to the point of becoming liquid, the impurities float right to the top. When working with molten gold, which glows, the impurities are black and they stand out. As they come to the surface, the craftsman can carefully wipe them away, gently trying not to remove any of the gold along with it. By increasing the heat again, even more impurities...ones that were hidden inside...move up to the top to be scraped off.

Once again, the heat is increased until the gold is glowing almost red. Once again, more dross floats to the surface. Just when you think there can be no more impurities, the heat is turned up. The amount of junk in the gold is unbelievable...until you see the finished product. It is stunning in its beauty. It glows and shines with a clarity that only the craftsman knew was in the original lump. He can see himself in it.

You are like that metal. The pressures of life turn up the heat. The dross rises. I scrape it off. Life throws more and more at you. I continue to stand with you in the fire and remove the gunk that shows up. I know the pressure and the heat are difficult. I know there are times you feel you cannot handle any more. You are right. You cannot. But I can. Do you trust me? Do you believe I am shaping and purifying? You are valuable. The things that hold you back have to be removed, and the fire is the easiest way.

# August 2

*For a people shall dwell in Zion, in Jerusalem; you shall weep no more. He will surely be gracious to you at the sound of your cry. As soon as He hears it, He answers you. And though the Lord give you the bread of adversity and the water of affliction, yet your teacher will not hide Himself anymore, but your eyes shall see your teacher. ~Isaiah 30:19-20*

Walk on. Have you been betrayed? Walk on. Has disappointment crowded in? Walk on. Has a bully gotten to you? Walk on. Have you crashed someone else's expectations of you? Walk on.

People in life have a way of knocking you down, over and over again. A sucker punch to the gut doubles you over and steals the air from your lungs. You crash to the ground, skinning your knees and hands, face down in the dirt. It may be real, or it may be figurative, but it certainly feels physical when you are caught off guard by a supposed friend turned enemy. When words are hurled at you that you cannot believe, they are like blows which bruise your soul. It can be a friend or family member or a stranger. It can be a pastor or a teacher. It can be a spouse or a child. Anyone you thought was for you, but turns against you, becomes can a bully. Betrayal is one of the most traumatic experiences you can weather.

It can crush your weary spirit like fighting with a heavyweight. The hardest part is when you don't see it coming. Surprise attacks are the most dangerous because it takes you awhile to figure out what is happening. Your mind cannot grasp the punches and it grapples to make sense of things.

Beloved, before you rise up, take a moment down there on your knees to seek My face. These life blows can cripple you if you let them fester. Those skinned hands and knees, the black eyes, and the aching ribs will make you bitter. You will dwell on how others have wronged you and you will feel justified in your unforgiveness. It is a bitterness which poisons you and leaves you sulking in the dirt. There are so many who never rise from the places they were victimized. They get stuck there, wallowing and licking their wounds.

The wounds are real, My Love. They are bloody and messy. They cannot be ignored, so when I say walk on, I do not mean disregard your pain. No, the pain has to be attended to. While you are on your knees invite me in to begin your healing. Let me pour antiseptic on your wound and scrub out the dirt. It will hurt, but it is necessary for complete healing to let me dig out the infection before it spreads. Let me see the tears. Let me feel your hurt. Bring it to me and let me minister My grace to you.

Once I have cleaned it, let me cover it with a healing balm. Allow yourself time; you took quite a beating. But once we have dealt with the internal wound and we have processed the pain, it is time to rise.

Get up. Brush yourself off. Forgive. Walk on. Do not look to the right or the left. Do not look back. Focus your eyes on me. Listen to My voice. Put blinders on so you will not be pulled into the trap again. I am the one who tells you the truth about yourself. Listen to me. Plug your ears to those who wag their tongues against you. Trust that I know what it is like to be beaten with words, and even more so My body. I can carry you through this kind of pain. I can help you to your feet. I can teach you to move forward again so you can walk on.

Do not let these kinds of attacks harden your heart. Do not protect your heart in the future by covering it with armor. No, leave it open to others. The only way to do that in a healthy way is to trust me. I will give you discernment regarding your heart. It is a treasure to me, and I do not want it pummeled again. Focus on My words to you so that the hurtful words of others do not hurt and then...walk on.

# August 3

*And the angel of the Lord appeared to him and said to him, "The Lord is with you, O mighty man of valor." But the Lord said to him, "Peace be to you. Do not fear; you shall not die." ~Judges 6:12, 23*

Hello, Victorious One. Yes. I am talking to you. I know you don't feel like one who walks in victory, but you are. Each morning you wake up is an act of defeating the enemy. Each breath you take is a statement of life. Oh, I know there are days where it is all you can do to swing your feet out of the bed. Do not let that discourage you; instead view it as a gift. Every time you choose to move forward instead of cowering back, no matter how small the effort, you are walking in victory. You see, if you had strength enough in yourself, you would not appreciate your health. You would not recognize your need of me. You would feel you could handle anything life throws at you on your own. But to walk in areas where you feel easily overcome, places where your strength fails you, is to walk dependent on me.

Think of Gideon. He was fearful. He was weak. He didn't believe he could do anything, and he wasn't sure I could either! He tested me many times before he trusted what I told him to do. Yet, I called him Mighty Warrior from the beginning. I saw something in him, which he could not see in himself. I called it out of him. I do the same for you, Victorious One. You may not believe me. You might require evidence of My ability to speak victory into your life because you have felt un-victorious for so long. But I promise you, I know what I am talking about. I know you have victory living inside of you. I know it can overflow into your days and your actions.

How do I know this? I have set you upon the earth for such a time as this. I know what you need. I know what you can do with me at your side. I will route your enemies. Every time you inhale, you will defy the plan the enemy has against you. It is that simple. Living is victory. Living to your fullest is your most effective weapon. It shows those around you that you are not caving in. You are not giving up. It is inspiring.

Did you know that in getting out of bed each day you could be an inspiration to others? It's the truth. To be seen and known is to be victorious. No matter what state you are in, if you share yourself with others you will cease to be a victim and become a victor. If you look at yourself as I look at you, you will see the truth. So, let me call you by your name. Do not disagree with me on this. You are My Victorious One.

# August 4

*For He Himself is our peace, who has made us both one and has broken down in His flesh the dividing wall of hostility by abolishing the law of commandments expressed in ordinances, that He might create in Himself one new man in place of the two, so making peace. ~Ephesians 2:14-15*

The world you live in doesn't make sense, Dear One. Trying to wrap your head around why things happen the way they do will not be helpful. It is a sin-filled world with an enemy who has been given free reign. Logic and reason can't make sense out of such things. It is so very far from what I created it to be, yet I cannot walk away from it. I will not. Even if My creation abandons me, I will not abandon it. When My children choose freely to walk away it breaks My heart. When they choose pain over healing, or bondage over freedom, it is hard for me to understand, too. Why won't they choose me? Do they not know I am for them? Do they not know I can make them whole?

Instead, they choose to lash out at each other. They choose crime. They choose drugs. They choose toxic relationships. They choose hate. They choose any number of things to numb themselves, only they don't realize in choosing those things they give the enemy more of a foothold, not just in their lives, but in the earth as a whole. Then, the ones called by My name live in a darker and darker world, trying to logically figure out the whys of daily struggles, which are really age-old tactics which have run amuck. It is mind boggling to see how far things have fallen since the garden.

You must know that *why* is the wrong question. Why never has an answer. It seeks to place blame. Finger pointing and blaming keeps the focus off of the real question. It is a diversion. The real question is *what*. What do you do now? What can you learn? What is My role in your own life? Do you find someone to blame or do you make the most of the hard things? I am not saying it is easy, but if you shift your focus from the situation in which you find yourself, to what you can gain from it, the burden will lighten. If you give me control as best you know how, I will come in to help you. The ways of the world are such that you will always have trouble, but I have made a way out. Not for the future in heaven, when you come to be with me, but for now while we are yet apart.

Seek me and you will find me. Seek only cognitive answers and you will find none that make sense fully. The enemy is playing not only a mental game, but also a spiritual one. If he can keep you believing it is simply about having more understanding and knowledge and who is to blame, he can keep you in shackles. Don't trust your own understanding; it is not dependable. Trust in me. Look to me. Read My words, for they are My heart. Listen to My voice. Then you will live *in* the world, but not *of* it.

# August 5

*And when they had prayed, the place in which they were gathered together was shaken, and they were all filled with the Holy Spirit and continued to speak the word of God with boldness. ~Acts 4:31*

When the world is shaken, hold your ground. The truth doesn't have to be proven. It will remain while all else groans and shakes. Sometimes it doesn't feel secure around you and then you realize what you truly believe. When circumstances happen that are beyond understanding, will you cling to me? When world events don't make sense, will you still believe in me? The earthquake moments in life shake off all that is not grounded. The things that fall are the things that are not important.

Sometimes it is hard to know the difference between the big things in life and the little things. When tremors begin to shake things up, the difference between them becomes clear. Conversations with loved ones are the big things. Hope, faith, joy...all big things. Job is a small thing. Money, ambition, stuff...all small things. Usually the times your world is rocked, things turn upside down and it is difficult to wrap your mind around it. Give yourself grace. Stand still and hold the space.

Making too many changes in life can be overwhelming, especially if they are beyond your control. Start slowly. Wait for the shaking to end first, then walk with me to put things back together. You will decide some things can be tossed. Some things will need to be repaired to be used again. Others will shine like the morning sun once they are cleaned of the dust. You will find you had treasure all along, but didn't even know it until it was knocked loose.

After an earthquake, you will know how close I am to you. You will feel My heartbeat for you. You will see others through My eyes. The scary times of shaking unify you with My truth. The false things you have believed, the lies, fall away. Leave them on the ground. Do not pick them back up to carry again, once things are still again.

Hold tightly to what you learn in a quake. Once you have the truth, it cannot be taken from you. Walking in intimacy with me solidifies the experiences and makes them forever lessons. They are integrated and carved into your heart forever. No one can steal them from you because you experienced these lessons in the midst of hardship. They go from theoretical to real. Real things will remain. They have staying power.

# August 6

*I thank you that you have answered me and have become my salvation. ~Psalms 118:21*

Beloved, My answers don't always look the way you thought they would. Sometimes they are harder to accept, and others are a breath of fresh air. It is because I have other people in mind besides you. I am working on many levels all the time. None of the answers I send are to harm you. I want you to know that. I want you to understand that each part of My plan is for your good and My glory.

In your world, you define hardships as an answer that means I am somehow against you. Nothing could be further from the truth. Hardships are a mixture of your choices, the choices of others, the plan of the enemy, and My plan all rolled into one. They are the defining moments of your life. They are when the growth spurts are the highest. Do not underestimate the power of hardships to create change in you. They shape you and give you compassion for anyone who experiences anything similar. I do not cause them, but I certainly use them for your benefit.

Other answers are gloriously wonderful. It seems the stars align and everything falls into place. Those are the happy times when you feel My favor, but make no mistake, you always have My favor. Good times are not related to good performance, nor are bad times related to bad performance on your part. Do not try to simplify your relationship to me in this way. I am not a performance related God. I am a God of grace. I am a God who gives generously despite the circumstance in which you find yourself.

If you have been pummeled by life, do not wait for the other shoe to drop when something goes right. I know it is hard to just receive the good things without wondering when they will end, or when the truth will be revealed that the good thing wasn't really for you. I know you question every good thing with suspicion. But Beloved, I long for you to have good things. I long for your bread to be something other than pain and hardship. You must believe this about me.

I do not sit and wait to give you something you prayed for only to pull it out from under you. That would be cruelty to My children. I am not an abusive father, no matter what thoughts the enemy puts in your head. I want the best for My kids just as all parents do. Sometimes that looks like the perfect answer at the perfect time. Other times the answer seems far away or like there is no answer at all. No need to question, I am for you and want to bless you beyond what you can imagine. Let me.

# August 7

*You have captivated my heart, my sister, my bride; you have captivated my heart with one glance of your eyes, with one jewel of your necklace. ~Song of Solomon 4:9*

I am proud to be seen with you. Does that surprise you? It shouldn't. You are My creation, uniquely made exactly as I planned. A work of art. Really, I mean it. You are not a disappointment to me. I am not embarrassed or ashamed of you. I would gladly take you anywhere and be happy to be by your side.

I love it when you talk about me and tell others what I mean to you. It is a joy for me to know your feelings are deep and real. When you show compassion, I smile. When you are faithful, I rejoice. Each part of you makes me happy. Every time you walk in who I have made you to be, it brings me joy.

I know you don't see these things. You focus on your flaws. You hold onto your mistakes. You think I couldn't possibly love you because of these things. What you need to know is, I couldn't NOT love you. It is impossible for you to shake me. I see those areas as places of growth. Places that will be worked out over time. You know them, and so do I, but I do not see them as something to be ashamed of. Instead, I see them as part of the complexity of who you are and who you will be. They are the layers that make the painting more beautiful. The places you need to walk out of, only add to the beauty of the overall piece.

You have stolen My heart. One glance of your eyes has grabbed it and will not let it go. When you look at me, I am undone. When you seek me, I am enamored. I long to be with you. I am transfixed by you, and abundantly blessed that you take an interest in me. You and I belong together. Do not let the decisions you have made keep you from me. My forgiveness is complete and it cleanses you. You need only to receive it. Then you will know My love for you isn't dependent on perfection. I could have made you perfect from the beginning, but I chose not to. Instead, I chose messy for the texture. I chose colorful for the variety. I chose muted tones for the contrast. I know what I am doing with you. Trust me, won't you? Step out with Me and allow Me to display My work in you. I am so very proud of you.

# August 8

*Behold, I am doing a new thing; now it springs forth, do you not perceive it? I will make a way in the wilderness and rivers in the desert. ~Isaiah 43:19*

I am doing a new thing for you, Desert Dweller. You have been in a dry place...parched with no life-giving water to soothe your thirst. A new season is upon you. Can you see it? Where there has been drudgery, there will be action. Where there has been a void, you will be filled up. Something fresh is coming your way. The motivation you have lacked due to the dry place will return to you. There is hope again.

There are seasons in life just as there are in nature. The drought seasons will always come...but only for a time. The rains follow the drought and with them come the flowers and the fruit. Growing things. Life. The question is, do you see it? Since these are spiritual places, they are not visible to the eye, but the heart knows. Can you feel your heart beating with hope? Can you see a new place of health and wholeness? It waits for you.

When you are in the desert, the eyes of your heart play tricks on you. The lack of the water of My Spirit changes your viewpoint and causes mirages. You see things that are not there. Things as you wish them to be. But when the desert turns out to be different than you thought a heaviness sets in and doubt takes root. You wonder how you ever believed something so beautiful could be in the desert. However, when the seasons change, and the floods come, the beauty of the desert comes alive. The place you thought was going to kill you, springs to life to greet you. The harsh places are soon covered with green plants and they flourish.

Your heart is going to flourish in this new place. The dry parched places will fade in your memory, but will always be noted for their ability to change your perspective. The garden that springs forth in the deep places of your soul will bring beauty, peace, and comfort. You will no longer crawl, begging for water. You will skip and dance in the new season I am providing for you. You will no longer be in the wasteland. The wilderness will fall away. Should you ever return to this hard place, you will remember it is survivable. You will wait for me to deliver you because I always do. I will not leave you to die in the desert, My Love. I will pour out My blessings on you and do a new thing!

# August 9

*Therefore, the Lord waits to be gracious to you, and therefore He exalts Himself to show mercy to you. For the Lord is a God of justice; blessed are all those who wait for Him. ~Isaiah 30:18*

The word on my heart today is surrender. Is that so hard to do? Just put your hands up and give up trying so very hard to do it all yourself. Surrender has a bad connotation in the world. It means to submit to another. To cease resistance. Beloved, when you work to make things work in your own strength you are battling me, not the enemy. As long as you are laboring, I will wait. Yes, I will wait for you. I sit with My hands tied while you strain to carry it all on your own. It is only when you lay it down that I move on your behalf. I long to take your burden from you. You were not meant to carry it alone.

Weary One, there is a difference between carrying a burden and bearing a burden. Carrying is the act of lifting something and moving it to a different place. Bearing refers to supporting a load. You can bear a burden if I am the one carrying it. I do the heavy lifting and you support me. Whenever you attempt to carry, you will be weighed down. Life will feel heavy because it will be. When you release your burden to me, it doesn't mean the hard times disappear. Not at all. It simply means I will carry the brunt of the load. It makes room for My grace to lift your shoulders.

If you do things in your own strength, you will think it is up to you. You will look at your circumstance and say 'look what I have done' or 'look at what I have to do.' But when you surrender it to me, you will know you are not carrying it. You will still feel the weight, but because you are bearing instead of carrying, it will not be heavy. The worry and fret which roll around in your mind will get quiet. My grace will surround you in the midst of it. When you wait for me, I will come. It will be a shared burden.

You will not be striving any longer. You will allow My strength to operate in your weakness. You will know it is not up to you anymore because when you surrender to me, you are giving up control. It is then that I step in and move. It is then My glory is made known and I shine through you. You cut yourself loose from the heavy things and you raise your hands to me. I will lift you, and your burden, to Myself. My heart will burst with the willingness to help My child in need. It will look differently in different situations, but My help is limitless. I am the Bearer of Burdens.

# August 10

*For God, who said, "Let light shine out of darkness," has shone in our hearts to give the light of the knowledge of the glory of God in the face of Jesus Christ. ~2 Corinthians 4:6*

You are a carrier of My glory. It's true! Your body is made of flesh and bone. It is corruptible and frail in comparison to My Spirit that lives within you. I have made it that way on purpose. You are a container for a triune God. I know that sounds complicated, but it is simpler than you think. You are a triune person with your body, mind, and spirit. We are a triune God - Father, Son, and Spirit. When we come to inhabit you, at your request, everything aligns perfectly.

You see, your humanness results in imperfection and brokenness. It wasn't always that way, but living in a fallen world shrouds everything I created and causes it to decay. Yet, when you allow me to put the pieces back together, I create a masterpiece which is defined by the cracks. In shining My light through them, the light within is glorious. You shouldn't try to hide your broken pieces. Bring them to me and let me build you. I can take the ick and make it part of the tapestry that is your life. You can be torn apart, brokenhearted, depressed, or lonely. You can be angry, sick, or overwhelmed. It may feel like it, but you will not be destroyed. You walk in the dark places of life, the unexplainable ones, and you survive them. Why is that? How is it you feel like you cannot make it one more day, but you do?

It is My life that pumps in your veins. It is My breath in you that holds you together. It is My presence that holds you up. You are not alone, or forgotten. You are broken, sure, but so was My Son. His body torn, but My glory was revealed through Him. And it will be through you as well.

# August 11

*The name of the Lord is a strong tower; the righteous man runs into it and is safe.*
*~Proverbs 18:10*

I am your refuge. When you need a place to rest and recover from life, it is me. I hide you under My feathers, like a bird covers her chick. When you feel desolate, choose me. When you feel sad, choose me. When you are pressured from without, choose me. When you are pressured from within, choose me. When your grief overtakes you, choose me.

In hard places, it seems trouble has found you and surrounds you on every side. In those moments, it is hard to remember you still have a choice. It seems every choice has been made for you. You do not always choose your circumstances. Grief finds you. Broken hearts happen to you. Illnesses show up. Oppression is real. Most times these foes arrive unannounced. They turn your world upside down and in just a moment, everything changes. Everything...but me.

I am always the same. I do not change and you always have a choice to seek me as your refuge. I will always understand. I will always relate and get it. There is nothing that escapes My experience. I have felt what you feel. My Son's human experience was varied and the full range of brokenness and pain was spilled onto Him. His faithfulness is your shield. His steadfastness, your hiding place.

Fear does not become you, Beloved. It hangs over you like a cloud waiting to spill a downpour. You tremble with the load you carry. Your mind churns at all the invisible possibilities. It causes your focus to be on all the things that could go wrong. At every turn, you see the worst. Do not be afraid. Let me protect you. I will be your dwelling, a place you can abide. I will lift you up and encourage you. I will have My angels take watch over you. I will make you an overcomer.

There are so many complex and elaborate choices on your mind, yet My choice is quite simple. It is plain and straightforward. Take My hand and let me lead you to My tower of safety. Run with me out of the fray and into the quiet of My sanctuary. It is a place of rest. A place I will hide you from the enemy. Please, let me take you there. It is your choice, in the midst of all that life throws at you. Take My hand.

# August 12

*Christ redeemed us from the curse of the law by becoming a curse for us—for it is written, "Cursed is everyone who is hanged on a tree"— so that in Christ Jesus the blessing of Abraham might come to the Gentiles, so that we might receive the promised Spirit through faith. ~Galatians 3:13-14*

So many times, Weary One, you feel unworthy. Unworthy of love. Unworthy of life. Unworthy of blessings. The enemy has convinced you that you cannot approach me and therefore, you steer clear. You feel somehow less than; you cower and shrink back from me, instead of standing tall...in your imperfection.

I am aware of my flawlessness. There was a time I had to keep separated from you because of it. But that was only until the cross, when My Son took the imperfection upon Himself, so you could stand unashamed before me. Yet, it seems like you don't really believe it. You are caught up in the old trap of how unworthy you are. Fortunately, it is not up to you to determine your worthiness. It is up to me, and I deem you worthy.

After you lose your temper, I deem you worthy. After you disappoint yourself, I deem you worthy again. After you make a mistake or a bad decision or hurt a friend or lie, I deem you worthy again. Again. Again. Again. My love isn't conditional, Dear One. Your behavior or actions do not keep me from loving you.

Instead of bringing all your broken pieces to me directly, you avoid me. My love is pure, and shines a light on all the dark and dirty places in your heart. Standing in front of me, with no way to answer for yourself, you have to allow My love to wash over you. It is a humbling thing. A cleansing thing.

To resist My love sends you into hiding, holding onto your shame like a cloak. You think it is keeping your wounds invisible, but the opposite is true. Shame highlights the crevices where the pain resides. It pulls the scab off and pours salt into your wound, refusing to allow healing. The whispers of shame drip with how unworthy you are and...you listen.

Instead listen to the voice of your RE-deemer. The one who deems you worthy, again. I can redeem time wasted. I can redeem relationships ruined. I can redeem death into life. You may not believe me when I tell you, but look around you. There are others. They have stories of redemption. They glow with the pure love I poured over them when they brought their shame into My light.

Weary One, I want to redeem you. I want you to receive all I have for you. I deem you worthy of it all...again.

# August 13

*I love you, O Lord, my strength. The Lord is my rock and my fortress and my deliverer, my God, my rock, in whom I take refuge, my shield, and the horn of my salvation, my stronghold. ~Psalms 18:1-2*

Beware of burnout. It's a real thing. The world you live in creates it. The constant running on a hamster wheel wears you down. Day after day of busyness causes exhaustion, physically, but also mentally and emotionally. Remember you are a triune being, so stress in one area of life can affect all areas.

Burnout is different from stress. Stress is temporary and circumstantial. Once the situation has changed, it relents. Burnout is when stress becomes unending and it beats you down to a state of numbness. Your over-caring shorts out your motivation. Burnout happens when My grace for the task has lifted. Life becomes difficult and you live in exhaustion. The joy of My call to a task is gone, replaced by cynical, painful hard work.

However, this is not the only kind of burnout, Beloved. There is a kind which is beyond job/ministry satisfaction. Sometimes you can be burned out on life. This is an entirely different kind of issue, and it is on the increase in your world. You are burned out on grief. You are burned out on loss. You are burned out on chronic illness. You are burned out on relationships. You are burned out on parenting your prodigals. You are burned out by the oppression of your people. You are burned out on caring for so many.

Life itself is overwhelming. At first, it is painful, but as burn out increases you succumb to numbness...or you artificially create it. Emotions are cut off because they hurt too badly to feel them. Mentally, thoughts are in a downward spiral. Physical exhaustion is the norm. Beware of this kind of burn out because it leads nowhere good.

I am the remedy. When you look up, you can see My light, but for it to cut through the darkness you have to look up regularly. The circumstances around you make you feel as if you are going to drown, so don't study them. Look up. Sometimes just by looking at me, everything changes even though nothing has changed. It is one of My mysteries. A change in viewpoint.

For those who walk in circumstances which will always be challenging, you must find me in the midst. It is the only way. Come to me. Rest. Wait for me to show up, because I do. Every. Single. Time. If you look My way, I can be found. I will infuse you with thankfulness for the blessings that burnout has tried to get you to overlook. I will pour kindness into you for those who walk a similar road as you. I will give you a place to rest, even when the activity in your life is constant. I will bring others across your path so you do not feel all alone. Burnout is one of the most diabolical strategies of the enemy, because it uses your compassion against you. Your caring starts as helping others, but spirals into zapping you of your strength. Do not fall for it. Wait for me. Only take on the things I direct you to. Good things are not always God things.

Saying no sometimes allows me to raise up others for a task. It is never all on you. The thought the enemy plants make you believe that if you don't handle it, the world will fall apart. Nothing could be further from the truth. I hold the world in My hand, and nothing you can do will cause me to drop it. Trust me, My Child. Look up.

# August 14

*But He gives more grace. Therefore, it says, "God opposes the proud but gives grace to the humble." ~James 4:6*

My Child, your secrets are killing you. Do you think I am unaware of the thoughts and actions you believe to be hidden? The outside is only half of what I see. I know everything about you, and yet I love you, anyway. You do not believe it but it is true. I hate to see the turmoil you live in because of the hidden things in your life. Anxiety only increases when secrets are not exposed. You think things will only get worse if you confess your brokenness, but you are wrong. The load lifts when the light comes in. The burden will seem easy in comparison to now. Tell me your secrets and be free of them.

Sometimes the issue is that you are unaware of the things you are holding in your heart. The outside looks good, but the inside is harboring dirt. When you cannot see this dirt, I use the circumstances to show you. I will certainly tell you if you seek me out. If not, your secrets will come to light one way or another. When you belong to me, you have given me permission to work in you for your good and My glory. I am an artist who is trying to release the fullness of My creation. I shape and reshape. I smooth. I add texture and color. All of these transformations come about when the secrets are exposed.

Attitudes. Thoughts. Judgements. Self-righteousness. Pride. Superiority. All so easy to see in others, but not so much in the mirror. The enemy makes sure you never look inward on those kinds of things, but they are there, nonetheless. If they continue to be invisible to you, they will continue to hinder your freedom. The choice you have is to humble or harden your heart. I vote humble.

# August 15

*Behold, God is my salvation; I will trust, and will not be afraid for the Lord God is my strength and my song, and He has become my salvation. ~Isaiah 12:2*

You are My Dry Ground Walker. How many times have you been backed into a corner with no way out and suddenly there was a path before you? How many times have you felt you were going to drown, only to have dry ground open up for you to pass through? I do not delight when you are in hard places. My joy comes in seeing you walk through them in the way I provide for you. Deliverance is a hobby of mine and I am good at it.

So many times, when the enemy is surrounding you and things are dark and hopeless, I get the blame. It is the age-old question from way back in the garden: "Did God really say...?" The question that leads to all the others. Did He lead you here? Where is He now? Why has He left you? Who does He think he is? Is He trying to kill you? Why would He let this happen to you? The enemy always tries to make you doubt My character. He plants doubt as if there is a famine in the land. He sews the seed and he reaps a harvest, triple what he plants. You would think he would have changed tactics by now, but why would he do that when his strategy works so well?

I allow him to continue for one reason; I want to prove him wrong. I want to show My children his ploy, and deliver them. His plan is to drive you to the point of hopelessness so you will turn to him. Yet, as your enemies chase you through the desert I have already made a way of escape. Of course, I could open the sea before you arrive at it, but then it would appear to be coincidence or Karma, perhaps. No, I prefer to wait until there is no doubt where the deliverance came from. In the future, when you feel trapped again, you will believe that I will come to rescue you.

At least, I hope that you will have faith in me. What I find instead is that you need many reminders. Your memory is short, Dry Ground Walker. You can be on the other side of deliverance, having witnessed a powerful path open up before you. You can watch your enemy be swallowed up in front of your very eyes, but when the next obstacle presents itself, you worry and fret. All of your questions about My trustworthiness come flooding back, just like waves in the sea which cover your enemies.

Why is it this way? I have proven Myself a worthy deliverer over and over again. Why you listen to the enemy, instead of believing I will come through, astounds me every time. Yet I still love you. I still long to deliver you. I desire to make a way for you to go through the waters on dry ground so you will see My heart is for you, and there is no other like me who so longs to be with you. In the hard places, remember. Remember what I have done for you before. Remember how the sea opened up for you. Remember I did not lead you to a place so I could abandon you. I would never abandon you, Dry Ground Walker.

# August 16

When grief is a daily occurrence, come to me. When you are overwhelmed with a loss, come to me. The death of a child, a spouse, a parent, or a friend is beyond hard. Come to me. The world seems to be falling apart. Come to me. You think you want to be alone, but your heart needs me.

Death isn't the only kind of grief. You can grieve the loss of a friendship, or a marriage. You can grieve the changing of your roles in life. You can grieve when someone you love moves away, or when circumstances never change. You can grieve the loss of your dreams, the change in physical status, the decline of your health, or someone else's. You can grieve when things around you are uncertain and fear covers you like a blanket. Grief is a part of life, My Teary One. It isn't going anywhere, so it is best to learn to bring it to me.

Grief manifests in tears of course, but not always. It can also be exhaustion…which comes in two forms, sleeplessness or hibernation. It stalks you, trying to throw a heavy blanket over your life, like an old, abandoned house with sheets over everything, void of life, gathering dust. Grief is choking you, sitting on your chest and waiting for you to wither away. It steals your motivation, and brings sadness to you every day. Sometimes, it gets angry and refuses to relent its bitter poison.

Grief is a result of pain, but it is actually My answer to it. It may surprise you; grief was My idea. Like any parent, I wanted My kids to be pain free, but their choices led them down a different path. The loss of paradise was a huge blow. The reality of a life filled with pain was overwhelming. Having a way to process this was critical. Grief allows all of the hurt to be expressed. It takes different forms because I created complex individuals. Allowing yourself to feel is a healthy thing.

Of course, the enemy wants you to get stuck. He always takes what I intend for good and twists it. But, if you can walk through your grief instead of camping in it, you will be healthier. I designed grief to allow you to release your pain, but a key part of that process is bringing it to me. Each time it threatens to overtake you, bring it to me.

Grief doesn't go away. It is not supposed to. It is a marker that something significant was lost. A memorial of sorts, to hold the space where something important to you once was. Layers of grief will be in your life to represent the loss. However, the sharp pangs that happen at first, the struggle to get up or even to breathe, those will fade. Time doesn't heal the wound, but it does develop a beautiful scar, and that shows your depth of love. It is not a bad thing; it is the right thing. If you let me, I will help you with the deep pain. I know that pain. I have felt it. You are made in My image, remember? Therefore, you feel what I feel. It may surprise you; I feel pain. What better way to unburden your heart than to share it with another who gets it? I get it.

Bring it to me. Let me carry it with you. Let me celebrate the beauty of what was, and walk you towards what is to come. You will never leave it all behind, or get over it, because grief is what makes you who you are. And I think who you are is pretty fantastic. I don't want you to be stuck, I want you to heal so you can show others the way to let grief have its way, and still live a healthy life.

# August 17

*Blessed is the man who trusts in the Lord, whose trust is the Lord. ~Jeremiah 17:7*

My Child, what are you afraid of? Losing your home? Losing your loved? Losing your sanity? Losing your health? Losing your life? Those who have the most are usually the most afraid, because they have the most to lose. When your life becomes complicated, fear begins its work in you. Remember when you were a child and things were simple? Riding bikes down enormous hills was a thrill. Climbing to the top of the jungle gym or a tree was a challenge. Running along the road was a release. Skateboarding was the proof of skills. You didn't think of falling or getting hurt. You just did whatever it was to the fullest. There was freedom in that joy of love, even if wisdom was lacking.

But then, time brought pain with it. The first lost love brought a broken heart. The death of a friend brought grief. A broken bone brought hesitation. Your soul learned to fear. To withdraw when something was risky, to avoid taking chances. The more you grew, the more things you obtained, the more fear loomed large. You have not called it fear though. The enemy knows that would be too obvious.

No, fear disguises itself as wisdom, but you can see the truth when it whispers its questions. Is it a good idea to travel internationally? It's not really safe. Should you start your own business right now? The economy might collapse, you should wait. Changing careers this close to retirement is foolish. You can hang in there just a few more years, then you can do what you want. Do you need more insurance? What if there is a disaster and you are not prepared? Should you let your children go? They might get hurt.

These are all fear-based questions. They hold you back. They rule your mind and prevent you from stepping out in what I have for you. Trust me to be the wise one. I will give you the wisdom you need to make decisions. I am not for being reckless, but I also want you to have freedom. The chains of fear bind too many of My children.

The remedy for fear is trust. Trusting My hand to provide. Trusting My character to protect. Trusting My mind to be for you. Trusting me with your life. Knowing the simplicity of belonging to me and the innocence of stepping wherever My footsteps lead you without fear of loss. I am trustworthy, My Child. Take a step without fear and you will see how free you can be.

# August 18

*Do not let your adorning be external—the braiding of hair and the putting on of gold jewelry, or the clothing you wear— but let your adorning be the hidden person of the heart with the imperishable beauty of a gentle and quiet spirit, which in God's sight is very precious. ~1 Peter 3:3-4*

Comparison is a trap. Do not let the enemy catch you in the snare of "less than." The only way you can feel "less than" is to compare yourself to others who you deem 'more than'. Your foe is a crafty one. He uses technology to reinforce your perceptions that you are not enough...not smart enough, good looking enough, rich enough, funny enough, brave enough, or good enough. It is a lie, but you don't believe that on most days because you compare yourself to others.

These thoughts usually start with looking in the mirror at your perceived flaws. Your hair isn't like others. Your nose is too big. Your freckles too many. Your eyes too close together. Your skin is too dark, or too light. I am amazed at the smallest details you find with which to criticize yourself. Outward appearance isn't all either. You move onto your own character and attack yourself for not being generous enough, or diligent, or responsible, or kind enough. No matter what traits you have the enemy will convince you they are not the right ones, or they are less than what they should be. What strategy the enemy uses to get you to help him destroy you! He is wicked, and it never ceases to amaze me what he can convince people to do for him.

Weary One, have you ever wondered at My words of assurance that you are fearfully and wonderfully made? Full of fear doesn't seem something that would be a good trait when I was creating you, right? I mean who wants to think they struck fear into the heart of God? Yet, there is another definition, which means extremely. Or exceedingly, exceptionally, remarkably, uncommonly, extraordinarily, incredibly. It means you are a unique, well-crafted work of art...just as you are. No need for self-condemnation.

On the contrary, look in the mirror and see what I see. The exquisite, intricate detail that is you. Each freckle painted in the correct place by me. You are the right color. Every hair is numbered. The sparkle of life in your eyes was put there by My hand. When you criticize yourself, you are saying I made a mistake. I can assure you that you are NOT a mistake. I was very intentional when I created you. There is no one like you anywhere in the world. Therefore, none can compare to you nor can you compare to others. Each of you is made in My image, which is beyond your comprehension. I am wider and deeper and multifaceted than humans can imagine. It takes billions of people of all shapes and colors to even begin to touch My image.

You tire of yourself, but I never will. I knew exactly what I was doing when I created you. I know exactly why you are the way you are, and I know exactly where you belong. And you do...belong. Don't listen to lies which say otherwise. You belong to me and with me. You are My favorite. I burst out with joy when I see you and a smile comes across My face when you wake up each day. Don't forget you are beyond compare.

# August 19

*Blessed is the man who remains steadfast under trial, for when he has stood the test he will receive the crown of life, which God has promised to those who love Him. ~James 1:12*

Don't give up. I know some days you feel like it. It seems like things never change, like the circumstances you live with are never ending. I promise giving up won't help, and even though it seems like it would release the pressure, it would only be temporary. No. Quitting is not the way to go. Going through, rather than around, is the solution. Sometimes during hardship, it feels as if each day takes years. Sometimes, it is years before there is some bit of breakthrough.

These chronic ongoing broken times are exhausting. They drain you in every way possible. And honestly, there is really no way to quit; it is more of a disengagement from life, a pulling away. When you pull back, Dear One, it isn't healthy. I know when circumstances are rough it seems easier not to have to explain it all to others. It is difficult to explain what you yourself do not understand. Also, it is simpler to go it on your own, rather than to involve and converse with me. When it feels like I have abandoned you, why would you want to talk to me? You might even harbor some resentment towards me and bitterness towards those in your life who will never understand because they appear to have no issues.

Beloved, do not hold onto resentment or bitterness. If you have to quit something, quit those two attitudes. They will steal any joy you might have during this time. Your journey is uniquely yours, hardships and all. Your life is what it is because you are strong enough to handle it. You know how to dig deeply and how to hold on when things are beyond your ability. You are excellent at putting one foot in front of the other. You know to breathe, even when your head is barely above the water. You do not panic. You do not quit...even though you want to just to get some rest. You persevere. It is one of the things I most love about you. You continue to look to me, even when you don't understand, even when you are hurting. You are tenacious.

Days may be hard for you now, but it will not always be that way. Though the circumstances you are in may remain the same for a long season, the outcome of change. Your days will get easier as you adjust. Remember it is a season. And remember you are not alone. I am always with you. Do not quit; instead plow ahead, right into the middle of the pain. Lean into me and let me hold you up. I will heal your heart. I will pour My balm over you and your season of humility, of bowing down in order to survive. This season will bear lasting fruit. You will know what is important and what is petty. You will find that the things you once cared about no longer matter. Life and death will be evident. What brings you life? That is what you embrace, Precious One. Then you quit the things that suck the life out of you. Hang in there. With me, you can do anything.

# August 20

*Then they cried to the Lord in their trouble, and He delivered them from their distress. ~Psalms 107:19*

Are you in need of rescue? I am a first responder. You feel trapped or that you are sinking beyond help. The water is over your head and life is continually battering your soul. You call out to me on a bed of tears, or sometimes you just cry. My Love, your tears are your cries for help. They are liquid prayers and they speak volumes to me...more than your words ever will. Tears are honest and real prayers. They are beyond understanding of the mind, they are heart language. I am fluent in heart language. Your cries do not bounce off the ceiling, they rise to My throne. They are stored in bowls of prayers which emit a sweet fragrance to me. They move me to tears. They move me to action. I am your rescuer.

I will find you. I will not allow you to sink in the waves or wither up in the desert or take your last breath in the tangled wreckage of life. Wherever you find yourself struggling, I will be there. I will come for you. Be looking for me. You will see me. Sometimes in the smiles or hugs of others. Sometimes in the scripture on the page. Sometimes in a song melody. Sometimes in a painting, or work of art. Sometimes in the touch of the wind, or the sway of the trees. Sometimes in the light of the moon or twinkle of the stars.

You will see me and I will speak to you...beyond words. Just like your tears are beyond words, so is My rescue. It is your soul I touch. I fill it up with My presence. My peace is like the jaws of life that cut you out of your tangled mess. My joy lifts you to breathe again. My goodness is water in the dry and arid places.

I am holding space for you. I am waiting for you to see me. Look intentionally towards me and you will find me. I hold you in the palm of My hand. I sit with you in your tears. I am the first responder who is on the scene in the immediate need. I help clear your vision. I soothe your emotions and speak gently and kindly to you. When you need rescue, I come to you. I find you and I sit with you while I heal your heart. I have heard your cries. I will not abandon you in your distress. I will come and save you.

# August 21

*For all who are led by the Spirit of God are sons of God. For you did not receive the spirit of slavery to fall back into fear, but you have received the Spirit of adoption as sons, by whom we cry, "Abba! Father!" The Spirit Himself bears witness with our spirit that we are children of God, and if children, then heirs—heirs of God and fellow heirs with Christ, provided we suffer with Him in order that we may also be glorified with Him. ~Romans 8:14-17*

You are not an orphan. Why do you act as though you are fatherless? Rejection stalks you and you harden your heart. You do not share your troubles with me, you act as if I am not a part of your life. You build walls around your heart to keep me out. Walls you are not even aware of. You seal up your feelings and your worries inside.

It is not wise to hold in your fears and frustrations. A volcano will erupt when the pressure gets too much. With the eruption comes an explosion which is dangerous to anyone around it. Debris flies through the air and smashes anything in its path. The hot lava spews, burning everything, it touches. Ash floats up, blocking all light and making it impossible to breathe. You may think your holding things in doesn't hurt anyone, but you couldn't be more wrong.

Instead, release your burden in healthy ways. Give it to me and let me be your Father. I am not a slave driver who marks down any mishap. I do not keep a list of rights and wrongs. I do not expect you to work for My affection. I willingly, lavishly even, give My love freely. It is My choice to love you. I do so with abandon. I leave all the lists and I run to take you in my arms as a Father welcomes his son/daughter. We laugh. We bond and we share our visions, dreams, and our pains. It is a two-way relationship where we are in it together. It brings life. There is no build up or explosion.

To be in relationship with me means you are free to share EVERYTHING without fear of rejection. It is a relief not to carry it all by yourself. When you start feeling as if everything is up to you, say, "I am not an orphan. I am not on my own to earn approval or to garner affection. I am loved by God as a son/daughter of the Most High. I am of royal lineage. I choose life and to open my heart to my Father."

# August 22

*That I may know Christ and the power of His resurrection, and may share His sufferings, becoming like Him in His death, that by any means possible I may attain the resurrection from the dead. ~Philippians 3:10-11*

The night seasons are the hardest seasons. I know that. Void of light, you cannot even see one step in front of you. They are crushing to your soul. Every doubt, every question rises up during these agonizing times. It is beyond just brokenness. The dark places churn in the depths of your soul. Feelings roll around with nowhere to land. Understanding and knowledge take flight. Confusion comes in like a flood. Writhing, wrestling, and wondering are earmarks of this heavy place. Everything you thought you knew goes out the window. You don't have words with which to describe the place your heart is. Some have called it the dark night of the soul because the depth of pain brings blindness with it.

Beloved, when you are blind here in this season of distress, you have to depend on me for your sight. You cannot use your own awareness or knowledge. In the dark night of the soul, you are purged of yourself. It must be this way in order for you to become one with me. This season leaves you with only me. Your awareness of all else fades, until I am your only option. There is nothing left other than to allow me to take you deeper because you surrender. You may not know that is what you are doing in the moment. You are giving up because as your soul is purged you realize the truth…I am.

It is in this place our intimacy grows. It is in this place I find you and I heal you. Here, you allow me to use the darkness for your growth. Here, you realize none of it has anything to do with you…it is all grace. No action is needed on your part. I love you extravagantly no matter what. I pour out My love in this place in ways you cannot see at other more distracted times. It takes the blindness, the questioning, the groping in the dark, to find this secret place in me. New meaning comes to the phrase walk by faith, not by sight.

Beloved, you are in good company. All the saints of old had night seasons. You can read about them, including My Son in the garden. He even sweat drops of blood. His anguish was so great. He questioned My plan. He believed I had forsaken Him. He descended to the depths to bring resurrection from the dead to you. Your season of darkness was bought with a price. It comes with a gift. A gift of intimacy. A gift of oneness with me. A gift of presence. In the midst of your suffering, you are not alone.

# August 23

*He brought me out into a broad place; He rescued me, because He delighted in me.*
*~Psalms 18:19*

What brings you life? Making things? Painting? Dancing? Nature? Designing things? Growing things? Athletics? Singing? Reading? Baking? You are heavy hearted. I have given you many things which you are passionate about, but you have put them to the side. Life has crowded them out. Time has filled until there isn't one-minute left for them. Part of the enemy's plan, you know, is to keep you busy. Keep you resentful and bitter and oh so busy, that you don't have any time for the life-giving activities. The grief, pain, and hard path of life have stolen much from you, Beloved.

Stop. Take a moment to remember. Remember your craft. Remember your talent. Remember your gift. Remember what makes your heart beat faster. Remember what brings you joy. Remember the things you put to the side when the kids arrived or the accident happened or the disease came in or the trauma took over. It was a season, Dear One. A season which required sacrifice of yourself, laying down your loves and picking up responsibilities. You did it willingly…or not…but you did it. And now, you have lost your loves. The life that sparkled has faded under the weight of your burden. But, it was just a season, not meant to be forever.

It is time to find those joys which set fire to your hope. The ones which resonate deep in your innermost being. I planted those desires and dreams inside of you. They were never meant to be forgotten or put on a shelf permanently. Even with the daily struggles you live with, there is a place for them. A place for you to breathe again. Seek them out. Dust them off. Write them down. Tune your guitar. Sing your song. Dance in the moonlight. Build something beautiful.

You are most like me when you are creating. When you allow the gifts I have placed within you to rise to the top and express themselves, you thrill My heart. Can you feel My pleasure in you? Do not neglect your life-giving activities. I gave them to you to bring you joy. In the midst of hardship, they will delight you, just as I delight in you. Seek life. Find life. Let me show you how. My word to you is, REMEMBER. I have not removed the desire from you. It is buried beneath the cares of the world, but it can be unearthed. Think of it as buried treasure. It has always been there. It just needs to be uncovered. Dig, Dear One. Find it. It will bring you life.

# August 24

*The Lord your God is in your midst, a mighty one who will save; He will rejoice over you with gladness; He will quiet you by His love; He will exult over you with loud singing. ~Zephaniah 3:17*

I sing over you. You might not always be aware of it, but if you pay attention you can hear it. Have you ever listened to the wind and felt it on your face? Have you heard a summer shower pattering on the ground? Peals of thunder? The birds' morning song? Laughter of a child? A bubbling stream? Waves on the shore? It is me. Rejoicing and sharing My joy with you. Even the stillness of a lake or the silence of the stars is part of My song over you.

Have you ever worshiped and felt an urge to get on your knees in reverence? Or have you ever felt the need to join in the song and shout? Both are your response to My song. Both are appropriate. I love it when you join me in My singing. When I am making a melody, you can feel it in your spirit. It lifts you up and encourages you. Your circumstances fade away and I become your focus. The worshipers understand this. They long to sing with me every day. They are acutely attuned to My voice, but anyone can learn how to hear My song, Dear One.

Set your mind to listen. That is all. Simply listen for it. I am pouring out music all the time. The songwriters hear it. The composers, too. The musicians play it. The birds and beasts know it well. The rain and waves are in sync. It is all around you. You don't have to be a musician to allow it to flow over you. Let it well up inside of you. Start by listening. Close your eyes, Dear One. Listen to what is around you. Tune your ears to My voice. Just as you listen for My words, you can listen for My song. It might be on the radio, the most obvious place, or it might be the crickets and tree frogs. Anywhere I am, there is a song. Anywhere you are, because you are my child, you are surrounded by My song. It is a bubble around you.

I rejoice in you. You are My joy. You are My creation. I love you with an everlasting love. How can I not sing about that? Love songs are an outgrowth of falling in love, and I fall in love with you again every single day. You are always in My thoughts. You are never forgotten or forsaken. I rescue you with My song. I adore you.

Singing over you is the most natural thing in the world for me. Do not discount it. Do not push it away, or ignore it. Tune in. Let me embrace you with My music. It is My way. It is My hug to you. Linger with me in My arms while I sing over you. It will heal you, Beloved. It will align our hearts. It will fill in the cracked and dry places. Join me in My song.

# August 25

*O Lord, you have searched me and known me! You know when I sit down and when I rise up; you discern my thoughts from afar. You search out my path and my lying down and are acquainted with all my ways. Even before a word is on my tongue, behold, O Lord, you know it altogether. You hem me in, behind and before, and lay your hand upon me. Such knowledge is too wonderful for me; it is high; I cannot attain it. ~Psalm 139:1-6*

There is something you should know, Weary One. I know you. I am not just talking about your name. I KNOW the deepest parts of you. Your thoughts. Your motives. Your every move. How could I not? Your spirit rests in mine. You are part of me and I of you. We are united by the sacrifice of My Son.

On the nights when you are up caring for others, I know it. You are seen. In the days when you cannot take another step for fatigue, you are understood. When the grief of loss is unbearable, I have you in the palm of My hand. It is true, Beloved. You are valuable to me so much so that I have attuned My ear to your voice. When you cry out, I feel your pain. When you laugh, you light up My face. You are important to the creator of the universe. Why, you ask? Because I love you. Because your every breath is a miracle. Because you matter. Because you are just how I made you. Because you are My happy thought.

All your talents were My idea. It overjoys me when you use them. Your personality is unique to you on purpose. I didn't want you to be like anyone else. I am aware of your flaws, too. You didn't really think you were hiding them from me, did you? Weaknesses are chances for growth. I didn't put them there for nothing. They are part of the puzzle of you. Move them around, smooth them out, put them away, but whatever you do, let them do their work. Ultimately, you will be more like My Son when you use the weaknesses to expose My strength in your life.

You are not forgotten or abandoned. You are cherished. You are beloved. That means you are written in My heart. Every moment you are alive is a treasure to me. So, as you sit in the dark of the night with a loved one, or as you walk through your days without one, I am aware of you. Your every pain is known. Your every move is noticed. You will never be invisible to me. My hand is on you. Covering you. Protecting you. Guiding you. Never forget that, My Love.

# August 26

*Our soul waits for the Lord; He is our help and our shield. For our heart is glad in Him, because we trust in His holy name. Let your steadfast love, O Lord, be upon us, even as we hope in you. ~Psalms 33:20-22*

Do you trust me? I know sometimes it seems a hard thing, but in reality, trust is something you choose to do or not to do. You trust the vehicle you ride in, and the people around you on the road in theirs. You trust a stranger to fly your plane across the ocean. You literally put your life in the hands of others, most of whom you do not know. Why then is it so much harder to trust me, the one who created you and loves you abundantly more than you can comprehend?

Is it so hard to leave your children in My hands? Your spouse? Your marriage? Your job? Your future? Your daily life? I am worthy of your trust. You will see if you give it to me. I am faithful. If you choose to put your belief in me, you will not be disappointed. I long to guide and direct you to the spiritual freedom I designed for you. Every part of your life plays into the healing of your heart. Each relationship is a piece of the plan. If you trust me, I will set your heart free. Free to be yourself. Free to love others well.

Some people put me in a box. They make me too small to be trustworthy. Some build walls around their lives. Fear holds them captive and releasing things to me is too terrifying. What they don't know is that control is just an illusion. They think they are handling life, but when reality hits, the illusion will be shattered and the boxes and walls will not be enough. Trust will be the only way.

You may not even be aware that your trust is limited. It takes me to expose the restrictions you put on me. I do so love showing you how much you can rely on me. Beloved, you don't know how much you trust me until you have to. It is common to say with words that you trust me, but when the difficulties of life actually require it, the incongruities between what you say and what you actually believe come to light. Where there is a big, gap I am there to close it. If you will walk with me, growth will be the result. Security will replace your insecurity. Confidence will replace your doubt.

Think of trusting like the peeling of an onion. The first layers of trust are small, but the longer you live the deeper the trust becomes. Soon your trust blossoms into faith and stepping out becomes as natural as breathing. You learn your trust is not misplaced. You find I am steadfast. I am faithful. I am worthy of your trust.

# August 27

*And Jesus stopped and said, "Call him." And they called the blind man, saying to him, "Take heart. Get up; He is calling you." And throwing off His cloak, he sprang up and came to Jesus. And Jesus said to him, "What do you want me to do for you?" And the blind man said to Him, "Rabbi, let me recover my sight." And Jesus said to him, "Go your way; your faith has made you well." And immediately he recovered his sight and followed Him on the way. ~Mark 10:49-52*

You are blind, My Love. It is hard to believe I know. When you seek me daily, it seems you should be able to see clearly, but it is not so. You live in a sin-tainted world, and by its very nature, sin causes spiritual blindness. I am the only one who can open blind eyes, but you can prevent it when you believe you see everything clearly.

You have to humble yourself to see with My eyes. You have to let me show you My heart. My ways are not your ways, Dear One. So many times, they are the opposite. Up is down. Death brings life. When you believe you know My heart for yourself and others, you can fall into deception. Pride brings blindness with it.

I do not want you to find out later that you were leading others astray because you assumed you knew My heart on a matter rather than seeking me out to show you. Even the disciples thought they knew, but when the plan didn't go as they thought, they ran. They denied. They feared. They cursed My name. Until that moment they didn't know they were blind. The regret and sorrow were instant. They took quite a beating from their own thoughts and fears. It was a humbling thing for them.

When you seek me to open blind eyes, make sure you are asking for your own to be opened, Beloved. I took the scales off of Paul's eyes. My Son healed a man blind from birth, among others. He also healed blind Bartimaeus because he called out, "Have mercy on me!" When My Son asked him what he wanted he said, "I want to see." That My Dear One, is the statement that brought healing. I want to see.

Do you want to see? Do you want me to show you the areas in which you are blind? I will be happy to show you, if you want me to. It is up to you.

# August 28

*For He will command His angels concerning you to guard you in all your ways.*
*~Psalms 91:11*

I am your protector. You may know me as your provider or healer, but those are only two of My roles. My protection is given to all My children without request. It is who I am. You are made in My image, so the instinct you have to safeguard children comes from me. I have the same desire to defend and shelter the ones I love, so much so I send My angels to cover you. You should know there are such things.

The unseen realm is real, Beloved, more real than the physical world in which you live. Angels follow My command and the demons ignore it. The father of lies thinks he owns everything and everyone. He is mistaken of course, and there will come a day he will know just how wrong he is. His chief weapon is to make you think all the good and bad in the world come from either human kindnesses or human weaknesses. He does not want you to believe in the unseen forces at work. He convinces you that flesh and blood are your rivals. He is gleeful when humans dismiss him and his demons to fight one another.

There are a few who can see in the spiritual realm. They see what is happening, because I give them the ability to see, for My purposes. Yet, all humans can sense it. Have you ever walked into a place and become very uncomfortable, as if there is a blanket of darkness weighing on you? Or have you ever been caught up in worship and felt your spirit bubble up in unquenchable joy? Have you ever had a near miss and recognized the physical impossibility that you escaped without a scratch? You are aware of the unseen. You simply have to tune into it to see with the eyes of faith. It is much more difficult to believe without seeing, yet you will, if you tune your senses to My ways.

You have angels all around you. They operate in My ways, which become your ways as you grow up in me. I have given them charge over you, to watch you, to care for you, to minister to you, to protect you. The demons try to circumvent them by whispering lies in your ears. The dark ones know that if they can get you to agree with them, it will limit what the angels can and cannot do. They ride on the wings of your prayers. They move on your behalf when you seek me. When you wait for me, I dispatch even more to surround you. My Love, you are under My protection. I am your shield. I cover you. Always.

# August 29

*Rejoice in hope, be patient in tribulation, be constant in prayer. ~Romans 12:12*

Weary One, you are not defined by your circumstances. Your grief is not a badge of honor. Your day-to-day suffering isn't your identity. Your losses and traumas are not punishments. Your hardships are not who you are. They do not make you 'less than', nor do they make you "more than."

Some people weather their trials by becoming victims. They wallow in sympathy because it feeds their need to be validated in their suffering. Each sorrow they endure is fuel for another woe-is-me moment. They walk through life feeling as if they have messed up so terribly that I am punishing them. This is a lie, of course. But their eyes only see through the lenses of their pain. Everything centers around the chaos in their lives.

Other people think that their difficulties are a reward from me. They feel they must be righteous enough that I have given them suffering, because they are worthy. To them every trial validates their view of themselves as holy enough to suffer. This is also a lie. Yet, in their self-righteousness, they find a way to make the hard things a badge of honor.

Beloved, neither of these extremes is true. Circumstances cause you to cling to me. To depend on me alone. In the above scenarios, neither is looking up. Both are only looking around themselves at the storms. There is a desperate need to explain hardship, but the why question always derails the process of growth. If you can find out why something happened to you, it can be explained away. You don't have to dig deeper. If the why of your suffering is because you are a victim, you are not responsible for the result. You can't help it. If the why of your hardships is because you deem yourself somehow holy, you are elevated on a pedestal and you are not responsible for your reactions.  Not to mention it makes me a cruel God who smites My children with trauma to show their righteousness. This could not be further from the truth.

Your difficulties, all of them, do not define who you are. I am the only one who can give you your identity. You are not abandoned. Nor are you alone. You are not going to suffer forever, even though it feels like it sometimes. You are not rejected by me. You are not holier or somehow more deserving of My love than anyone else. You are not righteous. It is not about you. Take your eyes off the why. Turn them instead to what.

What do I do with My suffering? What good can come from it? What is God doing in me through it? Do you see the difference, Dear One? I will tell you what I know about you. You are worthy. You are beautiful. You are stronger than you know. You are valuable. You are the apple of My eye. You take My breath away. You are a new creature. You are My child, not a servant.

# August 30

*So, we are always of good courage. We know that while we are at home in the body we are away from the Lord, for we walk by faith, not by sight. ~2 Corinthians 5:6-7*

Walk by faith. Not by sight. You cannot see what I see. I know what I have for you. I can see the whole of your life. To you, it is foggy. The things you endure do not make sense. You wonder if I have forgotten you. I assure you, I have not. These times and seasons you walk through are temporary. Temporal. Passing. Momentary. They seem to take forever to you, but trust me, forever is much longer than you understand.

This short time is carved out for you and me. It is the time for you to climb into My lap and let me hold you. It is not a time for words. It is a time for me to comfort you, as a father comforts his child. I understand you. I know the hurt you live with. I see your wounds. You can rest in me. Sitting with me bonds your heart to mine. We become a team unified in peace. These times are precious to me. I cannot tell you how much they mean to me.

It is here, in these intimate moments, that your burden lifts. Even if for only an instant, you can see with My eyes. After the afflictions bring you to me and deposit you at My feet, they fade away. I pull you to Myself and I hold you there so you can hear My heartbeat for you. Would you come if it weren't for the afflictions? It is in this place of rest you will find your strength to continue. It is here you will be infused with My love. From here you can go forth, not by what you see, but by what you KNOW.

This is the place faith is born. It is conceived in intimacy with me. In knowing me, not about me, but truly knowing me, you will find it increases. Faith is simply having confidence in me, Weary One. In knowing My character. In knowing I am for you, no matter what it looks like around you.

Think about how your confidence grows in other areas of your life. Practice. Not being afraid to try. Not being afraid to make mistakes. Experience over time. Being open to new things. The more you experience something, the more you get comfortable with it. You no longer hesitate to step out. You overcome the fear. You don't let it hold you back, or allow you to put whatever it is on the shelf.

It is the same with me. Come to me. Put your fear aside. Let me take your broken pieces in My hands and cement them back together with My love. Do not believe what you see with your eyes. Look with your heart. Then the faith to walk your path will rise. Your confidence that momentary suffering leads to eternal communion with me will increase.

# August 31

*For we who live are always being given over to death for Jesus' sake, so that the life of Jesus also may be manifested in our mortal flesh. ~2 Corinthians 4:11*

The whole world is groaning. Can you feel it, Weary One? It is not just you. You live in a broken place, but it is not your home. You are merely passing through. Your affliction is momentary compared to eternity. Keep that in mind as you navigate your daily life. It is momentary.

I know it seems longer and there are days that seem like years, and years that seem like centuries. The pressure is great. It comes from all sides. It feels like a pressure cooker about to explode. You were born for such a time as this. Are you surprised by that statement? Don't be. I knew the weight of the world. I knew your weakness, and yet I placed you here with the circumstances you are in. I knew that you would be one who would let me shine through you.

You are My representative in this time. I trust you to reveal My heart and character despite the swirling chaos. I know you walk with me in such a way that you will share My compassion. You will not reach out in judgement like the Pharisees did. You will be My voice in a declining world. You will let me use your pain to heal others.

You will walk so that others can see you, really see you. Your hardship will serve you well in times like these. When resurrection comes, you will give me glory. When you cease to be a victim of your circumstances and instead become a victor in the midst of them, you will be a light to others. While the world is groaning, and dying, you will be living. Shining My light in the darkness for others to follow.

# September 1

*What man of you, having a hundred sheep, if he has lost one of them, does not leave the ninety-nine in the open country, and go after the one that is lost, until he finds it? And when he has found it, he lays it on his shoulders, rejoicing. And when he comes home, he calls together his friends and his neighbors, saying to them, 'Rejoice with me, for I have found my sheep that was lost.' Just so, I tell you, there will be more joy in heaven over one sinner who repents than over ninety-nine righteous persons who need no repentance. ~Luke 15:4-7*

I go after lost sheep. It is not that I don't care about the others in My care, but I want ALL to be with me. Therefore, I go after the one. Passionately. I will go to great lengths to draw ALL men/women to me. I have always done this. See how many lost sheep My Son found along His journey? Nearly every day He was talking, healing, eating with one of My lost sheep. In fact, I sent Him to do just that. He revealed My heart for the hurting. My desire to find the ones left behind.

I leave no one behind. I will always go after the one. I send people across the world to find them, and in their own neighborhoods. I find the prodigals in the dark places. I go to find the oppressed. I lift them up. The marginalized are in My heart. I do not force them to love me, but I will never stop loving them. Remember, Dear One, My love is unconditional. It is a hard concept for you to grasp. Your human mind wants to categorize others and to make My love dependent on their actions, but that is the human way, not mine.

My way is to love them. To look beyond actions into the heart I created. I build every person as a conductor of My love. To both receive love and to expend it. Before you can give it out, you have to receive it. Lost sheep have a hard time receiving from me. They have been off the path, alone, rejected, and so very scared for a long time. They don't expect anyone to come after them. When I rescue them, it takes them some time to recover from their wounds. They do not want to leave My side. They receive and receive My love and lap it up because they are so thirsty. Over time, the briars are removed. The scrapes heal over. Scars appear from their journey.

You were once a lost sheep, Beloved. Do you remember that time? Do you recall what it was like to be without direction, wandering aimlessly through the tough parts of life? It was such a scary place. Do not ever forget that. Always have compassion for those wanderers. Always be kind and express My heart. Because there may be a day, I send you to retrieve one of them. There may come a time when you will be My voice to the lost sheep and your kindness will begin the healing for them.

I will always go after the one. Always.

# September 2

*But the Lord said to Samuel, "Do not look on his appearance or on the height of his stature, because I have rejected him. For the Lord sees not as man sees: man looks on the outward appearance, but the Lord looks on the heart." ~1 Samuel 16:7*

When you think of yourself what do you think about? Do you think about how you look? The color of your hair or skin? The shape of your body? The color of your eyes? The wrinkles or gray? Or maybe you think about what you do? Where you work? What extra you give to others? How you care for your family? What your business is doing? How much money you bring in?

I have some news for you, Dear One. I don't think about any of those things when I think of you. Nope. Not in My thoughts at all. Even your good works are like filthy rags to me. You see, these thoughts you are thinking are all based on your performance. Did you do the right things to appear the right way? So much of what humans do is for those appearances. I didn't intend for it to be that way. Before the fall, we could just be. Together. No striving to impress. No comparison. No awareness of appearance at all. One day, we will be back to that place and you will love it!

Until then, remember I don't want you to strive and compare and wrestle with your appearance in the mirror. I don't want you to worry over all these things that are only temporary. I look at the heart. If you want to put in time and effort, think about the deep places. Sit with me there and really look at what is hiding there. I will show you. When you address the heart, you are dealing with spiritual concepts, not temporal ones. Come away from the mirror. Sit with me and I will show you who you are.

# September 3

*All this assembly may know that the Lord saves not with sword and spear. For the battle is the Lord's, and He will give you into our hand. ~1 Samuel 17:47*

There are giants in the land. They are big and they carry themselves in ways in which they stand out among all the others, and it has nothing to do with stature. Anyone can be a giant. Between David and the giant, the small man won the fight. So, who was the real giant? It seems backwards, and you know how I love to turn things inside out. Some giants are all talk. They blow hot air. Other giants are quiet but powerful. Their voices are soft, but they never waver in their determination. What is the difference? Where does their confidence lie?

In the story of David and the giant, David had confidence, not in armor, not in the king or the army, but in me. He couldn't understand why the army was cowering in fear. It is because he spent time with me. He was confident I would defend Myself. He simply followed me. He used his own gift with a sling instead of trying to be a warrior. He knew he was a shepherd and he acted within that role. Later on, he would become a warrior and then a king, but that was all in My timing. He became a giant.

On the other hand, the giant had all the confidence in the world. He mocked My people. He bragged about all his accomplishments. He mostly made My warriors afraid to stand up to him. Bullies are like that. Yet, for all his confidence, he was felled by a shepherd with a stone.

In your world, the giants are not always who you think they are. Your circumstances seem like giants, coming to take you out. The hardships you face are difficult and it seems as if they have overcome you. They are not real giants. You are the real giant. You are the one who knows me intimately. You know how I rescue. You know My ways because of what you perceive to be giants in your life. But that isn't how I see things.

The voice I have given says, "You come against me with sword and spear and javelin, but I come against you in the name of the Lord of Hosts, the God of the armies of Israel, whom you have defied." This is the message of a giant. Always listen for this message, Dear One. It is how you will know the difference between those who think they are giants and those who actually are. You are one of My giants.

# September 4

*And I am no longer in the world, but they are in the world, and I am coming to you. Holy Father, keep them in your name, which you have given me, that they may be one, even as we are one. ~John 17:11*

I am your home. I am where you belong. You fit in me and I in you. When you wander away, everything gets out of sorts. Just as when a child wanders off and suddenly finds everything is unfamiliar. You may be lost even now. Do you find yourself confused? Are you wondering which way to go? What is your next step, or do you feel forever stuck where you are?

Learn, My Love, what it feels like to wander away. Recognize the signs so you can correct your course. Many times, weariness is one of the biggest red flags. It can mean you are relying on your own strength. Even in normal life circumstances you still must let me help you carry the load. It is the only way. Especially with all you find on your plate. I long to walk it out together.

Confusion is another red flag. Remember when your steps seemed clear? Everything was vibrant in the beginning of your love for me. Decisions seemed to make themselves because love was the plumb line. Then life happened and fog settled in the corners of your mind. You decided you don't understand me anymore.

Bitterness waves itself proudly in your heart and mind. The unfairness of life can plant that in you. When you forget to look to me, and instead allow the hard things you endure to take the front seat, home seems farther and farther away. Victimhood is shortly behind, and depression takes up residence in your soul.

Come home, Weary One. Come sit with me like we used to do. Let's converse. We can cry together and laugh. We can enjoy one another's company. Do not put it off. I come to be with you every day. I look on the horizon for you. I am just waiting for you to join me.

# September 5

*Now to Him who is able to do far more abundantly than all that we ask or think, according to the power at work within us, to Him be glory in the church and in Christ Jesus throughout all generations, forever and ever. Amen. ~Ephesians 3:20-22*

I am bigger than your problems. Do not doubt that for a minute, Dear One. Even a worldwide event is a small thing to me. You might not understand how this could be, but remember I created the universe. The whole thing, not just the part you know about. I know all things. You live on a blue dot, but that dot has My attention. And the people on that dot are My precious ones. You are one of them.

I know the big and I know the small. I know the intimate details down to the cells in your body. I am so immense; I know from the largest to the smallest details across the universe. Do not forget this when you are living day-to-day. When circumstances seem to be stacked up against you. When there is oppression. When there is uncertainty. When it is all overwhelming to you.

Remember, I am bigger. Bigger than job problems. Bigger than relationship issues. Bigger than people who oppose one another. Bigger than your grief. Bigger than your illness. Bigger than your stress levels. Bigger than depression. Bigger than all the "big" problems in your life. Hand it all over to me even if it has to be a minute-by-minute surrender.

Change your thinking. Change your mindset. Ask for big. Imagine big. Know that I am not too limited to help you. I am not so small that I cannot see your circumstances. Set your thoughts on the enormous God you know. Do not think small, Weary One. You will get stuck in smallness. Look to me and I will show you just how big I am. Bigger than you can imagine. Bigger than you can ask or think.

# September 6

*And the master said to the servant, "Go out to the highways and hedges and compel people to come in, that my house may be filled." ~Luke 14:23*

I have plans for you. Sometimes, Dear One, you think I only have plans for others. That somehow you are not worthy of plans, and there is no purpose for you. Or somehow you have missed your purpose because of the circumstances of your life. Nothing could be further from the truth.

Not every purpose of mine is in the spotlight. In fact, many of the men and women of faith were solitary in their journeys. They were quiet and, in the background, doing what I directed them to. Raising their children. Going to their jobs. Doing the daily activities of life in normal ways. But in doing My will, they lived profound lives. Lives I used to forward My kingdom of love.

During their lifetimes no one may have even known their names, but later on, everyone knew their stories because of the way they lived in the day-to-day. Missionaries lived among remote tribes. Families rescued those running from oppression by incorporating them into the mundane of their lives. Doctors and nurses saved lives on battlefields that went unnoticed at the time.

The stories you read in My word are the same. Those heroes of the faith didn't know they would be written into a book which would tell their stories for centuries. They were just two women going to the tomb to care for a dead friend. They were just men following a teacher who had some radical ideas. She just went to the well to draw water. The father just ran to welcome his son home. They were going about their lives and I interrupted, and then recorded their stories for others. They never even knew.

It is no different for you. You are just taking kids to school. You are just taking care of elderly parents. You are just working a boring job. You are just taking care of your own health. It is all "just" doing life. But doing life with me changes the world, Dear One. Doing life with me makes a difference now, but it also travels out from now into the future.

You do not know how I will use your life, Weary One. How I will tell your story, or when. Keep living it. Keep doing the hard work you are doing. Know that nothing you have been through or are going through is wasted. It is all a part of My plan to spread My light to others. Yes, even the smallest of details will be used, so do not fret. Do not write yourself out of My story.

# September 7

*As each has received a gift, use it to serve one another, as good stewards of God's varied grace: whoever speaks, as one who speaks oracles of God; whoever serves, as one who serves by the strength that God supplies—in order that in everything God may be glorified through Jesus Christ. To Him belong glory and dominion forever and ever. Amen. ~1 Peter 4:10-11*

What do you carry, Weary One? Besides your weariness, I mean. Do you know? I have given you parts of me to carry to the world around you. Think about it for a minute. My gifts that you carry are usually obvious to those closest to you, even when you yourself may not recognize it. Do you carry compassion? Is it beauty? Maybe it is hope? Motivation? Order? Creativity? What about grace? Or joy? Mirth? Humility?

The gift you bring is something that is easy for you. It seems like nothing. You wonder why anyone would find it difficult. That is because it is natural for you, like breathing. Without thinking about it, you may be giving grace to others and empathizing with them. Or maybe bringing encouragement is your autopilot. Whatever your gift is, people will seek you out for it. They may or may not recognize that is what they are doing, but you will find yourself in situations where you are using what you carry. Do people tell you their life stories all the time, everywhere? You carry empathy. Do people want you on their team on a project? You carry organization.

What you bring to the world is something only you can bring. You are a unique combination of gifts. Wherever you go, you carry them with you. Even in your own household you can distribute what you carry. Even in difficult circumstances. It is important to remember that on days where you feel small. It is important to remember that on days you feel worthless, or weary, or too tired to keep going.

If you don't know what you carry, ask those around you. They likely know. When do people seek you out? When do you feel most like yourself? Take note of it. Write it down. Do a little investigating about yourself. When you find it, your eyes will see your importance to My kingdom.

Where will you carry your gift? At home? At work? In the carpool line? On the street? You have it with you always. I give gifts and I do not take them away. You can tap into this anytime. I have given it to you freely. Be confident in who you are and what you carry. Let it flow out. It will change your outlook. It will change the world.

# September 8

Run to me in times of trouble. Do not hold the suffering inside. It will only build up in there and start to transform your heart into stone. To be tenderhearted is not a weakness, My Child. It is what makes you vulnerable and compassionate. Those are not bad things. In fact, the world needs more tenderhearted people.

When you are having difficulties, the tendency is to pull back. To protect yourself. Sometimes it is necessary to separate yourself from others so you can have some space to breathe. But, Beloved, do not separate yourself from me. I know at times it feels as if I am far away. It feels as if I don't care, but nothing could be further from the truth. I love you with an everlasting love. I am a safe place to run to. You do not have to hold back your feelings from me. You can pour them out until you are empty. I will not leave or forsake you.

The hurt caused by others will sting. When you take what they say into you, it is like a poison. Your life is one of hardship, and you will find others are uncomfortable with that. Whatever cannot be explained easily brings judgement from them. They grasp for why hard things keep happening to you and they must find a reason. They will blame you. They will blame me. They will blame the devil. They do not often realize that living in a sin-tainted world means hardship is a companion for some through no fault of their own.

Let their words roll off. Put them down on paper, wad them up, burn them. Get the pain out of your heart, Dear One. Carrying it around with you only causes harm. Run to me. Spill it all out. I will begin the healing process. Your heart will remain soft if you can remember to come to me instead of internalizing your feelings.

# September 9

*Behold, I have refined you, but not as silver; I have tried you in the furnace of affliction. ~Isaiah 48:10*

You are in a fiery place. The flames are licking your feet and you feel as if you will burn up. Do not mistake this place for hell, though it feels similar. The difference is that I do not dwell in hell. It is devoid of My presence. The place you are in now; I am in the midst of it with you. It is the refiner's fire. Here, there is heat. High heat. Yet, there is also purpose. A refiner knows that in order to create something pure and beautiful, the dross has to be scraped off. I am a refiner. A creator of beautiful works of art.

The fire is blistering. The metal has to be molten, so it is put into the hottest part of the flame. It is melted, but not just melted...purified. If the metal has dirt or impurities within it, they rise to the surface in the heat. Like a blob of gunk, they float up to the top of the molten metal. They are easy to spot there, like an island of imperfections. I scrape them off at just the right time to keep the metal intact.

It may seem as if the process is finished, but a good refiner knows it takes many times to get out all the dross. Another hit of the heat knocks more dirt loose. It would surprise you how much ilk can be in a small amount of metal. I am not surprised, but I am diligent in My creations. I want them to shine with My reflection. In fact, that is how I know it is complete. When the heat no longer brings up the impurities, the molten metal will go from a dull gray to a shine in which I can see Myself. It is an amazing moment.

One truth I don't want you to miss here, Beloved, is that I never leave the process. My eye is always on the metal, especially when it is in the fire. I have to watch every second to make sure the metal isn't damaged. I have to wait for the yuck to bubble up so I can capture it and remove it, otherwise it would weaken the metal and cause it to break. When I am refining you, I never abandon you. I sit and wait and I am always watching for the moment My reflection shines out. I do not keep you in the fire one moment longer than necessary.

# September 10

*Now faith is the assurance of things hoped for, the conviction of things not seen.*
*~Hebrews 11:1*

Substance has weight. It is a solid presence. It is the quality of being important, valid or significant. You have substance, Precious One. It is more than just mass. It is more than connecting your feet to the ground. I am invisible. You cannot see My mass, but you can feel My substance because I have it.

Many do not believe in me because they do not see a physical presence. Yet others don't see me, but they feel My substance, and so they believe. I have a tangible presence. You feel it whenever you need comfort. In the midst of tragedy. During your day-to-day activities. You feel the weight of My glory in worship. When creating. During moments of satisfaction. When all feels right and when things are terribly wrong. My substance is always around you.

You are My child. You carry My DNA, so to speak. You have a tangible presence everywhere you go. It is easier to see yours since you also have a physical body. Yet, your substance is more than just skin and bones. It is the essence of who I have made you to be. It is your spirit. Your personality. Your strengths. Your weaknesses. All of you. There is not a part of you that is not valid, important, and significant.

Remember that, as you move through your days. Remember that, as you interact with others in your life. You carry your substance with you. You arrive with it. You leave with it. You are a human being, and being substantial is who you are. Don't forget it.

# September 11

*This is the message we have heard from Him and proclaim to you, that God is light, and in Him is no darkness at all. ~1 John 1:5*

The sun comes up every morning. It is indiscriminate in the way it shines. On good days. On bad ones. It is there to remind you the world doesn't stop spinning, Weary One. When unthinkable things happen in your life, look at the sun. It is still in the sky and the sky is not falling, it only feels that way sometimes.

The light of My love is steady like the sun. It is there always as a source of life. When it feels as if the world is going to crush you, my love stands in the gap. It is a comfort when nothing else makes sense. Do you know, Beloved, that My love is present in every circumstance? Not just the happy ones, but the hard ones too. The confusing, never-understood times are still rooted in My love, like the light of the sun shines always.

It might seem difficult to understand how it can be true, but think of your own personal trials and tribulations. Even in the midst of the hardest ones, I am with you. You will see me in the care of others around you. You will see me in the natural world. You will feel me in the hug of a friend and hear me on the phone call of a well-wisher. It is all in your perspective. My love is greater than the suffering around you, but you have to look for it. Otherwise, you will be waylaid by the words of the world.

You will forget the sun shines every single day. It came up today and it will come up tomorrow. It is an object around which the Earth turns, not the other way around. My love is the same. Immovable. Unquenchable. Unstoppable by the spinning of days. It brings warmth and life. It promotes healing. Look for it to shine even today. No matter what the circumstances of your life or your world, look for the rays of My love to break into your day.

# September 12

*And when He had finished speaking, He said to Simon, "Put out into the deep and let down your nets for a catch." And Simon answered, "Master, we toiled all night and took nothing! But at your word I will let down the nets." And when they had done this, they enclosed a large number of fish, and their nets were breaking. ~Luke 5:4-6*

One step. Dear One, it only takes one step to move forward. My children tend to think of climbing a whole mountain. To pursue a dream, the first step is the only one that matters. Without it, the dream will not happen. It doesn't matter what follows if you never begin.

When you are tired and life has beat you down, dreaming of the future seems futile. In fact, the plans you had seem to have disappeared in the wind. Thinking of them only brings disappointment to the surface. The hopelessness wrought by your life path is a daily burden you carry. But, Beloved, I have not put your path to the future away. I have not removed My plans from your life. There is still a purpose, and to get to it you must take the first step.

Do not be fearful. Do not believe that you are not capable. Do not fall for the lie that I am finished with you already. Even those with big dreams still must start with the first step. So, let me show you how to begin. You can go slowly. You can find healing in the forward movement. After feeling stuck for so long, just considering where you are going next can be its own sort of beginning.

The first step? Allow your heart to hope again. That's all for now. Just sit and consider the dream for a bit. Has it transformed and changed since the beginning? Is the goal still the same or have you been inspired in a different direction? You know, My Love, everything you do, even the hard things, prepares you for the next thing.

Down the road of life, you will find that pieces you have collected all along the way will serve you where you are going. It is My way to prepare you long before you even know where you are going. Hindsight will show this to be true. Sometimes you have to look back in order to move forward. When the terrible thing happened, and you didn't understand, it took time to get some perspective. But looking back, you can see My hand guiding, even through trauma. You can see My provision, even in the loss. And now, you can see what strength you have because of it. How it shaped you as a person. How it transformed your beliefs.

All of those hard places prepared you for the next step. Don't let them steal from you by convincing you not to take a step. That the dream is too hard, or too big for you. Or that I have passed you by and that dream is dead. No, it is not. Timing is everything, Dear One. Take the next step and see what I mean.

# September 13

*I will give you the keys of the kingdom of heaven, and whatever you bind on earth shall be bound in heaven, and whatever you loose on earth shall be loosed in heaven.*
*~Matthew 16:19*

I hold the key. It might sound dramatic to you, but it is the truth. The key to life and death is me, My Child. I don't just mean literal life and death, but also spiritual life and death. When you experience abundance in your spirit, a time of growth and excitement, a time of life flowing out of you, I am the key. I am the source and I unlock the door to those seasons.

When you experience hardship and heartache, a time of death and heaviness, when all seems lost, I am the key. I don't mean I cause these hard seasons, rather I can unlock how you can survive them. I am the key to lifting of heaviness. Everyone has these seasons, Weary One. It is part of being alive in the world. However, not everyone knows that the key to getting through them is me. Some struggle for years before they turn to me for help, and others never do. You already know that I am the key to unlock the way out.

What you might not know is that you hold the key to My heart. Does this surprise you? Your worship touches me deeply. Your time spent talking to me fills me up. When you walk out compassion, or faith, or healing, My face lights up. Even in your seasons of hardship, especially then, it moves me when you look to me.

Keys to the kingdom of heaven rest in My hands. And the kingdom begins now. No need to wait until you see me face to face. Let me open the door to My heart now. Let me use My key to show you life, even in dark places. I am the key.

# September 14

*Lift up your eyes on high and see: who created these? He who brings out their host by number, calling them all by name; by the greatness of His might and because He is strong in power, not one is missing. ~Isaiah 40:26*

You may have noticed; I am a star breather. It is a gift I happily share with the world. I love it when you look up and take notice of My work. Just as artists share their art, I love to display My fascination with light and dark for those who will appreciate it. I know this skill I have is enormous. It likely makes you feel small, but I hope that My skill assures you that I am big enough to handle whatever life has thrown at you.

I am also the maker of the wind. I send it to and fro. The trees dance for me. It is My joy to see them swirling and releasing their leaves in abandon. The colors are magnificent and add to My palate of wonder. The wildflowers are looking up and shining their smiles towards me, too. They are precious dabs of color which I enjoy immensely. They are so tiny and intricate; I hope they show you I am in the tiniest details of your life.

No matter where you are in the world, or what is on your plate, you can see me around you in the big and in the small. I created all the world to show you Myself. It is what an artist does, uses materials to share a part of Himself with his audience. It is the evidence that I am around you and with you always.

Whatever your life holds at this moment, you simply need to step outside to know I am with you. Breathe the fresh air. Take in the sounds of many waters, bubbling creeks, or wide, full waterfalls. Find a quiet place. Sit by a lake, or paddle down rushing rivers. Walk in the park. Hike a mountain. Climb a tree, or sit under the night sky. Find nature. I am a star-breathing God. If I can speak to light, and the waves obey me, how much can I do for you? You are never alone, or forgotten. Just look at what I can do. If I call the stars by name, and there are billions of them, how much more do I know you?

# September 15

*No temptation has overtaken you that is not common to man. God is faithful, and He will not let you be tempted beyond your ability, but with the temptation He will also provide the way of escape, that you may be able to endure it. ~I Corinthians 10:13*

What if nothing changes? What will you do if everything stays the same as it is right now? Does that make you too tired to think about? Does it scare you? My Love, I know you feel you could not handle it. I know the idea of things staying the same is not one you want to consider. You have heard the statement, "God won't give you more than you can handle," but it is untrue. First of all, I am for you. I don't "give" hardship...life gives hardship. You live in a fallen world and as such, bad things happen. Hard things. Things with no explanation. Many of these things get falsely attributed to me, mainly because people do not know My character. I use these things, but I do not put them on you.

They are more than you can handle...without me. If you are working in your own strength, the burden will be too great. Sometimes, even with me, it is overwhelming to you. That is perfectly normal. What you are living with is difficult. I know that. You are not alone in your thoughts. I see your concern and fear of things staying the same forever.

My question to you is am I enough? Am I enough for you, if there isn't a breakthrough coming? Do you seek me for the breakthrough or do you seek me for me? What if it is just you and me every morning? What if what you are asking me for never happens? Will you still love me and follow me? Are you seeking me for what I can do for you, or because you want to be with me?

These are hard questions for me to ask you. I am scared of your answers, even though I already know them. If I could dictate answers to you it would be different, but the choice is yours. Your circumstances define the way you see me, the way you relate to me. They put doubt of My goodness in your heart. This saddens me, because I know if you and I could spend time together outside your circumstances, you might see things differently. I hear, "But you have control of my circumstances, you could change things if you wanted to." You might state it calmly, but within the words is an accusation. That somehow, because things aren't going your way, I am responsible for your pain. That if I would just wave a magic wand and "fix" things, your life would be better and you would love me more.

I have found that in hardship, dependence on me is increased. In good times, it is decreased. Not true for every human, but the majority. If I could wave a wand and make all things right in the world and every person love me deeply, I would. However, this thing called free will is a limitation I put on Myself. I don't want you to love me because you have to. I want you to desire me on your own, because of me, not because of who I am or what I can do for you. Can you love me like that?

# September 16

*Whoever believes in me, as the scripture has said, "Out of his heart will flow rivers of living water." ~John 7:38*

There is such a thing as living water. It is that part of me that flows out of you no matter the circumstance. It is hope mixed with grace for the moment in which you are living. It is the ability to put one foot in front of the other despite what is happening all around you. It cleans the mess, and forgives the mistakes. Living Water is not a thing, it is the person of the Holy Spirit. He is your counselor. He is the one who rises up in difficulty to hold you up. In the daily routine of hardship, He flows out, even when it's not pretty.

In your body, thirst is something you feel when you are depleted of water. Dehydration causes your mouth to crave liquid. If you do not get it, your body will begin to have problems. Headaches, weakness, fever, nausea. In essence, you will be imbalanced.

In a spiritual sense, it is the same. Look at the woman at the well. She longed for Living Water, though she didn't know it. She came for the physical, but My Son met her with the spiritual answer she needed. She knew her life was a mess, but she didn't share that with Him. He knew it already. He saw her need before she even recognized it herself. He knew she was exhausted by her life. Her need for love had caused her to seek it out from men repeatedly, each time failing to find what she was looking for. But on this day, she found the source of hope and the grace for life she had been unknowingly searching for all along. Her eyes and heart were opened when she believed what He said.

Beloved, the Living Water gives you what you need when you are weary. It flows from your innermost being. Have you ever been to a fast-moving river? You know how the water swirls and races around rocks and anything else in its path. It makes a joyful noise, even in the face of obstacles. It goes around them. It even has the power to smooth the rough edges over time. The obstacles do not disappear, but they are transformed. The water does that. It falls toward the lowest place and humbles itself in joyous abandonment.

Without the Living Water, you will not be able to surrender to the obstacles that remain in your life. You will be bitter or resentful. Life will always seem unfair. With the living water, there is grace to endure, but more than simply endure, but to move with joy. It may seem impossible, but I assure you it is not. Believe me and let the water flow.

# September 17

*The night is far gone; the day is at hand. So then let us cast off the works of darkness and put on the armor of light. ~Romans 13:12*

The birds sing My praise. The sun rises with colors impossible to name. They are different every day. The rooster crows, welcoming the day, and annoying the neighbors. Tree frogs and crickets fade into the light after a long night of singing. I do so love My creation. I love that you love it too. I want it to be fresh and new every morning, just like I want you to spend it with me. I do have words for you daily, and if not words, pictures. The picture of the sunrise is like the dawn of a new day, Weary One. It is fresh and clean. No need to hold onto yesterday with all its heaviness. Look up.

I speak to you because I see you. I know it is hard. I know you need encouragement. Look around you. The trees blow My wind to kiss your cheek. The shadows disappear as the orange sherbet sky lights up. I am not kidding when I say THIS is the day I have made. Rejoice. Despite hardship. Despite grief. Despite ongoing trials of all kinds. Stop for a moment to rejoice. It is not for me you rejoice, but for you. It builds your spirit. It lifts your eyes. You have another day. It is a gift. Do not waste it complaining. Erase your bitterness with joy. You know My joy is your strength. I find joy in you. I find My own happiness wrapped up in you.

Some say I am far away, but it is not true. I am right here with you. I am in the moment...actually I am above the moment...above time. Your day-to-day timeline is not the way time works for me. I can see the beginning and the end. I can see your place in time. It is now. Looking back will not help you, Dear One. Looking forward is speculation. You have 'now.' Be intentional with your now. Intend to make today a joyful one. Intend to listen to My birds sing to you. Intend to show kindness and love to those around you, wherever you are. It is not difficult to be in the moment. It is the anticipation of the unknown moments which take a toll on you. For now, breathe in. Breathe out. Breathe in. Breathe out. Release the stress of yesterday and breathe in the fresh new day ahead of you. Re-joice...show joy again. You can do it, just as the dawn does each morning.

# September 18

*The hand of the Lord was on me, and He brought me out by the Spirit of the Lord and set me in the middle of a valley; it was full of bones. He led me back and forth among them, and I saw a great many bones on the floor of the valley, bones that were very dry. He asked me, "Son of man, can these bones live?" I said, "Sovereign Lord, you alone know." ~Ezekiel 37:1-3*

There once was a valley of dry bones. They were long since dead and there was no life in them. I took My prophet to see them and he walked among them to witness just how dead they were. Then I told him to call them back to life. It was a grand sight to see the bones come together and form bodies. Then he prophesied to the breath. My breath came. They inhaled. They stood. They moved, a whole army of them. It is a great story, but there is a meaning here for you, Weary One.

You feel dead inside. You are burned out. You are grief-stricken. You are tired. There is a dryness within your heart. It is brittle, which makes it easier to break. The pieces never seem to go back together. The constant hot winds which surround you suck any life from you and leave you in the desert, dry as a bone.

I ask you, the same as I asked the prophet. Can these bones live? Dear One, can you live again or have you given up and decided to lie in the desert? You want me to speak to your circumstances, but in the story, it was the prophet who did the speaking. He spoke to the bones; He spoke to the breath.

Speak to your bones, Beloved. Tell them this is what the Lord says...you will live. You will not allow circumstances to dry you out. He will make you whole again. He will breathe His breath into you. You will come together and you will stand. You will not give up.

Then speak to the breath. Tell the breath to come as the Lord says. Come breath, and breathe into the bones. Blow life into them so they can live again. Raise them from circumstances and hardship. Raise them from hurt and woundedness. Raise them from grief and bitterness. Raise them from abandonment and loneliness. Raise them from feeling invisible in the day-to-day monotony. Raise them from exhaustion and busyness. Raise them from being sick and tired. Raise them from caring for others, to caring for themselves. Raise them from death and destruction to life.

I am the resurrection. I am the life. When you see yourself walk out of the valley of dry bones, you will know these things about me. No one will ever be able to convince you otherwise, because you will testify. Your bones will no longer be dry. You will no longer be in the valley of death. You will be in the land of the living. You will walk and breathe freely because you have spoken My words over your bones. My words bring life...always.

# September 19

*I will give in My house and within My walls a monument and a name better than sons and daughters; I will give them an everlasting name that shall not be cut off.*
*~Isaiah 56:5*

Take courage. I have things for you. I have names you have forgotten. Things spoken in childhood which you put to the side when life got busy. When you think on those things you feel forgotten, overlooked, but Dear One, nothing could be further from the truth. When I name something and call it forth, it stands for all time.

If I call you Writer, you will write. If I call you Musician, you will make music. If I call you Singer, you will sing. If I call you Teacher, you will teach. If I call you Minister, you will minister. If I call you Encourager, you will encourage. It is not a matter of *if* you will or will not do what I have called out in you; it is a matter of *when*. When will you gain the courage to step into the name? When will you believe My word to you enough to go for it?

Don't get me wrong, you may already be following your calling...you probably are in some capacity. You might sing in the shower, or write in your journal every day, or any number of other things that are partial acceptances. When I put something inside of you, there is no removing it, and so it is there, somewhere in your life, lurking around, tucked away in your mind and heart. You may have given it an outlet of some kind, but are you owning the title that goes with it? It is as much a part of you as the tired parts, actually more so. It is the flicker of passion that rises up when you get close to it. It is hope and purpose, which you have felt was lost.

The promised gift is still in there, the thing previously spoken, and some new ones as well. My children have multiple gifts and you are no exception. Even the hardship you live with is part of the future I have for you. It has honed your compassion and it will shape your gift.

The question is, do you have the courage to receive the name? Do you trust me? Will you step from the shower to the stage? Can you go from the journal to the page? Will you tell your story...our story? It is in the stepping out you will find the freedom you seek. It is there you will find the purpose for your pain. It is there you will stand tall and own the name I have written on your heart. Take courage, Weary One. I have something for you, which you cannot comprehend; you need only to believe me.

# September 20

*For all that is in the world—the desires of the flesh and the desires of the eyes and pride of life—is not from the Father but is from the world. And the world is passing away along with its desires, but whoever does the will of God abides forever. ~1 John 2:16-17*

There is a certain pride that comes when you follow me. I am aware of it and how it grows over time. To be associated and intimately connected to the creator of the universe is a big jump from feeling as if you are nothing. It is understandable that there would be pride, however, pride is a tricky thing, slippery.

Pride begins by praising an event or complimenting a job well done, but then morphs into how much better one person is than another. It starts as one thing and transforms into comparison and judgement. Insidious really. It does this in a way unbeknownst to people, and before you know it, they become full-blown Pharisees telling everyone else how to think, and using themselves as examples of how to do things the right way.

Broken One, the brokenness you live in prevents pride from taking hold. When you are living with pain, emotional or physical, you know your weaknesses. You struggle to have energy for each day, with none left to be critical and judgmental of others. Broken people are some of the humblest people. You know you don't have the answers, and sometimes you don't even know the questions, but you are okay with it. You have learned through your pain that it is not all up to you. You are in survival mode and just being in the moment day-to-day is enough for you.

The why of your circumstances isn't important. It is a question that cannot be answered to your satisfaction, but part of the answer is the humility which comes from the hard places. It is not a cause and effect relationship, however. I do not intentionally put My children through difficult things in order to humble them. That would be against My character.

However, I do use the hard things that come through living in a sin-filled world for My purposes. Humility and intimacy with me are a couple of ways I redeem the difficult seasons. I make you more like My Son because of the circumstances that happen. I draw even closer to you, to lift you up, to encourage you, to show you My heart for you. In turn, your heart for me grows and you spend more time cultivating your soul. It is a win-win, even in the midst of brokenness. It also helps to avoid the pitfalls of the pride of life.

# September 21

*And we all, with unveiled face, beholding the glory of the Lord, are being transformed into the same image from one degree of glory to another. For this comes from the Lord who is the Spirit. ~2 Corinthians 3:18*

Health of relationships is important, My Love. In the many relationships you have in life, your beliefs are tested by fire, so to speak. There are so many relationships. They are the fire where what you say you believe is tested. When you walk with me and you read My words, when you strive to be transformed by me, sometimes you believe you are further along the path than you are. In a way, your relationships with others are a measuring stick.

It is easy to put on masks of kindness, but not actually be kind in your heart. It is easy to pretend to care, when you actually could care less. Coworkers annoy you, and you smile and walk on past, rather than looking at your heart. Friendships are born from similarities, but move into judgements. Family relationships are the most volatile because they are not ones that can be easily abandoned. Even if you are estranged from your family in some way, it never changes the fact they are family.

The relationships closest to you are usually where the truth can be seen. The health or lack of, is visible almost immediately. Yes, it is a two-way street. The other person, spouse or child, has a part in how things go as well. However, you can never change someone else. You only have the power to change your own health. But first, you have to see the unhealthy parts.

I want to open your eyes to see your part in all this. I want you to quit giving others the power over your life, and I want you to let me lead you into health and wholeness. It starts with you. It starts with you seeing and acting IN YOUR LIFE, not the lives of others.

This change will require help. From me. Maybe from others whom you trust. Friends. A minister. A counselor. A safe person. The key is to take stock of all your relationships. See what they all have in common and think of your role in them. Let me show you your masks. Let me bring you real transformation.

# September 22

*"For I will restore health to you, and your wounds I will heal," declares the Lord, "because they have called you an outcast." ~Jeremiah 30:17*

How do you care about yourself? Do you? Because I do. I care deeply for you, and I know that when life is hard all the time, it is difficult for you to care for yourself. You are busy caring for everyone else. But Dear One, *you* have to care for *you*. Otherwise, you will burn out. You will crash.

I have future plans for you other than what you are experiencing now. You have places to go and people to meet. Your story matters. It is the place you have come to know me deeply. It is the voice others need to hear. If you are so inward focused from being in hard places for so long, it will be difficult for you to speak up and out.

I want to breathe care back into you. I want you to feel hope again. I want you to know I am here with you. Sleep can be an escape. Food or drink is an outlet. But sometimes they bring you down instead of up. You have to step out of the place you are drowning. I know you feel as if you cannot. But I am throwing you a rope. Get up. Sit with me. Let me breathe into you.

Find your way to health. Baby steps. Seek me for what is needed. I will show you. I will connect you with others so you are not alone. Consider caring for yourself by trying the following: Support groups, therapists, joining a gym, prayer groups, book clubs, hiking clubs, massages, cooking classes, any kind of group who does the same things you do. Find your passion and find others who share it. Find a group who understands your specific hardship. Any way you can join with others who care about their own health. It will rub off on you.

I need you, Dear One. I need you to care about what I care about and that is you. All the other things in your life that cannot wait must take a backseat somehow. You must find a way to include time for yourself into what you do on a daily basis. It is imperative. I cannot tell you enough how much I love you. I want you to thrive even in the hardship where you live.

It is important to me for you to be as healthy as possible for the place you are in. That doesn't mean you have to run marathons; it simply means you need to do what you can where you are. Walk to the mailbox or hike a mountain. Write a note or a book. Paint a picture or build a house. Whatever you can do where you are. No comparison with others. They are not dealing with what you are dealing with. Do not allow judgements into you. They don't know where you are. Just focus on me. I get it. I understand. I see you. All I ask is that you see yourself, too. That you do not count yourself invisible, because you are not. Not to me. I watch you every day. You are My Love.

# September 23

*There is therefore now no condemnation for those who are in Christ Jesus.*
*~Romans 8:1*

Forgiveness is critical. It is not optional. It is not only sometimes. It is always and everyone. I can show you any unforgiveness in your heart if you want me to. Just ask. Forgiveness is crucial, Beloved, and you should not neglect it. It is a key to your freedom, and more than anything, I want you free.

To forgive is the essence of who I am. When you can bring yourself to choose forgiveness, you are choosing life over death. It is difficult, I know. If someone has hurt you, or your family, it can feel impossible. If your child has hurt you, it is even harder sometimes. A spouse can rip your heart out and the bitterness and unforgiveness that follow are all-consuming. A friend's betrayal, really any betrayal, is most difficult to let go of. I promise that I will help you if you are willing to try. It may take some time, and I know it will take effort, but it can be done. I promise. I forgave those who killed and were brutal to My Son. There are some who still are, but I not only forgive them, I love them and offer them the freedom he bought for them. It is that important.

When you hold onto unforgiveness, it brings you down. Your heart fills with revengeful thoughts, and your replay the unfair actions of others who acted against you in some way. You get stuck, and moving forward in life seems impossible. There is something sickeningly sweet that draws your thoughts towards getting even. Once those thoughts are entertained, they take up residence and begin spreading throughout your mind. Choosing forgiveness doesn't make those thoughts disappear, but over time it does expose their lies. It also requires you to recognize them and put them out of your head.

Now the tricky part is when you don't know you are holding onto unforgiveness. Usually, you have more than one person to forgive. The one who wronged you, but also yourself for allowing it. Humans often have trouble forgiving themselves. The way you blame yourself for things in which you are in no way responsible causes such heartache. You turn on yourself and beat yourself up.

Stop. It can cause you to become a bitter person. You must let me carry away the unforgiveness of yourself you are keeping. My Son demands that His blood be enough for you. You cannot add a penance for yourself in addition to His sacrifice. It cheapens the grace offered. It says to him and to me that the free gift we offer isn't enough for you. That you must do more or that you do not deserve freedom. It is not up to you who gets offered freedom, it is up to me. So, forgive yourself. Let me help you, unless of course you haven't forgiven me.

# September 24

*Come now, let us reason together, says the Lord: though your sins are like scarlet, they shall be as white as snow; though they are red like crimson, they shall become like wool. ~Isaiah 1:18*

Beloved, whatever your lot, whatever your hardship, do not blame me. I know it is hard to see why I didn't stop a particular event terrible thing from happening. I am all powerful, right? Why did I allow this death, illness, loss, broken thing to happen? It is a fair question and I do not run from it. I do however, desire you to listen in the midst of your anger with me.

Just because bad things happened to you doesn't mean I don't love you. Just because you cannot understand, doesn't mean I never cared about you. Do not lump the hard thing with My love as if it is a cause and effect. My love for you is not moved by what you do or do not do. It is always the same. I do not punish based on My love, or based on your actions. I am not looking for a performance to earn My love. My love simply is. It is for you and with you; it always has been and always will be. Challenging situations do not happen in life because I have slighted you.

They happen because I gave men free will to choose me or not. When they do not choose me, they choose death instead, causing a chain reaction of effects for which I am not responsible. A person chooses a drink and the result is a drunk driver who kills. A person chooses another lover and the result is a broken family. A person chooses suicide and the result is devastation of their loved ones. The culmination of all of these choices results in a bruised and broken world where bad things happen. Life doesn't make sense then, becoming convoluted and confusing as a result of choice upon choice.

I long for the pain to stop. For you and for me. I long to have a relationship where you trust me and you know that My grace and love for you are immense. I want you to know My heart is for you. As long as you hold unforgiveness against me, you will not see My true nature. You will always mistrust My intentions. You will never fully believe I can love you fully and completely. That is why it is imperative you allow me in, to take the unforgiveness you cannot seem to let go of.

It is a matter of choice, and even in this I cannot make your choice for you. I designed it that way on purpose. I don't want those who have to love me...I want the ones who choose me. Who pursue me. Who run after me. Isn't that what you want, too? To be pursued and loved for who you are? To be wanted and known? I want the same things you do, Dear One. Truly.

What happens when you figure out I am telling you the truth? Your heart opens to me, forgiveness comes and with it, freedom to love fully. Not to hold onto hurt, but to release it to me where I can put it to rest. Will you allow me to do that for you? I love you so much more than you know. I long to show you, if you can only forgive me.

# September 25

*Every good gift and every perfect gift is from above, coming down from the Father of lights, with whom there is no variation or shadow due to change. ~James 1:17*

Change is never easy, Dear One. Even good changes are stressful and require adjustment. Then there are the hard changes which come from unexpected places. Job loss. Broken relationships. Sudden illness. Accidents. Those unexpected ones are really tough, because no one ever anticipates or plans for disaster. Catastrophe rushes in like a flood and leaves destruction in its wake.

You long for normal, but nothing is ever normal after these kinds of changes, Beloved. People say, 'You will find your new normal,' and that is true to a point. But remember following a sudden change, one of the effects is a change in you. So even if everything went back to the way it was, it would still not be 'normal' because you are different.

Wishing for change to disappear is not a useful approach. It is preferable to notice how the outward circumstances are changing you inwardly. Are you more fearful? Are you depressed? Are you walking on egg shells? To survive the hard changes, you have to become pliable. Flexibility will keep you from breaking to pieces. Longing for the past isn't going to help in this endeavor. As much as good memories of former times and places are nice to have, you cannot live in those memories. You have to live in the present reality. Things change. People change. Culture changes. It is the way things are.

My word to you, Beloved, is to hold onto me during the changes in life. When your outside world is crumbling, hold My hand. Let me do the internal work of the heart and make you into My image. Do not let bitterness creep in, or unforgiveness have its way. They only make your heart harder to mold.

When good changes come...a new place to live, a good job, a marriage, a baby...any time where life is flowing into you, continue to hold My hand. Let me help you manage the good stress and appreciate the forward movement. I am with you in the good and the bad changes, and even the ones which are a mixture of both. Bitter sweetness is the landscape of change. Your desire is always for the sweet without the bitter, but without it, the sweet wouldn't be as lovely. The key is to remember I am in your midst when change is swirling around you.

# September 26

*For even when we were with you, we would give you this command: If anyone is not willing to work, let him not eat. ~2 Thessalonians 3:10*

You are the glue, Weary One. You hold everything together by the skin of your teeth. Everyone looks to you. They may not even realize they are doing it, but they are. You feel the weight of such a load yet, you also feel the importance of the role. You want to unstick sometimes, but you know you cannot.

What would happen if you were not the glue? What if you let all the balls drop? All the plates stop spinning? Sure, things would go undone, but would you, could you, stop feeling the weight of all that you carry?

What if you let me carry it for you? That is a scary thought, isn't it? If you let everyone take responsibility for themselves, their own choices, the consequences of the choices, their own lives, if you stopped carrying so many. It would free you. Of course, children need supervision. Although some cases require dependency, reducing these levels of dependency would improve your health.

I am the real glue that holds the universe together. Since you are made in My image, being the Sticky One is expected in some instances. However, I am big enough to handle it. As a human, you are a finite being. Your capacity is limited. You cannot hold the world together, not even your world. I am the only one who can do that but you have to let me. I know it is easier said than done.

You care deeply. It is why I love you so. Your compassion uplifts. It might seem harsh to let some things go but the consequence of not doing so is killing you. The trick is knowing which things truly need you and which things do not. Stepping back is tricky. Beloved, look at each thing you hold. Does it bring you life or does it suck the life from you? If you have more life-sucking activity than actual life, make some adjustments. Let me help you. Ask me. I promise I will take those things and show you how to turn it around. I love you enough to walk with you. I want you to have freedom to love fully without being buried under responsibilities. I will show you. Let go and let me be the glue.

# September 27

*So, we do not lose heart. Though our outer self is wasting away, our inner self is being renewed day by day. ~2 Corinthians 4:16*

In life, there are seasons of rest. Or there should be. These seasons look different from the productive ones where you are going non-stop. Both types are delivered to you by My hand. Both are equally important. You have to be careful to recognize each kind because if you don't, you will burn out.

Burn out is when you physically or emotionally collapse due to overwork or stress. Most who are in a state of burn out think they cannot stop, so they try to 'push through' and cause further damage to themselves. Some do not even recognize it when burn out arrives at their door. They invite it in, thinking that being responsible for more and more is what leadership looks like.

Look at My Son. Even in His time on Earth He knew seasons of rest. He built them into His schedule. He regularly pulled away to talk with me. He knew where His strength came from. Dear One, you must learn to recognize seasons of rest, for if you do not, you will crash and burn out will become your only option. Rest will be forced upon you by your body, or your circumstances. Your life will begin to fall apart. Relationships will suffer. People will leave. Hurt will happen.

Stop. Right now. Stop and think. Are you in a season of fruitfulness or is that a facade? Are you productive and feeling life flowing or has My grace lifted and you are carrying all the burden? What season are you in? A season of rest is coming, one way or another. The choice is yours when it comes.

# September 28

*Be gracious to me, O Lord, for I am in distress; my eye is wasted from grief; my soul and my body also. ~Psalms 31:9*

The tears you shed, when you have no words, still make it to My ears. I keep them in a bottle. I have seen each one. Not one has fallen without My knowledge. There are times you wonder about that...if I have forgotten you, but I assure you I have not. The tears are real and when you cry My heart cries too. They are liquid prayers which find their way to me. I am with you as you cry yourself to sleep. I am with you when the frustrations overflow down your cheeks. I am with you when the pain is too much to bear.

I am like parents who hate to see their children suffer. It hurts My heart. I long to heal the pain and sometimes I do. Other times you must walk through it, but not because I enjoy your pain. Not because I am punishing you, but because it is a sin-filled world, a broken place. Wherever the enemy is given reign there will be pain and heartache. The good news is that I have overcome. The enemy will not wreak havoc forever. Until his day comes, when I bind him forever, there will be difficulty in this life. Yet, I do not abandon you to it. I am in it with you.

Most humans wrestle with having control of their lives, but the ones who walk with suffering already know control is an illusion. They allow me into their pain because they know My strength is made perfect in weakness. They know they are weak because life has been drained from them by their circumstances. Still, they do not give up. They do not quit. They refuse to renounce me because they walk in the deep places with me. Through the valley of the shadow. I am with them. I comfort them as they walk.

My Son was a man of sorrows when He walked the earth. He knew pain and suffering. Knows it still. He carries it for you. He walks beside you, so your load will not weigh you down. You must give it over to Him. You may not know how, but you must try to give it up. There is peace in the surrender.

# September 29

*Now may the God of peace Himself sanctify you completely, and may*
*your whole spirit and soul and body be kept blameless at the coming of our Lord Jesus*
*Christ. ~1 Thessalonians 5:23*

You haven't given up, Weary One. Your spirit lives somewhere deep inside you. The internal part of you that feels crushed. Some people call it your inner child. Others, your true self. Your human spirit. There are many names for the unique essence which I created and put within you. It is the part of you which rises up again and again to keep moving.

People will say they don't know how you do it. You wonder about that too. How do you manage? Beloved, it is the way I created you. When you acknowledge and receive yourself as My unique creation, you will feel hope rise. When I reside within you, My hope mingles with your essence and keeps you moving, even when it is difficult.

Sometimes you don't feel this part of you. You stuff it down. You ignore it for more pressing matters. It's not that you don't want to feel, it's that you don't have time. But, Beloved, you must make time to find this part of you again, because hope lives in this part.

Remember when you were a child and were free to roam. Think of that part of you that thrived when you were happy. Every day wasn't always happy, but there was an innocence that surrounded the child part of you before life got hard. It is that part that is still in existence. It is that part where your dreams live. Your interests, your big ideas. Life has tried to silence this part of you. I am here to bring it back.

I created this core part of you to be unlike anyone else I have ever created, and that is a lot of people. You are you because of this place in your heart. Add to it life experiences, both good and bad, personality shaped by your upbringing, all the individual talents and gifts you possess, and there is none like you. Take a moment to recall the feeling of freedom. Use some time to take inventory of all that you remember about that part of you. If you cannot remember, I will remind you. You need only to ask me why you are so wonderful. I have a long list.

You must not give up on you. Pain, loss, hurt, and continuous difficulty cannot snuff out the light I put within you, unless you let them. Don't let them. Look up. Look to Me. Listen to My list and take it to heart. Let me stir up the hope and light inside of you. Find ways to see it and to feed it. Set aside time to nurture it. Today, use five minutes. Tomorrow, go to 10. Small steps back to yourself. Write. Sing. Dance. Express yourself. I love it when you share yourself with the world around you.

# September 30

*Fear not, for you will not be ashamed; be not confounded, for you will not be disgraced; for you will forget the shame of your youth, and the reproach of your widowhood you will remember no more. ~Isaiah 54:4*

Are you looking back? Do you get stuck in the past, or does it propel you forward? Your past brought you to me, here and now. That is not a bad thing, Dear One. You might not be able to forgive yourself, but I forgive you. I do not hold it against you. In fact, I ask you to look at it through My eyes. Your way may have been crooked, or twisted through many hard places, but you were not alone.

Is it a surprise to you that I have been right beside you the whole time? Do not hang your head in shame...look back and see how I used things to clear your path to me. I do not hold things against you. The current place you find yourself has nothing to do with punishment. It has more to do with the consequences of living in a dark world. Hard things happen. Events turn out differently than you expected. The harsh reality is that sometimes life isn't fun. Sometimes it is hard. But do not allow your thoughts to be contaminated by the enemy. He wants you to think it is all your fault, or all My fault, or anyone else's fault but his. He deflects like that.

Your past is in the past. You cannot change it. You cannot forget it. It is part of you. It shaped you. The way you view the world is a product of what you do about your past. If you give it to me, it can renew your heart and bring a humility that is rare and beautiful, and so transformational that you bring My light to anyone who hears your story. If you keep your past for yourself, it will beat you up. It will cloak itself around you like darkness, so shame is your partner and with it, bitterness and unforgiveness. Which way would you prefer to live? In freedom and light or in shame and darkness? The answer is not a hard one, but it is up to you to choose.

Free will is a gift I give you. You make the choice. You are My beloved and I long for you to see yourself as I see you. I do not want you to make the past an idol which you bow to each day when you refuse to forgive yourself. I do not want shame to be your lifelong companion. Choose healing, Weary One.

# October 1

*For we are His workmanship, created in Christ Jesus for good works, which God prepared beforehand, that we should walk in them. ~Ephesians 2:10*

How many times have you had to get up after a season of loss, Weary One? You know, the days where giving up seems the preferable option? The days you don't want to get out of bed for the pain, or the loss, or the daily burden you carry. My point is, you get up anyway. You go forward. You might have days where it doesn't happen right away, and it is so much effort to do the tiniest little task, but you rose up.

You will always rise up. I have put the desire to live within you. To have purpose. To make a difference. To grow. To move forward. Even on days when it doesn't seem there is a forward movement to make, you stand up. You put one foot in front of the other.

Weary One, there are times you need to stand in the promise of what I have given you. There are times to remain steadfast and plant your feet to stand on My words to you. Hold fast. Stand tall in faith. Then there are times to pick up your feet and walk into the promise. Beloved, pick up your feet.

Pick up your feet to get out of bed. Pick up your feet and walk towards your goals. Don't have goals? Pick up your feet and set some. Standing is good. There are seasons of standing and holding on by your fingernails. There are seasons of barely hanging onto the promises. Then there are seasons of movement. Pick up your feet.

You are a child of God. You are the apple of My eye. You are loved. You are important. You are valued. You cannot be replaced. Your past does not define you. I call you out. I call you to pick up your feet.

# October 2

*Who is to condemn? Christ Jesus is the one who died—more than that, who was raised—who is at the right hand of God, who indeed is interceding for us. ~Romans 8:34*

I listen to My Son's prayers for you. Did you know that He intercedes for you night and day? His love is that great. And, if He is praying for you, how can your life go awry? It can't. Every mistake you make, sin you commit, or misstep you follow is redeemable. Some of them even prepare you for what I have for you in the future. Nothing is wasted with me, and His prayers are the reason that is true.

If you could hear His heart for you, you would not doubt. If you could hear His words about you, you would not fear. His powerful words are speaking on your behalf. The life you live is a hard one, with pressure on all sides. His words are required to survive it. And when your words join His, there is such power!

Spend some time with me. Join your prayers with the ones going up all around me. You will see. It will change your life. Not always the circumstances, but always your heart. You will notice anger fading away. You will feel peace in the midst of trials. It will revolutionize how you perceive the world around you. You will no longer feel alone in your suffering, because you will realize you are not alone. The man of sorrows and suffering is praying for you to make it through. He knows you. He knows what you feel. He knows your fear. He knows your anger. He gives you strength with the words he speaks over you.

# October 3

*For it is you who light my lamp; the Lord my God lightens my darkness. ~Psalms 18:28*

Is the dark getting darker? Is your world out of control? That's good news! That means the light is getting brighter. Did you know, Beloved, that the darkness serves the light? It is not the other way around. When the darkness comes, it seems like everything is being swallowed up by it. It seems as if nothing will ever work out because the blanket is so thick. Ah, but appearances can be deceiving.

At the cross, it seemed all was lost. At the tomb, it seemed all was dead. At the well, it seemed redemption was out of reach. In the street, it seemed accusation had won. At the table, it seemed betrayal was sure. At the pool, it seemed healing was impossible. On the shore, it seemed hunger would win. In the tree, it seemed injustice was here to stay. On the side of the road, it seemed blindness had shut out the light. At the gate, it seemed lameness was preventing movement. On the street, it seemed the disease would continue to ravage. In the graveyard, it seemed the devils had won.

But with me, Dear One, nothing is as it seems. With me the resurrection comes. The Living Water is served to the fornicator, grace is given to the adulterer. The betrayer is forgiven, the complacent find their feet. The hungry are fed and the blind see. The lame walk and the lepers are made whole. Even the demons release and remove themselves when I am near. I use the darkness to display the light.

So what darkness in this world taunts you? What is happening now that I cannot redeem? I will tell you. Nothing. There is nothing of which I am unaware. There is nothing that is so dark My light will not dispel it. Worry not. I have all things in My hands. My use of the darkness will bring about redemption, healing, freedom, hope, and life. It is who I am. I cannot be anything less. You are in good hands, Beloved. I will use your darkness to draw others to My light. Watch and see.

# October 4

*May the God of hope fill you with all joy and peace in believing, so that by the power of the Holy Spirit you may abound in hope. ~Romans 15:13*

You've probably heard that joy and happiness are two different things. Happiness is dependent on circumstance. When things are good, happiness is close by and when things are bad, it is fleeting. When you are walking a hard road because it seems like happiness is not possible, depression and loss of hope follow. Pursuing happiness is a futile task, because lasting happiness is only possible if you never have hardship, and life is full of hardship.

Joy, however, is a different animal altogether. Joy isn't dependent on circumstance. It is not really a feeling, but more of a knowing. You can be full of joy, even when you are not happy, because it is a deep well which never runs dry. In the dry seasons, there is still joy. In the hard seasons, there is still joy. It is a gift from Me; a fruit of My spirit, and thereby isn't dependent on you at all. You merely need to tap into it.

When you carry a heavy burden, you need joy more than ever, but it cannot be found apart from me. Look up, My Child. There are times for horizontal relationships, among friends or family, but there are also times to focus on your vertical relationship with me. When you find me, you find the bubble up kind of joy that comes from within. Your circumstances do not change...but everything is different. Joy filters your circumstances. Not in a rose-colored glasses kind of way that denies pain and suffering; no, joy is actually more present in those hard times. It can flourish in the midst of them.

Don't seek happiness, Weary One. It will only make you wearier. Honestly, don't even seek joy, seek me, then you will find My joy. It will well up within your heart, and it will comfort you. It will overflow to those around you. They will want to know where you get it in the midst of your trials. Then you can tell them. How you seek me and find me, even now.

# October 5

*O Lord, I love the habitation of your house and the place where your glory dwells.*
*~Psalms 26:8*

I want you to learn how to dwell with me. A dwelling is more than just a place. It is a state of being. To dwell with me means to think or speak or be with me at length. To live not just with me, but in me. To have your being in me. There is a unity in mind and spirit that happens when we are dwelling together. Peace bubbles up. Calm camps out. In hard times, Dear One, you want to come to me as your dwelling place.

Do not dwell on circumstances. Do not dwell on news. Do not dwell on the past. Where you make your dwelling place is important, My Love. It can make or break you. Once again, it is a choice you make.

In the morning when you rise up, you choose where you will abide. Which camp you will spend your time in. I want you to be in mine. Not getting stirred up and frustrated and angry with another. Not beat down or oppressed by others. Not caught up in the games the world plays. I want you to be sitting with me. Resting. Finding My peace internally that will carry you through your days, whatever they hold.

It is possible to dwell in me even when hardship is your companion. In fact, it is vital you learn how to do this. It will strengthen you. To come to me as your dwelling place will teach you how to walk in My protection. Your heart will be with me and that alone will protect it. Dwell with me and you will find the peace your heart is looking for on the difficult days. You will be in me and I will rescue you from the chaos around you. You will know me, and you know My peace.

# October 6

*The heart of man plans his way, but the Lord establishes his steps. ~Proverbs 16:9*

Unexpected things happen, and they can throw off your game. They interrupt life and get in the way. Or do they? It is really a matter of perception, Dear One, just a way of thinking about it. Say someone in your family suddenly gets ill or is in an accident. You have to cancel everything on your to-do list. It can be stressful and rearranging tasks is a big ordeal. If your mind gets stuck on that part of the interruption, it can ruin your day, week, month, or year. However, if you let me change your thoughts it can turn the entire event into an opportunity for you to shine My light, just in a different place than you had thought.

Hospitals, courtrooms, and funeral homes need My light. Who will take My light to them if not My children? If you never go there, how will they see it? In the circumstances which take you to these places, there are so many who need to know My heart is for them. That I am with them in hard times. You know that already, so you can show it to them just by showing up with a peaceful mindset instead of a stressed out one.

Stress certainly is present in unexpected situations. But figuring out how to manage the unexpected could change someone else's life, and yours as well. So, where does the stress come from? It is the weight of unmet expectations. If you expected to be home for a day of relaxation, stress may fill your mind with all that you are missing. If you were in charge of an event, stress may fill your mind with all of your obligations. If you had appointments which had to be cancelled, stress may fill your mind with all the people you are letting down, or all the time you will have to spend rescheduling.

However, if you accept the interruption as a divine moment, orchestrated by me for the purpose of sharing My light, stress takes a backseat. Sure, it is there, but once you arrive at the unexpected place, you begin to look for where My light is needed. Another family member needs a hug. A nurse needs a smile. Someone visiting needs a positive word. You become My hands and feet. The other stuff can wait. I promise you it can. It is not as important as it feels to you.

Just pay attention to me. Allow me to change your mindset. Allow me to show you who to share My light with. Allow me to speak to you in your own stressful circumstances and make them into opportunities. Sometimes, I send My children to be light for you too, Dear One. And sometimes, you are the interruption for others. Aren't you glad that those who come in your darkest times rearranged their schedules and showed up for you?

# October 7

*The Lord is gracious and merciful, slow to anger and abounding in steadfast love. The Lord is good to all, and His mercy is over all that He has made. ~Psalms 145: 8-9*

There is a difference between My mercy and My grace. Sometimes people define grace as My unearned favor, but that is actually mercy. No one can earn My mercy. It is freely given. Remember the servant who owed the king and he threw himself at the king's mercy? Mercy is My compassion and forgiveness shown toward you when it is within My power to punish. Mercy is My love blotting out your sin.

On the other hand, grace is My empowering presence. It resides within you where the Holy Spirit lives. It is the power to do things you thought impossible, like walk through hardship and tough circumstances. When you feel unable to take a step, My grace takes it for you. When you feel overwhelmed, My grace calms your heart. Grace covers you in the tough places of life.

You can also feel My grace resting upon you when you are walking in your calling. My grace flows when I place you in the right job. My grace flows when you have an idea that examines problems in a new way and solves issues around you. My grace makes you feel empowered even when your boss does not. My grace fills you up when you know your tank should be empty. My grace gives you bubble-up excitement when the circumstances are not very exciting. You feel it flow through you as a tangible energy source and you know it isn't coming from you.

My mercy washes you clean and My grace sustains you in your fresh new state. Both are amazing. Both are gifts. They work together in tandem with My presence. They are part of My character and they set you free from what binds you. They set you free to move in with My power.

# October 8

*You are my hiding place and my shield; I hope in your word. Psalms 119:144*

I am your defender. I am the one who protects you from attack. I shield you from danger. I know it feels like I am asleep at My post sometimes, but I am not. You cannot see all that I do. I assure you that I take the title of defender seriously. It is My character to protect what is mine.

Beloved, when you feel as if you have to defend yourself, stop and take a breath. Wait for me. I can defend you much better than you can defend yourself. When attacks come against you, it is hard to stand down. You want to come out fists blazing and tell everyone what is going on. That is not always the best course of action, Dear One. Sometimes it is best to stay quiet. Sometimes it is best to allow me to work within the silence. It is oh so hard to do, but there is little that can be done for you if you are wailing and shouting your own case.

When I defend you, you might not see it, but it is long lasting. When I am finished there is no doubt that I am the one who resolved the conflict. It causes you to humble yourself and to wait. I can work with you on the areas where your heart needs healing when you are in that posture. Whatever the situation is, it is in My hands while we work on the healing. I can move and work, because you are not in the way. If you are sitting and waiting for me, I can move. If you are moving, I have to sit and wait for you to finish.

Think of children in an argument. They are going at it, taking swings at each other and calling names. In the heat of the moment, they are not listening to each other. There is little chance they will work it out between themselves unless they have outside intervention. When a parent arrives and sits them down, they calm down to the point they can reason together. The parent guides them to a peaceful conclusion.

Then unbeknownst to the children, the parent begins arranging opportunities for them to work together again in the future, finding them their own places to shine. The parent knows what is needed and goes about arranging it. To the children, the situation is over and done, but the defender of freedom is still working. It is the same with me. I work on all levels, all the time. I just need you to let me. I need you to sit and take a breath. I need you to trust me. Can you do that?

# October 9

*"You will not need to fight in this battle. Stand firm, hold your position, and see the salvation of the Lord on your behalf, O Judah and Jerusalem. Do not be afraid and do not be dismayed. Tomorrow go out against them, and the Lord will be with you."*
*~2 Chronicles 20:17*

The battle is mine. It is not yours. I will take it up for you; you need only to be still. In some ways you are always under attack. Sometimes by the enemy, but other times by your own thoughts or the lies you believe. It is not possible for you to handle the burdens that weigh you down on your own. You have to have help. I am the help. I am the one who provides what you need to daily walk out your path.

The children of Israel had manna every day. I provided exactly what they needed in the hour in which they needed it. They did not need to worry about tomorrow's supply. It was a practice of trusting. After days and days, they began to believe.

In your battles, which come and never seem to end, there is a practice of trust. Have I fought for you before? Can you see My hand when you look back to remember? Yes, I have fought for you every time. You have never been alone, Dear One. You will never be. You can try to fight on your own but that is what wears you out. The armor you are trying to wear is too heavy and you just want to sit down. It is ill-fitting. The breastplate of bitterness. The shield of self-defense. The helmet of lies. The belt of regret. The shoes of resentment. And the sword of a sharp tongue is not the armor you need.

Take up MY armor: righteousness, truth, peace, salvation, faith and the sword of the spirit. Then take your position and stand firm. That is all I require. I fight the battle. You stand in My character. You are surrounded by it. My armor is protective. It isn't something which requires you; it is a gift from me. You cannot create righteousness out of thin air, nor any of the other pieces. Only I can do it.

I Myself am the one offensive piece of armor. Holy Spirit. You do not have to wield it because I am the sword. You carry me with you and all the battles will be won. After so many, you will believe. You will trust My provision and you can tell others how steadfast and faithful I am.

# October 10

*Oh, give thanks to the Lord, for He is good, for His steadfast love endures forever! Let the redeemed of the Lord say so, whom He has redeemed from trouble. ~Psalms 107:1-2*

I am the Redeemer. One who redeems. I compensate for your errors and weaknesses. I turn your weaknesses around and use them for My purposes. You may not believe I can redeem the things you have done. I beg to differ. I can flip any wrongdoing into something to show My glory.

With so many examples in My word, you would think people would see how I use them to redeem. The woman caught in adultery walked away free and the audience saw what My forgiveness looks like. The woman at the well shared her story with the town and they came to see for themselves. The demoniac stood clear-headed and the town marveled. From those times to now I have redeemed people, circumstances, and time.

You know people who have been redeemed. They are likely the fanatics and may be over the top with their emotions because he who has been forgiven much loves much. They are living testimonies of My mercy and grace. But it is not only people I redeem.

As the redeemer, I can turn anything around. You have not wasted your life as you might suppose. The years the locusts have eaten can be restored. Did drugs steal from you? Not anymore. Has a bad relationship hindered you? I can redeem that time. Have you lived in poverty, in want, or in wealth? Money, or lack of it, doesn't intimidate me. I can pour it out or dry it up to redeem its uses. Have you lost someone close? The darkness can be turned to light. Do you suffer from an illness? Is your mind broken? I am the healer and the one who holds all things together.

I deem you worthy to be restored. I deem you valuable. I deem you worthy. I re-deem. Which means I deem you all these things again and again and again. As many times as it takes. I take the broken places and make them whole.

# October 11

*Be merciful to me, O God, be merciful to me, for in you my soul takes refuge; in the shadow of your wings I will take refuge, till the storms of destruction pass by. ~Psalm 57:1*

The shadowlands are hard places. Everything is cloaked in darkness where you cannot quite make out the details. There are times in life where it seems everything around you is unclear and there is a foggy unknown about the future. But remember, Beloved, shadows can be deceiving. They are not the actual object but they blow up a shady version of it, which can be imagined to be something horrible.

When you were a child and you saw a shadow in the night, fear was your first reaction, not because of what you knew, but because of what you didn't know. Your eyes turned it into something other than the truth. Rather than investigate, it is more likely you ran to get under the covers. However, when your parents came, they turned on the light and the big dark object was gone, replaced by some benign one, like maybe a teddy bear or a baseball glove sitting on a chair.

When you grew up, you realized that shadows are merely exaggerated everyday items. When you see one now, it is immediately dismissed as nothing to fear. You don't even think about it, or if you do, you know to turn on the light to see what is really going on. The shadowlands, where the scary things live, have been banished from your mind by the truth you know as an adult, but didn't know as a kid.

The same is true for the shadowlands of life. They are foggy places where you cannot see clearly, and your imagination thinks the issue, whatever it is, will overtake you. The doctor's words, or the letter that came in the mail, or the phone call you never wanted to get...all seem monumental, like the monsters you saw in your bedroom.

I say, turn on the light. My light. See the shadows for what they are. Every life has what appears to be monsters, but My light can transform them into manageable everyday items. Not every shadow will disappear, but when you see even the hard things in life with My eyes, knowing that I am with you, the step by step journey through them becomes possible. It is so much better to rest in the shadow of My wings than to grope your way in the shadowlands. I am with you. Rest in My shadow and the light will expose all the rest for what they are.

# October 12

*For His anger is but for a moment, and His favor is for a lifetime. Weeping may tarry for the night, but joy comes with the morning. ~Psalms 30:5*

Make room for the mourning. Grief is My design. It is built into you. I know it is difficult, but it is necessary. Grief means you have loved deeply. Loss is part of living in a fallen world. My Son knew this better than most. He was acquainted with grief. He knew tears. He wept. He sweated blood. He knew the agony of loss.

Do not put your grief away, Dear One. Do not bury it deep. It will surface. Always. Because unprocessed grief is a trap for your heart, it will sit there and turn to stone if you do not acknowledge it. Does making room for grief open you up...for pain? Yes, but also for healing.

When you have significant loss, it is right to say so. When the loss hurts, it is right to say, "This hurts!" It does not make you weak to admit you are grieving. Tears are cleansing to the soul. Pent up tears block feelings and blocked feelings eventually shut down hearts. It seems the desired effect of closing off your grief may be to feel nothing.

You see, in seeking to be numb, you close off ALL emotions, not just the hard ones. Joy is fleeting. Hope disappears. Happiness is a mirage. Even love is tainted by unprocessed grief. Dear One, do you want a life without these emotions? It isn't worth it. Instead, follow My Son's example. Weep when you are sad. Cry out when you are in pain. Let others see your suffering. Share your story. There is healing in making room for your pain. Just as the happy times are part of your life, so are the painful ones. They are what make you...you.

Weeping endures for the night, but joy comes in the morning, as well as in the mourning. There is relief. There is room for your pain. Do not push it out. Make a place for it, a healthy place where you can see the scars, recognize their power, and use them for continuing your journey. When you see your pain as a friend who walks with you, and you accept it as a reminder of all the love you have experienced, there is a change of viewpoint. Do not discard it, but allow it to spill out. Then, the brokenness will begin to heal and the joy will flow again. Your emotions will reconnect with your heart. You will come alive, even with the grief in residence. You will see. Look for tomorrow.

# October 13

*Come and see what God has done: He is awesome in His deeds toward the children of man. He turned the sea into dry land; they passed through the river on foot. There we rejoice in Him. ~Psalms 66:5-6*

There are numerous places in My word where I tell My people to make a memorial. They take large stones and stack them up at places where significant things occurred. I asked them to do this, not to make an idol, but to remember what I did for them. Humans have a short memory. It isn't just the children of Israel; it can be seen all throughout history. A sudden event results in changed hearts and behaviors, only to fade over time. This tendency is why I ask for memorial stones to be set up.

It is important to look back at what I have done for you. Sometimes, in the moment, you cannot see My hand at work. However, when you look back in a year from now, it is obvious I cleared the way. The Egyptians were chasing Moses and My newly released children, who had already forgotten what I had done to buy their freedom. Fear does that. It wipes your memory. When you are anxious about something, it is difficult to remember. When My children looked back, they saw their enemies get swallowed up and on the other side of the sea and they celebrated.

The memorial stones you set up in your life will remind you to look back. When hard times come, you will remember I am with you. I am the deliverer. I bring you out of difficult places. Over and over again. When you have built places of remembrance into your life, it builds your confidence in me, that I will come through. Trust. Belief. It is a lesson of faithfulness. I am steadfast in your life. I always deliver. As the memorial stones stack up around you, remind your kids how they came to be. It doesn't have to be actual stones, though it can be. Put in place ways to remember. Tell the story. When you are tired and overwhelmed, tell yourself the story. Write it in a journal. Make a note in the margin. Paint a picture. Drive a stake. Create a holiday. Whatever way you can...remember.

# October 14

*As a father shows compassion to his children, so the Lord shows compassion to those who fear Him. ~Psalm 103:13*

Just as you remember me, I will remember you. I will not shrink back. In the hard times, I will remember. In the times when you are burned out and overwhelmed, I will come to the rescue. When life is difficult for you, it hurts me too. Do you not know that your broken heart breaks mine, Weary One? Your tears cry out to me.

Just as when your own child is hurting, your compassion wells up within you, so does mine. I take no pleasure in pain. Even when it is a consequence of your own choices, it still hurts My heart. I long for you to be whole. My desire is for you to be at peace and rest in me.

There are times in life when it seems you are forgotten, Beloved. Fear of abandonment rises up in your chest. Each step you take seems lonely and you wonder where I am. You think I am absent, or distant. The enemy wants you to think I am far away and indifferent to your plight. You cry out and every sound, every prayer, every tear is heard in My ears as if with a megaphone. Your torment is mine. Your grief is mine. Your heartache is mine. You are My child.

Could you forget your children? Don't you feel their pain? Don't you wish you could fix it for them? When you cannot, how helpless do you feel? I feel all of these things too. You are made in My image, Dear One. You feel things as I do. The truth is I have inscribed you on the palms of My hands. My Son sacrificed His life. He rescued you, by making a way for me to reach you.

To inscribe means to carve a permanent record of something. This writing on My hands isn't temporary. It is there to stay. It will stand forever. It is a scar that shows the injury which bought you freedom. How could I ever forget that?

# October 15

*Trust in Him at all times, O people; pour out your heart before Him; God is a refuge for us. Selah. ~Psalms 62:8*

Selah. Stop and listen. Pause and Reflect. In difficult times it is hard to pause. Or maybe you can pause, but the reflection part is the tough part. Beloved, it is critical that you make time to do these things.

I am in the pause. I am waiting for you to take a moment. It cannot always be a getaway vacation; you have to learn to take short breaks. In circumstances where you are a caregiver, or grieving, or in a trial of one sort or another, the pauses make all the difference. Even to breathe in and out a few times, will reorient you to My spirit.

Then listen, a birdsong is My love song to you. My tears join yours like a pattering rain. Open My word and hear what I have to say. There are many ways I speak. The sunrise or sunset. The sound of a bubbling brook, or a child's belly laugh. Sometimes silence speaks as loudly as anything else. Listen. Sit in what you hear. Bathe in it. Soak up every little sound. It can become a mini vacation to listen.

Reflect. What did you hear? What does it mean? I can tell you; it is important to reflect. The love songs I sing over you mean something. Can you guess? You are loved. You are important. You are not forgotten.

Pause. Listen. Reflect. Selah.

# October 16

*Why are you cast down, O my soul, and why are you in turmoil within me? Hope in God; for I shall again praise Him, my salvation and my God. ~Psalm 43:5*

If you are not careful, a spirit of heaviness will engulf you, Weary One. Being aware of despair in the midst of what appears to be a never-ending trial is crucial. This spirit feels like a wet blanket draped over you. It makes it hard to get up in the morning. It makes it hard to go through your day. It is part of what you are going through, but it shouldn't be all of what you are going through. Eventually, it will paralyze you and keep you from moving.

I see this spirit of heaviness hovering around, waiting for an opening when things are overwhelming and confusing. It comes through a broken heart, or a huge loss. It comes through poverty or bondage to addiction. Oppression or frustration. Grief opens the door and mourning welcomes it inside. This spirit wants to keep My children in darkness. But I have another plan.

I offer beauty for ashes. I offer freedom for captives. I offer light over darkness. I offer comfort for those who mourn, and joy instead of tears. I offer a garment of praise to throw off the cloak of heaviness. That wet blanket doesn't have to be your covering. It can be removed. It can be replaced with a robe of righteousness, and a garment of praise. It is what My Son offered when he spoke of the favor of the Lord.

You have My favor, Dear One. All these garments are already yours. They have been bought for you. I paid a high price, because you are worth it. Do not let the spirit of heaviness tell you otherwise. Surround yourself with people who know this truth and will speak it to you until you believe it. Allowing others to help you is not weakness, it is strength. In this upside-down world you live in, you must remember you are not alone.

# October 17

*Can a man hide himself in secret places so that I cannot see him? declares the Lord. Do I not fill heaven and earth? declares the Lord. ~Jeremiah 23:24*

No need to hide. Not in your house or out in plain sight. No need to withhold your heart from me or anyone else. Sometimes the harder places seem like hiding places. Broken heartedness is like a closet you go into and never want to come out. It seems risky. It seems if you expose your heart, it will shatter into dust. It is normal to try to piece it back together on your own, to trust no one else but yourself. After all, someone or something broke it, something outside of you, and so pulling back and isolating yourself seems the only safe solution. Find a place to lick your wounds; remove the chance it will happen again.

Dear One, when you hide from others you also hide from me. You remove me from getting close to you, as if you do not wish me to see the condition of your heart. It hurts. It is in pain. Broken heartedness is messy. In the day-to-day exhaustion it drains you even more. No wonder you hide. No wonder you try to sweep it under the carpet. You feel if you expose it to me I will require you to fix it or clean it up. You don't have the energy for that, so you pretend all is well, when inside you are shriveling up. You are dry and brittle.

I am the healing balm. You don't have to perform for me. I am the one who can make your heart soft and supple again. The circumstances may or may not change, but your reaction to them can. In your dark hiding place, I can bring light. I can illuminate the cracks of your heart and fill them in. You cannot hide from me, Weary One. I am everywhere you are, even in the broken-hearted closet. I will hold you, and guide you and bring My light wherever you are. You cannot be outside of My presence.

# October 18

*Submit yourselves therefore to God. Resist the devil, and he will flee from you.*
*~James 4:7*

There is more than one battle going on. The one against the enemy can be difficult, but it is already won. This battle is more of a nuisance than anything, like an annoying fly that buzzes around your head. The enemy has no power over you unless you give it to him. My Son took care of that. He defeated the darkness so you could walk in light and freedom.

Another battle is with yourself. Sometimes you think the battle is with the enemy, but it is really the lies he told you, which you believe to be true. It isn't him; it is you. Your mind. You wrestle and fight, but it is your own beliefs you are battling. It is why I say to take every thought captive. Every thought matters in how you live life. Defeated or inspired. Depressed or empowered. So many of your struggles are internal.

However, the biggest battle you fight is with me. That may surprise you, but it's true. You want so badly to hold onto control. You are not sure I am completely trustworthy, so you withhold parts of yourself from me. I ask for your whole heart and you give me a small part. I ask for your whole self, but you wrestle with me when I show you the parts you still have not given. I ask for surrender and you keep fighting.

Remember as a kid when you and a sibling or a friend got into a fight? It could be a fist fight, or a verbal one, no matter. The emotions rode high and sometimes pushing and shoving followed until one of you yelled, "Stop! I give up!" In a verbal sparring match, one walked away. Fuming and full of emotion, the frustration finally got through that this was an impossible situation. No use in continuing. Give up. Beaten. Surrender. Like soldiers in a battle you put your hands up and waved the white flag.

When you battle me, it is the same. I do not relent when it comes to your freedom. I know what you need and I will not stop until you have it. It is easier for you to surrender to me than to wrestle with me your whole life. The thing is, once you realize I am for you, and I am trustworthy with your heart, giving up is easy. The sooner you do, the sooner you move forward. The longer it takes, the more tired you get. The other battles, the one with the enemy and the one within yourself, will come into alignment in victory once you surrender to me. Don't fight me, Weary One. Put your hands up. Walk out of the battle and into freedom.

# October 19

*I wait for the Lord, my soul waits, and in His word I hope; my soul waits for the Lord more than watchmen for the morning, more than watchmen for the morning.*
*~Psalms 130:5-6*

While you are waiting, Dear One, do not fret. There will always be seasons of waiting: waiting for a breakthrough, waiting for a next step to become clear, waiting for a prodigal to return, waiting for the grief to lessen, waiting for your body to heal, waiting for the next season to begin, waiting for maturity, waiting for hope to resurface. There are so many kinds of waiting. I know you are scared to pray for patience because you are afraid I will give you circumstances that require it! The truth is, life requires patience and those who walk with me know this; but waiting is hard for all My children.

Limbo-land is a hard place. It is the in-between space where your vision isn't yet a reality. It is a space where you wonder if it ever will be. Sometimes it is a foggy place full of mist where you cannot see your hand in front of your face. Other times it is a place where you can see clearly, but cannot actually get to where you are going. Sometimes you know in part; others you don't know the first thing. Waiting One, impatience doesn't make it go any faster. Worry only slows things down and causes stress.

For me, your waiting seasons are like the blink of an eye. I stand above time and I can see the end from the beginning and everything in between, including My plan for your life. I am not taken by surprise when you are in a waiting place. I have not forgotten you and I am not silent.

For me it is not waiting...it is preparing. Preparing your heart for the future. It is preparing your life to be able to receive what I have for you. Think of me as a farmer who plants seeds. I prepare the soil. I dig the hole. I plant and nourish the seed. I water. I let the sun shine its warmth. All of these things I do for the good of the seed, so it can thrive and produce fruit.

There are dormant times, when I am preparing the ground deep inside, which cannot be seen on the outside. There are sprouting times, where everything is new and tender. There are fruitful times, where there is a harvest. There are pruning times, where the dead parts are cut away. Each of these times requires a different kind of waiting.

I am in no hurry because I know the preparation that is needed. Look around you. You are always waiting on something. I will not move until you are ready. Rather than begging for the next step, prepare your heart. Sit with me and let me prepare you. Wait, here with me.

# October 20

*For I know the plans I have for you, declares the Lord, plans for welfare and not for evil, to give you a future and a hope. ~Jeremiah 29:11*

The morning after the storm is the brightest. The dawn comes just after the darkest hour. Hope rises after all seems lost. In the midst of the storm, Weary One, do not forget the dawn is right around the corner. You might think it will never end, but it will. Your memory of previous dawns might be overshadowed by the present storm, but take a moment to remember. Has there ever been a storm you haven't come through? I walk you through each and every one. You have survived all of them. Do not be discouraged or afraid that this one is going to take you out. I will not allow that to happen.

There is coming a day, the sun will rise and the clouds will part. The rays will filter down, and your heart will unfold like the petals of a flower. You will raise your chin to warm your face and you will breathe again. It will be a glorious day. You will feel My love envelope you and wonder how you ever doubted that the new day was coming. When that day comes, mark it in your mind. Remember it and make a memorial in one way or another. Every storm has a dawn. Every cloudy sky breaks open to let the sun shine again.

I made the world that way. I intentionally created a storm cycle, which pours down and washes clean, and then clears up and shines brightly. What would the dawn mean if not for the darkness before it? When your heart leaps inside you at the beginning of a new day, it shows you are alive. When you feel excitement bubble up after a long absence, it is a gift. Hope is always around. No storm can snuff it out. It cannot be extinguished because it is me. I reside in you and around you. Even in the storm I am with you. Even when you cannot see me, I am there. Even when you cannot feel me, trust that I am there. Hold tight to the facts. The storm will end. The day will come. You will survive. Hope will rise again.

# October 21

*Be watchful, stand firm in the faith, act like men, be strong. ~1 Corinthians 16:13*

You have a voice. You may not think you do, but you do. When you are tired from life's storms there is a tendency to feel forgotten, or bypassed...like nothing you have to offer really matters to anyone. You may be sick, or grieving, or exhausted, or overwhelmed by life, or even confused. In those times, the last thing you think of is having a voice, but you do. You have a story to tell. It might not be a pretty story...they rarely are. The importance of your voice, your perspective, your experience cannot be understated. There are others who need to hear. There are others who are drowning and need a life rope to hang onto. Your story can be that for them.

It is a scary thing to share openly, when you have your own doubts. It requires transparency and vulnerability. You take a risk when you open yourself up. What if you don't know all the answers? No one knows all the answers, and those who think they do are wrong. What if no one listens? They may not say anything because they are in a hard place too, but they are listening. What if they don't like what I say? Leave that up to me. It is not your concern if you are liked by others, only that you are loved and adored by me.

I don't start you with a microphone in front of a crowd. No, if you pay attention to me, I will bring those who need to hear your voice to you. It might be a neighbor, or a co-worker. It could be a stranger in the grocery line, or a server at a restaurant. Pay attention to the nudges I give. If you say yes, and you speak your story, I may put you on a stage...or not. Just follow me. Listen to me. Your voice is like no other. No one else I have created has the story you do. I will bring purpose to the pain you have walked with. I will use it for healing. I will give you the courage to use your voice and you will become brave. The heaviness will flee in the moment of your speaking. I will give you the words. You will know what to say and how to say it. Trust me. Listen to your voice as it heals others because it can heal you, too. Use your voice to testify.

# October 22

*Heal me, O Lord, and I shall be healed; save me, and I shall be saved, for you are my praise. ~Jeremiah 17:14*

Trauma can change you. Whether it is an assault of some kind, an accident, or a horrific loss, trauma divides life into before and after. I know it causes you deep pain. I know it changes the way you see things. I know it causes your brain chemistry to change. It was My design for your brain to go into a heightened state of awareness in certain instances. A design for protection, for fight or flight, but in My design, it is only a temporary state. In this sin-filled world, traumatic events were not supposed to be as constant as they have become. I did not design brains to be on alert 24/7. Now, memories hold onto the pain. They replay it over and over, causing trouble.

I just want you to know I was with you. In the event. I saw the horror. I bore witness to the thing that happened to you. You were not alone. You are not alone now. I never wanted humans to choose to harm one another. The enemy is wreaking havoc and it affects people for life. I do not undo free will choices of My creations, but I can use the results of the pain they inflict for My purposes. I can walk beside the wounded and show them I love them despite the pain.

My heart breaks for the broken. My eyes see what happens in the day-to-day. The suffering is not lost on me. My Son's death was traumatic. It was gruesome. I had to look away. The cruelty of humans influenced by the enemy is far beyond anything in My design. My desire is to reconcile My creation back to the beginning, the days when we walked and talked together in the garden, where I was with you face to face. Where in the conversations we have together where you will find peace for your soul.

Sharing your pain with others where you will find some healing. If I had a magic wand, I would wipe away your tears and take away the pain, but I don't do magic. I do miracles, and I can assure you that each breath you take is one of those miracles. You are not less than. You are valuable. My compassion is surrounding you. I hold you in My hands. Rest in me. I see your heartache, and I love you. I will never stop loving you.

# October 23

*And He said to them, "Come away by yourselves to a desolate place and rest a while." For many were coming and going, and they had no leisure even to eat. And they went away in the boat to a desolate place by themselves. ~Mark 6:31-32*

Do you think self-care is selfish? Do you believe asking for help will impose upon someone else? Do you think taking care of yourself is in opposition to caring for others? Teary One, if you do not consider yourself important and you do not recognize how to take care of yourself, you will burn out. You will get overwhelmed, bitter, resentful and it will make you miserable. Whether it is caring for a loved one or My bride, the church, you will find yourself spread too thin. It is not good for your health, Beloved.

Take My Son for an example. He spent His ministry traveling with crowds who had expectations. They pulled on Him. They required so much care, and He loved them well. He fed them, and healed them, and taught them, but He also took time away from helping people. He wandered off to a garden or a lake. He spent time talking to me. He had dinner with His friends. He took solitary walks. He hung out with others, talking and joking. If My Son, 100% divine and 100% human who was actually sent to save the world, took time for Himself, how much more should you?

It is not wrong to put yourself and your mental health first sometimes. It actually makes you a better caregiver. It will do no one any good if you are depressed to the point you cannot function. Eventually, if you do not require yourself to rest, your body will require it of you. This is not a sprint, Dear One, it is a marathon. I urge you to find ways to make time for yourself. Learn to take deep breaths throughout your day. Take five minutes to sit alone and listen for My voice. Meditate on My word. Soak in some music. Talk to a counselor or a friend. Find some movement you can do regularly. Bike ride, hike, walk, run, swim, go to the gym, kayak, paddle board, whatever you can do to move will relieve your stress. You must manage it, or it will manage you.

My servants often feel guilty for taking self-care seriously. Walking away for a bit can feel cold and uncaring, but you are not a servant, you are a son/daughter. You don't work for me; you work with me. I need you at your best to join me in My work. I don't want you stressed, tired, and overwhelmed. My Child, take care of yourself so you can take care of others I have placed in your care. I selected you for this purpose, because you are the one who can love them like I do. Your students, your patients, your congregation, your coworkers, your family members, your children, all deserve the best you, just as you do. Listen to My words. Take care of yourself.

# October 24

*But you are a chosen race, a royal priesthood, a holy nation, a people for His own possession, that you may proclaim the excellencies of Him who called you out of darkness into His marvelous light. ~1 Peter 2:9*

Chin up, Dear One. I am not through with you yet. I will not leave you to fade away into obscurity. You are not a wallflower. You are My heart's desire. I long to spend time with you. You may not believe it, but it is true. There is no one like you, with the same personality, the same characteristics, the same heart, the same talents. None like you. I can say this because I know it to be true. You are the perfect combination of you. Do not let the enemy tell you otherwise.

Look to me to learn who you are. Look in My word. It tells you there plainly; you are the apple of My eye. My strength is made perfect in your weakness. You feel weak. You feel empty. You feel less than. Those are lies. You are none of those things. Hard times beat you down, but I will lift you up.

I bring life into dead situations. I bring light into the darkness. I bring healing to hearts and sight to blind eyes. I am the redeemer of lost causes, who were never really lost to begin with. I am the champion of the downtrodden. I am always for the underdog because everyone else is against him.

Look at My Son's track record. The adulterous woman. The woman at the well. The prodigal Son. The thief on the cross. The centurion. Even the demoniac was set free. Remember that Jesus demonstrated My heart. He is a picture of me in flesh and blood. My heart is freedom for all to see what I see in them. That includes you. Freedom to see yourself as valuable, worthy, beautiful, strong, and important. You are important to me. Your life is important to me. I have things for you to do, but more importantly, I have someone for you to be...yourself. Wholly and fully you. When you can embrace the person I see, you will stand in My love with your chin up and your back straight. You will walk in your identity in me.

# October 25

*But godliness with contentment is great gain, for we brought nothing into the world, and we cannot take anything out of the world. ~1 Timothy 6:6-7*

Simplify your life, Weary One. When it gets too cluttered up, your mind gets too full. Your heart is crowded. Your body lives in a state of constant stress. Simplicity is the quality of being easy to understand. If something is simple, it means it is not difficult. There is a discipline of simplicity.

Choosing a less complicated life, often makes things easier for yourself instead of harder. What does this look like? Being intentional. You don't have to go to every party you are invited to. You don't have to be on every committee you are asked to join. You do not carry an entire movement on your shoulders. In your home, you can share the load, instead of doing everything on your own. You can have hard conversations where you ask others to contribute. Even in seeking truth and justice, you can do so in a way that is simple and straightforward.

My point, Beloved, is that the more complex your life gets, the more you are owned by things, or events, or people. The more of a slave you are to your life, the less enjoyment you have. My Son didn't have a place to lay His head. He lived a simple life so He could focus on the people around Him. He went where I led Him. He took very little. He gave up complicated. Even in His death, when complicated was swirling around Him, you can see His commitment to simple truth.

The enemy always wants your life to be complicated because that leaves so much room for his smoke and mirrors. He thrives in the shadows of complexity. He knows the more complex things are, the more excuses humans make for not following me. I don't have time. My bank account is empty. My calendar is full. I have to be somewhere. Instead of being interruptible and in the moment, My people are scurrying around, unaware of the pain-filled world in which they live. They think the pain is far away, or on the TV. They ask, "What can I do? I am so busy and the problem is so far away."

My answer to that question is simplify your life. Take out the fluff. You don't have to live in a tent, but pay attention to all you possess and how much life it gives you and how much it takes from you. You might be surprised how freeing it is to let go.

# October 26

*O, give thanks to the Lord; call upon His name; make known His deeds among the peoples! ~1 Chronicles 16:8*

Come. Sit with me. Let me give you a fresh revelation for your day. Each day's a new beginning. Sitting with me allows me to speak over you. I can open up My word to you in ways you have never known it before. I can drop truth into your heart. Weary one, I am always longing to give you something fresh. No one likes stale things, least of all me!

Sometimes My favorite thing to do is to remove the scales from your eyes on a matter. When you have seen things in one way your whole life because of your experiences, and then all of a sudden, I give you fresh eyes, it brings joy to My heart. Fresh perspective is powerful, even though you might see things about yourself that are not pretty.

No one can know everything there is to know about me. No one can know everything there is to know about themselves either. But I know all of both. When you sit with me, I choose to reveal new places in your heart or new thoughts about Myself. It is one of My greatest joys to peel back another layer of My heart for you to enter. The layers are never-ending, meaning the revelation is always growing.

If your relationship with me is stagnant, it is not because I want it to be. I want the opposite. I want interaction. I want to show you great and marvelous things which you do not know. Come sit with me, Dear One, and get My fresh word for your life.

# October 27

*For you equipped me with strength for the battle; you made those who rise against me sink under me. ~Psalms 18:39*

You are a warrior. You may not feel like one, but you are. I have prepared you for this battle, and I am preparing you still. You do not just become a warrior; you have to be prepared to be one. You cannot go from sitting to a battle. There has to be training. Sometimes training exercises are tough. They feel like the real thing. I allow these exercises because then, you are experienced when the real battle erupts. You know what to do.

Hard things are not faced by the weak. You feel weak, but there is a strength in you which you are not even aware of. I put it there, Beloved. You are stronger than you know. You will not fully understand until you have to use the strength to make it through the day. It doesn't always feel like you are a victorious warrior. Sometimes it feels as if you are conquered. Sometimes it feels like you are defeated and beat up. The image of a warrior with a sword thrust overhead in victory is a powerful one, but not accurate. A warrior who has been in battle is exhausted, dirty, and injured. The power is in continuing to battle despite those conditions.

A true warrior doesn't give up when situations get hard. A true warrior has resilience to get back up, to continue moving even when the enemy is about to win. To know when to crouch and when to spring up. To know when to be silent and when to make a warrior's cry. To know the battle will end and to remember it is temporary. A true warrior knows I am the one fighting. I am the one who gives the strength and perseverance. A true warrior knows you cannot fight the battle alone.

I make your heart ready. I have prepared you for this. Do not shrink back. Do not give up. You will be victorious because I am victorious. You will win the battle, tired, dirty, and exhausted...but then the victory will infuse you with confidence. Then you will rise up and you will stand, sword of the Spirit in your hand, and you will cry out. It will be a glorious day.

# October 28

*The heavens declare the glory of God, and the sky above proclaims His handiwork.*
~Psalms 19:1

Arise, My Weary One. Take in the sunrise. Observe the light as it rises to greet the day. See the soft colors throughout the sky. Notice the clouds hovering above to create a stunning painting in the heavens. Bring your tired eyes to gaze upon it. Restore your soul with My beauty. Start your day looking up. Then all that is around you from that time forward will be seen with new eyes.

My handiwork has the effect of changing perspective. Wherever you are you can find a tangible sense of My presence if you look around you. Trees lift their arms in surrender to me. Mountains stand steadfast as a testament of faithfulness. In cities, birds still sing My praises. The sky opens wide My palette of colors. Rivers, valleys, and lakes all contain My essence. The night sky, with its diamonds twinkling and the moon shining, points to the light of the world.

My creation is a place of restoration. Let it seep into your bones. Let it light up your face. Breathe it in. Soak in the whole expanse of it. When you take a moment to intentionally pay attention, you will be surprised at how much life you will find. It will soothe your weary soul. It will uplift your tired body. It will give hope to your heart. It will cause you to look up more often.

The hard things in life are heavy. They bring you down, but My creation stands as a testimony of My glory. No matter what happens in your day, or your lifetime, there is always a testimony of My love surrounding you. You simply have to pay attention and look for me. I write you a love letter every day...every single day.

# October 29

*And you will know the truth, and the truth will set you free. ~John 8:32*

The truth will set you free. It is a simple concept really, but one that is difficult to apply in your life. Especially in these times where truth is up to the highest bidder. Weary One, I am the way, the TRUTH and the life. When you can be easily swayed by someone claiming to be telling the truth, you can also be easily fooled.

Instead, put your ear to My chest. Listen for My heartbeat. Even in the words of others you can hear it. Does My love come through? Is there compassion in the message? What about hope? Justice? Peace? Is there any of my character in the message? If not, dismiss it. Do not be taken. It is so easy to be pulled into the argument over whose truth is right. Beloved, My truth doesn't have to be proven. It stands alone.

No need to defend the truth. It defends itself. No need to get caught up in the swirling so called debate over who is right and who is wrong. That misses the entire point, which is expressing My heart. You are My representative on the earth. What would I say if I was standing beside you? Are you sure you know? Seek me and I will tell you the truth.

# October 30

*And no creature is hidden from His sight, but all are naked and exposed to the eyes of Him to whom we must give account.* ~Hebrews 4:13

Seek me and you will find me. Search. I will not hide from you. You may have already found me and do not realize it. I often don't look like you expect me to. Especially when your life circumstances are difficult. You might want a knight on a horse to ride in and whisk you away, but I come in a soft whisper to help you to stay. You may prefer a dramatic rescue, but I show up in a kind neighbor. I do rescues. I might do them in dramatic ways, and I might do them in subtle ways...but I do them.

You are worthy of My rescue, Beloved. Do not question that. When things are hard, do not believe it is because I do not love you, or because you are not good enough. Nothing could be further from the truth. You are the one I long for. You are the one I want to find me. If you have been distant because of what happened to you, ask me to show you Myself. I am never far. In fact, I am all around you even now.

Nothing is hidden from My sight. Not anger. Not tears. Not broken hearts. I will not shy away from messy pain. I will not walk away. I have not walked away. I am always here; you simply have to turn your face towards me. I will make My presence known to you if you search for it.

# October 31

*"Because he holds fast to me in love, I will deliver him; I will protect him, because he knows My name. When he calls to me, I will answer him; I will be with him in trouble; I will rescue him and honor him. With long life I will satisfy him and show him My salvation." ~Psalms 91:14-16*

You are not hidden. I am the one who sees. You are not lost. I see every move and feel every breath. Every whisper for help finds its way to My ears. I will surround you in the darkness with My angels. I will plot your escape from your enemies, those who want you to cave in, give up, or walk away. Do not give up, I am coming. I have designed the most elaborate rescue. Hold on. Do not write me off. Wait for it. See what I will do.

I am the changer of hearts. I can turn what is difficult one day into hopefulness the next. I can make the things you dread into gifts. I can redeem and I can replace mourning with gladness. It is My specialty. Do not mourn yourself into a dark place. Look up for My presence. You are not alone. There are others. There is a group I am coming after. You are all going to be My testimony. My warriors. My ones who show others the way.

I am coming for you. You will not have to cry yourself to sleep any longer. You will not have to wonder if you have been abandoned. You will see and you will know I am alive and well. You will see My hand fight for you. Defend you. Care for you. You are loved and you are worth every drop of blood My Son shed. You are worthy. He made you worthy. Do not doubt that.

# November 1

*You did not choose me, but I chose you and appointed you that you should go and bear fruit and that your fruit should abide, so that whatever you ask the Father in My name, He may give it to you. ~John 15:16-17*

I chose you. Before you knew I existed, I chose you to be mine. So many times, Dear One, people think they have chosen me first, but it is not possible for you to choose me until I have chosen you. You are not even capable of seeing the truth, unless I open your eyes.

Think about the disciples, minding their own business, until I chose them. They were fishing. But when I called them, they saw me. They knew. They did not choose me first, I chose them, but when I asked, they followed. It was an interaction, a two-way communication between us. I called. They answered.

Do not despise those who cannot yet see. All will see in My time. It is not up to you, except to speak when I say so. My voice will be heard at the appointed time. No need to feel the weight when someone doesn't decide to follow at the moment you are speaking to them. I have it well in hand. Just be obedient when I nudge you. That is all.

There will be fruit. Simply love one another. The fruit that comes from My love is always good fruit, lasting and changing hearts.

# November 2

*Lift up your heads, O gates! And be lifted up, O ancient doors, that the King of glory may come in. Who is this King of glory? The Lord, strong and mighty, the Lord, mighty in battle! Lift up your heads, O gates! And lift them up, O ancient doors, that the King of glory may come in. Who is this King of glory? The Lord of hosts, He is the King of glory! ~Psalms 24:7-10*

Awake O Sleeper. Do not let your life pass you by, Weary One. Do not sleep your life away. By sleep, I mean walking through your life as if your current reality is all there is. Standing in the foggy mist of discouragement clouds your view of what actually is true. Swing wide the gates. Invite me in. Let me into your circumstance so I can change your perspective. Ask me for My viewpoint, because it is eternal. I don't only see where you are now, I see what is being formed in you. It is a precious thing. You are not awake to it. Let the King of Glory come in. Let My Son show you all that is in store for you. Not darkness...glorious light, hope, and victory.

See your reality with My eyes. Longsuffering produces depth. Patience produces wisdom. Hardship produces compassion. You are not aware of the precious jewels being formed within you. Like diamonds are formed under pressure, so you are going to shine in a spectacular way. You already are; you just do not know it. Look, My Love. You carry brilliance and beauty, even now. Even in the mess of life, you are being formed for My eternal purpose. Swing wide the gates. Open yourself to me. Let me work through your pain and suffering.

You will find that joy comes disguised as pain. Hope is dressed as suffering. It is My secret. When you hold onto your circumstances as gifts from me, you will find you see them with new eyes. See. Your resurrection is at hand. Walk out of your grave.

# November 3

*And he arose and came to his father. But while he was still a long way off, his father saw him and felt compassion, and ran and embraced him and kissed him.*
*~Luke 15:20*

My arms are open. They are welcoming to you, and to your heart. Come fall into them. I will hold you like a father holds a child. I will not let you go. I will infuse you with My love. It will transfer from me to you as I hold you in My embrace. Love does not close its arms.

The prodigal son learned this. He thought he would be shunned, thought he already had been, but that was his perception, not his father's. He walked away from his father, full of his own ideas in his youth. Life's reality brought him back with his head hung. Imagine his surprise to find his father racing towards him with open arms. While he was still a long way off...the father was looking, waiting, and hoping. Hoping that on the horizon today would be the day his son would return. Hoping to see a familiar silhouette coming towards him. The father knew the day would come. He anticipated it. He had faith for it. He never gave up.

Then he ran. When the day arrived, he didn't wait, he ran to rescue his son. His joy was overflowing. He was ecstatic. His grace complete. The story of the father of the prodigal is My story. It is yours, too. I wait with open arms...always. It doesn't matter to me if you are in a faraway country, squandering My gifts, or if you are shut up in your own house in a dark pit.

I am in both places with My arms open. I long to embrace you and welcome you home. I am your home. I am the peace you are searching for. I am the way back to wholeness. I am the glue that joins your pieces together. I am the healer who will use the broken parts to create something beautiful of your life. I am running towards you with open arms. Come fall into them.

# November 4

*So, we built the wall. And all the wall was joined together to half its height, for the people had a mind to work. And each of the builders had his sword strapped at his side while he built. The man who sounded the trumpet was beside me. ~Nehemiah 4:6,18*

Guard your wall. Not the walls you build to protect yourself, Weary One. Those have to come down over time. No, I am talking about the wall of My presence. I am with you always. I have told you this, however; there are times that life crushes your belief that it is true. It is in the moment of doubt that the gaps and fissures in the wall allow the enemy to seep into your thoughts. If there are enough breaks in the wall, your belief will weaken. Then, it is child's play for the enemy to come in and break down the rest.

My children rebuilt the wall of Jerusalem under such circumstances. It had crumbled and was in disrepair. Nehemiah took My instructions and My favor to rebuild it. There was much opposition, but they worked with all their heart. They built with one hand and carried a sword in the other. They had to guard the wall because their enemies knew the power that would come when it was completed.

Beloved, when you fill the gaps that life has torn in your faith, strength will come. Guarding your wall, taking a stand and not compromising what I say about you is critical to your hope. It is easier to lose hope, to be defeated, when you let your guard down and begin to believe the lies of the enemy. He says you are crushed. You are not strong. You cannot do it. You are less than. Each of these lies is designed to break down your wall. You must guard it by speaking the truth over the lies. You are crushed, but NOT defeated. My joy is your strength. You can do all things in Christ's name. You are a child, not a servant. Find the truth to counter the lie. Speak it over and over. This is guarding your wall. Do not let the enemy breach it, because it crumbled under the pressure. Fill in the areas that are gaping open. Use your sword to rebuild.

# November 5

*If this be so, our God whom we serve is able to deliver us from the burning fiery furnace, and He will deliver us out of your hand, O king. But if not, be it known to you, O king, that we will not serve your gods or worship the golden image that you have set up. ~Daniel 3:17-18*

Holding on to me doesn't mean you won't have trials, Weary One. It doesn't mean there won't be times in your life when you struggle…or when you have to stand up for what you believe. However, it does mean I will be with you in those times. I will stand with you in the fire and you will not smell of smoke.

Look at the lives of Shadrach, Meshach, and Abednego. They were young boys. Taken from their home. They were asked to be something they were not. Not allowed to worship freely, or choose their own food, but My favor was on them in this trial. They trusted me implicitly. They were given titles and responsibilities and even in this, they remained true to who they were. They stood for me when no one else would. It cost them. It ruffled the feathers of the king, who simply wanted them to bow to him.

He took his rage at their refusal out on them and threw them into the furnace. But I was with them…inside the flames. They came out of the fire without even the smell of smoke. What a powerful testimony.

It will be no different for you, Beloved. You will wait on me. I will come to you in the midst of your trouble. I will be in it with you. I will walk with you and talk with you in the midst. Then you will come out and your testimony will show My power to the world around you. Stand up for me. Believe. Trust me. Take heed. You will walk in the fire, but you will not be burned.

# November 6

*Tell your children of it, and let your children tell their children, and their children to another generation. ~Joel 1:3*

Your life is a story I am writing. You may have heard this before, but it is true, Dear One. There are characters and a plot. There is action and movement. There are problems and resolutions. It is all a part of the narrative. I am a writer of lives.

What I do is not fiction. It is real. I do not create your story for drama or sorrow. I do not throw in horror to My narratives. I design them for you to be the character who becomes. That changes over time and all the ups and downs of the plot of life, will shape you. They will make you into who you are designed to be. The immaturity will fall away. The wisdom will grow.

Becoming takes time, My Love. You do not just wake up one day fully formed and mature. The trials of life smooth out the rough places. They draw you closer to me. They give you release from expectations. They show you judgement is not beneficial. They help you in your becoming. They are not always fun, these plot twists, but they are necessary to the whole of the story.

You cannot see the ending, so you have to trust I know where this is going. I have your best interest in mind. All will be resolved. You will see, Beloved. Do not fret when the problems come. They are merely chapters, needed to bring you closer to the end of the story where you are complete. Let me keep writing. The final story is a bestseller.

# November 7

*But he who is joined to the Lord becomes one Spirit with Him. ~1 Corinthians 6:17*

What if the things you are hoping for never happen? What if the prodigal doesn't come home? What if the illness isn't healed? What if the marriage isn't saved? What if...? Will you still love me? Or is your relationship with me dependent on what I can do for you?

These are tough questions, Weary One. But they are important to ponder. Weariness makes you tired and when you are tired, sometimes you give up...on me and on hope. When people walk away from me, many times it is because I didn't do something the way they wanted me to. Healing wasn't instantaneous. They lost something or someone so important to them they cannot see past the grief. Their life didn't turn out the way they thought it would.

Holding a grudge towards me is more common than you might think. I get the blame for most anything that doesn't go right. This view, that I can fix anything easily but choose not to, is not accurate. It puts our relationship in the performance category. If I perform, you will love me. If I do not, you resent me. This is not the kind of relationship I desire.

I long for a relationship where you love me beyond circumstances. Beyond the breakthrough you want. I want to sit with you in the hard places with no expectations that I will change it for you. I want to hold space for you to grieve and to allow My presence to be enough. I want to be with you. Can you do that? Am I enough for you?

You know what it feels like not to be enough, and to feel as if there is always more expected of you than you can give. You know how freeing it is not to worry about doing all the things, but just to sit and to be. To rest in who you are. You have friendships where you are received like that. Those are the people you go to in hard times and they are the ones who remind you who you are. That is what I want with you. To be one of those who isn't expected to perform, but just to be with you because you want me there. Then if I do a miracle, it is not tied to what you can get, but to how much I love doing things for those I love.

# November 8

*Therefore welcome one another as Christ has welcomed you, for the glory of God.*
*~Romans 15:7*

When My Son did miracles, He showed you My heart. I long to heal. I long to bring freedom and to rescue. But miracles are not tied to relationship. They drew the crowd. He saw the need and He filled it, sometimes even before He met the recipient. Miracles attract the attention of those who might never believe otherwise. They are tied to belief. They are for the observers, as well as the one receiving. They increase faith in me and are the soil in which the seed of the gospel grows. Miracles happened throughout the Bible, and they happen now.

There has never been a time that I didn't do them, but Dear One, I don't operate on demand. When I perform a miracle, it is intentional and has a specific purpose. Breakthroughs can come through miracles, but not always. Sometimes breakthroughs happen slowly, over time. The blind see, the lame walk, and I love to make those things happen instantaneously, but I also like to watch others, like you, reach out to the blind and the lame to meet them where they are. To welcome them with kindness. To show compassion and love to them, in order to heal their hearts when their bodies are broken. I use these kinds of situations for My children to show and experience kindness through relationship. Kindness is its own kind of miracle. It is a picture of My glory.

The showy kind, the kind that command the attention, are faith builders. But the kind that come in the day-to-day mess are the ones in which deep work is done. Every breath you take is a miracle. When you look at it like that, every day is filled with them. It is hard to see it this way when circumstances are difficult. When it appears there will never be a breakthrough.

Do not be discouraged or feel I have forgotten your miracle. Know that you are seen and I am doing a deeper work in you. One that takes time and compassion. One that is just as real, though not as flashy. To change your view of you, to show you how I see you and have you believe it, is the biggest miracle of all, but it requires your participation. It requires you to change your thoughts and actions and beliefs about me. It requires a deep relationship, not a quick fix.

# November 9

*Know therefore today that He who goes over before you as a consuming fire is the Lord your God. He will destroy them and subdue them before you. So, you shall drive them out and make them perish quickly, as the Lord has promised you.*
*~Deuteronomy 9:3*

When the world comes unglued, I am still here. When all is shaking, remember I am the one who holds the keys. I shake the earth and the heavens so that all things that are not of me fall away. This is true in your life, Beloved. O, Fearful One, do not shake in your shoes. I am behind the rattling. My shaking only removes that which is created by someone other than me.

Times of quaking create discomfort. They show that you are not in control which is hard to swallow. It requires trust in me. My ways are not your ways, Dear One. When suffering and uncertainty find their way into your life in one way or another, know that I am working. I am never caught by surprise. I am never unaware of you and what you need. Sometimes the things you need are not what you think they are, and sometimes you are stronger than you know. Times of trembling make this clear.

I am a consuming fire. I burn up all that is not from me. This includes external and internal things. Do you have hopelessness? Let me shake it from you. Do you despair? Let the quaking move it. Is there anger hidden in your heart? Let it roll away. These are the enemies I want to rid you of. I am in control. I have not ever stopped being in control. Even on your worst day. Let me hold you close, in times of shaking. Beloved, come to me for the healing of your heart when all that is left is me.

# November 10

*Blessed be the God and Father of our Lord Jesus Christ, the Father of mercies and God of all comfort, who comforts us in all our affliction, so that we may be able to comfort those who are in any affliction, with the comfort with which we ourselves are comforted by God. ~2 Corinthians 1:3-4*

Sorrow is a deep well. It is never ending. Just when you think your tears have dried up, a new flow begins. Dear One, let sorrow do its work. It is a cleansing flood. Pouring it out to me brings healing. No matter the circumstance which brings sorrow to your door, it is not unknown to me. My Son was a man of sorrows well acquainted with grief. There is nothing new under the sun and all that you experience has been experienced before. Take heart.

You are not alone in your grief. It may roll over you like waves on the sea, but I am there to comfort you. My Spirit is the comforter who covers you like a blanket. It connects and restores you to My heart. It is unexplainable really, how much peace comes during sorrowful times. Unexplainable to you, but not to me. Many times, My peace is wrapped up in tears. When you release tears and let them flow, healing will come to your heart. I am close to the brokenhearted and therefore, My peace is, as well.

Let me carry you. Let your sorrow lead you to me. Let me soothe your troubled soul, and life will flood you. Grief will do its work in you. You will look to me and I will comfort you.

# November 11

*This is My commandment, that you love one another as I have loved you. Greater love has no one than this, that someone lay down his life for his friends. ~John 15:12-13*

It is a noble thing to lay down your life for others. It takes courage and sacrifice. There are so many ways to give up what you desire, for the sake of others. Parents do it every day. First responders live their lives by laying them down. Soldiers give their all, sometimes to the death. It is not unlike My Son. Giving up His right to all the glory of heaven to save humanity. Sacrifice. Surrender. They are the same. You cannot lay your life down in sacrifice, until you have surrendered it. Surrender means to give over and above.

Every day you give away some of your life, be it at work, at home, or in your community. Different people deal with pouring out in different ways. Caregivers lay down their lives. Those who work with disabled people, or the elderly, have to surrender what they want, in order to care for those I have put into their charge. Teachers, nurses, and other service professionals surrender their own needs to help others.

When anyone puts the lives of others over their own, it is a picture of love. My kind of love. It does not come on human terms. It is a supernatural gift that allows self to be put aside and My love to take over. Not everyone who sacrifices understands where that ability originates. I try to speak into their hearts to share My love. They will understand at some point. I never give up on those who freely sacrifice. They are more like me than they know.

# November 12

*As in water, face reflects face, so the heart of man reflects the man. ~Proverbs 27:19*

I am exposing the heart of man. It is not a pretty sight, Dear One. Many will blame the devil for whatever difficulty happens. When hard things occur on the earth, he is the first to get the blame; many times, that is the correct place to look. However, so many of the hardships come not from his hand, but from the human heart. It is given over to its own desires and the fruit of it is obvious among men. Strife of all kinds. Even My own children have entered into name calling and finger pointing. Rather than reveal My heart, they rush to reveal their own.

I cannot tell you how this hurts me. It is a pain that, as a father, is hard to bear. I long for My children to express My love to the world. I desire for them to represent me instead of their own interests. My love is so much bigger than what you see. It is bigger than the division you see around you. Do not be fooled into taking up the cross as a hammer, with which to pummel others. Do not think I do not see the depth of grime in the hearts of men. It can no longer be hidden, because I am exposing it. All around you, can you see? Human effort, human will, human desires, run amuck.

The only remedy is My love. When the heart of man is exposed, the hope of a savior will also be seen. My love is bigger than all of it. It is also bigger than your circumstances, My Child. Whatever place you find yourself...downtrodden, heartbroken, wounded, grief stricken...I am there. Look to me. Allow me to expose your heart and heal it.

In healing your heart, I also reduce My own pain. My creation has gone far from My intent. I long to bring it all back to the original communion with me, which is My heart's desire. When the world is out of control, when your circumstances are filling you with sorrow, reach out to me. Talk with me. Walk with me. My hope is all will see My love, but it starts with one. It starts with you, Weary One.

# November 13

*But now, O Lord, you are our Father; we are the clay, and you are our potter; we are all the work of your hand. ~Isaiah 64:8*

You have heard that I am a potter and you are the clay. If you know anything about pottery, you know it takes many things coming together just right for the vessel to take the correct shape. The clay needs to have its air bubbles kneaded out, so it doesn't explode in the firing. Water is required to keep it moist in the shaping. The wheel must turn at the right speed. The pressure from My hands has to be just so, as not to crush, but to shape.

I gather pots from the potter's field, the place the world discards vessels, deemed unworthy. I repurpose them. I find the good and re-create what is broken, for My purposes. I use the powdered pieces and add water until the dry dirt is supple and moldable. I bring in the vessel from the field of throwaways and put it on the wheel under My hand. I shape and form, until it is exactly what I have imagined.

Then, I put it on the shelf to dry. It sits for the appointed time, until I take it down and add the dull glaze. My design doesn't look like what I want it to...yet. It is still unfinished. The glazes cover and absorb into the pores of the clay. They fill it in and make the colors come to life in the firing.

The heat is intense. It is so hot the vessels glow red hot. The glaze melts and forms a glassy surface. It is dark in the kiln, so you cannot see the result of all the heat. Then the vessels are cooled down, and there is another period of waiting. When they are removed from the kiln, they are spectacular. Bright and vivid. Fit for My purposes. Each is its own unique vessel.

Weary One, you are My vessel, with a purpose I have created. There are times of waiting. Drying times. Times of intense heat. You might have been thrown away, but you are not useless. You are My workmanship and I don't make trash. I will shape you and mold you to be everything I have created for you to be. Do not give up. Take heart, I am not finished with you yet.

# November 14

*But who are you, O man, to answer back to God? Will what is molded say to its molder, "Why have you made me like this?" ~Romans 9:20*

Does the clay talk to the Potter? Does the clay tell the Potter what it should be? No. Of course not. So Dear One, neither should you. By questioning My work in your life, you are like a pot questioning the potter. Your job, instead, is to remain pliable. To allow the circumstances of your life to mold you. Reacting against them and resisting the pressure is not helpful. It only delays the finished work.

I know it is all very uncomfortable for you. I know the day-to-day hardship gets old. I am aware of your pain. I know you are tired. But, Weary One, you are being prepared for a particular purpose. It cannot come forth unless you are shaped and molded a certain way. If the work is not finished, the vessel you are to become will not be useful for the purpose which I intended. So, the hardship you are begging to be rescued from is doing a work. I cannot pull you out before the allotted time.

But, Beloved, know this, when the time is right, and the shape is what I need, I will rescue you from My own hand, with My own hand. Until then, the pot does not tell the potter what to do. It humbles itself to the hand of the master. It doesn't speak on its own behalf because it trusts the maker. Trust me. Trust what I am doing.

# November 15

*Therefore encourage one another and build one another up, just as you are doing.*
*~1 Thessalonians 5:11*

Encouragement can do wonders for people in your life. I have created each of you to desire connection. Rather than independence, you are made for interdependence...on each other and on me. Handling life on your own is not My design.

The enemy has gone to great lengths in recent days to isolate humans from one another. He has done this by infusing division among you, causing offense with me and my body, using technology to create a virtual connection that looks real, but is false, and making independence an idol.

Unhealthy individualism is wreaking havoc on My children. Suicide is up. Depression is up. Anxiety is up. Confusion is up. None of those is fruit of My Spirit, but they are fruit of the adversary. You can look around and see his not-so-subtle campaign; it sickens me. My children are blind to him sometimes, and he keeps them in chains. He smiles and laughs at his success.

However, the enemy does not have the last word. I know the end of the story. He does not win. My children, once they see, understand how to love one another. They will remember. They will rise up to be encouragers. They will express My heart and become a body who reaches out with connection to those who are hurting. Some people call it revival. I call it remembering life. Remembering all that I have given you, remind others of what I have given them. Speak the truth to them about what an amazing creation they are. In little ways...like a kind word, or a note.

Altogether, when humans are interconnected, I am better represented. My life flows out, as does My love. Areas of bondage are broken because together you are stronger. Becoming the versions of yourselves that I see and know becomes possible when you are with me. I know the plans I have for you. They include hope and a future. They include connection to one another. They include encouragement and building up, not tearing down. They include unity in love and diversity in peace. I have plans for you, O Dear One, do I have plans!! Interdependence is critical and remembering how to connect is key. Trust me in this.

# November 16

*He who calls you is faithful; He will surely do it. ~1 Thessalonians 5:24*

I am faithful. Do not ever doubt that fact. The world around you will try to get you not to believe it, but you simply have to look to see me. Open your eyes. Where am I faithful in your life?

Do you have food? Do you have shelter? Do you have people who love you? All of those are the fruits of My faithfulness. Each day I shower you with them. No one else can produce them, only I can do that. I want you to have these things, and so I give them. Even your breath is evidence of My faithfulness.

So, when storms come and you feel as if you will go under, focus on My faithfulness. Look to what I have given you as evidence that I am for you, not against you. When your wayward child is far from home, look at all the examples of those who return home as proof that I can turn hearts. When you are faced with illness, look at those who are your support system; they are My gift to you to demonstrate My faithfulness. Whatever your lot, there are demonstrations around you. There are others who have tasted of them and can share their experiences with My grace.

I do not abandon you. I do not use you only for My purposes and then walk away. My heart is for you and I long for you to see how much I care. I want you to know My gifts are true and real. When you are suffering, My faithfulness is your anchor. It will hold you steady among the waves.

# November 17

*Look carefully then how you walk, not as unwise but as wise, making the best use of the time, because the days are evil. Therefore, do not be foolish, but understand what the will of the Lord is. ~Ephesians 5:15-17*

Take each day. One at a time. In your time-driven culture it is hard not to be caught up in planning for the future. It isn't a bad idea exactly, but it can pull you so far out of this moment that it hinders you from what I planned for you today. I live above time. I can see the end from the beginning. I know everything that has happened, will happen, and is happening now.

It is not wrong for you to think about how today will impact tomorrow, but tomorrow isn't guaranteed. It only takes one tragic event to drive that fact home. When you lose someone unexpectedly, or you have been diagnosed with a deadly disease, clarity follows. The big things and plans you have for the future suddenly seem small and insignificant. The little things you do every day, like conversations and time spent together, suddenly seem big.

My ways are not your ways. My thoughts are not yours. To you it may seem that your world is suddenly upside down, but to me, it is as if you finally see the reality. You only have today to live. That's it. Plan for tomorrow if you must, but do not count on your plan to see you through today. Do not spend so much time planning that you miss what is in front of you now.

Spend time on the important things. Your children. Your spouse. The family I have given you. Make them a priority. Be intentional. Your parents. Your grandparents. Your nieces and nephews. Your siblings. Let them know how you feel about them.

Pour into your friends. Your coworkers. Anyone your life intersects with is important. The job you have is secondary. The plans for tomorrow are only plans. All the running around you do, errands and activities are unimportant. All of it can become a vapor in an instant.

If you knew you would be dying in a week, what would you do with your time between now and then? Probably not clean your house. Probably not laundry. You would gather those you love most and laugh and cry together. You would tell them how you love them and why. You would probably quit your job. The big things, like working night and day for a promotion, would fall away. The little things, like sharing your heart with your kids, would be up front. Let me encourage you to think this way. Let me encourage you to remember that today is the most important day.

# November 18

*Do you not know that in a race all the runners run, but only one receives the prize? So, run that you may obtain it. ~1 Corinthians 9:24*

Trying counts. You don't have to get everything right, Weary One. Sometimes simply trying is enough. Finishing is the not the most important thing. Sometimes in life there is no finish line. The day-to-day try is what is important. Some days will go well. Others will not. How will you know which will happen if you don't at least try?

A determined attempt is better than quitting. I know there are times, when your circumstances are overwhelming, when it seems like quitting is your best option. I know you think in your head, "Why try? It's no use." But those are not My words to you. I am not the one saying, 'You'll never get it right. You are a lost cause.' No, Dear One, those are not My words over you.

I say, "Get up." I say, "You can do this." I say, "I am with you to get you through today." I say, "Do not quit. Try again." Did you know that trying again builds perseverance? Did you know when you keep trying it builds strength? It shows your children what it looks like to handle obstacles. You show yourself that you are strong enough to endure. It shows whose voice you are listening to. So, My Love, count trying as a win. Count it as a day well-lived. Do not get distracted by the finish line. It may still be a long way off. Focus on trying again and see yourself as one who is determined. That is enough.

# November 19

*And He who was seated on the throne said, "Behold, I am making all things new."*
*Also, He said, "Write this down, for these words are trustworthy and true."*
*~Revelation 21:5*

Start fresh today. You have the pen in your hand. You have the power to discard pages of your story or rewrite the ones that do not add to the narrative. We are co-writers, you and I. We collaborate. We consider the twists and turns of the story. Sometimes plot twists cannot be changed, but others are a choice. Those are the chapters I give to you to compose.

When you think you cannot go on, turn the page. When you think you have failed, turn the page. When you think the pain is too great, turn the page. You have the ability to start fresh. The old story doesn't have to continue on and on and on. You can make it more interesting. You are the main character, after all. Main characters are supposed to change over the course of the story. It is up to you how much change happens when the plot thickens. Sometimes your plot is as thick as pea soup. It leaves you feeling as if you are running in waist deep water. Turn the page.

Find something new. Write in a hobby. Add a dance. Design a deep dive with me as your guide. Move your body to increase oxygen to your brain. Listen to music or create it. Start fresh. Today. Now. Set aside time to begin again. You will not regret it. Even in the midst of a busy season, there is time to begin breathing again. Especially now.

# November 20

*For who is God, but the Lord? And who is a rock, except our God? ~2 Samuel 22:32*

You live in a painful place to which you have grown accustomed, but you carry pain well, Dear One. You have adjusted from what was expected, what you hoped for, even. You laid all that down for the path you now walk. It was so much different than your plan. No one plans for this. Yet, you have made the best of a hard situation. You have wanted to give up, but you have not done it. You have persevered.

The pain has transformed you. Longsuffering does that. It has given you seasons of grace. It has created compassion and softened your heart. You bear up under the pressure to the point people ask you how you do it. You smile and say you are not walking it alone. And you mean it, even though it seems a lonely journey at times, you know I am with you in ways others cannot understand.

You know what things are important because of the pain you carry. You know what real loss is and you understand its work. You allow me to carry you. In the dark. In the fog. In the woundedness of life. You have learned about deep. As you move through the hard places of life, you mature. Internally, you are in a place of acceptance and growth. Externally, you carry the pain with you. It is the internal journey that shows up externally. It is what causes people to ask you how you do it. It is the depth and wisdom of a journey walked in hard places.

You bear it well. I know you feel as if the pain will bury you at times. But you continue on, trusting in My ways even when you do not understand them. The humility that pain brings into your life shines out of you. Your awareness of how small you are and how fleeting your pain is causes me to rush to your side in hard moments. You know you are never alone, even when you feel you are. It is this knowing which bears up the hurt and loss. It is this knowing that creates a beauty inside you which cannot be described with words. It is this knowing that endears you to me.

# November 21

*But my eyes are toward you, O GOD, my Lord; in you I seek refuge; leave me not defenseless! ~Psalms 141:8*

Focus on me. I know it is hard sometimes not to focus on the circumstances you see around you. The day-to-day of finances, or lack of them, is a heavy load. So is the caregiving, or the grief, or the loss you endure. It is all so very burdensome. Beloved, if you focus on those burdens your heart will not be light.

However, if you focus on me and who I am, you will see your load begin to lift. Maybe not in your circumstances, but your spirit will be lighter. My identity as redeemer, counselor, healer, savior, and rescuer will be clearer. As your eyes see me for who I am, the things that seem so big around you will fade. They will no longer take up the majority of your view, but will be put in the places they belong.

You have seen what I can do. You know of My faithfulness. You have felt My rescue before. Those gifts are still available to you. Always. Let me show you again. Let me remind you. Do not lose heart. Keep your eyes on me. Not the waves around you. Not the boat that is sinking. Look to me. Focus your gaze. Lock your eyes onto me and do not look away.

# November 22

*But as servants of God we commend ourselves in every way: by great endurance, in afflictions, hardships, calamities, beatings, imprisonments, riots, labors, sleepless nights, hunger; by purity, knowledge, patience, kindness, the Holy Spirit, genuine love; by truthful speech, and the power of God; with the weapons of righteousness for the right hand and for the left; through honor and dishonor, through slander and praise. We are treated as impostors, and yet are true; as unknown, and yet well known; as dying, and behold, we live; as punished, and yet not killed; as sorrowful, yet always rejoicing; as poor, yet making many rich; as having nothing, yet possessing everything. ~2 Corinthians 6:4-10*

You do hard things. I see you. You sacrifice your own desires, your own dreams to do the hard things. You are not as alone as you suppose. I am with you and I see all that you do. More importantly than what you do, I see the heart behind your actions. I see compassion in the midst of your loss. I see love in the midst of your heartache.

I also see all that you cannot do. The frustrations you have over not being able to operate the way you would like to are not lost on me. Sometimes you feel as if you are spinning your wheels, not making forward progress. You wonder if anything you attempt is pleasing to me because often you cannot finish what you started. Trust me when I say that even your attempts are precious to me.

It is a beautiful thing for someone to try to do things to bless me. Just the idea that you thought of me at all stirs My heart for you. To look My way and consider me before you act is a blessing. It is a ministry to me. It encourages me when you want to see me glorified. Even if you don't accomplish what you set out to do, I see the heart to honor me and it lifts me up. Do not fret if you cannot always complete the task. It is not about what you do. I don't keep score or a list. I do not expect certain performances from you. I look at the heart, and who you are behind all the sacrifice.

In the midst of a life of hardship, you minister to others and to me. Yes, I called it ministry. The ministry of longsuffering, the ministry of the hard things. The ministry of difficulty. Not heard of much these days, but there are multitudes who are called to this kind of ministry. You call on me, you acknowledge me daily, even when life is hard and THAT is enough. There is no need to feel inferior because you cannot go and do what others do. No need to compare your life to theirs. You live under severe pressure all of the time. You depend on me in ways no one sees. No one but me. I see. I am blessed by you. That is enough.

# November 23

*Blessed are those who are persecuted for righteousness' sake, for theirs is the kingdom of heaven. Blessed are you when others revile you and persecute you and utter all kinds of evil against you falsely on My account. ~Matthew 5:10-11*

Don't take it personally, Weary One. When people do not understand you or your life circumstances, don't take it personally. They have no idea what you do, or what you are up against. They may feel like they know and they may share their opinions...loudly. They don't realize how hurtful the things they say are to you. They don't understand because they haven't walked where you are walking. You will hear their words, but do not let them penetrate your heart.

Trust me in the places you walk, Beloved. You are there because I have allowed you to be there. You are learning and growing in the dark places. Your roots are going deep, because I want them to. Your story will heal multitudes, but first you have to walk it out. Some will speak against you and your circumstances, but they don't know My heart is with you. They perceive I have abandoned you, but nothing could be further from the truth. I am here in the midst of all the pain, with you, surrounding you. I embrace the brokenhearted. I have a special place in My heart just for you.

People can be cruel. Their hearts are not compassionate. They speak before thinking. They speak out of ignorance. Yet, you continue on in your life, walking out the difficult places despite what others think. You are bold and brave. It takes guts to ignore words designed to hurt. Some people mean well, and others are simply self-absorbed. But you, Weary One, are learning to ignore those opinions; you are learning that I am the only one who matters.

I will use you to speak truth to those who will listen. Do not take their comments personally, instead use them to instruct. Take the compassion I am teaching you and use it to show them what a tender heart looks like. It requires a lot to make a heart of stone into a heart of flesh which quivers at My touch. You are My workmanship. You are My love. Do not let their words convince you otherwise.

# November 24

*But I do not account my life of any value nor as precious to myself, if only I may finish my course and the ministry that I received from the Lord Jesus, to testify to the gospel of the grace of God. ~Acts 20:24*

Stay the course. Do not allow the busyness of life to overwhelm you. You are not required to please all the people in your life at the expense of your own health. I know it feels important to do what is needed, but look at your heart, Beloved. Is the action going to bring life to you or death? Does it fill you up or empty you out? Pay attention. I know some circumstances cannot be avoided, but you have more choice than you know in these matters.

Hold fast to My hand. Listen to My voice. Stay on course and do not be waylaid by the season or the amount of activity you have around you. You know what works for you. Do what works. You know what drains you; avoid those things whenever possible. Realign your priorities with mine. Have you sought me in a while? Maybe it is time for us to sit down together and sort out what is pulling you away from the grace I have for you.

My grace empowers you. When you move outside of My grace, you will feel frustrated, tired, overwhelmed, and exhausted. Is that how you feel? Then go back and look for me. You may have left me behind.

# November 25

*Giving thanks always and for everything to God the Father in the name of our Lord Jesus Christ. ~Ephesians 5:20*

This is the time of year to be thankful. Being full of thanks, being intentional about gratitude and gratefulness is important for your mental health. Did you know that, Dear One? When you stop and take note of the things in your life that are exceptional, or even the little inconsequential things which might be unrecognized blessings, your attitudes will change.

You can visit an impoverished community and find joyful people, even when they have very little. Being grateful for every little thing keeps their attitude positive. You can acknowledge your gratitude, too. Notice. Write down. Think about all the things you are thankful for. Even the small things. If you begin writing them down each day, you will see your heart begin to change. The hard parts of life will not seem as hard. Trials will become privileges.

My question to you is this: why do you limit thankfulness to one time of year? Wouldn't it be better to cultivate a heart of thankfulness that is with you always? Do you think your life could be different if you had learned the discipline of gratitude?

It is not too late to do so. The shadowy places where suffering and loss reside are hard places to see the light of thankfulness. The pain of loss, or the longsuffering of caregiving, or the grief of the heart are heavy and exhausting. Yet, if you look beyond those things, you will see there are a multitude of blessings in your life. In fact, sometimes the hardest places become the biggest blessings. Look for them. I will show you all that you have; you need only ask.

# November 26

*For anything that becomes visible is light. Therefore, it says, "Awake, O sleeper, and arise from the dead, and Christ will shine on you." ~Ephesians 5:14*

Awake! Let My light shine upon you and through you. It is easy to be in a haze when life is difficult. Your senses dull. You feel numb. Going through the motions is the norm. The darkness slips in unnoticed, at first. Survival mode forces you into the shadows and soon, before you even realize it, you are enveloped in the dark. It covers you like a blanket. All sorts of companions live in this black place: depression, apathy, anxiety, anger, resentment, sorrow, bitterness. The list is a long one.

Do not sleep in the dark, Weary One. It seems the easiest way, but I promise you, it is not. The path of least resistance is usually a slippery slope. The voices that lull you to sleep do not want you to know My secret. My light is in you. You do not have to slumber. Awake!! Let My light shine on you and dispel the shadows. I can send them packing. My sunrise is coming. The dawn is upon you. Awake.

Do not overthink it. Let me do it for you. Just put one foot in front of the other. Walk it out. To do that, you must first get up. You have to wake up, stand up, and walk. My word will shine the light onto your path. It will guide you. Open it up. I will speak, and you will see My glory appear. It will rip through the darkness that crowds your mind. It will revive you. Trust me.

# November 27

*Jesus said to her, "Did I not tell you that if you believed you would see the glory of God?" ~John 11:40*

You have a voice, Weary One. You have something to say. It is important. Speak it. You may feel overwhelmed. You are tired. You have so much to carry that speaking up might feel too big or too much. You wonder who would even listen to you. I am telling you, there are those who need to hear what you have to say.

Your experience, hard as it may be, is a shared one. Do you not know this? You feel alone and isolated, but you are not. There are others who are feeling the same, as if no one could possibly understand what they are walking through. They sit in defeat because of it. Yet here you are, with experience and a silent voice.

What would happen if you would speak out? Who might break out of their isolation? Who might embrace hope again? You will never know unless you try. I will show you how to speak up. Pay attention to My nudges. At first, it is scary, but once you do, you will see what happens.

There are multiple ways to speak, Beloved. You may write for yourself at the beginning, then compose to publish later. You could share with a small group at work or a Bible study at church. You can tell a friend, or speak to a stranger in line. You are not limited by one way. When you share your testimony...your life experiences...however you do it, you set others free to share theirs. Connection happens. Isolation flees. It is a beautiful thing to observe, but even better to be a part of, and even better to initiate. So, step up and speak.

Watch the waves of hopelessness subside. See the waters part, not only for you, but for those around you. Calm the storm. I do all these things with My words. With My words in your mouth, nothing is impossible for you.

# November 28

*Give thanks in all circumstances; for this is the will of God in Christ Jesus for you.*
*~1 Thessalonians 5:18*

Self-pity doesn't become you, Dear One. It longs to clothe you and cover you like a cloak. Making you feel like a victim is its goal. Self-pity is when you feel sorry for yourself because life is difficult. For those who carry a heavy load, it is a temptation which never goes away. Do not let it get to you.

In reality, self-pity is a form of grief. Grief itself isn't bad; in fact, it is designed by me, to release sorrow and to process hurt. The problem with self-pity is that it makes "self" the focus. It becomes all about you and instead of releasing the pain, it actually increases it. The pain of life makes you question me and my goodness. It makes you wonder if you are forgotten. It gives you the desire to tell everyone your troubles and how bad things are. Self-pity stagnates your life so you want you to sit down and just allow life to happen so you can whine about it, rather than standing up and being persistent. Stand up and find joy in each day. Stand up and make the day beautiful in the midst of difficult things.

There is a difference between self-pity and normal grief of loss. When you walk and loss is your companion, it is important to acknowledge it. You then recognize that some part of your life didn't go as expected. There is a permanent change and circumstances are not like you wanted them to be. Expressing your new reality out loud and acknowledging the pain of it is actually healthy. It is hard. It isn't fun. Trauma happens. Hardship happens.

Although living in a sin-filled world comes with difficult challenges, they don't define you. Your hardships do not become your identity. Self-pity focuses on the trauma, not the overcoming. It gives you a woe-is-me attitude that is unbecoming. It is easily slipped into. You must learn to recognize it and put it away. Instead of focusing on the circumstances which wounded your heart, focus on me and My grace to walk in the midst of them. Focus on being healthy in the place in which you live. Do what is needed to get past the past.

# November 29

*Why are you cast down, O my soul, and why are you in turmoil within me? Hope in God; for I shall again praise Him, my salvation and my God. ~Psalms 42:11*

I know there is hope for the future, but are you hopeful? Hope deferred makes the heart sick. Is your heart sick, Beloved? Do you wonder if things will ever be different...your body will stop hurting, your loved one will ever be independent, your grief will ever lift, your heart will ever heal? So much pain when hope is not visible. This time of year is a season of hope, but so many times it makes you realize how little hope you have. Others are smiling and joyful, when you are just trying to keep your head above water.

Breathe, My Love. Just breathe. Do not compare yourself to others. Nothing good can come from comparisons. You are on your own path. Please do not be afraid of hope. Hope is not out to get you. It is not playing hide and seek, though it probably feels that way to you. It does not hold a carrot out in front of you, never to be reached. It doesn't work like that...I don't work like that.

No, hope is embodied in a person...My Son. He doesn't withdraw from you, ever. He is always available. Hope is actually what keeps you going, even when you don't see Him or feel Him. The desire to move forward comes from Him. On days you don't desire to go forward, He is still there.

Hope is a spark which is built deep into you. The issue with hope is your expectation that it will behave in a certain way. That suddenly, all will be right and pain will be gone because hope has come. That expectation is what makes you sick when it is deferred. My ways are not your ways. Hope doesn't abandon you, just as I don't. It lives on, even when you push it away. The fear that the other shoe will drop is a sign of woundedness. I hate that you are in the place where you fear My provision for you. It was not My plan for you to feel this way. I understand it, but I want you to know hope is evidence I am near. It is like My shadow, with me always. You are not without me nor without hope.

# November 30

*It is like a grain of mustard seed, which, when sown on the ground, is the smallest of all the seeds on earth, yet when it is sown it grows up and becomes larger than all the garden plants and puts out large branches, so that the birds of the air can make nests in its shade. ~Mark 4:31-32*

Small steps. Pay attention to small steps in your daily walk. Do not be overwhelmed by activity. Do not let busyness steal your health. Small steps will bring life to you. Only do what you have the energy for. Stop trying to do it all. For example, if you do not love to cook for events, don't do it. If you do not have time to make all the events, say no to some of them...or all of them. Do not worry what others think; it is not up to them to live your life. They do not know what you are up against. Find people who understand if you have to cancel. The ones who love you in the midst of your difficulties, and do not judge you for them. Those are the ones to surround yourself with this season. They will bring you joy.

I have given specific people to you for that purpose. You know who they are. The ones who make you feel relief when you are with them because you don't have to explain yourself. You can just be. A key to making it through the holiday season without being depressed or down is to spend time with the people I have sent to you. On the phone, or in person doesn't matter. Just allow them to walk beside you. Let them help you set boundaries for protecting your health.

This time of year is the celebration of the birth of My Son. The redemption plan in action. He came to renew, revive, and restore My relationship with mankind. That included you. I knew even then; you would come to know me. I knew even then; where you would be at this moment. I knew even then; you would need friends and family to be a support system for you.

Do the small things that bring you joy. Leave the other things out. Make cookies. Listen to music. Enjoy the lights or the stars. Make your holiday schedule in small steps of only what you want to do. Drop all the fluff. It is a simple holiday. No need to complicate and dilute its meaning. Less is more. Small steps.

# December 1

*But Mary treasured up all these things, pondering them in her heart. ~Luke 2:19*

The gifts I have promised you will come, Dear One. They are promised, and I don't break promises. The time before they are revealed is the time to treasure them in your heart. To let them do an internal work on your faith. You do not have to wait for them to be completed to rejoice. There is a kind of rejoicing that comes in the waiting. Knowing that I have a plan. Knowing that I will not rest until My plans are accomplished, helps in the waiting.

There is a song in your heart for this time of waiting for My promises. It has to be sung before they are completed. It is just for this time. Once the hope is fulfilled, there is a new song to sing. Both require faith. Both require your whole heart to be engaged with me. So, sing the waiting song. Do not hold back your tune. Do not sit in your circumstances and say, "I will be silent until it comes to pass." You will shrivel up. You will be downcast.

Praises are made for this moment. They are to uplift your heart and countenance. In fact, they are wholly different than songs sung in the victory because they are sung during the unknown. These songs of faith rise up and trust me even without seeing the end. Stepping out. Believing. Your spirit rises up at the sound of the notes because it knows the truth. It tells your mind that My promises cannot be broken. It tells you that you are not forgotten.  Ponder the promises in your heart. Sing your song.

# December 2

*I appeal to you therefore, brothers, by the mercies of God, to present your bodies as a living sacrifice, holy and acceptable to God, which is your spiritual worship. Romans 12:1*

I am an audience of one. No need to try to impress others. Stop your striving, Weary One. I do not require a performance. Not ever. You do not have to oversee, or plan, or direct. When you know I am your audience, you only need to sit, listen, hear, and respond to what I say.

With me it should be easy and light. If it is not, Beloved, then you are performing. No need. Just be with me. Sit. Rest. Do not let your complicated life interfere with our time together. I know this is not always easy for you. You do so much for so many. Be released. You do not have to work like that for me. Let me be your safe place.

When you are striving, you feel exhausted or driven all the time. It is one way you know you are working in your own strength. When you feel the pressure building and you cannot rest, take stock. How did you get to this place? How can you get out of it? I understand there are obligations and commitments in life. I understand people count on you for so much. But, if you do not learn to rest, they will not be able to count on you anymore. You will burn out.

Get rid of anything that you can which causes you to feel you have to strive. You can say "no" to much of what you think is causing you to be frenzied. You do not have to attend every event, every meeting, every gathering. You can decline without excuses. Just a simple "no." No need to explain yourself. You are worthy of taking care of.

I am the only one you need to please. And I am already pleased with you, Precious One. Do you not know this? Well, you know it now. Your audience is pleased. Put down your performance role. Rest.

# December 3

*The creation itself will be set free from its bondage to corruption and obtain the freedom of the glory of the children of God. For we know that the whole creation has been groaning together in the pains of childbirth until now. And not only the creation, but we ourselves, who have the first fruits of the Spirit, groan inwardly as we wait eagerly for adoption as sons, the redemption of our bodies. ~Romans 8: 21-23*

I want to talk to you about waiting, again. I know you are tired and weary of hoping for things to be different. But, Beloved, please stop waiting for the other shoe to drop. Waiting with the attitude that what is coming will be more hardship is not what I intended for you. I am sorry that life has created this expectation of disaster in your heart. It makes me weep with sorrow that you feel it is all you can expect, or that you somehow deserve adversity.

No, there is another kind of waiting. This is the season of waiting...longing really...for the appearance of the Savior of the world. The people were aching for his arrival. They may not have known it, but they could feel something stirring inside that brought them hope and groaning together. The whole earth groaned for His arrival. It wasn't just his physical birth. No, the earth still groans for Him. You still groan for Him. It is built into you to do so.

You see, even as you go through trials and suffering, My Son can appear at just the right moment. So instead of expecting more of the same, expect the light to shine in the darkness. It is a shift of thought. Where is He? When will you allow Him to come into your circumstances? When will you see Him? Looking for Him is equivalent to the wise men and shepherds seeking Him out. Knowing He was somewhere close, and following My direction to find Him. Beloved, I tell you, He is close. You can follow the path I put in front of you to find Him. Active waiting. With hope-filled expectation.  Tis the season...to wait.

# December 4

*He gives power to the faint, and to him who has no might He increases strength.*
*~Isaiah 40:29*

Have you killed anticipation, Weary One? Is it too hard to bear it? Are you afraid to anticipate the promise? My promises to you are true. They are not for everyone else but you. I am the Promise keeper. You are My heart. You are the reason for the promise in the first place. My desire is for My children to know me, deeply. I have anticipation of what that will be like. I long for it. Does that surprise you? That I long for you? It shouldn't.

I have given everything I have to make our relationship possible. I do so love you. I know you feel I have abandoned you, and that breaks My heart. I could not do such a thing. You cannot see what I see. You do not know the outcome of your life, or where your path will lead, but I see it all. I see the promises fulfilled. I see the long-awaited breakthrough. I see what you will do with the treasure you are gaining in the hard, dark places.

Dear One, you can live in the moment and still look forward. You can dig deep to hold tight to My hand and at the same time open it to let go of the things holding you back. Letting go of bitterness and unforgiveness towards others, towards me, and towards yourself is freeing. You can let go of negativity, while holding onto My grace. You can let go of hurt, while soaking in My love. You can let go of woundedness, with your hand wrapped around My healing.

I know I appear to be a dichotomy sometimes. This is one of those times. Let go. Hold on. Both can be done at the same time. Faith will bubble to the surface. It will be exciting, because you will believe in the promise again. You will know I keep My promises to you.

# December 5

*The Lord is my light and my salvation; whom shall I fear? The Lord is the stronghold of my life; of whom shall I be afraid? ~Psalms 27:1*

Discouragement sneaks in like fog on a cold morning. It makes it hard to see anything else. You wonder if the shadowy shapes are what they appear to be, but then you don't really know and so you stop trying to figure it out. You give up on the promises and dreams that once fueled you. Discouragement does just what it says, takes courage away from you and leaves you in a state without it.

Precious One, it takes courage to believe. It takes courage to follow after dreams long dead. It takes courage to get back up again and piece together human promises broken. The shapes they take are different because of the shards that have to be glued back together with hope. The bravery it requires to continue your journey is monumental. Trust me, what I am asking you is not easy, but it is not impossible either. I am not asking you to forget or just get over whatever it is that caused you to find yourself in the fog. No, that would be a waste of your pain. I waste nothing.

I am asking that you get up and try again despite the disappointment. Allow the place you find yourself to motivate you rather than define you. Take courage. When you reach for it and you get up again, it is exhausting at first. You have lived in the fog for a while. It will require great effort to remember what it feels like to be encouraged. My words are like an infusion that seeps into you each day. Someone who takes a moment to smile or be kind to you will also encourage you.

Weary One, did you know you can actually infuse yourself with courage...encourage yourself? Try an act of kindness. Try smiling at a stranger. Try sending someone a note or a text and you will find that in encouraging others, you also receive encouragement.

I am telling you; the sun is coming to burn off the fog of discouragement that has camped at your door. I will shine My light, but I am asking you to be ready for the fog to lift, and to know that even if it sits low every morning over you, you can stand up and take courage.

# December 6

*I will give thanks to the Lord with my whole heart; I will recount all of your wonderful deeds. ~Psalm 9:1*

Can you receive words and gifts from me in your current circumstances, or are you waiting until things get better? Or until something changes? Or until the kids are grown? Or until you have a better job? Dear One, I have so much to give you now, and you are waiting for someday.

Do not resist the place in which you are walking. It may be a challenging walk for a long time. It may have already been difficult for years. The longsuffering is a gift of the spirit, but it isn't an easy one. It is one which requires acceptance. Acceptance is the action of consenting to receive something offered. You can consent to the circumstance or you and resist it. No one wants to suffer grief for a long time. But if you learn to live in the midst of it, acceptance will follow.

When you consent or surrender to the path you are on, freedom comes. Not always in the way you think. Freedom doesn't always mean you will walk away from the pain never to feel defeated again. Sometimes embracing the sorrow and letting it have its way in you is the better way. My Son was acquainted with grief. He was a man of sorrows. Not depressed, but filled with the kind of compassion that moved His heart. It was different than being stuck and wallowing in pain. It was aligning Himself with My heart for My people. My love for the world broke His heart.

My love for you and your difficulty is the same. Feeling defeated is difficult, but My love is sending your roots deep. It is giving you wisdom. You are growing in empathy for others. You are less harsh, and more kind. You are more careful with your words and actions. You are beautiful under pressure. Your light is getting brighter because of all you have been through.

Acceptance of the gift. Acceptance of the pain. Acceptance that your path is the right one for you. You are not finished. I have not left you alone, on the contrary. I am as close as your breath. I am near to the broken-hearted. I am broken-hearted Myself, and so I long to be with those like me.

# December 7

*Behold, we consider those blessed who remained steadfast. You have heard of the steadfastness of Job, and you have seen the purpose of the Lord, how the Lord is compassionate and merciful. ~James 5:11*

How strong do you feel, Weary One? Not very? You are tired. Tired of trying. Tired of sorrow and grief. Tired of life. But you keep going. You keep getting up. Dear One, that is the opposite of weak. It takes guts to keep going when you don't feel like it. Courage. There are two kinds, raw courage and bold courage.

Raw courage doesn't feel the same as bold courage. Bold courage comes out with a roar, swinging and thundering into battle. It is pumped up. It is loud and boisterous. It makes you feel confident. Bold courage always runs ahead with abandon into whatever the battle is, dressed in armor and war paint.

Raw courage disguises itself as weakness. It feels as if you are barely moving, barely surviving. It is quiet. It is not confident. You might even say it is insecure. There is no rushing, roaring, or running. There is no battle cry, unless you count the silent tears cried in private. Raw courage holds on. It feels holding on is all that is possible.

Sometimes raw courage takes more guts than bold courage, because you don't know what you are up against or how long you will have to endure. It is not a one-time battle, but an ongoing one. The ground under you feels unstable, and getting your footing each day is a struggle. Yet, you do it. You find your way each day. You do not give up, even though you want to.

I love this about you...your determination to keep going. This is raw courage at its best. Beloved, you are not weak. You are anything but. You are solid. You have a depth and understanding of life very few will comprehend. You are not wasting time; you are fast forwarding growth. The depth of your sorrow is a tool of strength, not a weakness. Be en-couraged.

# December 8

*And God is able to make all grace abound to you, so that having all sufficiency in all things at all times, you may abound in every good work. ~2 Corinthians 9:8*

I have everything covered, before you even know you need it. I make a way for you in the wilderness. The journey you are on with me has every provision you need included. The wilderness is a wild place, with unknown obstacles and dangers all around. It is an adventure, but also a challenge. Your life has never followed the "regular" path. That is by design. It has been unpredictable and wild. It has come to you in unexpected ways which often include hardship. But just as you adapt when you are in the woods or on a trail, you adapt in life as well.

As you move onto the path I have called you to, you will find everything you need. Sometimes, before you even ask me, I have already lined up the next provision. What is an afterthought for you is a forethought for me. If you are dealing with an illness, I have put people in your path who have gone before you and can guide you. If it is a loss of a loved one, or a broken relationship, I have given you support groups and counselors who are specifically equipped by me to help you. If you are living without basic needs, I place ministries nearby who help people get back on their feet.

I am in the business of making a way where there is no way. I have placed you on this journey to the promise. I will keep My promise. I will walk you all the way to it, despite the hardship and the difficult journey. I am in it with you. I will give you everything you need at the moment you need it. Not before. Not too late. I am right on time. Trust me.

# December 9

*Little children, you are from God and have overcome them, for He who is in you is greater than He who is in the world. ~1 John 4:4*

How do you define victory? Is it someone being carried off of a field of play on the shoulders of their teammates? Is it shouting and spraying champagne? There are many images which display what it is like to defeat a foe. Most of them are joyous and full of celebration, but victory doesn't always look that way, My Love.

There are days where victory looks like getting out of bed, or the triumph of getting dinner on the table, completing a work day, or making important phone calls. Sometimes conquering your fear, rising above your depression or moving through your pain is worth a celebration. There are small victories and larger ones.

Weary One, when you make some progress that you think is small, redefine it as a victory. Use those moments to celebrate. When you realize you are a victor, not a victim, your perspective changes. Victims have no control over their circumstances. Victors use their circumstances as fuel to move forward. To keep growing. To keep learning. Sometimes, when the outward situations do not change, the inward seeds of strength of character are fertilized. The inward lessons are the important ones. The wisdom you gain and the compassion in your heart grow like weeds. The insight into others and their suffering expands so that you feel for them, like I feel for them. In My book, that is victory.

What you need to know, Beloved, is that I am the victor who has conquered your enemy. My Son did that. He overcame death. He overcame everything that tried to rise against you. You can grow because of what He did. You can be an overcomer because He was. Do not let your circumstances define you. Make note of each and every victory because you, My Love, are victorious.

# December 10

*Let me hear in the morning of your steadfast love, for in you I trust. Make me know the way I should go, for to you I lift up my soul. ~Psalms 143:8*

I am the God of unfailing love. That means I cannot fail to love you, Weary One. Ever. No matter what. It means that My plan for you cannot fail. It means failure is not an option. You cannot mess up My plan, or My love for you. It is never ending.

Love is who I am. I don't do it, I *am* it. Since it is My nature, nothing I do is without love. You may feel as if you are unlovable, but you are wrong. You may feel as if you don't deserve My love, or that I only love you because I have to. Beloved, I choose to love you. Even in the messy times. Even on the hard days. My love surrounds you. Don't let the enemy tell you otherwise.

My love is its own atmosphere. You breathe because of it. It surrounds you and like air, you might not realize how dependent you are on it. It is easy to take it for granted because it is easy, like breathing. You swim in it. You soak in it. It is with you always. Turn your intention towards me and you will begin to see how My love permeates everything. It is as close as your breath.

If you cannot count on one other thing in your life, count on My unfailing love. It always wins. It is always present. It is tangible. Can you feel it? Yes. But even if you cannot, it is still there. Set your mind on it. Recognize it. Attach your hope to it. When all seems hopeless, you can depend on My love for you. Really. You can. I am trustworthy in this. My inability to fail is something you can count on in a world where you feel nothing is sure. I am sure. Trust me.

# December 11

*Be still before the Lord and wait patiently for Him. ~Psalms 37:7*

Is it hard, this life you are living, Weary One? Hands up. Surrender. Give it to me. Sometimes you have to give it to me daily. Surrender isn't a one-and-done thing. It is ongoing.

I am not sure why it is so hard for you to let go. It seems to me, knowing I can take control to guide and direct would take the pressure you feel away. It would allow you to breathe easier. But for some reason it is frightening. Terrifying even. Fear always likes to make things out to be bigger than they actually are.  Fear wants you bound, and if you knew how freeing it is to let go, you would laugh at fear and run to me.

I am running to you, but you have turned and fled the scene. Controlling your life is all important to you. Doing things your way, because you think My way will hinder you in some way, is your preference. Nothing could be further from the truth. I do not hinder; I set free. It is for freedom I have come. It is for freedom I am invested in you. I want to see you free in every way.

Surrender to me equals freedom for you. Alignment with me brings obstacles low. Notice, I didn't say takes obstacles away. No, aligning with me won't remove barriers, but it will make them easier to overcome. It will no longer seem like you are pushing a boulder up a mountain. Life doesn't have to be as hard as it is right now. You can surrender and let me do the work. Don't move until I give you direction. Don't barge ahead of My plan.

My plan will require you to listen. To tune your ear to My voice. To wait until you know My directive. One of the main reasons people hold onto their own lives is that they are afraid of what I will say to them, or what I will ask them to do. Dear One, everything I say is born out of love for you and wanting the best for you. Everything. Trust My words. I will not send you somewhere I have not prepared you for. I do not sit around and make up jokes to play on people. It is not My way. That is the way of the enemy.

If you feel like you are being taken advantage of, or that there are constant pranks in your life, do not look to me. I am not the one who is invading your thoughts. It is My desire to break that cycle and show you a better way. Will you let me?

# December 12

*His master said to him, "Well done, good and faithful servant. You have been faithful over a little; I will set you over much. Enter into the joy of your master." ~Matthew 25:23*

Well done! You may not hear these words often. You may not feel you are doing things very well. I will be the judge of that, and I say you are doing well. Days when you feel overwhelmed, you continue to make an effort. That is doing well. Sometimes you don't know which way is up and you feel confused or unable to continue, but you do. That is doing well. Beloved, you must give yourself some grace. I do. I allow for your humanness. I know you are not perfect. You never will be. You will never be able to carry all of this on your own. I created you to need a Savior. I am not surprised by your abilities or inabilities. I allow for them.

When you do things to the best of your ability, when you pour all you have into something, even if all you have isn't very much, I say, 'Well done.' Every person has differing abilities. Every person is created to be unique. It is My plan. Not everyone will be the same or have the same ability. Some have more challenges than others. Some overcome more obstacles just to get through their day. That does not make them less than others. Some seem to fly through life with nothing stopping them. They look as though they don't have a care in the world. Beloved, do not compare. You cannot know all the details of someone's life. Only I know that.

When I say well done to you, receive it. Let it lift you up. Trust me to tell you if there is something that needs adjustment. Listen to My voice. Well done. Walking through pain. Well done. Caring for others. Well done. Moving forward. Well done. Seeking me. Well done. Getting out of bed. Well done. Getting food on the table. Well done. Working a thankless job. Well done. Not allowing difficulties to stop you. Well done. Persevering. Well done. Suffering long. Well done. Holding onto My hand. Well done. Beloved. Well done.

# December 13

*There is no fear in love, but perfect love casts out fear. For fear has to do with punishment, and whoever fears has not been perfected in love. ~1 John 4:18*

I have noticed that when you feel everything depends on you, your fear rises. I think it is because you know you cannot do it all. It is too much for you, Weary One. So, when your plates are spinning and it seems there is not enough of you to go around, you get afraid. Afraid something will fall through the cracks. Afraid you will collapse from the effort. Afraid the bills won't get paid, or that the children will not have what they need. Afraid bankruptcy will come. Afraid the relationship will break.

Dear One, that is too much fear to carry. If you know that perfect love casts out fear, it means you know how much I truly love you and you also know I will take care of you. It might not look like you expect it to, but each item that brings fear into your heart is My challenge to meet. I can help you, but you have to let go. Let go of all the pressure you put yourself under. Let go of the fear that does nothing but suck the life from you. Worry is setting your mind on things below. I want you to set your mind on things above. When you do, even when the circumstances do not change, your mind does. You see with My eyes.

My eyes see My strong hand instead of your shaky one. I see My unlimited supply instead of your limited resources. I see My unlimited love instead of your strained care. I see My restoration instead of your broken relationships. I see healing instead of hurting. When you see from My eyes, you will drop fear like a rock. Worry will fade away, and trust will rise up.

I do not pridefully demand My way. I offer it freely to you, so you can avoid living in fear. I humbly submit it to you as a choice you have. Perfect love or fear? You decide.

# December 14

*And He said to them, "Come away by yourselves to a desolate place and rest a while." For many were coming and going, and they had no leisure even to eat. ~Mark 6:31*

Come away with me, Beloved. Even just for a moment. I know an extended time away is rarely possible. But you can come for moments at a time. I long to have the time with you. I want to pour strength into you. To give you hope. To encourage you. I cannot do these things if you never pull away. A quiet moment is all it takes. Morning or evening or the middle of the night.

Time with me is a necessity for someone in your place. The weary places you walk in require renewal, refreshing, and revival to survive. The only way to get those things is to come away. Burn out will take you down otherwise. I know your heart doesn't want to be irritable or grumpy. I know the stress of this season isn't what you want to be weighed down with. Instead allow me to infuse you with hope and joy. Allow me to lift your chin to look me in the eyes, so you can see My love for you. You can feel My presence in the loneliness, the exhaustion, the worry, the loss. I am in all the places in your heart where you are. Come away from them, just for a moment with me, and let me show you what this season is about.

This season is not about what you don't have. I am not talking about material possessions. I am talking about the circumstances you long for, whatever they are. There is a heart hole and a longing for what you can't have. It eats at you. The joy you do have is taken away. Remember, you have a lot. Count your blessings. If you come away and sit with me, I will show them all to you. One by one. Your eyes will not wander to what others have or to what your expectations were, but you will see the truth of what I have given you. The depth you have from the constant struggle and resistance in your life has built in a depth of relationship you are not even aware of. I want to show it to you. Will you come away with me?

# December 15

*But she was greatly troubled at the saying, and tried to discern what sort of greeting this might be. And the angel said to her, "Do not be afraid, Mary, for you have found favor with God." ~Luke 1:29-30*

Push through. There is opposition to most forward motion that comes your way. It is true. Rarely is anything worthwhile free of effort. Dear One, you have to push through the resistance. Dreams you had seem to have died. But it isn't true. You are experiencing resistance. Don't give up, push through. Ideas and visions of your future may not have come to pass in the way you thought, but don't give up. Push through.

When a baby is born, there is a time of transition. Everything is saying stop. Give up. This is too hard. It is too painful. Stop the pain. Quit. Yet, pushing through the pain is what is required to birth the baby. There are nine long months of preparation, forming the future. There are some discomforts, but also some beautiful moments. Feeling life growing, knowing it is coming, the anticipation, the longing to meet the baby. All of it is part of the process. But when the appointed time comes, it is anything but easy.

Some have quick deliveries. They just seem to be born to birth babies. Others, take longer. They labor in their labor. It feels like the time will never arrive, and often there are complications. Yet, both types of delivery have the same result, the baby is born. The difference is that the one who has a quick delivery may not be as tired as the one who labors long.

Weary One, you are one of those who has labored long. You are in a weakened state. You want to quit, but you cannot. You are tired and exhausted. The dreams I have planted and you are birthing are meeting resistance. Yet, you are in the process of bringing life into the world. There have been complications, but you can push through. Your birth story is different than that of others. It is unique to you. The labor is long, but the result is the same. Life. Dreams. Visions. Push through.

Mary experienced resistance. The mother of Jesus, struggled at every turn. Yet, she brought My Son into the world to save it. Her delivery experience didn't look like everyone else's, it didn't look like she expected. There were complications. It was a long path with resistance at every turn. The appointed time came and she pushed through the pain and gave birth to life and you can too. She pushed through from the birth, to the death, and even to glorious resurrection.

# December 16

*But the meek shall inherit the land and delight themselves in abundant peace.*
*~Psalms 37:11*

Meek is not the same thing as weak. Meek and mild describes My Son: quiet, gentle, easily imposed upon, submissive. However, this does not mean He was weak. On the contrary, He was powerful. He submitted Himself fully to the plan. He did not have to exert His authority loudly, He simply walked in it. He used it to heal, to do miracles, and to set people free. He combated the religious leaders sharply, but without a fight. He used His meekness as His weapon. They didn't know how to reply. They didn't know how to fight someone who didn't fight back. Of course, they thought they figured it out. Yet, even in His death He allowed them to impose their will upon Him. What they didn't know is that it was all part of the plan.

You mistake meekness for weakness, Weary One. Your lot in life has made you quiet and pensive. Yet, you feel strongly about certain things. Things that are important to you. Things I have planted deep within you. Those are the things you fight for, in a meek way. Your life experiences in the past have broken you. When you are broken, you absorb the pain, but it makes you a meek and mild warrior. Those attributes are not mutually exclusive. They can and do go together, often. Look at some of the heroes of history. They went forward with determination, not insults. They stood alone, quietly, and changed the world.

Do not mistake meekness for weakness. You are not weak. You are deep. You are meek. You are a warrior. My strength lives within your meekness. It rises up at injustice, or at the enemy, or at your circumstances. Sometimes it is overwhelming to live the life you have, but it is also My way of creating a warrior who will make a difference and use meekness and mercy to win the world.

None of those before you had it comfortable or easy. It is a mistake to think walking with me will provide comfort because the seasons in the wilderness rarely have comfort built into them. All My children have wilderness in their lives; some paths are just more visible than others. Watch me use meekness to walk you out of the desert in your life. Your meekness can make you powerful enough to fight for everything dear to your heart.

# December 17

*All these things My hand has made, and so all these things came to be, declares the Lord. But this is the one to whom I will look: he who is humble and contrite in spirit and trembles at My word. ~Isaiah 66:2*

Blessed are the poor in spirit. Poor in spirit doesn't mean poor in the natural. It means humble. Humble people are aware of their need for me. They know they cannot make it without me. They do not resent that fact; they embrace it. They seek me out. They listen to My voice. Rather than speaking *about* me, they speak *to* me. They wait for me to speak and they obey. They bow their own will and align with mine. They do so quietly, calmly, and meekly.

It isn't a secret that the poor in spirit inherit My Kingdom. I have said it plainly in My word. I long to share space with these ones. They do not fight to rule. They do not proclaim their authority. Much of the time, they are not even aware they have authority. They bow their knee to me out of honor and love. They don't want leadership, but it finds them. They simply want to be with me. It touches My heart. The poor in spirit are happy to sit in My presence and nothing else. They do not clamor for position. They are free of ambition born of pride. They know their place is beside me.

You are one of them, Beloved. The hardships you face have humbled you. You don't rush to take. You are content to sit with me when you can. The struggles have taught you that you need me. You know you cannot do things on your own. You are aware that being with me is enough. Sometimes, I am all you have. That's what poor in spirit means. I am all you have. You are poor in every way spiritually. Bankrupt. You know you have nothing to give, so you give me yourself.

You sit and listen to My heart. It is enough to be. It is a special time, and rarer than you might think. You don't draw attention to your plight. You live it day in and day out, with me by your side. You quietly go about your days and you sit in My presence. You are aware of me.

You bring My kingdom wherever you are because you carry it. I reside with the poor in spirit. They abide in me. It is a two-way relationship, which I cherish. It is what My kingdom is all about, not programs, not buildings, not numbers, not big things. It is about being with me. That is all. Everything else falls into place after that. It is why I trust you to inherit My kingdom. You can be trusted with My ways because you have been humbled. You are poor in spirit.

# December 18

*Be sober-minded; be watchful. Your adversary the devil prowls around like a roaring lion, seeking someone to devour. ~1 Peter 5:8*

Make ready for His coming. Consider mothers who build nests in anticipation of a baby. It is a natural process to prepare. It might look frenzied, but it is a built-in instinct. She is overwhelmed with a desire to clean things she had not noticed before, preparing for new life. A weary expectant mother may suddenly become overwhelmed with the desire to make ready. It seems clutter is her enemy. She goes to war on dust and dirt. The activity makes her feel like she is accomplishing something for her child. It is her welcome mat.

Have you made ready for Him? You can build a nest too, Dear One. Build it in your heart. Clean out bitterness. Sweep out hurt. Discard unforgiveness. A long time waiting gives these feelings time to build up. You might not have even noticed, but now cleaning out lets you see clearly. There is work to be done to prepare. In this season, My Son is remembered for breaking into the world. Great light. Glory. All for a baby. But the question remains, are you ready for Him?

You can't purify yourself. Only I can take away sin. Yet, you must prepare your heart for His work in you. You can give up and surrender those things which have piled up. They prevent your freedom. You must let them go. It is the season for giving. Give them to me. My Son has so much to give you, but if your hands and hearts are full, there is no room in the inn. Do not turn Him away, Beloved. Invite Him in. Offer Him shelter. Give Him your heart. You will never regret it.

# December 19

*Then the Lord God formed the man of dust from the ground and breathed into His nostrils the breath of life, and the man became a living creature. ~Genesis 2:7*

Breathe, Weary One. In and out. Deep cleansing breaths. Do you know I am the Breath of Heaven? When you breathe, you are the closest to me. My Holy Spirit indwells your breath. It makes you one of My creations. When man and woman were formed, they were works of art. Sculptures. Beautiful in every way. But the inhabitants of heaven collectively held their breath when I leaned in to blow breath into the clay. There was a gasp in heaven that day. A wondering. What would these creatures do with My breath? When their hearts began beating, blood flowed and their chests started to rise and fall, heaven fell silent. Heaven listened for the inhale and exhale of breathing artwork.

My breath is life. It brings life. If you are alive, I am giving you each breath. Do not take them for granted, Beloved. Each one is a gift. To remove even one takes what I have intended away. When life is difficult, take a moment and focus on each breath. Breathe out your stress. Breathe in My love. Breathe out frustration. Breathe in comfort. Breathe out grief. Breathe in hope.

Each breath in your body transports oxygen to your cells that cannot live without it. If you are too busy to feel your breathing, you are not getting My oxygen to your cells. This results in all manner of ailments, so easily solved by breathing. Get the oxygen flowing and you will see a difference. How? With busy and complicated lives, it is hard to make a time to fit me in, yet all that is needed is an awareness of the rise and fall of your chest. Intentional focus on the Breath of Heaven, who lives within you.

Pay attention. Listen to me. Hear My gift flow through you. It is your daily sustenance. It will remind you of whose you are. Your breath is My life force, saying that you are My creation, telling you that you are more than a beautiful lump of clay. You are united with the Breath of Heaven which is My Holy Spirit. He lives in you and through you. No matter what your day holds, I am with you in it. Breathe in. Breathe out. Breathe in. Breathe out. You can do this day.

# December 20

*And an angel of the Lord appeared to them, and the glory of the Lord shone around them, and they were filled with great fear. And the angel said to them, "Fear not, for behold, I bring you good news of great joy that will be for all the people."*
*~Luke 2:9-10*

The angel said, "Fear not." He said it to them all, "Do not be afraid." Angels are intimidating creatures, if you are not in the habit of seeing them. To hear what they said, humans had to first recognize they were messengers with "good tidings of great joy" and not there to harm. "Fear not" seemed a good way to start the conversation. But the angels were not the only things not to fear.

They used those words because fear of change, fear of what was going to happen, was also something to consider. When I reveal a plan of mine there is likely going to be change involved. It is always this way. To walk into who I have created you to be, you have to step out of your old ways. You have to do things differently. You may have to face those who disagree with you or discount what you feel I am saying. Mary and Joseph certainly had to do so. Fear not. I am with you.

Weary One, hear me. Your fear is a different kind of fear from most. You do not fear change, you long for it. You do not fear a new path, you desire it. You fear things staying the same. The same life of pain or loss. The same life of caring for others. The same life of grief. The same life of illness. You are afraid that nothing will change and you will be in this hard place forever. Listen to My words to you. Fear not.

Do not fear sameness, Beloved. You will not be left behind because your life is stuck in one place. You cannot be stuck. It only feels that way to you. I have a plan for you, in your current circumstances. It requires great faith to stay where you are, but still believe in My plan. You will not have to take a donkey ride to another city. You will not have to flee a king. You will not have to figure out where to deliver your baby. However, you will find yourself on a spiritual journey. You will have to flee the temptation to give up what I have called you to do. The vision I have given to you will be born. Do not give up on these hopes. Do not fear that I have forgotten you, or left you behind.

Fear not, Beloved. You are right where you are needed. You are doing what you need to do: walking out of hard places with me by your side. Take courage. You are not alone. I bring you good tidings of great joy! There is a plan. You are part of it. You will see something birthed in your life and it will be miraculous. Fear not!

# December 21

*The people dwelling in darkness have seen a great light, and for those dwelling in the region and shadow of death, on them a light has dawned. ~Matthew 4:16*

Dark places can bring heaviness. They are hard places. Yet, in the dark places, the light is so much more brilliant when it comes. It is blinding, really. Like the star. Like the angels. In the night of uncertainty, the light broke through the darkness. It confirmed that the words spoken previously were true. It clarified things.

Have you ever had an idea you knew to be true...you were certain it would come to pass? Then it didn't? Were you disappointed? Did you think you had missed it? Dreams are this way. There are interests you had and a way you thought life would work out. All the excitement of the future is laid out ahead of you.

Then the plot twist you didn't expect. The story that changed everything. Nothing was the same after: the diagnosis, the phone call, the death, the divorce, the career crash, the illness, the DARKNESS. It came in like a flood. Unexpected and taking out everything in its path, including your hopes and dreams. Your future. And since then, you have been living under a blanket of darkness. It is heavy, this blanket, and it keeps you from seeing the light around you.

There is light, you know? Have you not seen it? Are you so caught up in the disillusionment that you have missed the light in your life? It shines, guiding your way. You can ignore it, or even completely miss that it is there, but it directs. It shows you the path. It is brilliant, and it illuminates the landscape around you enough to be able to move in a direction. Look up at the light. Around you there is so much heaviness, but above you is the light that breaks through the shadows. It will lead you to me. It will point you in the direction of My plan. Pay attention.

I do not offer freedom from the darkness. No, the darkness serves My purpose of exposing the light. It works both ways, you know. Many times, My light exposes the darkness. It shines on the corners of your life where shadows hold you back. But other times, the darkness exposes My light.

When you are in the dark night of the soul, sweating drops of blood, and wrestling with heavy, difficult dilemmas, the light breaks through. It splits the night and opens your eyes to SEE. You can see me, even in the darkest of nights. When the light comes and shines, be it a star, an angel, a candle, or a spark of hope, your heart knows these lights. They reside there, inside your battered soul. Let the darkness of your heaviness expose My light, Dear One. Let it grow inside you until you can SEE, even in your challenging circumstances.

# December 22

*And Mary said, "Behold, I am the servant of the Lord; let it be to me according to your word." And the angel departed from her. ~Luke 1:38*

This time of year, people think of My Son, and how He arrived to save humanity. They hear the story of Mary and Joseph and their long journey. They are amazed at Mary's humility and her ability to ponder these things in her heart. She took me at My word. She conceived and she carried my Son to a faraway land by donkey, all while great with child. Then to give birth to Him in a stable, among the animals. She did all of this with Joseph by her side.

I wonder if you see the parallel, Weary One? She did not have things the way it was done in those days. She was pregnant before marriage. She travelled a long way just before the birth to another city. She had the world against her, in cultural terms. She and her betrothed were in difficult places, hard places, from the very beginning. They walked it out wondering what this life was going to be like for them. Parenting God. Did it even make sense? Were they imagining things? Questioning, while holding true to what the angels said. It is said of Mary that she was storing these things in her heart. Having God's baby. The seed of Him growing within her. Bringing Him into the world. Showing Him to shepherds and kings. All of it, so unexpected.

Nowadays, you have the same opportunity. What Mary did in the natural, you are created to do in the spiritual. Listen to My voice. Believe what I say. Allow the intimacy of the Holy Spirit to grow within you. Nurture it. Bring My Son into your world. Share Him with those in your path. You can be like Mary in these ways. You have a journey to carry My seed. The womb is a place of safety, but babies don't stay in the womb forever. They are birthed into the light. In darkness they are formed, but in the light, they bring life to the world. You bring life to the world. Even in hard and unexpected places when your life isn't as you planned it to be. Consider these things, Beloved. Ponder them.

# December 23

*Wait for the Lord and keep His way, and He will exalt you to inherit the land; you will look on when the wicked are cut off. ~Psalms 37:34*

Watch. Wait. It is the key to seeing what I am doing versus living frantically. Watch for me. Wait for me. In this season, the strategy of the enemy is to keep you distracted. Keep you busy. So busy, you forget to watch. Watching for me in the midst of crazy holiday seasonal activities will help you remember the deeper meaning of Christmas.

Waiting for me is critical to what I am birthing in you. Timing is everything, just ask Mary. It may seem like the timing is off, or that things are taking too long. You might be miserable in the waiting, uncomfortable even, but still you wait. You wait for me. You wait for something miraculous, but it doesn't come in the way you want. It isn't easy or magical. It comes in the messiness of life. A stable is different than a palace, but a stable is reality. It is in the realities of life's trials where you find me. Watch. Wait.

It is sometimes easier to see all the shallow, but enticing things. They distract and when you walk a hard path, distraction is welcome. Yet, you know it is temporary. It will not hold you. It will not sustain you on the long hard days. It is flashy. But like a vapor it is gone, leaving you aching. Watch. I am all around you. No need to go to the mall, or any one of the thousands of activities swirling about. I am beside you and with you in the quietest and most mundane places.

Wait. I know the longing you feel for something to change. For a miracle to appear and fix everything. It is the desire for wholeness. I have put that ache in you. If you wait for me and look to me, you will see My plan. But only in My timing will the vision be fulfilled. Until then, you are in good company with others, like Mary and Joseph, who await the promise.

# December 24

*And suddenly there was with the angel a multitude of the heavenly host praising God and saying, "Glory to God in the highest, and on earth peace among those with whom He is pleased!" ~Luke 2:13-14*

Silent night. Holy night. All is calm. All is bright. The words of a song which do not fit in a stable. Animals are not silent. Hay doesn't seem holy. A teenage couple having a baby all alone is not calm. The star was bright outside, but inside it was dark and damp, and scary.

The silence was in the heavenly places. Angels were stunned when the plan was revealed to be a tiny human baby. As understanding dawned, there was a holy hush in heaven. All was calm, as heaven held its breath to see. The light from My throne, from My very presence, glowed brighter than ever before. It was a moment unlike any other before it.

Yet, with all the wondering and watching, there was also excitement. The long-awaited promise arrived. The waiting was over, the promise was beginning. No one knew the plan in its entirety, except me. The wrinkles of the tiny God were sweet like any other baby. Not one scar on Him. Lovely in every way, was the baby born in the dark.

Then the heavenly hosts were given permission to show themselves. How could they not? How could they remain silent? They couldn't. And on such a monumental occasion I could not resist allowing the joy to overflow into the seen realm from the unseen. It was a spectacular event. It required attention from every station. Lowly and noble. Every tribe and tongue. Notification came cloaked with glory that glowed and spilled out over the earth. And it was good. Very good.

# December 25

*For to us a child is born, to us a Son is given; and the government shall be upon His shoulder, and His name shall be called Wonderful Counselor, Mighty God, Everlasting Father, Prince of Peace. ~Isaiah 9:6*

The long-awaited promise has come. All the prophecies fulfilled. All the waiting, longing, birthing, over. The celebration commences. It was all at once an ending, but also a beginning. That is the thing about My plans, Dear One, they are multi-layered. Just when you think an end is near or complete, a new beginning appears. This day was the culmination of so many promises, so much anticipation. Yet, there was so much still to come.

It is the same now. The promises I have given to you are multi-layered as well. You may not see their fulfillment all at one time. They may not come as one tiny gift wrapped in heavenly glory, but they are still going to be fulfilled at the appropriate time. The gift of My Son was the embodiment of My promises kept. Every promise I have made to you is wrapped up in this one event. It was a physical reminder of a spiritual truth. I keep My promises. I make a way. I do not forget.

With each promise, comes a journey, from conception all the way until the resurrection. Weary One, there is a resurrection promise. You will not be downtrodden forever. The baby points the way. The man walks in humility. The savior uplifts with power. Overcoming power. It is all there. It is available to you because of this day. The day of the promise.

# December 26

*I wait for the Lord, my soul waits, and in His word I hope. ~Psalms 130:5*

Upon the arrival of the promise, people think the work is complete, but nothing could be further from the truth. Once the promise has arrived, there is more preparation to continue the journey. Each journey I create BEGINS with a promise, not the other way around. Somehow it has become popular to believe the fulfillment of My words, the promise, is the culmination of the journey. However, the opposite is true; My words come first. They prepare the way. You join with them to prepare your heart. Every bump in the road along the journey you are on is another chance to prepare for what is coming.

Beloved, nothing is wasted. Not one tear. Not one long hard day. Not one sleepless night. I use everything to prepare for what is coming. As you walk through the dark, I am preparing the light. As you walk through the grief, I am preparing the hope. As you walk through the loss, I am preparing the future. One cannot be found without the other. You may not have thought about it like that. If you don't have any doubt, you cannot have faith. If you don't know what it feels like to be in darkness, the light will mean nothing. There is tension in difficulty which emphasizes the beauty in the messiness of life.

I made you a promise. You believed me. You started walking the path I showed you. The promise seemed to disappear. You questioned me. You wrestled with me. You wrestle still. I asked you to trust me. You fumbled through the darkness, the grief, the unknown. You wonder. You wait. You watch. I show up, on time, every time. You long for the promise. I accomplish it. You benefit. After all the wrestling, you KNOW what is real. What is true. It is me. I am in you.

# December 27

*No man shall be able to stand before you all the days of your life. Just as I was with Moses, so I will be with you. I will not leave you or forsake you. ~Joshua 1:5*

Your burden is weighing you down. The unknown of it. The harshness of reality. It is taking its toll. Dear One, it is physically exhausting to carry an emotional burden. Do you hear what I am saying? Give yourself grace. You carry a load of heartache. It will drain you, if you do not recognize and acknowledge the truth of where you are.

The truth is, if you hold all the heartache inside of you, it will suck the life from you. Do not bury the emotion, or it will bury you. There must be an outlet. It is why I created tears. They release the pain and lighten the burden. Crying tears is a healing process. You may cry more of them than you think you have, but I have made you an unending supply so you can release the pressure in which you are living.

Another way to alleviate heartache is to find someone who has walked a similar path to the one you are on. A shared load is a lighter load. I put people in your path who can join you in your reality. A pastor, teacher, counselor, or friend. It is up to you, but they are all there. All around you. You do not have to feel so isolated. Look around you, they are there.

If you cannot see them, you can always find me. I never leave you or forsake you. I love it when you come to chat. One of the things I love about you most, Dear One, is when you ask me to be in your life. I love to talk with you and to let you pour out your heart. When you go ahead and begin speaking, then wait for My reply, I will always respond. Just listen for me. You will recognize My voice. I will lead you on the path.

# December 28

*For thus said the Lord God, the Holy One of Israel, "In returning and rest you shall be saved; in quietness and in trust shall be your strength." ~Isaiah 30:15*

Learn to love the lull. A lull is the in-between-place. This time of year, it is between the end of one year and the beginning of another. Anytime in life there is one season ending, but the next one hasn't begun yet, there is a lull. You have an opportunity when it happens. You can be frustrated with the limbo, or you can embrace it. You can trust My timing is perfect, and so the in-between-moments are actually opportunities for growth.

Pacing yourself is critical. I created lulls in life so that you would not rush too fast into things. So that you would have to stop and think. So that you would look to me instead of to yourself. If there were no in-between-moments, there would be little time to breathe. There would be continuous planning, endless activity, and frantic action. The culture demands it of you. Keep moving. Never stop.

Lulls are like hitting the pause button. If you let them, they will become the place to rest between one season and the next. Rather than fretting about them, allow them to be places of refreshment. It is these moments when some of My best work happens. Waiting for the birthing, or waiting for the new year, or waiting for the middle, between the beginning and the end. Not one ever preaches about the middle-lands. They are understood to be the monotonous places of life. The places you hash out the glorious vision, into the completed vision.

Do not skip over the lulls. Do not forget to rest and renew. Do not let a lull discourage you, or deter you from your path. The lull is where the hard things happen to bring you to the completed vision. They are not only necessary, they are vital to arriving at the promise. Love the lull.

# December 29

*So also, you have sorrow now, but I will see you again, and your hearts will rejoice, and no one will take your joy from you. ~John 16:22*

Sometimes you have to fight for joy. When your life is overwhelming and threatens to take you into depressed places, fight for joy. When your burden is heavy, fight for joy. When you cannot take one more day of grief, fight for joy. I am not referring to striving or performance. What I mean is to recognize that joy is something every person needs. Not only that, but I have provided it for every one of My children. So, you need it, and I have it. You just have to remember to connect those two dots.

My joy is your strength. Forgetting My joy zaps you. It drains you. With the journey you are on, that is the last thing you need. If anything, you need a double portion. Finding joy will build you up from the inside. It will rise up and overflow.

One way to find it is to look at your blessings. When you are in weary places you might forget how many good things there are in your life. Look around you. Write them down if you have to. Joy will begin to flow. You will feel it starting to bubble up. Look at your memories. All the places in your life where you laughed. Share them with others. When a group has a collective memory lane, it can bring back the joyfulness of years past.

Joy is different from happiness. Happiness is circumstantial. Joy isn't. You are happy when things are going your way. When they are not, you are sad, depressed, or lonely. Joy is different because it is dependent on me, not on you. The love I have for you is tangible. You can feel it, and when you do joy is the result. Come to me and ask me to show you. I promise I will. The secret is knowing how much I love you. Find that and you will always have joy. Look for it in My words. Look for it in My actions. Look for it with those around you who love you. Once you know, I mean really know, how much I love you, joy will be your constant companion. That is what it means to fight for joy. Don't let the enemy distract you. Fight to find it, then rest in it.

# December 30

*But when you pray, go into your room and shut the door and pray to your Father who is in secret. And your Father who sees in secret will reward you. ~Matthew 6:6*

Life is a solitary journey. There is a difference between solitary and lonely. Do not confuse the two. Solitary means you go it alone. You are unaccompanied. At the end of life, it will only be you and me, but in reality, that is all it is now. There are friends and family, sure, but in the day-to-day, you and you alone, are the one responsible for how you live your life. No one else can do it for you.

You may have figured this truth out already. It is part of the maturing process to realize there is no one else to blame for your shortcomings. Or when you are going through hard times, even with the support of loved ones, you are on your own to figure things out. It is difficult too, because you cannot follow someone else's path. You must walk your own. Solitary can be scary at first. It can definitely feel lonely. But solitude is not a bad thing. It is a place where you learn contentment. It is a place where you find I am with you in the midst of your aloneness.

The people around you, your friends, your family, your coworkers and colleagues are all there along the way. You can learn and grow with these relationships, but ultimately, you are on your own. You might find this out when you experience a serious illness. It is you and me. You might come to understand when you lose someone close to you. It is you and me.

People come around, and they mean well, but they just cannot feel what you feel. They cannot be where you are. Do not knock them for not knowing how best to reach you. They have compassion, and they try. However, it isn't about them. It is about you and how you and I relate in the tough stuff. I am all you have that is solid and sure in the solitary times.

When you see that, and you learn how to reach out to me, you will not feel so alone. You will be infused with energy from your solitary time with me. You will gain wisdom and insight. You will no longer be afraid to sit with me. You will know our silence together is companionship. Even solitude is different with me. Don't be afraid of it.

# December 31

*For by Him all things were created, in heaven and on earth, visible and invisible, whether thrones or dominions or rulers or authorities—all things were created through Him and for Him. And He is before all things, and in Him all things hold together. Colossians 1:16-17*

Be still and know that I am God. It is a commonly quoted scripture. Today, Beloved, be still. Take a moment to reflect on the past year. Think of the good things that happened. Revisit the bad things. All of them together make up your year.

There are some years where the earth shakes under your feet. All circumstances feel as if they are falling away and new opportunities arrive. The unstable years lead to changes, like it or not. These years are ones to which you say good riddance on this day. Hope is renewed that something better will come, has to come, in the next year.

There are other years when things are calm and life flows along smoothly. Appreciate them. Learn to admire them, rather than taking them for granted. It is a sweet time when life is expanding. Adding to family, getting a new job, increasing your wholeness in life, are all changes to celebrate.

Most years are a combination of both the good and the bad. This time of year, as you are still, take stock of how the blessings came in spite of the hard times. How the two go together in ebb and flow. Pondering will give you hope.

What did you learn? Did you grow? How did the events change you? These are important questions. Before you leave this year, take stock. Write down your thoughts about the year. It is important to process events, both good and bad, to see where you were at the beginning of the year and where you are now because of what happened this year.

Know. Know that as you look forward, I will be with you. Know that I am in control, even when things feel out of control. Know that I will never leave you. Know that the new year and new events are never a surprise to me. Know me. Make it a point to come to me and get to know me better. I am deep and wide and there is always more of me. I would love to share Myself with you in new ways this year.

# Epilogue

In a novel, the epilogue is a section at the end of the book that tells what happened after the story.  Even though my book is non-fiction, I wanted you, my readers, to know what happens next.

After God speaks to you, there will be peace in your heart no matter what is happening around you.  You will be victorious because God has said so, and His word never comes back void. You will have breakthroughs. You will have quiet moments. You will hear his voice. The loose ends of your life will not be wrapped up in a big happy-ending bow. I wish I could give you that ending, however, the real-life journey will be richer because I cannot write away the pain. You will care greatly and love deeply along your way because God has taught you how to walk in brokenness with grace.

You, as a character, are complex and constantly being developed. You are a multi-faceted force to be reckoned with and the power of God flows through you. Even in what seem to be never-ending circumstances, you are the Beloved of God. He will continue his work in your life and you will be transformed into His image of love. The end of your story has yet to be written, but I do know that one day you will live happily ever after.

# Acknowledgements

There are no words to express how thankful I am for those who support me in my writing. Yet, I will try to unearth and string together some sentences in order to give credit where credit is due.

The love of my life, my husband Bill, has been my biggest cheerleader in this endeavor. He is the one who encouraged me to write books and he is convinced I have many more inside of me yet to come. I am humbled by his belief and motivated by his faith in me. You are my rock, Bill Gunnin.

My kids, who are no longer kids, have read my words for years. I am grateful they still do. They are witnesses to the life I write about and they love me anyway! I can count on them for feedback when I need an opinion, and I always know they are pulling for me no matter what I write. You are all my heart.

All of my dear friends, too many to name, who have encouraged, pleaded, and demanded that I write a book. They would not let it go no matter how many excuses I used to put it off. Thank you, my friends for your tenacity and boldness. I was listening, even if it didn't look like it!

My family who have never wavered in their love for me. Their love is like a blanket I wear everywhere I go. With every word I write, I think of them, especially Mom, who I know would be so proud of this book if she could remember who I am. I know she is in there somewhere and in her deepest self she knows her life of devotion to God led me to this book by example.

The Creator of the Universe, but also my friend, God the Father. The life-long relationship I have with Him is at the core of this book. My desire for everyone to know Him on an intimate level is my motivation for writing. He is such an encourager and He freely gives me the words I share. I could never repay his kindnesses to me and thankfully I will never have to.

**Some practical thanks:**

To my friend and former boss Betty Means, mega thanks for allowing me to promote my book and gather beta readers from the Facebook pages you manage. Your constant support of me is appreciated more than you know.

To all my beta readers, you have been such a help for feedback, editing, and encouragement. It made this book better.

To my friends Clint and Amie Bokelman, if you hadn't needed the words, printed them out, and told me over and over how much healing they brought, I would have never written this book. Your belief in the need for this book and your encouragement not to wait but to proceed with self-publishing has made *Words to the Weary* a reality.

To my friends and neighbors Suzanne and Gary D'bate, I couldn't have done this without your editing and formatting skills!! I would never get the dreaded semicolons correct and my pronouns would all be without antecedents. I'd be crying at the kitchen table trying to figure out section breaks. Yikes! Seriously, THANK YOU!

To my husband, who endured many of my teary evenings during the editing, formatting and self-publishing process. And who spent literally hours, capitalizing references to God throughout this manuscript. There is no way anyone would be reading this book without your support and help!

**Most importantly**...To my readers, this book would not be in existence without you. Your stories have inspired me. Your hearts are generous and no matter what, you keep on moving forward. To you, I say an enormous THANK YOU. I am honored you would read the words I write.

# About the Author

Michelle Gunnin is an everyday woman who is a wife, a mom of four grown children, a teacher, a colleague, a sister, and a daughter. She is a cancer survivor as well as a caregiver who loves deeply. She is determined be in the moment, and live fully…both things life has taught her. She has endured some incredibly difficult trials along life's way that only the grace of God could have brought her through. In those hardships He has transformed her heart.

In addition to Words to the Weary, she is the author of The Nature of God, a coffee table book she wrote as a gift for her father, combining his nature photos with her words. Michelle lives in Cleveland, Georgia with her husband and their 3 dogs. Visit her blog at michellesmosaic.com

# Books by Michelle Gunnin

*The Nature of God* is a coffee table book about the attributes of God with beautiful photographs. The photos were taken mainly in the mountains of Georgia and North Carolina, with a mixture from other locations as well. The text is encouraging in its message and will inspire the reader to see more of the Nature of God within the natural world.